International Marketing Strategy

International Marketing Strategy

Analysis, Development and Implementation

Second Edition

Isobel Doole and Robin Lowe

INTERNATIONAL THOMSON BUSINESS PRESS
I(T)P® An International Thomson Publishing Company

London • Bonn • Johannesburg • Madrid • Melbourne • Mexico City • New York • Paris
Singapore • Tokyo • Toronto • Albany, NY • Belmont, CA • Cincinnati, OH • Detroit, MI

International Marketing Strategy – Second Edition

Copyright © 1999 Isobel Doole and Robin Lowe

Thomson Learning Logo is a registered trademark used herein under licence

British Library Cataloguing in Publication Data
A catalogue record for this book is available from the British Library

First edition published 1994 by Routledge, London
Reprinted 1996 by International Thomson Business Publishing

Second Edition 1999
Reprinted 2000 by Thomson Learning

Typeset by LaserScript Limited, Mitcham, Surrey
Printed in the UK by TJ International Ltd, Padstow, Cornwall

ISBN 1-86152-472-2

Thomson Learning
Berkshire House
168-173 High Holborn
London WC1V 7AA

http://www.thomsonlearning.co.uk

Dedication

We give special thanks to our families: to Gordon and Sylvia and to our children, Robert, Libby and William, Catherine and Jonathan, for their loving support.

Contents

Introduction

Aims and objectives

Knowledge and an understanding of the markets in which companies operate is important for all business activities. In international markets because of geographical distances and the complexities of operating in a number of disparate markets where risk and uncertainty are high, the need for knowledge and understanding becomes of paramount importance. It is this issue which is central to Part I of this book. The chapters within this part concentrate on helping the reader generate a greater understanding of the concepts of the international marketing process and the international environment within which companies operate. It aims to extend the range of understanding to enable the reader to deal with international marketing situations and develop the skills to analyse and evaluate non-domestic markets to enable their firms to compete effectively in world markets.

Learning outcomes

On the completion of Part I the reader should:

- understand the international marketing strategy process
- have developed an awareness of the environmental influences in international marketing
- be able to understand the changing nature of the international trading environment
- understand the social/cultural influences which affect buyer behaviours and marketing approaches in international markets
- be able to apply frameworks to enable a systematic analysis of cultures within and across countries

- have developed an understanding of the processes and practices necessary in identifying and evaluating marketing opportunities across the globe
- know how to carry out a market research study in foreign markets and understand the issues in multi-country research.

Indicative content

In Chapter 1 we focus on the international marketing environment. The book uses the SLEPT approach to understanding the complexities of the environmental influences on international marketing, thus enabling the reader to acquire an appreciation of the complexities of marketing on an international basis. We examine what is meant by international marketing and examine the reasons for success and failure in international marketing strategies and the characteristics of best international marketing practice.

In Chapter 2 the focus is on gaining an understanding of the international trading environment. We first examine, at a macro level, the development of international trading structures and the changes in trading patterns, as well as examining the major international bodies formed to foster world trade. The evolution of trading regions are analysed and the implications to international marketing companies assessed.

In Chapter 3 we take a fairly detailed approach to examining the social and cultural influences in international marketing. The components of culture are examined and the impact of these components on international marketing. We then look at how cultural influences impact on buyer behaviour across the globe both in consumer markets and in business to business markets and discuss methods that can be used to analyse cultures both within and across countries.

In Chapter 4 the focus is on the identification and evaluation of marketing opportunities internationally. Segmentation of international markets is discussed and how to prioritise international opportunities. The marketing research process and the role it plays in the development of international marketing strategies is also examined. The different stages in the marketing research process are discussed with particular attention being paid to the problems in carrying out international marketing research in foreign markets and coordinating multi-country studies.

In Part I we include a special focus on China. China is attracting the interest of many firms internationally and is seen to have huge potential as a growth market over the next ten to twenty years. In the special focus we examine the market entry barriers and the implications for international companies. The final section of Part I gives the reader the opportunity to test their skills through a number of short case studies which have been included here as they reflect a number of the issues we have been discussing in the first four chapters.

The development of analytical skills is a critical pre-requisite to the international marketing manager's ability to make effective decisions. In order to develop such skills the manager needs a sound knowledge of the marketing environment in which they operate and a systematic research methodology. By studying Part I of this text it is hoped the reader goes at least some of the way in developing such skills.

Chapter 1
An introduction to international marketing

Introduction

Managers around the globe are recognising the increasing necessity for their companies and organisations to develop the skills, aptitudes and knowledge to compete effectively in international markets.

As we move into the next millennium, the emergence of a more open world economy, the globalisation of consumer tastes and the unabated construction of global electronic highways all increase the inter-dependency and inter-connections of nation economies across the globe. The need for managers to develop the skills to respond to these pressures affects companies of all sizes.

In this chapter, the reader will be introduced to the concepts of international marketing, enabling them to acquire an appreciation of the complexities of marketing on an international basis and of how this activity differs from operating purely in domestic markets. In the following sections we will define international marketing, examine the important trends in the global marketing environment and introduce the reader to the international marketing management process.

The strategic importance of international marketing

Last year's international trade in merchandise exceeded US$5.5 trillion and world trade in services is estimated at around US$1 trillion. Whilst most of us cannot visualise such huge amounts, it does serve to give some indication of the scale of international trade today.

This global marketplace consists of a population of 10 billion people which is expected to reach 11 billion by 2020 according to the latest projections prepared by the United Nations.

Global wealth is increasing and this is again reflected in higher demand. Increasing affluence and commercial dynamism has seen nations across Asia and South America and Eastern Europe emerge as high growth economies. Increasing affluence and demand simply means that consumers will actively seek choice with the result that competition is emerging as companies compete to win the battle for disposable income. Countries or at least large sections of them are moving into a world away from commodity purchases of eg: maize or rice, consumer goods into packaged and marketed to their citizens' personal needs.

Population growth and increased affluence together has helped create a 'global youth culture'. In many countries, particularly the newly industrialised economies (NIEs) more than half the population is pre-adult, creating one of the world's biggest single market, the youth market. Everywhere adolescents project worldwide cultural icons, Nike, Coke, Benetton, Sony Walkman, and now Sega, Nintendo and the Sony Playstation. When 'virtual reality' is commonplace, the one-world youth culture market will exceed all others as a general category for marketers. Parochial, local and ethnic growth products may face difficult times.

Older consumers are also increasingly non-national, not in their personal identity but from the perspective of the consumable fabric of their lives. They drive international cars, watch international programmes on television, use international hardware and software. International consumption is accelerating and boundaries of product ownership are increasingly blurred.

On the supply side, multi-national and global corporations are increasing in size and embracing more global power. The top 500 companies in the world now account for 70 per cent of world trade and 80 per cent of international investment. Total sales of multi-nationals are now in excess of world trade, which gives them a combined gross product of more than some national economies.

To deal with the size of the global economy, companies are consolidating through mergers, acquisitions and alliances to reach the scale considered necessary to compete in the global arena. At the same time, there is a trend towards global nationalisation, seeking world standards for efficiency and productivity. Toyota and General Motors have a joint plant in California called Nummi. BMW have taken over Rover (UK) and the Rolls Royce brand, whilst VW have taken over the Bentley brand and UK production facilities. Glaxo and Wellcome formed a global alliance in the pharmaceutical market and are looking to further extend their global alliances. General Electric recently formed a strategic alliance with the French Aircraft Company Snecma.

The global marketplace is simultaneously becoming inter-dependent, economically, culturally and technically through the consistent thrust in technological innovation. Information moves anywhere in the world at the speed of light and, what is becoming known as the global civilisation, is being facilitated by the convergence of long distance telecoms and cuts in the cost of electronic processing.

The combination of all these forces have meant that all companies need to develop a marketing orientation which is international and have managers who are able to analyse, plan and implement strategies across the globe. It is for these reasons that international marketing has become such a critical area of study for managers and an important component of the marketing syllabus both of the Chartered Institute of Marketing and University Business Schools.

So perhaps now we should turn our attention to examining exactly what we mean by international marketing.

What is international marketing?

Many readers of this textbook will have already followed a programme of study in marketing but, before explaining what we mean by international marketing let us, for a few moments, reflect on our understanding of what is meant by marketing itself. The Chartered Institute of Marketing defines marketing as the 'Management process responsible for identifying, anticipating and satisfying customer requirements profitably'. Thus marketing involves:

- focusing on the needs and wants of customers
- identifying the best method of satisfying those needs and wants
- orienting the company towards the process of providing that satisfaction
- meeting organisational objectives.

In this way, it is argued, the company or organisation best prepares itself to achieve competitive advantage in the marketplace. It then needs to work to maintain this advantage by manipulating the controllable functions of marketing within the largely uncontrollable marketing environment made up of SLEPT factors, i.e. Social, Legal, Economic, Political and Technical.

How does the process of international marketing differ? Within the international marketing process the key elements of this framework still apply. The conceptual framework is not going to change to any marked degree when a company moves from a domestic to an international market, however, there are two main differences. First, there are different levels at which international marketing can be approached and, second, the uncontrollable elements of the marketing environment are more complex and multi-dimensional given the multiplicity of markets that constitute the global marketplace. This means managers have to acquire new skills and abilities to add to the tools and techniques they have developed in marketing to domestic markets.

International marketing defined

At its simplest level, international marketing involves the firm in making one or more marketing mix decisions across national boundaries. At its most complex, it involves the firm in establishing manufacturing facilities overseas and coordinating marketing strategies across the globe. At one extreme there are firms that opt for 'international marketing' simply by signing a distribution agreement with a foreign agent who then takes on the responsibility for pricing, promotion, distribution and market development. At the other extreme, there are huge global companies such as Ford with an integrated network of manufacturing plants worldwide and who operate in some 150 country markets. Thus, at its most complex, international marketing becomes a process of managing on a global scale. These different levels of marketing can be expressed in the following terms:

- **Domestic marketing** which involves the company manipulating a series of controllable variables such as price, advertising, distribution and the product in a largely uncontrollable external environment that is made up of different economic structures, competitors, cultural values and legal infrastructure within specific political or geographic country boundaries.

- **International marketing** which involves operating across a number of foreign country markets in which not only do the uncontrollable variables differ significantly between one market and another, but the controllable factors in the form of cost and price structures, opportunities for advertising and distributive infrastructure are also likely to differ significantly. It is these sorts of differences that lead to the complexities of international marketing.

- **Global marketing management** which is a larger and more complex international operation. Here a company coordinates, integrates and controls a whole series of marketing programmes into a substantial global effort. Here the primary objective of the company is to achieve a degree of synergy in the overall operation so that by taking advantage of different exchange rates, tax rates, labour rates, skill levels and market opportunities, the organisation as a whole will be greater than the sum of its parts.

This type of strategy calls for managers who are capable of operating as international marketing managers in the truest sense, a task which is far broader and more complex than that of operating either in a specific foreign country or in the domestic market. In discussing this, Terpstra and Sarathy (1997, p.9) comment that 'the international marketing manager has a dual responsibility; foreign marketing (marketing within foreign countries) and global marketing (co-ordinating marketing in multiple markets in the face of global competition)'.

Thus, how international marketing is defined and interpreted depends on the level of involvement of the company in the international marketplace. International marketing could therefore be:

- **Export marketing**, in which case the firm markets its foods and/or services across national/political boundaries.

- **International marketing**, where the marketing activities of an organisation include activities, interests or operations in more than one country and where there is some kind of influence or control of marketing activities from outside the country in which the goods or services will actually be sold. Sometimes markets are typically perceived to be independent and a profit centre in their own right, in which case, the term multi-national or multi-domestic marketing is often used.

- **Global marketing**, in which the whole organisation focuses on the selection and exploitation of global marketing opportunities and marshals resources around the globe with the objective of achieving a global competitive advantage.

The first of these definitions describes relatively straightforward exporting activities, numerous examples of which exist. However, the subsequent definitions are more complex and more formal and indicate not only a revised attitude to marketing but also a very different underlying philosophy. Here the world is seen as a market segmented by social and cultural, legal, economic, political and technological (SLEPT) groupings.

In this textbook, we will incorporate the international marketing issues faced by firms, be they involved in export, international or global marketing.

For all these levels the key to successful international marketing is being able to identify and understand the complexities of each of these SLEPT dimensions of the international environment and how they impact on a firm's marketing strategies across their international markets. As in domestic marketing, the successful marketing company will be the one that is best able to manipulate the controllable tools of the marketing mix within the uncontrollable environment. It follows that the key problem faced by the international marketing manager is that of coming to terms with the details and complexities of the international environment. It is these complexities that we will examine in the following sections.

The international marketing environment

The key difference between domestic marketing and marketing on an international scale is the multi-dimensionality and complexity of the many foreign country markets a company may operate in. An international manager needs a knowledge and awareness of these complexities and the implications they have for international marketing management.

There are many environmental analysis models which the reader may have come across. For the purposes of the textbook, we will use the SLEPT (Social, Legal, Economic, Political and Technological) approach and examine the various aspects and trends in the international marketing environment through the social/cultural, legal, economic, political and technological dimensions, as depicted in Figure 1.1

Figure 1.1 The environmental influences on international marketing

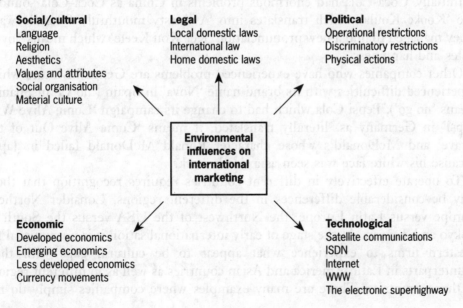

Social/cultural
Language
Religion
Aesthetics
Values and attributes
Social organisation
Material culture

Legal
Local domestic laws
International law
Home domestic laws

Political
Operational restrictions
Discriminatory restrictions
Physical actions

Environmental influences on international marketing

Economic
Developed economics
Emerging economics
Less developed economics
Currency movements

Technological
Satellite communications
ISDN
Internet
WWW
The electronic superhighway

Social/cultural environment

The social and cultural influences on international marketing are immense. Differences in social conditions, religion and material culture all affect consumers' perceptions and patterns of buying behaviour. It is this area that determines the extent to which consumers across the globe are either similar or different and so determines the potential for global branding and standardisation.

A failure to understand the social/cultural dimensions of a market is a prime reason for failure as McDonald's found when they moved into India following the opening up of that market a few years ago (see Illustration 1.1).

Cultural factors

Cultural differences and especially language differences have a significant impact on the way a product may be used in a market, its brand name and the advertising campaign.

Coca-Cola had to withdraw their two-litre bottle from Spain when they found that Spaniards did not own fridges with sufficiently large compartments. Johnson's floor wax was doomed to failure in Japan as it made the wooden floors very slippery and Johnson's failed to take into account the custom of not wearing shoes inside the home.

Initially, Coca-Cola had enormous problems in China as Coca-Cola sounded like 'Kooke Koula' which translates into 'A thirsty mouthful of candle wax'. They managed to find a new pronunciation 'Kee Kou Keele' which means 'joyful tastes and happiness'.

Other companies who have experienced problems are General Motors which experienced difficulties with its brand name 'Nova' in Spain ('no va' in Spanish means 'no go'), Pepsi Cola which had to change its campaign 'Come Alive With Pepsi' in Germany as, literally translated, it means 'Come Alive Out of the Grave' and McDonald's whose character Ronald McDonald failed in Japan because his white face was seen as a death mask.

To operate effectively in different countries requires recognition that there may be considerable differences in the different regions. Consider Northern Europe versus Latin Europe, the Northwest of the USA versus the South or Tokyo and Taiwan. At the stage of early internationalisation it is not unusual for Western firms to experience what appear to be cultural gaps with their counterparts in Latin America and Asian countries as well as in different regions of those countries. There are many examples where companies simply do not

Illustration 1.1: India spices things up!

The McDonald's formula, hugely successful as it is, was always going to have to be adapted to a place where killing cows is sacrilege. But burger joints are not the only ones that need to be careful, other western firms tempted by India's growing middle class have had to be sensitive to the country's definite tastes.

McDonald's, which now has seven restaurants in India, was launched there a year ago. It has had to deal with a market that is 40 per cent vegetarian; with the aversion to either beef or pork among meat-eaters, with a hostility to frozen meat and fish, and with the general Indian fondness for spice with everything.

To satisfy such tastes, McDonald's has discovered that it needs to do more than provide the right burgers. Customers buying vegetarian burgers want to be sure that these are cooked in a separate area in the kitchen using separate utensils. Sauces like McMasala and McImli are on offer to satisfy the Indian taste for spice. McDonald's promises to introduce a spiced version of its fries soon.

Although its expansion has been faster in India than some other Asian countries such as Indonesia, it has hardly been rapid. Yet, at least, the firm has avoided the disasters of some other big American names.

A few years back, violent protests in Bangalore in southern India over the quality of its food temporarily closed KFC which sells fried chicken.

Three years ago, Kellogg made a splash pitching breakfast cereals as a healthier alternative to the heavy Indian breakfast. Indians were unimpressed. Kellogg facing mounting losses is now selling to a westernised niche market instead.

Foreign companies have got three things wrong in India. They overestimated the size and disposable income of the much-touted Indian middle class. They underestimated the strength of local products in the markets they were entering and they overestimated the value of their reputation. Indian consumers seem unimpressed by the glamour of the western brands, food companies are scaling down their plans accordingly.

Others are playing it safe. For years Wimpy has restricted itself to only a few outlets. Burger King has stayed out of the market altogether. Three years after Heinz went into India by taking over Glaxo's food business, it is still chewing over the idea of introducing Indians to the joys of tomato ketchup. An extra pinch of spice might do the trick.

Source: *The Economist*, 22 November 1997.

find their way into a market or where their performance is less than successful. Only a very small proportion of the failures or the major difficulties are made public. EuroDisney in France received considerable media attention but any careful scrutiny of the performance of a company in different markets will show the number of disappointments in foreign markets exceeds the success.

Derwent Valley were highly successful in the UK but met huge problems facing the cultural complexities of the continental European market which they were totally unprepared for (see the case study on Derwent Valley at the end of Part I).

On the other hand, there are visible trends that social and cultural differences are becoming less of a barrier. This has led to the emergence of a number of world brands such as Microsoft, Intel, Coca-Cola, McDonald's, Nike etc., all competing in global markets that transcend national and political boundaries.

However, there are a number of cultural paradoxes which exist. For example, in Asia, the Middle East, Africa and Latin America there is evidence both for the westernisation of tastes and the assertion of ethnic, religious and cultural differences. These differences do not necessarily constitute unbridgeable cultural chasms in all sectors of a society. Instead there are trends toward similarities both in cultures and outlooks of consumers. There are more than 600 000 Avon ladies now in China and a growing number of them in Eastern Europe, Brazil and the Amazon.

In northern Kenya you may find a Sambhuru warrior who owns a cellular telephone. Thus, whilst there is a vast and, sometimes, turbulent mosaic of cultural differences, there is also evidence that a global village is potentially taking shape which as Kenichi Ohmae (1994) said, 'will be a nationless state marked by the convergence of customer needs that transcends political and cultural boundaries'.

The social/cultural environment is an important area for international marketing managers and will be returned to in a number of chapters where we examine the various aspects of its strategic implications. In Chapter 3, we devote a full chapter to the examination of the social and cultural influences in international marketing. In Chapter 6, we will examine the forces driving the global village and its strategic implication to companies across the world.

Social factors

Growth and movement in populations around the world are important factors heralding social changes. Figure 1.2 details the changes in the regional population around the globe. As can be seen, whilst world population is

Figure 1.2 Regional breakdown of global population

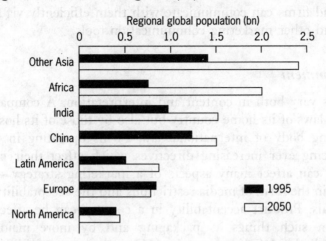

Source: Population Division, Department of Economic and Social Affairs, United Nations Secretariat, *World Population Prospects. The 1996 Revision*, United Nations, New York.

growing dramatically, the growth patterns are not consistent around the world.

Over the next half century, Africa's population will almost treble. In 1995 700m people lived in Africa: by 2050 there will be just over 2 billion. China's population will rise much more slowly from 1.2 billion to 1.5 billion. With a population of 1.53 billion people, India will have more inhabitants than China in 50 years time. Europe is the only region where the population is expected to decline.

There are also visible moves in the population within many countries leading to the formation of huge urban areas where consumers have a growing similarity of needs across the globe. The world is moving into gigantic conurbations. The population of Greater Tokyo is soon to be close to 30 million and Mexico 15 million. Cities such as Lagos, Buenos Aires and Djakarta will soon outstrip cities such as Paris, London and Rome. In the year 2015, no European city will be in the top 30 and 17 of the world's mega cities of 10 million plus will be in the Third World. This has powerful implications for international marketing. These cities will be markets in themselves. Urban dwellers require similar products (packaged conveniently and easy to carry). Similarly, they demand services, telephones and transportation of all kinds and modern visual communications. It also means for the incoming company that customers are accessible. They are identifiable and firms can communicate with them efficiently via supermarkets, advertising and other marketing communication tools.

Legal environment

Legal systems vary both in content and interpretation. A company is not just bound by the laws of its home country but also by those of its host country and by the growing body of international law. Firms operating in the European Union are facing ever increasing directives which affect their markets across Europe. This can affect many aspects of a marketing strategy – for instance advertising – in the form of media restrictions and the acceptability of particular creative appeals. Product acceptability in a country can be affected by minor regulations on such things as packaging and by more major changes in legislation. In the USA for instance, the MG sports car was withdrawn when the increasing difficulty of complying with safety legislation changes made exporting to that market unprofitable.

It is important, therefore, for the firm to know the legal environment in each of its markets. These laws constitute the 'rules of the game' for business activity. The legal environment in international marketing is more complicated than domestic since it has three dimensions: (1) local domestic law; (2) international law; (3) domestic laws in the firm's home base.

- *Local domestic laws.* These are all different! The only way to find a route through the legal maze in overseas markets is to use experts on the separate legal systems and laws pertaining in each market targeted.

- *International law.* There are a number of 'international laws' that can affect the organisation's activity. Some are international laws covering piracy and hijacking, others are more international conventions and agreements and cover items such as IMF and World Trade Organization (WTO) treaties, patents and trademarks legislation and harmonisation of legal systems within regional economic groupings e.g. the European Union.

- *Domestic laws in the home country.* The organisation's domestic (home market) legal system is important for two reasons. First, there are often export controls which limit the free export of certain goods and services to particular marketplaces and second, there is the duty of the organisation to act and abide by its national laws in all its activities whether domestic or international.

It will be readily understandable how domestic, international and local legal systems can have a major impact upon the organisation's ability to market into particular overseas countries. Laws will affect the marketing mix in terms of products, price, distribution and promotional activities quite dramatically. For many firms, the legal challenges they face in international markets is almost a double-edged sword.

In many mature markets they face quite specific and, sometimes, burdensome regulations. In Germany for instance, environmental laws mean a firm is responsible for the retrieval and disposal of the packaging waste it creates and must produce packaging which is recyclable, whereas in many emerging markets there may be limited patent and trademark protection, still evolving judicial systems, non-tariff barriers and an instability through an ever evolving reform programme.

Recently, McDonald's had a legal case they brought to win the right to use their brand name in South Africa dismissed, on the grounds that it was already used by several indigenous firms in the fast-food market. Some governments are reluctant to develop and enforce laws protecting intellectual property partly because they believe such actions favour large rich multi-nationals.

Piracy in markets with limited trade mark and patent protection is another challenge. Bootlegged software constitutes 87 per cent of all personal computer software in use in India, 92 per cent in Thailand and 98 per cent in China, resulting in a loss of US$8 billion for software makers a year.

India has been seen by many firms to be an attractive emerging market beset with many legal difficulties, bureaucratic delay and lots of red tape. Companies such as Mercedes Benz, Coca-Cola and Kelloggs cornflakes have found the lure of the vast potential of India's market somewhat hard to break into. Its demanding consumers can be difficult to read and local rivals can be surprisingly tough. Political squabbles, bureaucratic delays, infrastructure headaches and unprofessional business practices create one obstacle after another. Foreign companies are often viewed with suspicion. However some firms have been innovative in overcoming difficulties as can be seen in illustration 1.2

Economic environment

Amongst the 200 or so countries in the world, there are varying economic conditions and levels of economic development and GNP per capita. Thus it is important that the international marketer has an understanding of economic developments and how they impinge on the marketing strategy. This

---

Illustration 1.2: Reebok learn lessons on importing to India

Restrictions imposed by governments often cause major problems for companies wishing to enter a market. Reebok had to adopt a very innovative approach to overcome legal difficulties when attempting to start shoe production in India. Protection of local industry prevented them from importing even a single pair as a sample. Some manufacturers overcame the problem by importing the left shoe into Bombay and the right shoe into Madras. Reebok were determined to find a legal alternative and met with government officials time and time again until they managed to convince them that the foreign prototypes would help upgrade Indian industry. Eventually the government granted them a special license to import 10 000 pairs.

---

understanding is important at both a world level in terms of the world trading infrastructure such as world institutions and trade agreements, at a regional level in terms of regional trade integration and at a country/market level. Firms need to be aware of the economic policies of countries and the direction in which a particular market is developing economically in order to make an assessment as to whether they can profitably satisfy market demand and compete with firms already in the market.

One of the key challenges facing companies trying to develop an integrated strategy across a number of international markets is the divergent levels of economic development they have to deal with, making it often very difficult to have a cohesive strategy, certainly in pricing.

The Economist 'Big Max' Index is a useful illustration of the impact this has on firms. This index gives a guide to the comparative purchasing power across countries by examining their economies in terms of how many minutes somebody needs to work to buy a 'Big Mac'.

Figure 1.3 shows that the average worker in Caracas has to toil for 117 minutes to earn enough money to buy a Big Mac. At the other extreme, a worker in Tokyo needs to work for only nine minutes and a New Yorker 20 minutes.

The developed triad economies

The triad economies of NAFTA countries, European Union and Japan account for 80 per cent of world trade. For many firms this constitutes much of what is termed the global market. It is in this triangle that the global consumer with

Figure 1.3 Working time required to buy a Big Mac (in minutes)

Working time required to buy a Big Mac
(in minutes) 1997

| | 0 | 20 | 40 | 60 | 80 | 100 | 120 |

Caracas
Moscow
Manila
Shanghai
Mexico City
Bogota
Warsaw
Bangkok
Sao Paolo
Johannesburg
Singapore
Paris
Kuala Lumpar
London
Frankfurt
New York
Tokyo

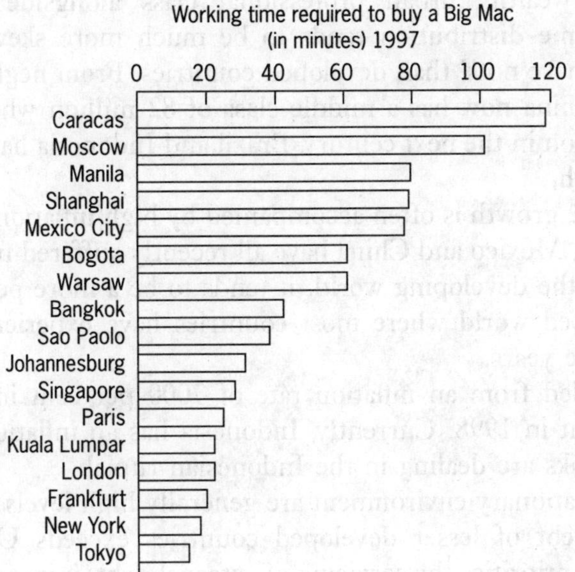

Source: Adapted from *The Economist,* 11 October 1997.

similar lifestyles, needs and desires emanates from. However emerging markets are now becoming more economically powerful and moving up the ranks such that by the year 2020 it is projected that China, South Korea and Taiwan will be amongst the top tier of national economies.

The emerging economies

In countries such as China, Brazil, Vietnam and India there is a huge and growing demand for everything from automobiles to cellular phones. Many of the countries which were seen only a few years ago as 'lesser developed countries' (LDCs) now show a healthy economic advancement and fall under the umbrella of emerging markets. Countries such as Indonesia, China, Mexico, Brazil, Chile, Hungary, Poland, Turkey, the Czech Republic and South Africa are all viewed as key growth markets.

In these emerging markets, there is an evolving pattern of government directed economic reforms, lowering of restrictions on foreign investment and increasing privatisation of state owned monopolies. All these herald significant opportunities for the international marketing firm.

Such markets often have what is termed as a 'dual economy'. Usually there tends to be a wealthy urban professional class alongside a poorer rural population. Income distribution tends to be much more skewed between the 'haves' and the 'have nots' than developed countries. From negligible numbers a few years ago, China now has a middle class of 82 million which is forecast to grow to 500 million in the next century. Brazil and Indonesia have middle classes of 15 million each.

High economic growth is often accompanied by high inflation. Countries such as Poland, Brazil, Mexico and China have all recently suffered from high rates of inflation and, in the developing world, it tends to be a more persistent problem than the developed world where most countries have experienced single digit inflation for some years.

Brazil has reeled from an inflation rate of 7000 per cent in 1994 to one of under 11 per cent in 1998. Currently, Indonesia has an inflation rate of 40 per cent and few banks are dealing in the Indonesian rupiah.

Tied to an inflationary environment are generally high levels of external debt. Total external debt of lesser developed countries exceeds US$1 trillion. As countries have to prioritise the servicing of external debt, it invariably leaves little availability of hard currency to buy imported products.

Less developed countries (LDCs)

This group includes underdeveloped countries and developing countries. The main features are a low GDP per capita, a limited amount of manufacturing activity and a very poor and fragmented infrastructure. Typical infrastructure weaknesses are in transport, communications, education and healthcare. In addition, the public sector is often slow-moving and bureaucratic.

It is common to find that LDCs are heavily reliant on one product and often on one trading partner. In many LDCs this product is the main export earner. Amongst twenty-eight LDCs seven receive over half and nine receive between 25 and 50 per cent of their export earnings from their main export commodity. In addition, three-quarters of LDCs depend on their main trading partner for more than one-quarter of their export revenue. The risks posed to the LDC by changing patterns of supply and demand are great. Falling commodity prices can result in large decreases in earnings for the whole country. The resultant economic and political adjustments may affect exporters to that country through possible changes in tariff and non-tariff barriers, through changes in the level of company taxation and through restrictions on the convertibility of currency and the repatriation of profits. In addition, substantial decreases in market sizes within the country are probable.

The typical pattern for single-product dependence is the reliance on one agricultural crop or on mining. Colombia (coffee), Cuba (sugar), Ghana (cocoa), Mali (cotton), Rwanda (coffee) and Somalia (live animals) are examples of extreme dependence upon agriculture. Gabon (oil), Jamaica (base metal ores), Mauritania (iron ore), Niger (uranium and thorium ores) and Nigeria (oil) are examples of reliance on the extraction of minerals.

A wide range of economic circumstances influence the development of the less developed countries in the world. Some countries are small with few natural resources. For these countries it is difficult to start the process of substantial economic growth. Poor health and education standards need money on a large scale, yet the pay-off in terms of a healthier, better-educated population takes time to achieve. At the same time, there are demands for public expenditure on transport systems, communication systems and water control systems. Without real prospects for rapid economic development, private sources of capital are reluctant to invest in such countries. This is particularly the case for long-term infrastructure projects and, as a result, important capital spending projects rely heavily on world aid programmes.

Currency risks

Whilst we have examined economic factors within markets, we also need to bear in mind that in international marketing transactions invariably take place between countries and so the exchange rates and currency movements are an important aspect of the international economic environment.

World currency movements, stimulated by worldwide trading and foreign exchange dealing, is an additional complication in the international environment. On top of all the normal vagaries of markets, customer demands, competitive actions and economic infrastructures, foreign exchange parities are likely to change on a regular if unpredictable bases. In 1998, instability has been seen across the world due to the currency crisis in the Asian markets and the consistent fall of the Japanese yen. Sterling has been exceptionally strong making it particularly difficult for UK exporters to compete internationally.

In Europe, the move towards European Monetary Union will lead to greater stability for firms operating in the market but will have important implications for pricing strategies as we will discuss in both Chapters 2 and 12; in Chapter 2, when we examine regional trading agreements and in Chapter 12 when we look at pricing issues in international marketing.

Political environment

The political environment of international marketing includes any national or international political factor that can affect the organisation's operations or its decision making. Politics has come to be recognised as the major factor in many international business decisions, especially in terms of whether to invest and how to develop markets.

Politics are intrinsically linked to a government's attitude to business and the freedom within which it allows firms to operate. Unstable political regimes expose foreign businesses to a variety of risks that they would generally not face in the home market. This often means that the political arena is the most volatile area of international marketing. The tendencies of governments to change regulations can seriously affect an international strategy providing both opportunities and threats. One only has to consider the volatility of the politics in the former Yugoslavia, Russia and in China over the past few years to appreciate the need for firms to monitor the political risk factors.

The opening up of Central Europe, the disintegration of the Soviet Union and Yugoslavia and the formation of the European Union have all had enormous implications for companies operating in the European markets. Parts of Europe are now perceived as areas of relatively high political risk and yet potentially of huge market opportunity. An unstable political climate can expose firms to many commercial, economic and legal risks that they would not face in their domestic markets. New risks also emerge, of course, as companies from the emerging markets start to compete internationally.

Political risk is defined as being: 'A risk due to a sudden or gradual change in a local political environment that is disadvantageous or counter productive to foreign firms and markets'.

The type of actions that governments may take which constitute potential political risks to firms fall into three main areas:

1 *Operational restrictions*. These could be exchange controls, employment policies, insistence on locally shared ownership and particular product requirements.
2 *Discriminatory restrictions*. These tend to be imposed on purely foreign firms and, sometimes, only firms from a particular country. They tend to be such things as special taxes and tariffs, compulsory sub-contracting, loss of financial freedom.

3 *Physical actions.* These actions are direct government interventions such as confiscation without any payment of indemnity, a forced takeover by the government, expropriation, nationalisation or even damage to property or personnel through riots and war.

Lesser developed countries and emerging markets pose particularly high political risks (see Illustration 1.3). This manifests itself by threats of civil disorder, creeping expropriation, mercurial government policies. Rising opposition to incumbent governments, e.g. as in Indonesia and the Chinese economic area, all deter potential investors.

Civil unrest is often accompanied by high illiteracy, poor health and a large proportion of the population living in poverty; 73 per cent of the population in Brazil live in poverty compared to 7 per cent in Spain.

Investment restrictions are a common way governments interfere politically in international markets by restricting levels of investment, location of facilities, choice of local partners and ownership percentage.

When Microsoft opened its Beijing office in 1992, it planned to use its Taiwan operations to supply a Mandarin language version of Windows. The government not only wanted such an operating system to be designed in China but also insisted on defining the coding standards for Chinese characters' fonts, something Microsoft had done independently everywhere else in the world. In a flurry of meetings with officials, Bill Gates argued that the marketplace not the governments should set standards. But the Chinese electronics industry threatened to ban Windows and president Jiang Zemin personally admonished Gates to spend more time in China and 'learn something from 5000 years of Chinese history'. Gates sacked the original management team and promised to cooperate with Beijing.

However, the recent trends of trade agreements, privatisation and market reforms are all working to remove trade impediments.

Globally, trade agreements have been making consistent progress over the last forty years. The World Trade Organisation (formerly known as GATT) has led to a series of worldwide agreements which have expanded quotas, reduced tariffs and introduced a number of innovative measures to encourage trade amongst countries. Together with the formation of regional trading agreements in the European Union, North and South America and Asia. These reforms constitute a move to a more politically stable international trading environment. An understanding of these issues is critical to the international marketing manager which is why in Chapter 2 we examine in some detail the patterns of world trade,

Illustration 1.3: Nigeria – the ups and downs of a major LDC

Nigeria has the potential to become a major political and economic force in the world. Within Africa, one in every five Africans south of the Sahara is a Nigerian.

Counting the number of people in Nigeria, reliably, has proved difficult. The last census discovered that Nigeria had 20 million fewer people than had been estimated previously. In a population of some 100 million people, Muslims are the largest religious group in the country, followed by Christians and then by animists – believers in spirits and witchcraft. The Muslim faith is important but has a more relaxed impact on life in Nigeria than in some Middle Eastern and other African countries. For example, the Muslim Yoruba tribe drink beer.

Nigeria has three big ethnic groups: The Hausa-Fulani in the north, the Ibo in the east and the Yoruba in the west. Each group speaks its own language. In total, there are about 250 languages in Nigeria. There is intense rivalry between the three main ethnic groups. Language, religion, culture and history helping to emphasise the differences.

Business is difficult in Nigeria. The system of paying for favours, 'dash', results in contracts having excessive profit margins to pay for the various favours granted.

Furthermore, the system of permits allows more people to 'charge' for the issue of permits. Business expansion and foreign direct investment is discouraged. An environmental regulation may be invented by an official to provide an extra opportunity for dash. Recently the rules of business have, at one level, been relaxed. Profits can be repatriated, new business can be wholly foreign-owned, and foreign staff will be given entry visas and work permits. However, approval from officials still needs to be obtained. This approval from the right official can take a long time and much persistence to obtain.

Since gaining independence in 1960, Nigeria has suffered considerable political and military instability. In thirty-three years there have been five military coups, four attempted coups, six military leaders and only nine years without soldiers in power. Oil is a major influence in Nigeria accounting for 82 per cent of government revenue. Inflation is above 100 per cent. Economic difficulties at a macro-level have their impact on every Nigerian. In just over ten years the average GDP per person has declined from over $1000 to under $300.

Source: Adapted from *The Economist*, 21 August 1993.

the regional trading agreements and the development of world trading institutions developed to foster international trade.

The political and economic environments are greatly intertwined and, sometimes, difficult to categorise. It is important, however, that a firm operating in international markets assesses the countries in which it operates to not only assess the economic and political risk but also to ensure they understand the peculiarities and characteristics of the country's market they wish to develop. In Chapter 4 we will examine in some detail the procedures, tools and techniques which can help the analysis and evaluation of opportunities. In this chapter, Figure 1.4 provides a summary of the key political and economic factors firms need to evaluate in a foreign country market in order to assess the associated levels of risk.

Technological environment

Technology is a major driving force both in international marketing and in the move towards a more global marketplace. The impact of technological advances can be seen in all aspect of the marketing process. The ability to gather data on markets, management control capabilities and the practicalities of carrying out the business function internationally over the past few years have been revolutionised with the advancement of electronic communications.

Satellite communications, the Internet and the World Wide Web, client server technologies, ISDN, cable as well as e-mail, faxes and advanced telephone networks have all led to dramatic shrinkages in worldwide communications.

Shrinking communications

Shrinking communications means, increasingly, that in the international marketplace information is power. At the touch of a button we can access information on the key factors that determine our business. News is a 24-hour a day service. (CNN offer global transmission and communication of events throughout the world.) Manufacturers wanting to know the price of coffee beans or the relevant position of competitors in terms of their share price or in terms of new product activity have it at their immediate disposal.

As satellite technology renders land cables and telephone lines redundant, developing countries are abandoning plans to invest in land-based communication. They are bypassing terrestrial communication systems, enabling them to catch up with and, in some cases, overtake developed countries in the market place. In emerging economies consumers are jumping from no

Figure 1.4 Country associated risks

Economic factors	Political factors
Population and income • Size and sectoral distribution • Economic growth and per capita income • Population growth and control • Income distribution	*Composition of population* • Ethnolinguistic, religious, tribal or class heterogeneity • Relative shares in economic and political power • Immigration and outmigration
Workforce and employment • Size and composition • Sectoral and geographic distribution • Productivity • Migration and urban unemployment	*Culture* • Underlying cultural values and beliefs • Religious and moral values • Sense of alienation with foreign or modern influences
Sectoral analysis • Agriculture and self-sufficiency • Industrial growth and distribution • Size and growth of the public sector • National priorities and strategic sectors	*Government and institutions* • Constitutional principles and conflicts • Resilience of national institutions • Role and strength of the army, church, parties, press, educational establishment, etc.
Economic geography • Natural resources • Economic diversification • Topography and infrastructure	*Power* • Key leaders background and attitudes • Main beneficiaries of the *status quo* • Role and power of the internal security apparatus
Government and social services • Sources and structure of government revenues • Sectoral and geographic pattern of expenditures • Size and growth of the budget deficit • Rigidities in spending programmes • Regional dependency on central revenue sources	*Opposition* • Strength, sources of support, effectiveness *General indicators* • Level and frequency of strikes • Riots and terrorist acts • Number and treatment of political prisoners • Extent of official corruption
General indicators • Price indices • Wage rates • Interest rates, money supply, etc.	*Alignments* • International treaties and alignments • Position on international issues, UN voting record
Foreign trade and invisibles • Current account balance and composition • Income and price elasticity of exports and imports • Price stability of major imports and exports • Evolution of the terms of trade • Geographic composition of trade	*Financial support* • Financial aid, food and military assistance • Preferential economic and trade linkages *Regional ties* • Border disputes • External military threat or guerrilla activity • Nearby revolution, political refugees
External debt and servicing • Outstanding foreign debt, absolute and relative levels • Terms and maturity profile • Debt servicing to income and exports	*Attitude towards foreign capital and investment* • National investment codes • Polls of local attitudes towards foreign investors
Foreign investment • Size and relative importance • Sectoral distribution • Geographic (by origin) and regional distribution • Court proceedings in disputes	*General indicators* • Record on human rights • Formal exiled opposition groups • Terrorist acts in third countries • Diplomatic or commercial conflict with home country
Overall balance of payments • Trends in the capital account • Reserve position • Capital flight and 'errors and omissions' *General indicators* • Exchange rates (official and unofficial) • Changes in international borrowing terms	

Source: El-Kahal S (1994) *Introduction to International Business*

telephone to a cellular telephone. China currently has 10 million mobile telephone users.

British Airways operates its worldwide 'exceptional request' facility, such as wheelchair assistance needed for a passenger, from a centre in Bombay. The ease of hiring computer-literate graduates by the hundred, who are intelligent, capable, keen and inexpensive to hire, as is local property to rent, make India an attractive location. The cost of transmitting data processing from London to Bombay, a distance of some 7000 miles, is no more than sending the same information 7 miles. It has been suggested that British Airways plans to run its worldwide ticketing operation from Bombay sometime in the future.

The Internet and the World Wide Web (WWW)

The Internet and the access gained to the World Wide Web is revolutionising international marketing practices. Firms ranging from a few employees to large multi-nationals are only now starting to realise its potential and joining the rush to develop home pages and register domain names (see Illustration 1.4).

A projected 175 million people will be connected to the Internet by 2001. Metagroup predict that goods purchased on-line worldwide will grow from, at present, US$10 billion to US$200 billion by 2001. *PC Week* predict business to business electronic commerce will grow from, at present, US$8 billion to US$300 billion by 2002.

Illustration 1.4: Advertising on the Internet

As little as two years ago, advertising on the Internet was unheard of. Now, the Internet is being hailed as the most effective promotional tool available to international marketing managers.

The number of companies with registered domain names is growing at an increasing rate. GE, IBM and Ford, for example, have all registered domain names, with Proctor and Gamble reserving 52 trademark names and Kraft foods registering as many as 132 domain names such as 'Cheez-whizz.com'. This action may seem extravagant, especially since few companies have any specific plans for how they would use a multitude of product websites. The practice seems to be protective rather than a promotional measure since, in the wrong hands, a domain name such as 'burgerking.com' could result in the company becoming the victim of adverse publicity.

This explosion of international marketing activity and the associated emergence of the global information highway will impact on all businesses.

Quelch and Klein (1996) argue that the Internet will lead to rapid internationalisation of SMEs, reduce global advertising costs making it much easier for small niche products to find a critical mass of customers and, because of low entry costs, permit firms with low capital to become global marketers. There are, therefore, quite significant implications for small and medium-sized enterprises (SMEs) which will be examined further in Chapter 7, where we discuss in some detail the issues in international marketing pertinent to SMEs.

Hamill (1997) in his study argues that the implications of the WWW to international marketing practices will be far reaching.

First, he argues that the Internet will lead to the increasing standardisation of prices across borders or, at least, to the narrowing of price differentials as consumers become more aware of prices in different countries. Second, the Internet by connecting end-users and producers directly, will reduce the importance of traditional intermediaries in international marketing (i.e. agents and distributors). To survive, such intermediaries will need to begin offering a different range of services. Their value-added will no longer be principally in the physical distribution of goods but rather in the collection, collation, interpretation and dissemination of vast amounts of information. The critical resource possessed by this new breed of 'cybermediary' will be information rather than inventory. Third, the Internet will become a powerful tool for supporting networks both internal and external to the firm. Fourth, the Internet is an efficient new medium for conducting worldwide market research, gaining feedback from customers.

Thus the Internet produces a fundamentally different environment for international marketing and requires a radically different strategic approach affecting all aspects of the marketing process. As such, the reader will find that we will examine the impact of the Internet and the WWW on the relevant marketing practices and processes as we move through the chapters of the book.

The dual technological/cultural paradox

On the one hand commentators view technological advancement and shrinking communications as the most important driving force in the building of the global village where there are global consumers who have similar needs. On the other hand, to access this global village a person invariably needs a command of the English language and access to a whole range of equipment. In many markets we yet again stumble against the paradox that whilst in most countries there is a market of well educated and computer literate people, there are others that the global electronic highway completely bypasses.

Despite all that has been said in previous sections, many developing and emerging markets are characterised by poor, inadequate or deteriorating infrastructures (Nakatat and Sivakumar 1997). Essential services required for commercial activity ranging from electric power to water supplies, from highways to air transportation and from phone lines to banking services are often in short supply or unreliable.

The huge population shifts discussed earlier have also aggravated the infrastructure problems in many of the major cities in emerging markets. This often results in widespread production and distribution bottlenecks which, in turn, raises costs.

'Brown outs' for instance are not uncommon in the Philippines, even in the capital city Manila, where companies and offices regularly lose electric power and either shut down in those periods or revert to generators. Fragmented and circuitous channels of distribution are a result of lack of adequate infrastructure. This makes market entry more difficult and the efficient distribution of a product very difficult. Pepsi Cola in Eastern Europe have a large number of decentralised satellite bottling plants in an attempt to overcome the lack of a distribution infrastructure.

In Chapter 11, the strategic implications of fragmented distribution channels and the strategies firms develop to overcome such challenges will be examined in some depth.

Differences between international and domestic marketing

As we have seen in the previous sections, there are many factors within the international environment which substantially increase the challenge of international marketing. These can be summarised as follows:

1 *Culture*: often diverse and multi-cultural markets
2 *Markets*: widespread and sometimes fragmented
3 *Data*: difficult to obtain and often expensive
4 *Politics*: regimes vary in stability – political risk becomes an important variable
5 *Governments*: can be a strong influence in regulating importers and foreign business ventures
6 *Economies*: varying levels of development

7 *Finance*: many differing finance systems and regulatory bodies
8 *Currency*: varying and unstable – strong likelihood of transaction risk
9 *Business*: diverse rules, culturally influenced
10 *Control*: difficult to control and coordinate across markets

Porter (1986) identified that the forces driving international marketing could be divided into currents and cross currents.

Currents are the macro forces such as the growing homogeneity of markets, the drive towards regionalisation, the rise of the emerging markets and shrinking communications.

Cross currents are the emergent trends in international marketing strategies which are driving international competition to behave in new and, sometimes, innovative ways which are changing the bases of international competitive advantage. Cross currents, therefore, are such things as strategic alliances, the growth of marketing on the Internet, R & D (research and development) cooperation, increasing involvement by governments in international trade, the growth of pirating and gray marketing.

The international competitive landscape

A major difference for managers operating on international markets is the impact all these currents and cross currents have on the competitive landscape. Wilson and Gilligan (1997) define marketing as 'getting the competitive advantage and keeping it'. The task of achieving this in a competitive environment where firms are subject to local (see Illustration 1.5), regional and global competition can be immensely challenging. This is especially so if indigenous local competitors are supported by the government of the country.

Across international markets, advanced countries are seeing significant competition from both emerging markets and less developed countries who are exploiting modern technology and their own low labour costs to compete in markets no longer so protected by tariff walls.

The complexity of competition is also heightened by the strategic use of international sourcing of components by multi-nationals and global firms to achieve competitive advantage.

This means, given the nature of the challenges and opportunities identified above and the speed of change within the international environment, substantially different pressures are being placed upon management than if they were purely operating in domestic markets. It follows from this that the

Illustration 1.5: Nescafe means instant coffee?

When Nestle launched Nescafe into Israel in 1995 they found that Nescafe was the generic word for instant coffee. Israelis had always assumed that it was an abbreviation of the Hebrew word *namess* ('dissolving'). Further complicating Nestle's arrival was the country's trading cafe culture. For some forty years, Israeli citizens were content to spend hours at sidewalk cafes drinking low-quality powdered coffee or *nescafe*, produced by Tel Aviv-based food company Elite.

So besides having to break a bad-coffee habit, Nestle's major challenge in entering Israel's US$60 million a year instant coffee market was to get consumers to understand *nescafe* wasn't the instant powdered coffee from Elite they knew and loved, but was really the brand name for Nestle's instant granular coffee.

Nestle rose to the challenge by acquiring a local producer, launching a new brand, Nescafe Classic with an intensive advertising campaign.

To tempt Israelis to try its new product, Nestle sold Nescafe Classic for only about 10 per cent more than the Elite powdered coffee. The company also relied on its policy of taste-testing at points of sale.

The total cost has been estimated to be US$5 million in the first year. However, it has been a highly successful campaign.

After just a year with Nescafe Classic on the market, more than 50 per cent of the instant coffee market was granulated coffee and, within that year, Nestle took 30 per cent of the instant coffee market in Israel.

Source: Adapted from Sugarman (1997) *Ad Age International*, April

manager of international marketing needs a detailed knowledge and under-standing of how particular environmental variables impact on a firm's international marketing operations.

In the next section we will examine the characteristics of international marketing strategies that both fail and succeed before finally going on to consider what are the necessary components of a successful international marketing strategy.

International marketing strategies

Reasons for failure

As we have seen from the various examples given throughout the chapter, sometimes, firms fail in their efforts to develop the international markets they have targeted.

Perlmutter (1995) examining the reasons why firms did not manage their international markets effectively identified nine cross-cultural management incompetences which led to failure across a spread of country markets. He defined these core incompetences as 'the bundle of activities and managerial skills that are mis-matched in a great variety of countries where firms do business'.

The first three are interrelated and relate to the failure to be market driven.

1 Inability to find the right market niches.
2 Unwillingness adaptively to update products to local needs.
3 Not having unique products that are viewed as sufficiently higher added-value by customers in local markets.
4 A vacillating commitment. It takes time to learn how to function in countries such as Japan.
5 Assigning the wrong people. Picking the wrong people or the wrong top team in an affiliate.
6 Picking the wrong partners. There is a list of difficulties in building alliances. A main limitation is picking partners who do not have the right bundle of capabilities to help reach the local market.
7 Inability to manage local stakeholders. This includes an incompetence in developing a satisfactory partnership relationship with unions and governments.
8 Developing mutual distrust and lack of respect between HQ and the affiliates at different levels of management.
9 Inability to leverage ideas developed in one country to other countries worldwide.

Reasons for success

Hamel and Prahalad in their best-selling book *Competing for the future* argue that the firms that will survive in the twenty-first century will be those that perceive the changes in the international environment and are able to develop strategies which enable them respond accordingly. The firms that will do well will base their success largely on the early identification of the changes in the boundaries of markets and industries. Management foresight, therefore, could become the bases of a firm's competitive advantage.

In the dynamic international markets, therefore, if a firm is to succeed it must develop the ability to think, analyse and develop strategic and innovative responses on an international, if not, global scale. Perhaps, such as Mrs Lofthouse did for the Fisherman's Friend in Illustration 1.6.

Characteristics of best practice in international marketing

It is apparent, therefore, that firms and organisations planning to compete effectively in world markets need a clear and well-focused international marketing strategy that is based on a thorough understanding of the markets in which the company is targeting or operating. International markets are

---

Illustration 1.6: Fisherman's Friend

Fisherman's Friend lozenges were initially developed for sailors and trawlermen who were working in severe Icelandic conditions. For a whole century the company made around 15kg of lozenges a month for the UK market. However, when Doreen Lofthouse became managing director, her ambition transformed the company by turning attention to overseas markets. Norway was a logical starting point and is now the market with the highest sales per head of population. Surprisingly, the lozenge was a success in many hot countries too, Italy being the largest foreign customer before recently being overtaken by Germany. Although the product needs no adaptation – a cough needs no translation – promotion of the product differs greatly. The traditional concept has been the centre of advertising in the UK, but overseas, promotional themes are quite different. Italians are shown a girl who breathes so deeply that the buttons pop off her blouse to reveal large naked breasts; in Denmark a man breathes fire; in the Philippines, butterflies flutter against pastel shades, accompanied by gentle music. The brand name is now registered in fifty-four countries and packets come in twenty-one different languages. Exports account for 80 per cent of the £12 million a year turnover.

dynamic entities which require constant monitoring and evaluation. As we have discussed, as markets change so must marketing techniques. Innovation is an important competitive variable, not only in terms of the product or service but throughout the marketing process. Counter-trading, financial innovations, networking and value-based marketing are all becoming increasingly important concepts in the implementation of a successful international strategy.

The challenge then of international marketing is to ensure that any international strategy has the discipline of thorough research and an understanding and accurate evaluation of what is required to achieve the competitive advantage. Doole (1998) identified three major components to the strategies of firms successfully competing in international markets:

- *A clear international competitive focus* achieved through a thorough knowledge of the international markets, a strong competitive positioning and a strategic perspective which was truly international.

- *An effective relationship strategy* achieved through strong customer relations, a commitment to quality products and service and a dedication to customer service throughout international markets.

- *Well managed* organisations with a culture of learning. Firms were innovative and willing to learn, showed high levels of energy and commitment to international markets and had effective monitoring and control procedures for all their international markets.

It is the hope of the authors that, as we take the reader through the chapters of this text, the reader will develop the management skills and capabilities that firms who successfully compete on international markets demonstrate. In order to achieve this the three broad issues which managers need to address are:

- The identification, analysis and evaluation of opportunities.

- The establishment of a strategic perspective and development of an international marketing strategy.

- Building added-values through marketing mix strategies internationally.

These three issues form the base of the international marketing management process undertaken in developing an international marketing strategy. This book is, therefore, organised to take the reader through this process.

Figure 1.5 illustrates the international marketing strategy process and how the chapters relate to each part of the strategy process.

Figure 1.5 The international marketing strategy process

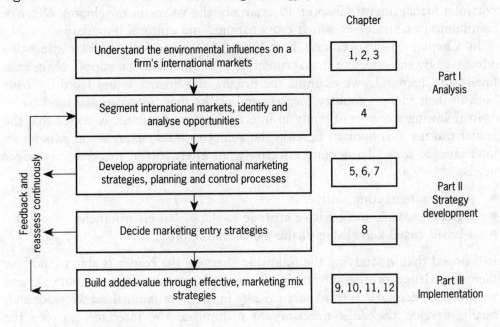

Chapter

Understand the environmental influences on a firm's international markets	1, 2, 3

Part I
Analysis

Segment international markets, identify and analyse opportunities	4

Develop appropriate international marketing strategies, planning and control processes	5, 6, 7

Part II
Strategy
development

Decide marketing entry strategies	8

Build added-value through effective, marketing mix strategies	9, 10, 11, 12

Part III
Implementation

Feedback and reassess continuously

Part I of the book is concerned with international marketing strategy analysis. The first three chapters address the issue of how international marketing management is affected by changes in the international trading environment and variations in social and cultural dimensions.

In Chapter 4, we focus on building analytical skills by examining the process of marketing segmentation and selection and the processes and tools needed for managers to research international markets.

Part II is concerned with the development of international marketing strategies, starting in Chapter 5 with the international planning process and how firms might be organised for international marketing.

The factors which influence the selection of an appropriate strategic option are then discussed, niche strategies for small and medium-sized firms in Chapter 6 and globalisation strategies for large firms in Chapter 7.

In Chapter 8 the alternatives available in foreign market entry strategies are then discussed.

The focus of Part III is how firms can build added-value to their international marketing strategies through their implementation programmes.

Chapter 9 discusses the need for innovative product strategies and effective portfolio management. Chapter 10 examines the issues in developing effective communication strategies which cross national and cultural boundaries.

In Chapter 11 we examine how firms can successfully build competitive advantage by the effective management of their international supply chain and, finally, in Chapter 12 we examine the pricing and finance issues faced by firms both in their foreign country markets and across their international markets.

In following a course of study in international marketing it is hoped that the reader can use this book to develop the ability to *think, analyse* and *plan* on an international scale. To operate effectively, an international marketing manager needs:

- proactive marketing skills
- a global outlook and positive attitude to the global environment
- a broad-based knowledge of the global marketplace.

It is hoped that in studying the following chapters the reader is able to increase their knowledge of the international environment, develop the outlook and perspective necessary to think strategically in the international marketplace and, finally, develop the skills necessary to manipulate the interface between the marketing strategies they develop and the complex environmental factors.

Conclusion

In this chapter we have discussed the growing strategic importance of international marketing and examined the issues associated with successfully competing in international markets. The environments that international companies must operate in are typically characterised by uncertainty and change – factors which taken together increase the element of risk. Given this, there is a need for management to have a properly planned approach to any international activity since, without this, the costs and likelihood of failure are likely to increase.

Major changes in the macro global environment have taken place as old political structures collapse, major trading blocs develop and strategic alliances are formed and the global village emerges through technological advances. Many nations are undergoing change and consumers generally are becoming more demanding and more discriminating. Faced with changes such as these, the implications for international marketing management are significant and it is to these challenges that we turn our attention in the following chapters.

The reader has been introduced to many of the concepts that are important to the international marketing management process and will have gained an understanding of the issues to be addressed. In the following chapter we will examine the international trading environment and the trends and developments in trading patterns.

Discussion questions

1 What are the major environmental influences which impact on international marketing? Show how they can affect international marketing strategies.

2 Using examples examine the reasons why marketing strategies fail in international markets.

3 Identify what you consider to be the three most powerful environmental trends and discuss how they are changing the way companies market goods and services internationally.

4 What skills and abilities are necessary requirements for an effective international marketing manager? Justify your choices.

References

Doole, I. (1998) 'Benchmarking the Competences and capabilities of SMEs successfully competing on International Markets', Ph.D. working papers.

El-Kahal, S. (1994) *Introduction to International Business*, McGraw-Hill.

Haliburton, C. (1997) 'Reconciling global marketing and one to one marketing – A global individualism response', in Doole, I. and Lowe, R. (eds), *International Marketing Strategy – Contemporary Readings*, ITP.

Haliburton, C. and Hunerberg, R. (1993) 'Pan European Marketing – Myth or Reality?' *Journal of International Marketing*, July.

Hamel, G. and Prahalad, C.K. (1994) *Competing for the future*, Harvard Business School Press.

Hamill, J. (1997) 'The Internet and International Marketing', *International Marketing Review*, 14 (5).

Herbig, P. and Hale, B. (1997) 'Internet, the challenge of the 20th Century', *Electronic Networking Applications and Policy*, 7 (2): 95–100.

Nakata, C. and Sivakumar, K. (1997) 'Emerging Markets and their impact on first mover advantages', *International Marketing Review*, 14 (6): 461–85.

Ohmae, K. (1994) *The Borderless World: power and strategy in the interlinked economy*, Harper Collins.

Perlmutter, M.V. (1995) 'Becoming globally civilised, Managing across culture', Mastering Management Part 6, *Financial Times*, 1 December.

Perry, A.C. (1990) 'International Versus Domestic Marketing: Four Conceptual Perspectives', *European Journal of Marketing*, 24 (6).

Porter, M.E. (1986) *Competition in Global Industries*, Harvard Business School Press.

Quelch, J.A. and Klein, L.R. (1996) 'Internet and International Marketing', *Sloane Management Review*, Spring.

Rank Xerox Ltd (1990) *CBI Initiative 1992, Marketing to the Public Sector and Industry*, Mercury Books.

Swift, J.S. (1991) 'Foreign Language Ability and International Marketing', *European Journal of Marketing*, 25 (12).

Terpstra, V. and Sarathy, R. (1997) *International Marketing*, Dryden Press.

Turnbull, P.W. and Cunningham, M.T. (1981) *International Marketing and Purchasing*, Macmillan.

Wilson, R. and Gilligan, C. (1997) *Strategic Marketing Management: planning implementation and control*, Butterworth–Heinemann.

Chapter 2
The international trading environment

Introduction

International marketing takes place within the framework of the international trading environment. If the reader is to have the skills necessary to develop international marketing strategies, some understanding of the parameters of the international trading environment in which they operate is needed.

In this chapter we examine the development of international trade in recent years. We will analyse the growth and changing pattern of international trade and discuss the institutions that aim to influence international trade.

We will also look at the changing regional trading blocs and the implications these have on trading structures around the globe.

World trading patterns

The world economy consists of over 250 nations with a population of 5.8 billion and an output (GDP) totaling US$30 trillion. In 1998 international trade in merchandise totalled US $5.5 trillion. Trade in services is growing at approximately 10 per cent per annum and is currently estimated to be about US$1 trillion. However, this may be well below the true figure.

Together, East Asia, North America and the European Union account for 80 per cent of world trade and 85 per cent of world direct investment.

Europe and the US alone account for 56 per cent of world GDP but only 11 per cent of the world population. Figure 2.1 displays the regional composition of the world economy.

The economic weakness of Africa, Eastern Europe, FSU and the Middle East is highlighted by their congregation in the lower sections. Cumulatively, these regions accounted for only 14 per cent of world GDP. In total, Asia represented

Figure 2.1 Regional composition of world GDP and population.

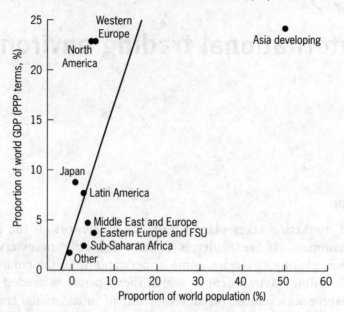

Source: Market Intelligence Department, NatWest Group (1998)

33 per cent of world GDP (including Japan) and 59 per cent of the world's population.

Japan registered very rapid economic and export growth in the early decades of the post-war period. However, progress in recent decades has been more subdued as the Japanese economy has matured and, during the 1990s, has encountered serious structural problems and financial sector weakness. In addition, much manufacturing activity has been transferred to economies with cheaper labour costs.

Over the past decade, Asia has expanded more rapidly than any other region. In 1998, following the Asian crisis, forecasts for growth have been down graded but the broad overall trend is forecast to continue. In the past thirty years, the developing economies of Asia have increased their share of world exports from 6.6 per cent to 18.4 per cent.

Despite concern over its trade deficit America remains by a wide margin the world's biggest exporter (see Table 2.1). In 1997 it sold merchandise worth US$689 billion accounting for 12.6 per cent of the global total. Germany accounted for 9.4 per cent of worldwide exports and Japan 7.7 per cent. Asian

Table 2.1 Percentage of the total of world exports in merchandise 1997

Country	Percentage %
United States	12.6
Germany	9.4
Japan	7.7
France	5.3
Britain	5.1
Italy	4.4
Canada	3.9
Netherlands	3.5
Hong Kong	3.4
China	3.3

Source: World Trade Organisation (web page)

turbulence notwithstanding, China continued to move up the rankings in 1997, to tenth place with 3.3 per cent of world exports.

The UK's share of global merchandise exports has declined appreciably over the past thirty years. Compared with a 7.5 per cent share in the mid-1960s, the UK currently accounts for only 5.1 per cent of global visible exports. The pattern of change over the period is very similar to that of the US exports with a sizable decline in the ten years to the mid-1970s followed by relative stability since. German exports by contrast held their share.

The pronounced change in the geographical structure of UK exports over the past three decades largely reflects the consequences of the UK's accession to the European Union. In 1970, less than a third of UK exports went to countries that now constitute the EU. In 1998 this proportion was 55 per cent. The main 'losers' in terms of the share of UK exports were Commonwealth countries such as Australia and New Zealand whose share fell to 2.0 per cent. The US, however, has 12 per cent share of UK exports. The advanced economies in total now account for over 80 per cent of UK exports compared with 70 per cent in 1970.

Future prospects

World trade volume is expected to maintain a growth of 7 per cent per annum. Table 2.2 examines the annual percentage change in gross domestic product (GDP) and consumer prices (inflation) forecast for the years 1999–2003.

Table 2.2 Forecasts in per cent changes in consumer prices and real GDP/GNP 1999–2003

Country	% inflation rate	% growth rate
Australia	2.7	2.9
Belgium	2.4	2.2
Brazil	6.0	4.2
Canada	2.4	2.6
China	6.8	7.6
France	2.3	2.2
Germany	2.3	2.2
Hong Kong	5.8	4.4
India	9.0	5.5
Ireland	2.8	5.5
Italy	2.7	2.2
Japan	1.8	2.2
Malaysia	3.9	5.4
Mexico	12.2	5.1
Netherlands	2.4	2.5
Singapore	2.6	6.1
South Korea	4.7	4.9
Spain	2.7	2.6
Taiwan	3.5	5.8
Thailand	5.8	4.4
UK	2.5	2.5
USA	2.5	2.6
Advanced Economies	2.4	2.5
EU	2.5	2.3
Eastern Europe	11.8	4.4
FSU	10.6	4.3
Asia Developing	7.1	6.2
Latin America	9.5	4.6

Source: Market Intelligence Department, NatWest Group (1998)

China, Mexico, India, Malaysia, Taiwan, Singapore and Ireland are all expected to maintain growth rates in excess of 5 per cent per annum. It follows that these countries are also expected to maintain a positive balance on the current accounts of their balance of payments (see Table 2.3) as is the European Union. The US, however, is still forecast to have a large trade deficit (US$178 billion) over the next five years. In Chapter 1 we discussed the difficulties of

Table 2.3 Balance of payments current accounts

	US$ billion
Australia	−14.0
Brazil	−13.0
Germany	+10.4
Japan	+87.0
UK	−6.6
USA	−178.0
EU	+78.2
Asia Developing	+27.6
Advanced Economies	−10.8
Non OPEC developing	−54.4
OPEC	+2.1

Source: Market Intelligence Department, NatWest Group (1998)

marketing to countries with high inflation rates. According to Table 2.2 firms are likely to have difficulties in such markets as Mexico, Eastern Europe and the Former Soviet Union where inflation is in excess of 10 per cent. Latin America for the first time for many years is now managing to bring inflation rates under control.

Reasons countries trade

International trade is a vital part of world economic activity but it is not a new phenomenon and whilst the growth of international trade has accelerated in the last forty years, it goes back far beyond then and has been developing throughout the ages since the time when barter was used.

The great growth period for trade was in the eighteenth and nineteenth centuries when many of today's important trading links were forged and developed.

A major source of many of the conflicts in the nineteenth century was the desire by nations to win the right to trade in foreign markets. One of the reasons why Great Britain went to war with Napoleon was to open the French markets to our newly industrialised nation. The colony of Hong Kong and the associated New Territories returned to China in 1997 were acquired by the UK in the early nineteenth century for trading purposes.

The reasons nations trade are many and varied: the two key explanations of why nations trade, however, are based on the theory of comparative advantage and the international product life cycle.

The theory of comparative advantage

The rationale for world trade is based largely upon Ricardo's theory of comparative advantage. At its simplest level, the theory suggests that trade between countries takes place because one country is able to produce a product at a lower price than is possible elsewhere. An illustration of this is provided by the way in which Japanese companies such as Sony and Hitachi came to dominate the European television market. Their strategy was based upon higher product quality, better design and, more importantly for our purposes here, the lower prices that were made possible by far greater economies of scale and better manufacturing technology than was currently being achieved by the European producers.

It is this notion of relative cost that underpins world trade, in other words, countries should concentrate upon producing products in which they have a comparative advantage over their foreign competitor countries.

How comparative advantage is achieved
A comparative advantage can be achieved in a variety of ways.

- **Sustained period of investment**. This may well lead to significantly lower operating costs.

- **Lower labour cost**. A firm operating internationally may locate a manufacturing plant in one of the newly industrialised economies (NIEs), to take advantage of the lower labour costs there. In 1998, the average hourly wage in the USA was $17.20, in South Korea it was $7.40, in Taiwan $5.82, in Brazil $4.28 and in China 25 cents! Many developed countries complain of the disadvantage this creates for them in trying to compete in international markets.

  This competitive disadvantage is further compounded by the government subsidies and support given in such countries. However, as illustration 2.1 points out, low cost is not the only factor in deciding the location of manufacturing facilities.

- **Proximity to raw materials**. This is another way to achieve comparative advantage as has been the case with Australia's reserves of coal and minerals ores.

Illustration 2.1: The global company – lowest cost isn't always the answer

Walk down the aisles of any western toy superstore and most of the basic products will say 'Made in China' or perhaps, Malaysia or Indonesia. Until that is you reach the Lego section. Suddenly the boxes are more likely to identify Denmark, Switzerland or the US as suppliers.

It might seem logical that a global company, selling into a multitude of country markets and measuring its market share in global terms, should place production facilities wherever costs are lowest and they often do. But life is not that simple: even in the toy sector price competition among retailers is ferocious, pressure on suppliers intense and manufacturing fairly unsophisticated. Lego, the

privately-owned Danish company, has for years concentrated its manufacturing in Europe and the US, arguing that this best satisfies design and quality requirements.

And, Lego is not alone in seeking something other than the lowest-cost solution. In a different sector, there is the example of Motorola's decision to set up cellular phone production facilities in Germany.

According to the latest United Nations Conference on Trade and Development data, developed countries took almost two-thirds of foreign direct investment inflows in 1996 while developing countries accounted for less than one-third.

Source: adapted from Tait, N. (1997) *Financial Times*, October 15.

- **Subsidies to help native industries**. When the US announced increased wheat subsidies to US farmers, they outraged the Australian and Canadian wheat farmers who saw it as a direct attack on their international markets. Without comparable government support, they felt they were unable to compete with US wheat in these markets.

- **Building expertise in certain key areas**. This is another way to achieve comparative advantage. The Japanese identified biotechnology as a key area where they have comparative strength and so have targeted it as a priority research area for the new millennium.

Some countries use international trade to buy in a comparative advantage, buying in highly developed products and so speeding up their development.

Porter (1990) suggests that countries can build a national advantage through four major attributes:

- *Factor conditions*: the nation's position in factors of production such as skilled labour or infrastructure necessary to compete.

- *Demand conditions*: the nature of demand in the home country.

- *Related and supporting industries*: the presence or absence of supplier industries and related industries that are internationally competitive.

- *Firm strategy, structure and rivalry*: the conditions in the nation governing how companies are created, organised and managed and the nature of domestic rivalry.

The international product life cycle

The theory of comparative advantage is often used as the classic explanation of world trade. Other observers, however, believe that world trade and investment patterns are based upon the product life cycle concept. Writing from an American perspective, Vernon and Wells (1968) suggested that on an international level, products move through four distinct phases:

1 US firms manufacture for the home market and begin exporting.
2 Foreign production starts.
3 Foreign products become increasingly competitive in world markets.
4 Imports to the USA begin providing significant competition.

This cycle begins with the product being developed and manufactured in the USA for high-income markets, subsequently being introduced into other markets in the form of exports. The second phase begins to emerge as the technology is developed further and becomes more easily transferable. Companies in other countries then begin manufacturing and, because of lower transportation and labour costs, are able to undercut the American manufacturers in certain markets.

The third phase is characterised by foreign companies competing against US exports to NIEs which, in turn, leads to a further decline in the market for US exports. Typically, it is at this stage that US companies either begin to withdraw from selected markets or, in an attempt to compete more effectively, begin investing in manufacturing capacity overseas to regain sales.

The fourth and final stage begins when foreign companies, having established a strong presence in their home and export markets, start the process of exporting to the US and begin competing against the products produced domestically.

It is these four stages Vernon suggests which illustrate graphically how American firms eventually find themselves being squeezed out of their domestic markets having enjoyed a world monopoly just a few years earlier.

Although the product life cycle provides an interesting insight into the evolution of multi-national operations, it needs to be recognised that it provides only a partial explanation of world trade since products do not inevitably follow this pattern. First, competition today is international rather than domestic for all goods and services. Consequently, there is a reduced time lag between product research, development and production, leading to the simultaneous appearance of a standardised product in major world markets. Second, it is not production in the highly labour-intensive industries which is moving to the low labour cost countries but the capital intensive industries such as electronics, creating the anomalous situation of basing production for high-value, high-technology goods in the countries least able to afford them. Nor does the model go very far in explaining the rapid development of companies networking production and marketing facilities across many countries. Thus global business integration and sharing of R&D, technological and business resources is seen as a more relevant explanation of today's world trade.

It is estimated that somewhere in the region of 50 per cent of international trade is now by global or multi-domestic corporations trading with each other. More and more industrial products sold throughout the world are assembled in one country from components manufactured in others.

Barriers to world trade

Marketing barriers

Whilst countries have many reasons for wishing to trade with each other, it is also true to say that all too frequently an importing nation will take steps to inhibit the inward flow of goods and services.

One of the reasons international trade is different from domestic trade is that it is carried on between different political units, each one a sovereign nation exercising control over its own trade. Although all nations control their foreign trade, they vary in terms of the degree of control. Each nation or trading bloc invariably establishes trade laws that favour their indigenous companies and discriminate against foreign ones.

Figure 2.2 Tariff and non-tariff barriers

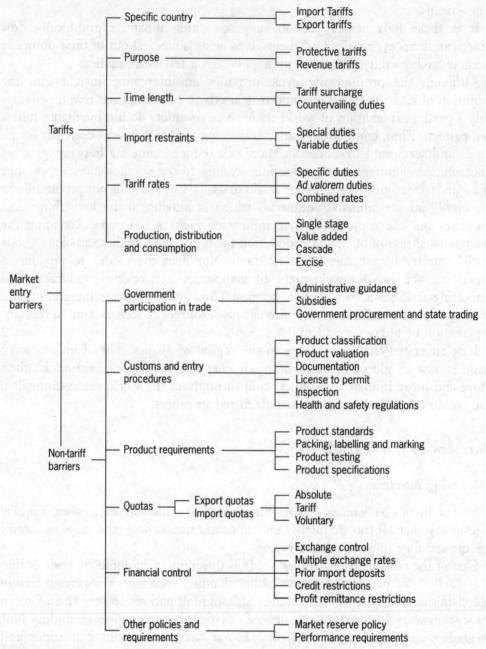

Source: Onkvisit and Shaw (1988)

Thus, at the same time as trade has been developing worldwide, so has the body of regulations and barriers to trade. Onkvisit and Shaw identify 850 ways of reducing imports and claim nations have been known to use all of them. Their research shows that large proportions of many manufactured goods are *overtly* protected, the main protagonists being the USA, Italy, France and Germany.

However, the major barriers to trade are becoming increasingly *covert*, i.e. non-tariff barriers which are often closely associated with the cultural heritage of a country and very difficult to overcome. The complex distribution patterns in Japan are one such example. Thus, whilst Japan is seen not to have many overt barriers, many businesses experience great difficulties when trying to enter the Japanese market.

Trade distortion practices can be grouped into two basic categories: Tariff and non–tariff barriers as illustrated in Figure 2.2.

Tariff barriers
Tariffs are direct taxes and charges imposed on imports. They are generally simple, straightforward and easy for the country to administer. Whilst they are a barrier to trade, they are a visible and known quantity and so can be accounted for by companies when developing their marketing strategies.

Tariffs are used by poorer nations as the easiest means of collecting revenue. The Bahamas for example has a minimum import tax of 30 per cent on all goods, some products are taxed even higher. Tariffs are also imposed to protect the home producer as in the US and Australia. Both of these countries have high tariff walls for certain industries they wish to protect – for example, cars and agricultural products. The trend towards the lowering of tariff barriers across the globe in recent years (the average tariff is now 5 per cent whereas in 1945 it was 25 per cent), together with the opening up of new markets to foreign investment, notably Asia and Eastern Europe, has greatly complicated the decision for many companies as to where to place manufacturing facilities.

These trends have made global production much more possible, but it has also reduced the need for many overseas plants. Markets that previously demanded local production facilities because tariff levels made importing prohibitive, can now be supplied from non–domestic sources.

A good example of these dynamics can be found in the Australian automotive sector. Over the past decade, the tariff on imported cars has fallen from 57.5 per cent to 22.5 per cent, whilst the number of imported cars has risen from less than 15 per cent of the total market to about half. One large car maker, Nissan, has abandoned Australian manufacturing as a result and other car makers, such as

Toyota, have threatened to follow suit unless the pace of tariff reduction slows down.

Tariffs can take many forms, as can be seen in Figure 2.2. The most common forms however are:

- *Specific*: charges are imposed on particular products either by weight or volume and usually stated in the local currency.

- *Ad valorem*: a straight percentage of the import price.

- *Discriminatory*: in this case the tariff is charged against goods coming from a particular country either where there is a trade imbalance or for political purposes.

Non-tariff barriers

In the last forty years, the world has seen a gradual reduction in tariff barriers in most developed nations. However, in parallel to this, non-tariff barriers have substantially increased. Non-tariff barriers are much more elusive and can be more easily disguised. The effect, however, in some ways can be more devastating because they are an unknown quantity and are much less predictable.

Non-tariff barriers take many different forms:

- Increased government participation in trade is one that is gaining more dominance and which is used by nations to gain competitive advantage as in the case of the US wheat subsidy previously discussed.

- Customs entry procedures can also impede trade. These take many forms; administrative hold-ups, safety regulations, subsidies and differing technical standards are just a few. France gained notoriety by insisting that all imports of video recorders came through one particular small customs point in Poitiers causing delays and hold-ups. Illustration 2.2 discusses the case concerning weighing machines which also achieved a certain notoriety.

  The need for customs modernisation and harmonisation has become a priority for companies which find their operations severely hampered by administrative delays at borders and who stand to be disadvantaged even more as economic globalisation gathers pace.

  Clearly the extent of customs delays and red tape varies enormously from country to country but everywhere there is a need for governments to take account of business needs for simple, transparent, coordinated and harmonised customs procedures.

Illustration 2.2: Scanvaegt – Denmark v. the French authorities

Scanvaegt is an exporter of weighing equipment which it successfully markets to Scandinavia, Germany and Britain where it has met few regulatory problems and much market success. When the Single European Market was formed Scanvaegt identified huge potential in the French agricultural sector.

Scanvaegt's semi-automatic weighing machines had been approved by an EU-approved testing centre in Denmark and sold in eleven other European countries. Moreover, an EC directive covering this type of equipment was issued just a month after Scanvaegt had set up a subsidiary in Brittany and won a large order to supply equipment for a factory being set up by the Anglo-French poultry concern Bourgoin Moy Park.

Scanvaegt feels that from the outset its application for approval of equipment met with undue delays, conflicting instructions and bureaucratic hindrances. The company says this was despite its best attempts to comply with escalating demands – attempts that put half its research and development team working flat out for several months in order to modify the machines.

The French weights and measures department initially said it could only consider granting licenses for machines fitted with electromechanical load cells that had been approved in France. In a bid to speed up the process, Scanvaegt consented to switch from British and Dutch-made parts.

But its dismay mounted during the two months of telephone calls, letter-writing to the French authorities and intercession by the Danish embassy that it took just to obtain a list of approved manufacturers of load cells.

Scanvaegt became increasingly caught up in the immense complexity of the French regulations which are contained in a series of intermeshing decrees dating back as far as 1941.

There then began a lengthy process of arranging to install modified versions of the machines at various test sites in France. Once again several design changes were requested – some of which Scanvaegt successfully contested on the grounds that they would have been unhealthy in the food industry.

Tempers frayed when it was found that several French-made machines had been launched on to the market without patent approval and without any objections from the French authorities.

Source: adapted from *Financial Times* (1993) 13 October.

- Quantitative restrictions such as quotas are another barrier. These are limits on the amount of goods that may enter a country. An import quota can be more restrictive than a tariff as there is less flexibility in responding to it. The Japanese car industry faced quotas both in Europe and the US and so developed manufacturing capacity in these markets as a means of overcoming the barriers. The US also imposes quotas on textile imports from China. However, China, according to the US, has been transshipping textiles through other ports such as Hong Kong in order to circumvent the quota. In 1998 it was estimated that transshipments of between US$2–4 billion had entered the US market illegally.

- In Europe the steel industry has felt very threatened by an influx of Polish steel as the European Union reduces barriers to East and Central Europe and is, at present, lobbying very hard to maintain quotas and barriers, arguing that price competition will decimate the European steel industry.

- Financial controls were last seen in the UK in the mid-1970s but are used today in Mexico and Eastern Europe where high inflation and lack of hard currency requires stringent monetary control. This is probably the most complete tool for the regulation of foreign trade as it gives the government a monopoly of all dealings in foreign exchange. A domestic company earning foreign exchange from exporting must sell it to the national bank and, if goods from abroad need to be bought, a company has to apply for foreign exchange. Thus foreign currency is scarce. As a result of the 1998 Asian currency crises, the International Monetary Fund placed stringent controls on several East Asian countries in particular, Indonesia, Thailand and Malaysia.

Countries practising exchange controls tend to favour the import of capital goods rather than consumer goods. The other major implication to companies operating in foreign markets is the restrictions on repatriating profits in foreign currency, requiring either counter-trade dealings or the use of distorted transfer prices to get profits home (see Chapter 12 on pricing issues).

Non-tariff barriers become much more prevalent in times of recession. In the US and Europe we have witnessed the mobilisation of quite strong political lobby groups as indigenous industries, which have come under threat, lobby their governments to take measures to protect them from international competition.

The last major era of protectionism was in the 1930s. During that decade, under the impact of the most disastrous trade depression in recorded history, most countries of the world adopted high tariffs and even Britain abandoned its hundred-year-old policy of free trade. After the Second World War there was a reaction against the high tariff policy of the 1930s and significant efforts were made to move the world back to free trade. In the next section we will look at the world institutions that have been developed since that time to foster international trade and provide a trade climate in which such barriers can be reduced.

The development of world institutions to foster international trade

In the 1930s international trade was at a low ebb, protectionism was rife and economies were strangling themselves. After the Second World War several initiatives were born primarily out of the 1944 Bretton Woods conference to create an infrastructure that fostered trading relations. These initiatives fell into three areas:

- Need for international capital: IBRD
- International liquidity: IMF
- Liberalisation of international trade and tariffs: GATT/WTO

International Bank for Reconstruction and Development (IBRD)

The World Bank, officially called the International Bank for Reconstruction and Development, was founded together with the International Monetary Fund (IMF) in 1944. The World Bank began operating in June 1946 and membership in the Bank is open to all members of the IMF. Currently, there are 130 member countries. The Bank is owned and controlled by its member governments. Each member country subscribes to shares for an amount relative to its economic strength. The largest shareholder in the World Bank at the moment is the United States.

The primary purpose of the Bank is to provide financial and technical help for the development of poorer countries. Currently it lends about £10 billion a year to help raise the standard of living in poorer countries.

The scope of the Bank's operations has increased phenomenally during the past two decades. For example, in the 1990s it provided more than five times as much financial help to developing countries than in any year of the 1960s. The Bank provides support for a wide variety of projects related to agriculture, education, industry, electricity, rural development, tourism, transportation, population planning, urban development, water supply and telecommunications. The Bank lends money only for productive purposes and gives serious consideration to the prospects of repayment before granting the loan.

Whilst the countries who are members subscribe to the share capital of the World Bank, it relies mainly on private investors for its financial resources through borrowing in various capital markets. In this way, private investors become involved in the development efforts of developing countries. Since the IBRD obtains most of its funds on commercial terms, it charges its borrowers a commercial rate of interest. Loans are usually repayable over a twenty-year period.

This has led, in the 1990s, to what has been euphemistically termed the 'debt crises'. Many of the poor developing countries who have been the recipients of large capital loans are now finding it impossible to meet the burden of debt facing them. Figure 2.3 illustrates the heavy burden of debt that some countries may face. In some cases the countries have debt burdens well in excess of their GDP and in the cases of Nicaragua, Guyana and Mozambique, in excess of 400 per cent of their GDP. There is now international agreement that international reforms are needed in order to achieve more sustainable debt platforms and

Figure 2.3 The heavy burden of debt (Debt burden as a per cent of GDP)

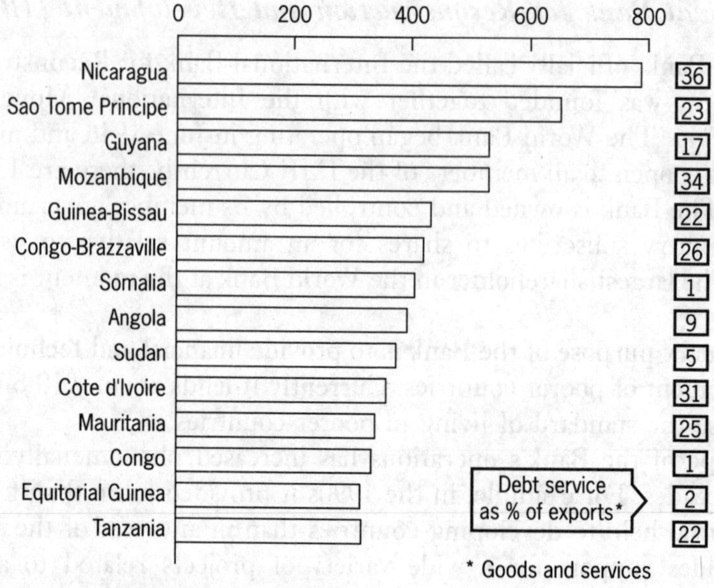

Source: World Bank (1998) (web page)

many campaigns are fighting for the debts of many countries to be written off completely.

International Development Association

In the 1950s it became obvious that many of the poorer countries needed loans on much easier terms than the World Bank could provide. The International Development Association was established in 1960 to help meet this need. It was made an affiliate of the World Bank and was to be administered in accordance with the Bank's established methods.

Almost all of the International Development Association's loans are granted for a period of fifteen years without interest, except for a small charge to cover administrative overheads. Repayment of loans does not start until after a ten-year period of grace. Both the IDA and the IBRD lay down quite stringent requirements that have to be met before any loans are granted. In many cases this has meant that in order to be granted the investment the countries have had to make quite dreadful political decisions in order to achieve the balanced budget required. In some cases this has led to severe hardship and social disorder for which the institutions have been severely criticised.

International Monetary Fund (IMF)

The objective of the IMF was to regain the stability in international exchange rates that had existed under the gold standard. Although the system of pegged rates failed to keep up with the growth in international trade, the functions of the IMF have continued to develop.

The main function is to provide short-term international liquidity to countries with balance of payments deficit problems enabling them to continue to trade internationally. The IMF with its 130 members provides a forum for international monetary cooperation enabling the making of reciprocal agreements amongst countries and the monitoring of the balance of payments positions of countries. Thus it serves to lessen the risk of nations taking arbitrary actions against each other as happened in the 1930s and also can sound a warning bell for nations with potential liquidity problems.

The World Trade Organisation

The predecessor of the World Trade Organisation (WTO) was the General Agreement of Trade and Tariffs (GATT). Established in January 1948, it was a treaty not an organisation with the signatories being contracting parties. Prior to the Uruguay Round (1993) there had been a series of seven trade liberalisation 'rounds'. These entailed tens of thousands of tariff concessions on industrial goods and covered trade flows worth hundreds of billions of dollars. Twenty-three countries participated in the 1948 opening round when 45 000 tariff concessions were agreed covering US$10 billion worth of trade. The Tokyo Round in 1979 saw ninety-nine participating countries and tariff reductions covering US$300 billion worth of trade. Under the first seven GATT rounds, the average tariff on manufactured products in the industrial world fell from around 45 per cent in 1947 to under 5 per cent in the 1980s. This has been an important engine of world economic growth which, in turn, has stimulated further increases in world trade. Signatories to the GATT treaty accounted for some 90 per cent of world trade.

Through all its rounds, GATT has preached a gospel of multilateral trade and most-favoured-nation status which obliges each signatory to the GATT treaty to grant the same treatment to all other members on a non-discriminatory basis. It has evolved regulations which it has tried to enforce through its adjudicatory disputes panels and complaints procedures.

The Uruguay Round which commenced in September 1986 with 107 participants was widely seen as the most complex and ambitious round ever attempted. This was due to the sheer volume of its coverage – fifteen sectors and US$1 trillion worth of trade – and because it sought to stem rising protectionist pressures through strengthening GATT's non-discriminatory trade rules and extending them into new areas including agriculture, textiles, services, investment and intellectual property.

The final GATT treaty was signed in December 1993 where it was agreed to reduce tariffs on a wide range of goods. A new General Agreement of Trade in Services (GATS) treaty for the first time agreed that principles of multi-trade rules will be applied to services. An important part of the treaty was the formation of the World Trade Organisation. The WTO currently has 132 members and another 29 countries including Russia and China who have observer status. The WTO replaces GATT and has the powers to arbitrate in trade disputes between countries. Since its formation, the WTO has been involved in several trade disputes between the US and China, particularly in the areas of copyright, piracy and the use of brand names.

The development of world trading groups

It is believed by some that during the fifty years of global economic expansion under the auspices of GATT, despite the long-term commitments to multilateral trade, there has been an unstoppable momentum of the creation of giant trading blocs.

The formation of the European Monetary Union in 1999 is, perhaps, the most significant of these. When the European single market was formed in 1993, the United States effectively became the second largest market in the world. Who will dominate the international markets of the twenty-first century depends upon the outcome of the competitive battle now commencing. The fear that the world economy may divide into three enormous trading blocs dominated by the world's three economic power houses – Germany, the United States and Japan – rather than a world of multilateral free trade is a recurrent fear. Some commentators argue that national economies are becoming vulnerable to the needs of the trading blocs within which trade is free, currencies are convertible, access to banking is open and contracts are enforceable by law. Whilst this scenario may be a long way from the present position, we are already seeing the formation of trading blocs such as American Free Trade Association (AFTA), Association of South East Asian Nations (ASEAN) and the formation of the European Monetary Union.

In this section we will examine in detail the regional trading blocs that are emerging but first let us examine different forms of trade agreements.

Forms of market agreement

There are nine levels of market association ranging from limited trade cooperation to full-blown political union (see Table 2.4). At the lower level of association, agreements can be purely for economic cooperation in some form, perhaps a decision to consult on or coordinate trade policies. At the next level of cooperation, there will be the development of trade agreements between countries on either a bilateral or multilateral basis. Often these are for a particular sector – for example the multi-fibre agreement in textiles. Sometimes such agreements, especially trade preference ones, will act as a forerunner to closer ties. As far as formal trade groupings are concerned, there are five major forms: free trade areas, customs unions, common markets, economic unions and political unions.

Free trade area

The free trade area type of agreement requires different countries to remove all tariffs amongst the agreement's members. Let us assume that there are three nations – A, B and C – that agree to a free trade area agreement and abolish all

Table 2.4 Main types of trade associations

Type	Description	Degree of policy harmonisation amongst members	Common external tariff	Free movement of capital and people	Example
Economic cooperation	Broad agreement for consultations on and possible coordination of economic trade policies	None/very low	No	No	Canada–EC framework agreement, APEC
Bilateral or multilateral trade treaty	Trade regulation and often, but not necessarily, liberalisation in one or more specified sector(s)	Low	No	No	The Peru, Chile accord
Sectoral free trade agreement	Removal of internal tariffs in a specified sector may include non-tariff barrier reduction	Medium (within specified sector(s))	No	No	The multi-fibre agreement
Trade preference agreement	Preferred trade terms (often including tariff reduction) in all or most sectors, possibly leading to free trade area	Low/medium	No	No	South African Development Cone (SADC)
Free trade area (or agreement)	Removal of internal tariffs and some reduction of non-tariff barriers in all or most sectors	Medium	No	No	ASEAN NAFTA Mercosur
Customs union	Free trade area but with a common external tariff, harmonisation of trade policy toward third countries	Medium/high	Yes	Possibly	Economic Community of West African States ANCOM, CACM
Common market	Customs union, but with provisions for the free movement of capital and people, removal of all trade barriers, elaborate supra-national institutions, significant harmonisation of internal market structure and external policies		Yes	Yes	European single market
Economic union	Common market, but with integration of monetary policies, possibly common currency, significant weakening of national powers of member states	Very high	Yes	Yes	European monetary union
Political	Full or partial federalism, including sharing of powers between supra-national institutions and national governments	Highest	Yes	Yes	Would resemble federal states (e.g. US, Canada, Germany)

Source: unknown

tariffs amongst themselves to permit free trade. Beyond the free trade area A, B and C may impose tariffs as they choose. The EEA (European Economic Area) formed between the EU, EFTA and the LAFTA (Latin American Free Trade Area) illustrate the free trade area type of agreement as does NAFTA, the agreement between the USA, Canada and Mexico and the ASEAN agreement.

Customs union

In addition to requiring abolition of internal tariffs amongst the members, a customs union further requires the members to establish common external tariffs. To continue with the example (countries A, B and C) under a customs union agreement, B would not be permitted to have a special relationship with country X – A, B and C would have a common tariff policy towards X. Prior to 1993, the EC was, in reality, a customs union. The objective of Mercosur is to form a customs union. Their cooperative effort started as a free trade area and now they intend to develop into a customs union.

Common market

In a common market type of agreement, not only do members abolish internal tariffs amongst themselves and levy common external tariffs they also permit free flow of all factors of production amongst themselves. Under a common market agreement, countries A, B and C would not only remove all tariffs and quotas amongst themselves and impose common tariffs against other countries such as country X, but would also allow capital and labour to move freely within their boundaries as if they were one country. This means that, for example, a resident of country A is free to accept a position in Country C without a work permit.

The European Union since 1993 is essentially a common market with full freedom of movement of all factors of production. The Andean nations in South America have formed ANCOM and the Central American nations have formed CACM. However, these are more association agreements than common markets.

Economic union

Under an economic union agreement, common market characteristics are combined with the harmonisation of economic policy. Member countries are expected to pursue common fiscal and monetary policies. Ordinarily this means a synchronisation of money supply, interest rates, regulation of capital market and taxes. In effect, an economic union calls for a supranational authority to design an economic policy for an entire group of nations. This is the objective of the

Maastricht Treaty agreed in 1991 by EC ministers. The European Union was officially formed on the 1st November 1993 and the European Monetary Union officially commenced in 1999.

Political union

This is the ultimate market agreement amongst nations. It includes the characteristics of economic union and requires, additionally, political harmony amongst the members. Essentially, it means nations merging to form a new political entity. Thus Yugoslavia, which was created after the First World War, was a political union as was the Soviet Union – both of which have now disintegrated.

Figure 2.4 shows the major trading regions which have significantly developed in the past decade together with their member countries. In the following sections we will examine these major trading groups and the developments they have undergone.

Figure 2.4 Regional Trading Areas

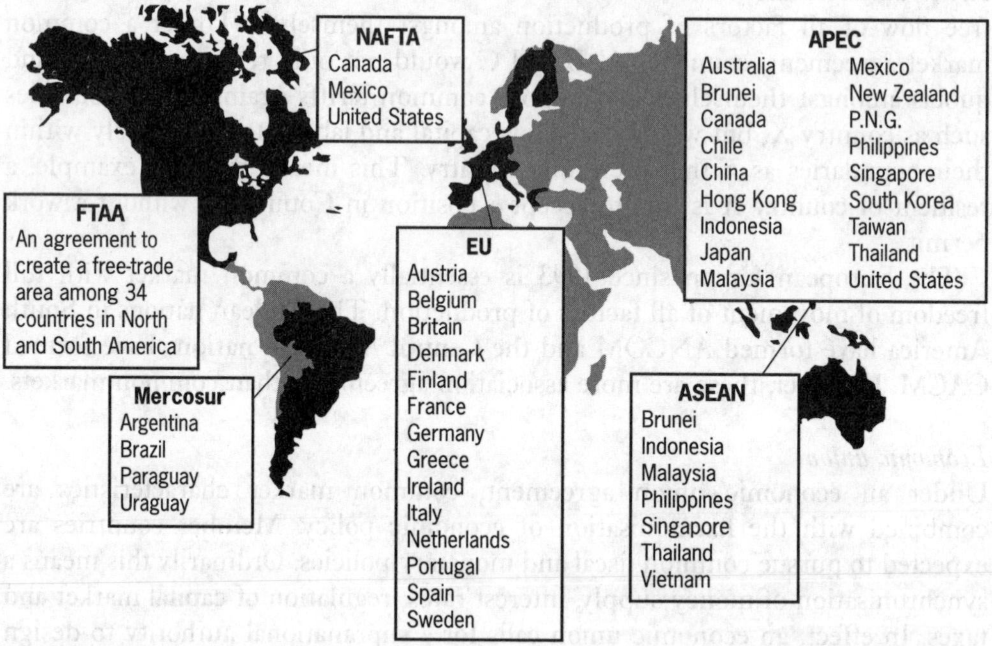

NAFTA
Canada
Mexico
United States

APEC

Australia	Mexico
Brunei	New Zealand
Canada	P.N.G.
Chile	Philippines
China	Singapore
Hong Kong	South Korea
Indonesia	Taiwan
Japan	Thailand
Malaysia	United States

FTAA
An agreement to create a free-trade area among 34 countries in North and South America

EU
Austria
Belgium
Britain
Denmark
Finland
France
Germany
Greece
Ireland
Italy
Netherlands
Portugal
Spain
Sweden

Mercosur
Argentina
Brazil
Paraguay
Uraguay

ASEAN
Brunei
Indonesia
Malaysia
Philippines
Singapore
Thailand
Vietnam

Source: IMF (1998)

The European Union

Since 1987 and the signing of the Single European Act, Europe has undergone momentous changes, the key amongst these being:

- the Single European Market (SEM)
- formation of the European Monetary Union (EMU)
- the opening of Central and Eastern Europe and the disintegration of the Soviet bloc and Yugoslavia
- the unification of the two Germanys creating a powerful economic force in the centre of Europe
- the expansion of the European Union (EU) to include members of the European Economic Area (EEA) and the planned extension to Central and Eastern Europe.

The Single European Market

The formation of the SEM meant that Europe became the largest trading bloc in the world with a population of 380 million people making it a powerful competitive force in the global markets. This, of course, was the key objective of the moves towards a unified market. In the early 1980s it was recognised that if European companies were to compete successfully in the increasingly inter-dependent and global economy, a free and unbridled large internal market was necessary. This would enable companies to develop the critical mass needed to compete globally. The highly fragmented and restricted European market was seen as a major barrier to the ability to compete in global markets.

The SEM was formed as a result of the signing of the Single European Act in 1987 which created, within Europe, 'an area without internal priorities in which the free movement of goods, personal services and capital is ensured in accordance with the provision of the Treaty of Rome'.

The key changes were:

- **Removal of tariff barriers**: a single customer-check at all intra-EU borders enabling goods and services to move freely across Europe.

- **Removal of technical barriers**: a major impediment to trade was the differing complex standards required in each country. Harmonisation of these standards has paved the way for product standardisation throughout Europe.

- **Public procurement**: public procurement amounts to 15 per cent of EU GNP, only 2 per cent of which went to foreign suppliers. By opening up the market to all European suppliers and by ensuring its enforcement, it is estimated that 17.5 billion Euro are saved per annum.

- **Free movement of labour and workers' rights**: nationals of member states now have the right to work in other member states.

- **Opening up of professions**: through mutual recognition of qualifications, professionals in certain categories have their qualifications recognised by other member states.

- **Financial services**: the opening of banking, insurance and investment services through the introduction of a single banking license and the harmonisation of banking conditions.

- **Transport, haulage and coastal cabotage**: road haulage permits and quotas have been abolished. A more competitive air transport industry is also being pursued as is unlimited cabotage for transport through the SEM. Thus, trucks are now allowed to pick up goods in any EU country and drop them off where required without the bureaucracy of permits and border documentation.

- **Company law**: several European developments in the area of company law are taking place in the fields of take-over bids, health and safety, cross-border merger, etc. The road to greater control from Brussels is now becoming especially apparent in this area.

- **Fiscal barriers**: there are many EU variations of fiscal policies, e.g. VAT. The UK has a standard rate of 17.5 per cent whereas France has six rates varying from 2.1 to 33.33 per cent. Moves are being made to reduce these disparities.

- **The environment**: the European Environment Agency was established to try and provide an integrated and Europe-wide policy for environmental protection.

Most analysts agree that the SEM greatly enhances market opportunities for European companies. As a result of its formation, there is a potential home market of 380 million consumers for companies within its walls.

Intra-regional trading amongst EU members accounts for 70 per cent of all intra-trade. With such inter-dependency, it is little wonder that so much effort has been put into completing the unified market.

European Monetary Union (EMU)

The idea behind a single European currency has been around since the early 1960s. As trade between member countries increased, various attempts were made to stabilise exchange rates. Previous systems such as the Exchange Rate Mechanism (ERM) attempted to create monetary stability through a system of fixed and floating exchange rates. This proved, however, to be incapable of coping with capital flows which resulted in problems for sterling and the lire in September 1992, with the remaining currencies also facing problems the following year. Pressure for further integration in the Community resulted in the move to monetary union and a single European currency following as a logical conclusion to the Single Market. EMU commenced in 1999 in the sense that the European Central Bank took control of interest rates. Businesses, however, will not have to trade or pay wages in Euros until 2002.

EMU has started with eleven founder members. The only country which qualified for entry into monetary union by achieving all the convergence criteria is Luxembourg. With a small manipulation of the figures Germany, France, Austria, the Netherlands, Finland, Ireland, Belgium, Italy, Portugal and Spain were all deemed eligible. The UK does not seem likely to join until at least 2002 and Denmark and Sweden have also opted out.

Even if Britain does not join the EMU until 2002, if UK firms trade in the European Union both the manufacturing and service sectors are likely to be affected by the introduction of EMU. Companies in both sectors will need to convert their customer invoices and accounts, credit notes and prices into Euros. Companies which use computer systems for their customer and/or supplier accounts will also need to adapt them to deal with Euros. The estimated conversion cost in computers, tills, packaging and billing is set at least at £1 billion. On the other hand, companies with customer and supplier bases largely outside the EU will face little or no impact unless Britain does decide to join.

Strategic implications

The strategic aspects of EMU are notoriously difficult to judge. EMU is not just a monetary event but one which is likely to have serious impacts on the real economy. Prices and wages will become transparent; consumers will shop around for the best deals; middlemen will try to exploit any prevailing regional price differences; margins everywhere will come under pressure. European business could face a messy transition scenario.

The competitive environment could be tougher under EMU. This seismic change will affect companies both inside and outside the EMU zone, except that it will force insiders to adjust quickly, whilst outsiders might take longer to adjust. Illustration 2.3 examines the impact on the car industry.

Illustration 2.3: Monetary Union drives motor industry changes

The European single market has prompted profound changes in the motor industry from the assembly line to the showroom but improvements to manufacturing and buying procedures need a single currency.

One of the biggest changes prompted by the single market has been increased willingness by motorists to buy cars made in other European countries.

Some traditionally more protectionist markets such as France and Italy have become more open to foreign products either as finished cars or components.

The single market has also made it easier for European car-makers to sell across national boundaries by lifting product approval and distribution barriers. Harmonisation of 'type approval' rules in the 1990s have eliminated the need for car-makers to undergo lengthy approval processes for each new model across Europe. That has accelerated product development times at a time of rising competition from non-European car-makers. However, obstacles remain in freeing up the European car market.

Amongst the continuing distortions are differing national tax structures for vehicle ownership and differing fiscal groups which complicate pricing strategies in the industry.

However, the biggest obstacle to a more efficient market was the lack of a single currency. Some car-makers spread their component purchases across a number of suppliers in different countries to hedge against exchange rate fluctuations. EMU will encourage the trend towards concentration on a smaller number of sources for greater economies of scale. Currency differences also inhibited transparency in the car market for consumers. Pricing under a single currency should eliminate regional distortions.

Source: adapted from Simonian, H. (1997) *Financial Times*, 4 July.

In some cases, it may take outsiders longer to sense the changes that are going on in the inside. By the time the UK eventually joins EMU, UK companies might find that their competitors may be significantly ahead, both in their logistical as well as strategic preparations.

Some large German companies – BMW, Daimler-Benz and Siemens for example – are already using the Euro as their in-house currency. Hewlett Packard have abolished national prices for office supplies. Schering recently introduced a new drug for multiple sclerosis at a single pan-European price. Marks and Spencer quote all prices in Euros as well as the local currency.

Which industries will win and which will lose from the Euro? Amongst significant losers will be the banks which will lose their business of buying and selling European currencies and carry most of the costs of the transition. The biggest difference, however, will not be between industries but between efficient, flexible companies and those that stick to their old national ways.

Companies which have concentrated on their national markets will be particularly vulnerable to takeover or extinction at the hands of their more far-sighted European competitors. Those businesses already used to competing internationally will have a strong advantage. As sources of supply widen, specialisations based on national talents will develop further. French and German companies, for example, are already running call-centres from Dublin, where multilingual Irish operators (or continental expatriates who prefer life in Ireland) provide advice or take orders over the telephone more cheaply and flexibly that would be possible in the companies' home countries.

Another effect of the single currency will be to open the European market for those small and medium-sized companies which have, so far, concentrated on their domestic customers. Salomon Brothers estimates that currency fluctuations and the costs of dealing with them have deterred a third of small and medium-sized German companies from venturing abroad. Many that do export have concentrated exclusively on countries where currencies are informally linked to the D-Mark, such as Austria and the Netherlands. In France, a study of small companies in the Paris region by Andersen Consulting found that nearly half expected to start selling in new markets as a result of the single currency's introduction.

Widening European membership

Since the fall of Berlin Wall in 1989, central Europe has been the scene of a series of political advances.

After the re-unification of Germany, developments continued with the independence of the Baltic Republics (1991), the achievement of good relations between the Czech Republic and Slovakia after partition (1992) and the sporadic relaxation of tension in major parts of former Yugoslavia (1996).

This political movement has been accompanied by a burst of economic renewal in most of these nations.

In 1990, the planned economies of central Europe could be better described as ill-developed rather than under-developed. They remained under the grey blanket of communism and exhibited different levels of economic advancement.

Since 1990, the style and pace of transition in the region has varied widely from country to country. Nevertheless, it has remained focused on a common set of goals; the attainment of political democracy, market economies and integration into the European Union and the international business community.

To date, ten central European governments have applied for EU membership; the three Baltic Republics, Bulgaria, the Czech Republic, Hungary, Poland, Romania, Slovakia and Slovenia.

In 1993 the European Council adopted the 'Copenhagen Criteria' for admission to the EU. These require that member countries attain the following:

- Democracy and the rule of law.

- A functioning market economy.

- Fulfilment of membership obligations.

Central European nations are moving rapidly towards the fulfilment of these criteria. Of the applicants listed above, the Council considers that nine have met the first criterion with only Slovakia failing in terms of democracy and minority rights.

From an economic standpoint, five of the ten countries pass the test (the Czech Republic, Estonia, Hungary, Poland and Slovenia) which indicates possible admission to the EU by 2003.

The five remaining nations are moving in the same direction. Romania, the second-largest post-communist economy in the regions, with 23 million inhabitants, has firmly engaged in the painful restructuring process and the transfer of initiative to the private sector. Even Bulgaria, which was hesitating to adopt such a policy, has made considerable progress.

In 1998, the growth rate in central Europe was 5.2 per cent, higher than the EU (2.4 per cent) for the third year running. It is reasonable to expect such a differential to continue in the medium term and, as such, central Europe may be considered a younger and faster-growing version of western Europe.

Depending on the country and industry, growth potential in central Europe is extremely high. The consumer goods market, for example, which was almost virgin territory in 1989 has undergone tremendous growth. Sony's sales in the region have risen 30 per cent annually in recent years whilst Skoda's sales in the Czech Republic rose by 21 per cent in 1996 (see Illustration 2.4).

Illustration 2.4: Skoda has the last laugh

Skoda Autos (of the Czech Republic), once a butt of jokes, has now completely over-hauled its image and its profitability with the help of its German partner. In 1991 Volkswagen bought a controlling share in Skoda. A new production line near Prague now makes one of a growing number of world-class mass-market manufactured products developed in Eastern Europe: the Octavia. Productivity according to Vratislav Kulhanek, Chairman of the Skoda Board, is around 90 per cent of western levels and rising; labour costs are around a quarter of those at VW's plants in Spain. Other car companies such as Audi (also part of the VW group) and Opel (part of General Motors) both of which have built engines and assembly plants in western Hungary tell a similar story.

Multi-national corporations that have had the vision and capacity to build a profitable presence in the region in recent years are now benefiting from the advantages of having been the first to move. With the most attractive locations, the best partnerships, the greatest opportunities through privatisation and, often the best people, these enterprises combine local strengths with the powerful weapon of cost-based global competitive advantage.

Volkswagen's presence in the Czech Republic and Slovakia through its subsidiary Skoda has three advantages. First, it increases Volkswagen's leadership in Europe through the conquest of local central European markets. Second, it increases competitiveness through local manufacturing and purchases. Third, it offers the possibility of using Skoda to penetrate other emerging markets in Europe, Russia and Asia. For example, Skoda is currently discussing a project for a new plant in India.

Source: adapted from *The Economist* (1997) 22 November.

The second major attraction for business is cost. In 1996 the average labour cost in the Czech Republic was only $4 per hour compared with $30 in Germany. Relative to other emerging regions, central Europe has a high level of education, a skilled labour force, a number of good and even excellent engineers and a strong technological and scientific tradition.

Third, trade provides a large advantage for companies operating in central Europe. In 1990 most trade was carried out within the region. A company such as Polkolor, which manufactures TV tubes in Poland, primarily targeted Polish and Russian markets. Gradually, many companies began considering exports back to their home countries and elsewhere in addition to the local market.

Since 1996 companies entering the region are likely to have had dual ambitions; dominance of the local and regional market and the development of an export platform for western Europe and other international markets (see Illustration 2.5).

The Free Trade Area of the Americas (FTAA)

NAFTA

In 1994, US, Canada and Mexico created the world's richest market by the creation of the North American Free Trade Area (NAFTA). NAFTA created a single market of 360 million people producing over US$6 trillion in annual output. Their combined intra-trade amounted to US$200 billion and commentators expected NAFTA to potentially add $30 billion per annum to the combined GDP.

The main provisions of the NAFTA agreement aimed to:

- Eliminate tariffs on manufactured goods.

- Eliminate tariffs on 57 per cent of the agricultural produce from Mexico.

- Harmonise and streamline customs procedures and bureaucracy.

- Liberalise telecommunications, transport, textiles, banking and finance.

- Establish a NAFTA trade commission to settle trade disputes.

The attractive feature of NAFTA is that by virtue of the fact that Mexico as at a different stage of economic development from the US and Canada, the potential for gains through specialisation should be relatively large. Although it is impossible to determine precisely, one would expect that the US would specialise

Illustration 2.5: ABB's central European strategy

ABB's surge in central and eastern Europe has two motivations: high local demand in energy-related businesses and low-cost manufacturing which enhances the group's global competitiveness.

Former ABB president Percy Barnevik often expressed his conviction that the only possible strategy for the division of labour was to manufacture high-tech products in the West and standard products in emerging countries. The current president, Goran Lindhal, confirms that ABB is reserving a large part of its new investments for emerging nations.

In central Europe ABB's presence has been massive and precocious. In 1997 the company employed 24 000 people in the region; worldwide it has 215 000 staff. The company's focus is on Poland, Hungary and the Czech Republic.

ABB's largest central European subsidiary (turnover $507 million in 1996) exports gas turbines, low-pressure turbine rotors and generators worldwide. Polish plants within the ABB group tend to export more than 20 per cent of their production.

This implies that local production meets the group's worldwide quality standards and that the group integrates all its activities into a unified manufacturing network. Since the cost of a turbine manufactured in Poland may be 40 per cent lower than competing products from western Europe, ABB's competitive advantage at a global level is increased.

Source: adapted from *FT Exporter* (1998) March.

in more complex products that are intensive in their use of knowledge, technology and capital equipment.

The available evidence suggests that this is precisely what has happened. US exports to Mexico of electronic goods and transport equipment have increased substantially. Meanwhile, most of the anecdotal evidence about US workers harmed by NAFTA comes from light manufacturing industries and agriculture.

However, it must be added that the scale of change induced by NAFTA is probably quite small relative to other factors impinging on the US economy such as technological change and reductions in defence spending.

For many, the creation of NAFTA was a US response to the formation of the single market in Europe. However, for others it has signalled the drive by the US to create a Free Trade Area across the Americas. This would create a free trade area consisting of thirty-four democracies by the year 2005.

This involves negotiations with the Central American Common Market, the Andean Community and Mercosur.

Mercosur

Mercosur is the incipient customs union linking Brazil, Paraguay, Uruguay and Argentina. Bolivia and Chile are associate members. This South American Southern cone is the fourth largest integrated market in the world and consists of 240 million people with a combined GNP of US$1 trillion.

The creation of Mercosur is seen as an integral part of the formula which has enabled its member countries to conquer inflation, expand the size of its markets and attract in substantial foreign direct investment.

Some of this investment is in Latin America's traditional extractive industries in response to new mining codes in countries such as Peru, Bolivia and Argentina. In manufacturing, it is the prospect of fast-growing domestic markets that attracts incomers. In many industries, acquisition is the easiest way to enter the market; it removes a competitor and offers instant access to a distribution network, local know-how and good connections.

Unlike China or Eastern Europe, Latin America is familiar territory for many multi-nationals which have been operating there for up to a century. Until recently, they behaved much like their local counterparts taking advantage of closed markets by charging high prices for goods of poorer quality or more old-fashioned design than they could sell at home. But as trade barriers have fallen, especially in intra-regional trade, many multi-nationals have brought Latin America into their worldwide strategy. For example, Unilever as part of its drive to dominate the global ice-cream industry bought Kibon, Brazil's largest ice-cream maker (see Illustration 2.6).

Three strategic issues have to be faced by companies endeavouring to build their presence in the Mercosur markets.

- **Infrastructural weaknesses**: although the region has achieved remarkable growth in internal trade in the past few years, its infrastructure has to be substantially improved to facilitate a more competitive flow of materials, machinery and goods. This will allow corporations to develop fully integrated regional strategies. As things stand, the inefficient infrastructure

Illustration 2.6: Unilever in $930 million ice-cream move

Unilever has strengthened its grip on the global ice-cream market by paying US $930m to acquire Kebon, Brazil's largest ice-cream business, from Philip Morris.

It meets two of Unilever's investment priorities – ice-cream is one of the seven 'starred' product categories selected for development and southern Latin America is one of the five sub-regions identified for expansion.

The acquisition gives Unilever more than 60 per cent of the fast-growing Brazilian market. The next largest producer is Nestle, the Swiss food group, which has 20 per cent.

Sales of ice-cream in Brazil average 1.2 litres per head a year and Unilever expects to increase this to the levels seen in other South American countries such as Argentina, where consumption is 3.3 litres, or Chile, where it is 4.2. As in those countries, it will introduce international ice-cream brands to Brazil such as Magnum, Vienetta and Solero.

Last month Unilever bought Mothelado, Argentina's second-largest ice-cream maker, also from Philip Morris. When the Brazilian deal is completed, Unilever will be the largest ice-cream maker in the $1.6 billion Latin American market.

Unilever sells ice-cream in eighty-five countries with sales worth about $6 billion a year – more than twice those of Nestle, its nearest competitor.

Source: adapted from *Financial Times* (1997) 21 October.

hampers companies' efforts to achieve the economies of scale needed for regional competitiveness.

- **The need to develop industrial 'clusters'**: a nation's successful industries are usually linked through clusters of vertical and horizontal relationships. The vehicle assembly industry based in São Paulo, which has been successful for decades, illustrates how clustering of related businesses (glass, rubber, pistons and steel) is a driving force behind an industry's competitiveness. Such clusters should increase the opportunities for small and medium-sized companies – not just the big corporations – to profit from the process of regional economic integration.

- **Entrepreneurial mindset**: the major obstacle for the development is not lack of opportunities or capital or technology; it is the business culture amongst traditional entrepreneurs. A mindset based on paternalism, centralisation of authority and casual opportunism is a fundamental obstacle to the empowerment and decentralisation of the decision-making process required for overseas expansion.

FTAA

The development of the Latin American markets is essential if the economies of the region are to compete effectively in a much larger area – as will happen if the FTAA (Free Trade Area of the Americas) becomes a reality. Mercosur, the Andean Pact and other trade agreements in the region are regional training fields for the new structures to come.

Companies are becoming familiar with the complexities of the new business landscape and designing innovative international strategies to increase their cross-borders capabilities. Whether they will flourish in the larger, more integrated, global economy that will be in place as the new millennium gets under way and the US pushes forward their aspirations for the FTAA, is yet to be seen.

The Asian Pacific Trading Region

Asia Pacific Economic Cooperation (APEC)

The US is also a member of APEC (Asia Pacific Economic Cooperation). APEC is essentially a forum amongst twenty-three Asia Pacific nations to discuss means and ways to build economic and trade cooperation. Some members of the group would like an Asia-Pacific trading bloc to emerge as they fear being excluded from traditional US markets. This would mean that Japan and the US would be in one regional bloc. Combining FTAA, East Asian and Australasian countries into one Asia-Pacific bloc would mean that nearly 70 per cent of their trade would be intra-regional. However, there is marked resistance amongst Asian members of APEC for an enhanced role of the group although the US is giving a high priority to the APEC grouping and intends to forge closer trade and investment ties across the Pacific.

The Asia Pacific region has had the fastest growth in the world for thirty years and, despite a downturn in 1998, East Asia is the principal export market for US products. In 1998 transpacific trade was 50 per cent greater than its transatlantic trade and more than 40 per cent of US trade is now in the Asian region. To foster this growth, the United States supports a more active APEC that will take on a role as a forum for consultations on trade policy and expansion of trade and investment, with a goal of lowering trade barriers in the region and supporting a multilateral system of free trade.

The Association of South East Asian Nations (ASEAN)

The members of the Association of South East Asian Nations (ASEAN) – Thailand, Indonesia, Singapore, Brunei, Malaysia and the Philippines, have agreed to form a free trade area by the year 2008.

This will create a largely tariff-free market of 340 million people. The scheme aims to reduce tariffs or internal trade to a common preferential tariff of 0–5 per cent.

However, some observers are sceptical about the development. Geographical distances and cultural disparities have meant that previous attempts at closer economic integration have failed. These nations are keenly competitive and previously have not kept to agreements to lower trading restrictions. Nevertheless, the Asian economies are pulling closer together than ever before and this trend is likely to accelerate in the new millennium. But where European (EU) and North American (NAFTA) integration has been based on treaties, in Asia it is based on market forces, the chief force being the region's fast rate of growth. By the year 2010, Asia should account for about a third of world production. Increasingly growth is also coming from intra-Asian trade which recent estimates have put as high as 30 per cent and which is expected to reach 40 per cent by the end of the decade.

Barriers to developing a cohesive trading region

Whilst an Asian Pacific trading bloc may never have the cohesion of either Europe or America as the fastest-growing economic region in the world, any move towards integration will be watched closely by international competitors. Investment there is dominated by Japanese companies which are providing 75 per cent of all foreign investment in China, Hong Kong and the ASEAN countries.

There are evident trends that Japan is building its own area of economic dominance in East Asia. Japan's exports to Asia exceed those to the US, and Japan is now the only country in the top twenty-three countries in the world who are not formally a member of a free trade area.

Thus in Asia, the trading bloc that is emerging could be one dominated by a Japan that is essentially building economic dependencies in ASEAN and the newly industralised countries of North Asia. However it is the fear of ASEAN member countries of becoming just such a dependency that may be the biggest barrier to any emerging trading bloc.

Some commentators include Australia as being amongst those countries which are now commercially dependent on Japan although the Australians themselves would argue against such a proposition. However, according to Austrade statistics, Japanese investment in Australia rose from A\$16 billion in the mid 1980s to A\$72 billion in March 1998 and Australia is actively seeking bilateral trading agreements with Japan.

Thus, even if ASEAN does not become a viable trading area, there are regional pressures beginning to emerge. Of key importance in this region is the reaction of Japan to the North American and European trading blocs. Both the EU and NAFTA have, in part, been formed as a reaction to Japan's emergence as a superpower. One option would be to expand the free trade area into the East Asian Economic Group (EAEG) including Japan and South Korea, Hong Kong and Taiwan, although Asian commentators see Japan and Korea as unlikely partners.

Ironically, the US is opposing any move towards an Asian free trade zone, emphasising the role of APEC which includes Japan, Australia, New Zealand and China.

There are particular barriers to developing a liberalised Asia Pacific trading bloc. Firstly, there is a huge diversity amongst the nation states, not just culturally but historical, religious as well as economic diversity. Japan has a GDP per capita of US\$20 000, Burma US\$200. Politically, the countries embrace very different political systems. Democratic structures in many of these markets e.g. Indonesia, are either non-existent or too weak to ensure the economic fairness necessary to sustain the progress to regulation of markets and trust in the rule of law which is crucial to any commercial relationship.

Furthermore the geographical area is huge and there is no natural groupings of nation states. There is also uncertainty as to the future intentions of Japan in the region but perhaps, more significantly, huge uncertainty as to the role China will play in this region over the next decade.

The Chinese economic area

The centre of gravity and dynamism of the Asia Pacific economy in the decade ahead is most likely to be the Chinese economic area. This consists of China,

Hong Kong and Taiwan. This is a prediction that could conceivably fall flat due to political circumstances. The implosion of China driven by the huge income discrepancies that are emerging within social groups and between regions on the one hand and the increasingly apparent illegitimacy of the Communist Party on the other is not a totally implausible scenario.

However, the past decade has seen a phenomenal rate of growth in China itself. China's GDP has been estimated by the latest 1997 World Bank figures as being around US$745 billion – driven by an average growth rate of 9.4 per cent between 1978 and 1997. Moreover, according to a study by China's Academy of Social Science (CASS), by 2030 it will have become the world's largest economy, surpassing even the US with a GDP of $155 billion. Some Western studies have even estimated that China's economy will have achieved top spot a decade earlier than this.

The World Bank report *China 2020*, estimates that China will achieve an annual growth rate of 6.5 per cent for the next 20 years – making it the world's second largest exporter after the US.

British exports to China were worth £740 million in 1997. The top five UK exports to China in 1997 were: specialised machinery (£112.5m), general industrial machinery and equipment (£98m), telecommunications and sound recording equipment (£91.5m, power generating machinery and equipment (£73m) and electrical machinery and appliances (£38.5m).

China has recently opened previously closed service sectors on an experimental basis such as: banking, retail, accounting, trade, real estate, tourism and insurance. For example, joint ventures between foreign accounting and inspection companies and Chinese companies are now possible.

Also levels of direct investment in China remain strong. Indeed, Britain is the largest European investor in China. The UK is pledged to invest US$11.93 billion in the next three years.

All this investment has helped China to achieve rapid economic development but it has been spread unevenly across the country. For example, the southern coastal regions of China, typified by Guangzhou Province, have grown out of all recognition with the rest of the country.

Figures supplied by the Chinese authorities underline this regional disparity; the eastern seaboard produces 53 per cent of China's GDP, the middle provinces 31 per cent and the western provinces 16 per cent.

Companies that have succeeded in China include Siemens, Johnson, Motorola and Volkswagen. It should come as no surprise that companies, however, have faced severe difficulties in establishing themselves in China and some car manufacturers especially have suffered huge losses. The main problems they have faced centre around the following problem areas: Chinese bureaucrats pushing for over-capacity, inconsistent regulations, red tape leading to significant increases in costs, and insufficient protection of intellectual property.

Conclusion

International trade over the past forty years has seen tremendous growth. In that time multilateral trade has flourished and a number of institutions have been developed to foster international trade.

The dawn of the new millennium, however, is seeing substantive changes in the global competitive structures as emerging markets strengthen their economic foundations and regional trading areas become more cohesive. Europe now has monetary union. Free trade areas are emerging in Asia, Pacific and the Americas, moving world trade away from global multilateralism to a more regionally focused trading pattern. China is developing the potential to dwarf most countries as it continues its rapid development and speedy economic growth.

Discussion questions

1 Identify barriers to the free movement of goods and services. Explain how barriers influence the development of international trade.

2 What do you consider the macro forces impacting on the development of world trade? Show by examples how they are changing the nature of international business?

3 In what ways does the creation of the European Union affect a firms global marketing strategy in Europe? Why have some firms reacted by acquiring and merging with other European firms?

4 Evaluate the importance of full monetary union within the European Union to a company marketing to the European market.

References

Buzzell, R.D. and Quelch, J.A. (1990) *The Marketing challenge of 1992*, Addison Wesley.

Doole, I. and Jones, R. (1992) 'Central Europe from blind spot to black hole', *MEG Proceedings*, July.

Garten, J.E. (1997) 'Troubles ahead in emerging markets', *Harvard Business Review*, May–June.

Henbig, P. and Day, K. (1995) 'Outgrowth of ASEAN a common market of the Pacific', *European Business Review*, 93 (2): 12–23.

IMF (1998) *Directions of Trade Statistics*, IMF.

Jeannet, J.P. and Hennessey, H. (1992) *International Marketing Management*, Houghton Mifflin.

Market Intelligence Department (1998) *Economic Outlook*, April.

'Mastering Global Business', *Financial Times (1998)*, Series January–March.

Onkvisit, S. and Shaw, J. J. (1988) 'Marketing Barriers in International Trade', *Business Horizons*, June.

Porter, M.E. (1990) *The Competitive Advantage of Nations*, Macmillan.

Vandermevwe, S. (1989) 'Strategies for a Pan European market', *European Journal of Management*, 7 (2).

Vandermevwe, S. and Huillier, M.A. (1989) 'Euro Consumers in 1992', *Business Horizons*, January–February.

Vernon, R. and Wells, L.T. (1968) 'International Trade and International Investment in the Product Life Cycle', *Quarterly Journal of Economics*, May.

Chapter 3
Social and cultural considerations in international marketing

Introduction

Markets in countries around the world are subject to many influences as we saw in Chapter 1. Whilst it is possible to identify those influences common to many country markets, the real difficulty lies in understanding the specific nature and importance of these influences.

The development of successful international marketing strategies is based on a sound understanding of the similarities and differences that exist in the countries around the world. The sheer complexity of the market considerations that impinge on the analysis, strategic development and implementation of international marketing planning is a major challenge.

In this chapter we will examine the social and cultural issues in international marketing and the implications they have for strategy development.

Social and cultural factors

Social and cultural factors influence all aspects of consumer and buyer behaviour. The differences between these factors in different parts of the world can be a central consideration in developing and implementing international marketing strategies. Social and cultural forces are often linked together. Whilst meaningful distinctions between social and cultural factors can be made, in many ways the two interact and the distinction between the various factors is not clear-cut. Differences in language can alter the intended meaning of a promotional campaign and differences in the way a culture organises itself socially may affect the way a product is positioned in the market and the benefits a consumer may seek from that product. A sewing machine in one culture may be seen as a useful hobby, in another culture a sewing machine may be necessary to the survival of a family.

Kotler (1995) included such things as reference groups, family, roles and status within social factors. Whilst this is a useful distinction from the broader forces of culture; social class and social factors are clearly influenced by cultural factors. Take the example of the family which is an important medium of transmitting cultural values. Children learn about their society and imbibe its culture through many means but the family influence is strong, particularly during the early formative years of a child's life. Furthermore, the way in which family life is arranged varies considerably from one culture to another. In some cultures the family is a large extended group encompassing several generations and including aunts and uncles, whilst in other cultures the family is limited more precisely to the immediate family of procreation and even then the unit might not be permanent and the father and mother of their children might not remain together for the entirety of the child-rearing process. Thus social and cultural influences intertwine and have a great impact on the personal and psychological processes in the consumer and buyer behaviour processes and, as such, play an integral part in the understanding of the consumer in international markets. Toys R Us found quite distinct differences in the type of toys demanded in their various international markets. Whereas the US children had preferred TV and movie endorsed products, Japanese children demanded electronic toys, South East Asian children wanted educational toys, and the more conservative cultures of the European markets expected a choice of traditional toys.

It is not feasible to examine all the social or cultural influences on consumer and buyer behaviour in one chapter, neither is it possible to describe all the differences between cultures across the world. In the first section we will highlight the more important socio-cultural influences which are relevant to buyer behaviour in international markets. In the following section we will focus on developing an understanding of the components of culture and its impact on consumer behaviour and the implications for international marketing strategies. We will then discuss the methodologies which can be used to carry out cross-cultural analyses to enable comparisons to be made across cultures, finally we will examine business to business marketing and the impact of culture in these types of markets.

What is culture?

Perhaps the most widely accepted definition of culture is that of Ralph Linton (1945): 'A culture is the configuration of learned behaviour and results of behaviour whose component elements are shared and transmitted by members of a particular society'. Or perhaps, more appropriately: 'The way we do things around here'. In relation to international marketing, culture can be defined as: 'The sum total of **learned beliefs, values and customs** that serve to direct consumer behaviour in a particular country market'.

Thus culture is made up of three essential components:

Beliefs: A large number of mental and verbal processes which reflect our knowledge and assessment of products and services.

Values: The indicators consumers use to serve as guides for what is appropriate behaviour, they tend to be relatively enduring and stable over time and widely accepted by members of a particular market.

Customs: Overt modes of behaviour that constitute culturally approved or acceptable ways of behaving in specific situations. Customs are evident at major events in ones life e.g. birth, marriage, death and at key events in the year e.g. Christmas, Easter, Ramadan, etc.

Such components as values, beliefs and customs are often ingrained in a society and many of us only fully realise what is special about our own culture, its beliefs, values and customs when we come into contact with other cultures. This is what happens to firms when they expand internationally and build up a market presence in foreign markets. Often the problems they face are a result of their mistaken assumption that foreign markets will be similar to their home market and so they can operate in a similar manner. Frequently in international markets the toughest competition a firm may face is not another supplier but the competition of different customs or beliefs as a result of cultural differences. This means for a company to succeed in that market they often have to change ingrained attitudes as to the way they do business. The beliefs and values of a culture satisfy a need within that society for order, direction and guidance. Thus culture sets the standards shared by significant portions of that society which in turn sets the rules for operating in that market.

Hofstede (1996) identifies a number of layers within a national culture.

Layers of culture

- A national level according to one's country which determines our basic cultural assumptions.

- A regional/ethnic/religious/linguistic affiliation level determining basic cultural beliefs.

- A gender level according to whether a person was born as a girl or as a boy.

- A generation level which separates grandparents, parents and children.

- A social class level associated with educational opportunities, a person's occupation or profession.

All of these determine attitudes and values and everyday behavioural standards in individuals and organisations.

Given such complexities, often market analysts have used the 'country' as a surrogate for 'culture'. Moreover, culture is not something granted only to citizens of a country or something we are born with, it is something we learn as we grow in our environment. Similar environments provide similar experiences and opportunities and hence tend to shape similar behaviours.

Terpstra and Sarathy (1997) identifies eight components of culture which form a convenient framework for examining a culture from a marketing perspective.

The components of culture

Education

The level of formal primary and secondary education in a foreign market will have a direct impact upon the 'sophistication' of the target customers. A simple example will be the degree of literacy. The labelling of products, especially those with possibly hazardous side-effects, needs to be taken seriously for a market that

Figure 3.1 A cultural framework

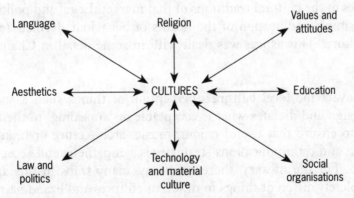

Source: adapted from Terpstra and Sarathy (1997)

has a very low literacy rate. ICI markets pesticides throughout the world. In developed countries its main form of communication is advertising and printed matter. In developing countries they rely heavily on training and verbally based educational programmes to get their message across.

Social organisation

This relates to the way in which a society organises itself. How the culture considers kinship, social institutions, interest groups and status systems. The role of women and caste systems are easily identifiable examples. If the firm has a history of successfully marketing to 'the housewife/homemaker' life becomes more difficult where women have no social status at all. House ownership is another. In Switzerland the majority of people rent rather than own their houses. They expect to rent property with domestic appliances already installed, this means the banks are the largest purchasers of washing machines, not individual families.

Technology and material culture

This aspect relates not to 'materialism' but to the local market's ability to handle and deal with modern technology. Some cultures find leaving freezers plugged in overnight, servicing cars and trucks that have not yet broken down, difficult concepts to understand. In instances such as these the organisation is often faced with the choice of either educating the population (expensive and time consuming) or de-engineering the product or service (difficult if you have invested heavily in product development).

Law and politics

The legal and political environments in a foreign market are often seen as consequences of the cultural traditions of that market. Legal and political systems are often a simple codification of the norms of behaviour deemed acceptable by the local culture. This aspect was dealt with in some detail in Chapter 1.

Aesthetics

This area covers the local culture's perception of things such as beauty, good taste and design and dictates what is acceptable or 'appealing' to the local eye. A firm needs to ensure that use of colour, music, architecture or brand names in their product and communications strategies is sympathetic and acceptable to the local culture. For the unwary, there are many, many traps in this area. Colour means completely different things in different cultures and brand names often do not travel well! (See illustration 3.1).

Illustration 3.1: Cadbury's: Lady Purple or Aunty Violet?

Not unlike ourselves, colours may or may not be aesthetically pleasing . . . but they all have a personality. When we look at a colour a whole spectrum of thoughts, feelings and emotions are evoked in our minds. Some of these associations are instinctive in us all, others we learn from the environment in which we live. From the passionate excitement of red to the playful happiness of yellow, colours are constantly eliciting subconscious responses in us all.

For international marketers this notion is particularly pertinent. In our efforts to cue the customer into positioning our brand in a certain way, the colours used in the design, packaging and advertising of a product can send very powerful messages about the personality of our brand. However, as the meaning of colour is often derived from the cultural environment, the messages and thus the personality, may fluctuate greatly across countries and cultures.

In a recent study, the Cadbury's brand was perceived very differently by UK and Taiwanese participants. Whilst in the UK Cadbury's was seen to be luxurious, stylish, expensive, classy and silkily feminine, the Taiwanese held the image of an old, warm, friendly, but essentially poor brand, low in quality and lacking in class.

In the same study, participants from the two countries were asked to discuss their perceptions of the colour purple – a colour that Cadbury's is currently attempting to register as a trademark.

Once again, the British made associations with luxury, style, sophistication, youth and femininity. The Taiwanese, on the other hand, talked of a warm, old, quiet colour, serious, a little sad but dignified. In both cultures, all the feelings, emotions and characteristics associated with the colour purple had been transferred to give very different meaning to the Cadbury's brand.

When taking colour abroad, therefore, marketers may do well to heed some of mother's most motherly advice . . . 'Looks aren't everything. It's the personality that counts!'

Source: Anthony Grimes (1999), Sheffield Business School

Values and attitudes

The values consumers from different countries place on things such as time, achievement, work, wealth and risk taking will seriously affect not only the products offered but also the packaging and communication activities. The methods used by a firm to motivate its personnel is also strongly influenced by the local culture and practice. Encouraging local sales forces to sell more by offering cars and more money, for example, may not work in all cultures. Values are important to marketers as they can be translated into consumption vehicles as illustrated in Table 3.1.

Table 3.1 Cultural values and their relevance to consumer behaviour

Value	General features	Relevance to consumer behaviour
Achievement and success	Hard work is good; success flows from hard work	Acts as a justification for acquisition of goods ('You deserve it')
Efficiency and practicality	Admiration of things that solve problems (e.g. save time and effort)	Stimulates purchase of products that function well and save time
Progress	People can improve themselves; tomorrow should be better than today	Stimulates desire for new products that fulfil unsatisfied needs; ready acceptance of products that claim to be 'new' or 'improved'
Material comfort	'The good life'	Fosters acceptance of convenience and luxury products that make life more comfortable and enjoyable
Individualism	Being oneself (e.g. self-reliance, self-interest, self-esteem)	Stimulates acceptance of customised or unique products that enable a person to 'express his or her own personality'
External conformity	Uniformity of observable behaviour, desire for acceptance	Stimulates interest in products that are used or owned by others in the same peer group?
Youthfulness	A state of mind that stresses being young at heart and a youthful appearance	Stimulates acceptance of products that provide the illusion of maintaining or fostering youthfulness

Source: Schiffman, L.G. and Kanuk, L.L. (1994) *Consumer Behaviour*, Prentice Hall

Religion

Religion is a major cultural variable and has significant if not always apparent effects on marketing strategy. For example, the identification of sacred objects and philosophical systems, beliefs and norms as well as taboos, holidays and rituals are critical for an understanding of a foreign market. Religion for example, will affect the food which people eat, when they eat it as well as people's attitudes to a whole range of products from deodorants to alcoholic drink.

In some countries religion is the most dominant cultural force. For instance, in Islamic markets, such as Saudi Arabia, no violation of religion by advertising and other promotional practices, no matter how insignificant, will go unnoticed or unpunished either by the government or the consumer. Major violations of religion are even punished in more liberal and so called secular markets within the Islamic world. Rules surrounding religious laws require heightened insight and empathy by international companies. Comparative ads are banned as, according to the laws of Islam, pegging one product against another diminishes the sense of unity and social community. Companies need to understand the difference between two key terms, Haraam and Makruh.

Haraa'm are subjects or things that are absolutely unlawful and strongly prohibited in Islam, such as alcohol and cheating. These taboo subjects are totally banned in advertising and other promotional activities in Saudi Arabia, Kuwait and Iran (see Table 3.2).

'Makruh' are the subjects which are seen as distasteful. They are discouraged in Islam but are not banned. Smoking is not forbidden in Islam but it is highly discouraged.

Language

Language can be divided into two major elements. The spoken language of vocal sounds in patterns that have meaning and silent language which is the communication through body language, silences and social distance. This is less obvious but is a powerful communication tool. Language to many commentators interlinks all the components of culture and is the key to understanding and gaining empathy with a different culture. In the following section we will examine the different components of language.

Table 3:2 Major 'Haraam' subjects in Islam

Pornography	Cheating	Alcohol
Adultery	Necromancy	Drugs (intoxicants)
Adulteration	Gambling	Pork
False promises	Usury (interest)	Prostitution
Immodest exposure[1]	Game of chance	Sodomy (homosexuality)
Bribery	Comarative adds	Murder
Backbiting	Abusive language	Arrogance
Idol worship[2]	Hoarding	Cruelty towards living beings
Interference in performing religious duties		

[1] Women must cover whole body except hands and face. Men must at least be covered from naval to knees
[2] Worshipping anything and any body other than the one and only Allah as the supreme power and creator

Source: Isobel Doole and Asif Yaqub (1997)

Language and culture

Spoken language

Spoken language is an important means of communication. In various forms, for example plays and poetry, the written word is regarded as part of the culture of a group of people. In the spoken form the actual words spoken and the ways in which the words are pronounced provide clues to the receiver about the type of person who is speaking.

Estimates of the main spoken languages around the world are given in Table 3.3. Chinese is spoken as the mother tongue (or first language) by three times more people than the next largest language, English. However, Chinese is overtaken by English when official language population numbers are taken into account.

It should be noted that official languages are not always spoken by the whole population of a country. For example, French is an official language in Canada but many Canadians have little or no fluency in French.

English is often but by no means always the common language between business people of different nationalities. Speaking or writing in another language can be a risky activity (see Illustration 3.2).

Table 3.3 Official languages and spoken languages

Mother tongue speakers	Millions	Official language	Populations (millions)
Chinese *	1,000	English	1,400
English	350	Chinese	1,100
Spanish	250	Hindi	700
Hindi	200	Spanish	280
Arabic	150	Russian	270
Bengali	150	French	200
Russian	150	Arabic	170
Portuguese	135	Portuguese	160
Japanese	120	Malay	160
German	100	Bengali	150
French	70	Japanese	120
Punjabi	70	German	100

Source: Guardian (1992) 11 February

Note: * Chinese is composed of a number of dialects of which Mandarin is the largest.

Illustration 3.2: Written English: but what does it mean?

Japanese hotel notice to hotel guests:

'You are invited to take advantage of the chambermaid'

Acapulco hotel notice regarding drinking water:

'The manager has personally passed all the water served here'

Visitors to a zoo in Budapest were asked:

'Not to feed the animals. If you have any suitable food, give it to the guard on duty'

A Bangkok dry cleaner to potential customers:

'Drop your trousers here for best results'

A Roman laundry innocently suggested:

'Ladies leave your clothes here and spend the afternoon having a good time'

A Hong Kong dentist claims to extract teeth:

'By the latest Methodists'

A Copenhagen airline office promises to:

'Take your bags and send them in all directions'

Source: adapted from *Sunday Times* (1992) 22 November

In advertising, particular attention needs to be paid when translating from one language to another. The creative use of copy to gain attention and to influence comprehension of the target audience can result in a clever use of words. However, inadequate translation often results in clumsy errors. In Germany a General Motors advertisement mentioned a 'body by Fischer' which became 'corpse by Fischer'. This is clearly a straightforward translation error, directly resulting from the mistranslating of the word 'body'. The Hertz company strapline, 'Let Hertz put you in the driving seat' became 'Let Hertz make you a chauffeur'. Instead of communicating liberation and action as intended this translation provided quite a different meaning, implying a change of occupation and status.

Silent language

Silent language is a powerful means of communication. The importance of non-verbal communication is greater in some countries. In these cultures people are more sensitive to a variety of different message systems. Table 3.4 describes some of the main silent languages in overseas business.

Silent languages are particularly important in sales negotiations and other forms of business meetings. They will, in addition, influence internal communications in companies employing people from different countries and cultures.

The example in Illustration 3.3 shows how difficulties can arise even between cultures which are geographically close to each other but have different perceptions of language.

Table 3.4 The main silent languages in overseas business

Silent language	Implications for marketing and business
Time	Appointment scheduling. The importance of being 'on time'. The importance of deadlines.
Space	Sizes of offices. Conversational distance between people.
Things	The relevance of material possessions. The interest in the latest technology.
Friendship	The significance of trusted friends as a social insurance in times of stress and emergency.
Agreements	Rules of negotiations based on laws, moral practices or informal customs.

Source: Hall and Hall (1987)

Illustration 3.3: Just a slight misunderstanding!

The meeting, planned over a number of weeks, was over in less than an hour. The German team was annoyed that their hard work was not recognised, the French team anxious that their lack of preparation for the meeting would not be revealed.

The real problem was concealed in the translation of one word. The Germans wanted a discussion of their *Konzept*. The French translation used the apparently similar French word, *concept*.

Unfortunately, the words have different meanings. To the Germans, *Konzept* meant a detailed plan of a proposed new product; to the French, *concept* meant an opportunity to discuss, propose and create a proposal which would eventually become the detailed plan. Unfortunately, the meeting never started with a firm mutually agreed framework. The result was a wasted meeting.

Source: adapted from *Guardian* (1993) 15 March

Cultural learning

The process of *enculturation*, i.e. learning about their own culture by members of a society, can be through three types of mechanisms. Formally, through the family and the social institutions to which people belong, technically, through the educational processes, be it through schools or religious institutions, and informally, through peer groups, advertising and other various marketing related vehicles.

This enculturation process influences consumer behaviour by providing the learning we use to shape the toolkit of labels, skills and styles from which people construct strategies of action, e.g. persistent ways of going through the buying process.

The process of *acculturation* is the process international companies need to go through in order to obtain an understanding of another culture's beliefs, values and attitudes in order to gain an empathy with that market. As we have seen, culture is pervasive and complex and it is not always easy for someone outside a given culture to gain an empathy with that market.

Having examined the main components of culture and the various important dimensions we will now look at how culture impacts on consumer behaviour.

Culture and consumer behaviour

There are several important ways in which the various components of culture influence a consumer's perception, attitude and understanding to a given product or communication and so affect the way a consumer behaves in the buying process. Jeannet and Hennesey (1993) identify three major processes through which culture influences consumer behaviour as depicted in Figure 3.2.

Culture is seen as being embedded in elements of society such as religion, language, history and education (cultural forces). These elements send direct and indirect messages to consumers regarding the selection of goods and services (cultural message). The culture we live in determines the answers to such questions as: Do we drink coffee or juice at breakfast? Do we shop daily or on a weekly basis? and so affects the consumer decision process.

The body of theory on which our understanding of consumer behaviour is based predominantly heralds from the USA. Usiner (1996) argues that the means by which international marketing managers understand consumer behaviour is flawed as sometimes the theoretical principles on which we base our understanding do not necessarily hold true across different cultures. He specifically highlights four important assumptions which international marketers should question:

1 That Maslow's Hierarchy of Needs is consistent across cultures.
2 That the buying process in all countries is an individualistic activity.
3 That social institutions and local conventions are similar across cultures.
4 The consumer buying process is consistent across cultures.

Figure 3.2 Culture influences on buyer behaviour

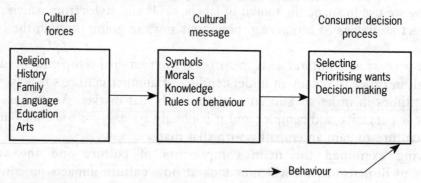

Source: adapted from Jeannet and Hennesey (1993)

That Maslow's Hierarchy of Needs is consistent across cultures

Culture influences the hierarchy of needs (Maslow 1970) on two levels. First, the axiom that one need must be satisfied before the next need can appear is not true for every culture and second, similar kinds of needs may be satisfied by different products and consumption types.

For example in some less developed countries, a consumer may go without food in order to buy a refrigerator and, therefore, satisfying the dominant need of social status before physical satisfaction. A study conducted by Chan and Lin (1992) identified that self-esteem needs were most important to Chinese consumers with the least important being physiological needs. Physiological needs include food, water, shelter, etc. whereas self-esteem needs include prestige and success.

In building a presence therefore in the Chinese market, companies would need to target consumers with high self-esteem needs by linking a product such as credit cards to success in business or beer to success in sporting activities (Assael 1992).

Likewise, similar kinds of needs may be satisfied in very different ways. For example, to a Hindu the need for self-realisation does not necessarily imply material consumption as in Western cultures but in fact abandoning all worldly possessions.

That the buying process in all countries is an individualistic activity

Many Western buying behaviour models are primarily based on individual purchases with reference to family decision-making in the context of husband and wife decisions. They assume buying decisions are focused on an individual's decision making process. In Asia a family may be a complex structure and so an individual would need to take into account all members of the family in making major purchase decisions. Thus the decision making is of a much more collectivist nature.

That social institutions and local conventions are similar across cultures

Institutions such as the state, the religious institutions, trade unions and the education system also influence consumer behaviour.

The UK company ROMPA which serves the market for people with learning disabilities, found enormous cultural differences across their European market due to the varying influences the national institutions had on how charities and social institutions should be organised. In Germany the market was highly organised and strongly supported financially by the state. In Spain the state lottery was the prime benefactor through major national charities, whereas in Italy the church was the major benefactor with very little involvement by the state.

The consumer buying process is consistent across cultures

There are many inconsistencies in the buying processes across cultures around the globe, three aspects which are particularly pertinent to our discussion are the differences in: the level of consumer involvement, the perception of risk in a purchase and the cognitive processes of consumers.

Consumer involvement

The Chinese are seen as having a low level of involvement when purchases are for private consumption but a high level of involvement when they are buying products for their social or symbolic value. Since the Chinese greatly value social harmony and smoothness of relationships within the extended family, the social significance of products are highly important be it to express status, gratitude, approval or even disapproval. Heineken very successfully tapped into this need for social acceptance in their innovative campaign in Hong Kong (see Illustration 3.4).

Perceived risk

The level of risk consumers associate with a purchase varies enormously across cultures and as such it is an important variable in consumer behaviour. It will determine whether a consumer will go for the comfortable purchase or is willing to try new products and services. Risk incorporates three components: physical risk, financial risk and social risk.

Whereas in some countries, *physical risk* may be important (e.g. the fear of BSE in the UK beef market), others may be more sensitive to *social risk* and the loss of social status if a wrong buying decision is made (i.e. the Chinese fear of losing of face). *Financial risk* closely relates to the level of economic development in a country. It is likely to be less in the more affluent economies where if a wrong purchase decision is made the financial hardship suffered may not be so profound.

The level of brand loyalty found in a market is also closely related to the perception of risk. There are huge variations in attitudes to brand loyalty across

Illustration 3.4: Heineken beats Carlsberg through the backdoor

Between 1993 and 1998 Heineken increased its market share in Hong Kong from 5 per cent to 25 per cent.

The Heineken brewer did not achieve these remarkable share gains directly. It was the local distributor which truly understood the cultural drivers of the Hong Kong beer market. The local distributor knew the market and understood that Heineken had an enormous task against the entrenched brands with huge market shares, large advertising budgets and very effective campaigns. To spend millions of advertising dollars to achieve anything against the two major and entrenched brands, San Miguel and Carlsberg who together had over 70 per cent market share, was considered unrealistic. The distributor basically tapped a key Asian value – make people believe the beer is popular!

The Heineken beer distributor in Hong Kong achieved this by pushing the product first in aspirational, on-premise outlets to develop an up-market niche. They then followed a programme of asking on-premise staff to leave the bottles on the table by not pouring full beers into glasses and not collecting the empties. Suddenly, little green bottles were seen everywhere, being drunk by white collar, up-market types in expensive, trendy outlets. This evolved until suddenly more and more people were drinking the beer and it eventually took on its own momentum.

This general approach was viewed as the only way to beat the entrenched brand loyalty. The biggest key to marketing in Asia is not necessarily actual market share but *perceived popularity*. If a firm can convince Asians that many of their colleagues are buying the brand by building high visibility then success is much more likely.

Source: adapted from Robinson (1997) *Journal Of Market Research Society*, 38 (1)

different cultures. In the US the standard buyer behaviour is that of *disloyalty*. A consumer will shift from one brand to another because it is standard behaviour to test several competitive products and so foster price competition. Thus in the US it is relatively easy for a new entrant to persuade Americans to try their product, it is much harder to get them to keep buying it.

In other cultures, consumers are more fundamentally loyal, less brand conscious and not so used to cross product comparisons. In Australia and South East Asia it is viewed that buyers have a greater need for brand security, are less confident with regard to trying unknown products and so are less willing to take risks.

Cognitive style

Western consumer behaviour models assume a logical buying process with rational steps including, the formation of awareness, the searching for information, reviewing the information, evaluating alternatives and finally making a choice.

Many authors argue that this process really only relates to the US and that internationally there are many different models of the buying process. Asian consumers tend to have a quite different cognitive style to Western consumers. The Chinese as well as the Japanese have a more synthetic, concrete and contextual orientation in their thought patterns, as opposed to the Americans who tend to have a more analytical and abstract decision-making process. Thus culture not only impacts on how we behave as consumers but on the whole decision-making process.

Analysing cultures and the implications for consumer behaviour

As we have seen in previous sections there are many social and cultural influences which determine our values, beliefs and customs which combine to form a cultural identity which in turn influences the process of decision making when buying products. All these aspects need to be examined to understand the consumer in any international market. The framework depicted in Figure 3.3 summarises many of the issues we have been discussing and may prove useful to the reader as a framework for assessing the impact of social and cultural influences in a particular market.

Engel *et al.* (1990) 'suggest' the following steps should be undertaken when analysing consumer behaviour in international markets. They propose if a company is to fully empathise with a culture they must pose a series of questions about buyer behaviour, culture and the suitability of various marketing communications approaches for that culture. These steps consist of:

- **Determine relevant motivations in the culture**: What needs are fulfilled with this product in the minds of members of the culture? How are these

Figure 3.3 Model of consumer behaviour in international markets

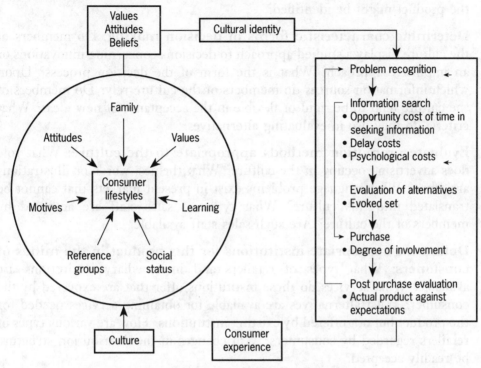

Source: adapted by Liv Kirby from Hawkins *et al.* (1992)

needs presently fulfilled? Do members of this culture readily recognise these needs?

- **Determine characteristic behaviour patterns**: What patterns are characteristic of purchasing behaviour? What forms of division of labour exist within the family structure? How frequently are products of this type purchased? Do any of these characteristic behaviours conflict with behaviour expected for this product? How strongly ingrained are the behaviour patterns that conflict with those needed for distribution of this product?

- **Determine what broad cultural values are relevant to this product**: Are there strong values about work, morality, religion, family relations and so on that relate to this product? Does this product denote attributes that are in conflict with these cultural values? Can conflicts with values be avoided by changing the product? Are there positive values in this culture with which the product might be identified?

- **Determine characteristic forms of decision making**: Do members of the culture display a studied approach to decisions concerning innovations or an impulsive approach? What is the form of the decision process? Upon which information sources do members of the culture rely? Do members of the culture tend to be rigid or flexible in the acceptance of new ideas? What criteria do they use in evaluating alternatives?

- **Evaluate promotion methods appropriate to the culture**: What role does advertising occupy in the culture? What themes, words or illustrations are taboo? What language problems exist in present markets that cannot be translated into this culture? What types of sales staff are accepted by members of the culture? Are such sales staff available?

- **Determine appropriate institutions for this product in the minds of consumers**: What types of retailers and intermediary institutions are available? What services do these institutions offer that are expected by the consumer? What alternatives are available for obtaining services needed for the product but not offered by existing institutions? How are various types of retailers regarded by consumers? Will changes in the distribution structure be readily accepted?

Self-reference criterion

As we have discussed it is of crucial importance when examining foreign markets that the culture of the country is seen in context of that country. It is better to regard the culture as different from, rather than better or worse than, the home culture. In this way, differences and similarities can be explored and the reasons for differences can be sought and explained. The differences approach avoids the evaluative and often superior approach based on one's own self-reference criterion.

James Lee (1966) used the term 'self-reference criterion' (SRC) to characterise our unconscious reference to our own cultural values when examining other cultures. He suggested a four-step approach to eliminate SRC.

1 Define the problem or goal in terms of home country cultural traits, habits and norms.

2 Define the problems or goals in terms of the foreign culture, traits, habits and norms.

3 Isolate the SRC influence in the problem and examine it carefully to see how it complicates the problem.

4 Redefine the problem without the SRC influence and solve for the foreign market situation.

The process of enculturation to gain empathy with a foreign country market is not an easy one and requires:

- *Cultural empathy*: the ability to place yourself in the position of the buyer from another culture. In this way a strong attempt is made to understand the thinking approaches, the decision-making process and the interactions between this and the cultural and other forces influencing the buyer.

- *Neutrality:* the ability to identify the differences that exist without making value judgements about 'better' or 'worse' cultures. Inevitably, self-reference will exist. If the focus is placed on differences rather than superiority, the chances of achieving accurate cross-cultural analysis are increased (Toyne and Walters 1993).

To ensure they achieve this, as we will see in Chapter 5, companies follow a number of policies. They may recruit foreign staff at their head office, collaborate with local firms when entering a new market or they may put managers through acculturation programmes. Guinness understood the importance of avoiding SRC in developing their knowledge base of the new international markets in which they were operating. It is for this reason they ensured they had a management team in each market which was truly multi-national as well as including managers with a local knowledge.

Cross-cultural analysis

So far our discussions have been primarily concerned with understanding what is meant by culture, examining their components and surveying its influence on consumer behaviour and how that differs across cultures.

However, strategists and students of international marketing need to move beyond this and endeavour to develop ways to compare and contrast consumers, market segments and buyers across cultures.

International marketers need appropriate frameworks or conceptual schemata to enable comparisons to be made and contrasts and similarities to be drawn.

For the most part, cross-cultural classification approaches tend to be either mere lists or incredibly theoretical complex structures (Triandis 1989). There is a recognised lack of a universal broadly generalisable framework within which to visualise national cultures. Consequently, the work of Hofstede (1980, 1994) and Hall and Hall (1987) are seen as holding the maximum potential for providing methods for cross-cultural analysis. In the following sections we will look at the work of each of these writers and examine how the concepts they propose can be used by firms in attempting to analyse consumer behaviour across cultures. We will then highlight some of the frameworks which have been developed by later authors building on their work.

Hall's high/low context approach

Hall and Hall's (1987) main thesis was that one culture will be different from another if it understands and communicates in different ways. He therefore saw languages as the most important component of culture.

The language differences between some cultures will be large and therefore there will be marked differences in their cultures. Language and value differences between the German and Japanese cultures for instance are considerable. There are also differences between the Spanish and Italian cultures but they are much less, both have languages based on Latin, they use the same written form of communication and have similar although not identical values and norms.

In different cultures the use of communication techniques varies. In some languages communication is based on the words that are said or written (spoken language). In others, the more ambiguous elements such as surroundings or social status of the message-giver are important variables in the transmission of understanding (silent language). Hall used these findings to classify cultures into what he referred to as 'low context cultures' and 'high context cultures'.

- **Low context cultures** rely on spoken and written language for meaning. Senders of messages encode their messages expecting that the receivers will accurately decode the words used to gain a good understanding of the intended message.

- **High context cultures** use and interpret more of the elements surrounding the message to develop their understanding of the message. In high context cultures the social importance, knowledge of the person and the social setting add extra information and will be perceived by the messages receivers. Figure 3.4 shows the contextual differences in the cultures around the world.

Figure 3.4 The contextual continuum of differing cultures

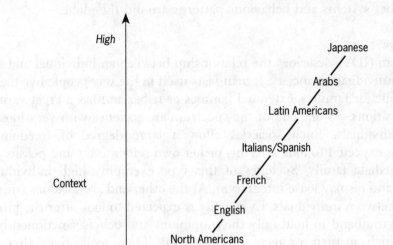

Source: Usunier (1996) adapted from Hall and Hall 1996

With the Swiss, in particular, having a high explicit content in their communications at one extreme are the low context cultures of Northern Europe. At the other extreme are the high context cultures. The Japanese have subtle and complex ways of communicating with people according to their age, sex and the relative and actual social positions of the people conversing.

The greater the contextual difference between those trying to communicate, the greater the difficulty firms will have in achieving accurate communications.

Hofstede's cultural dimensions

Geert Hofstede (1980, 1994) was primarily interested in uncovering differences in work-related values across countries. He identified four dimensions of culture: individualism, power distance, uncertainty avoidance and masculinity. These dimensions, it was argued, largely account for cross-cultural differences in people's belief systems and behaviour patterns around the globe.

Individualism

Individualism (IDV) describes the relationship between an individual and his or her fellow individuals in society. It manifests itself in the way people live together such as in nuclear families, extended families or tribes and has a great variety of value implications. At one end of the spectrum are societies with very loose ties between individuals. Such societies allow a large degree of freedom and everybody is expected to look after his or her own self-interest and possibly that of the immediate family. Societies of this type exemplify high individualism (high IDV) and display loose integration. At the other end are societies with very strong ties between individuals. Everybody is expected to look after the interests of their in-group and to hold only those opinions and beliefs sanctioned by the in-group which, in turn, protects the individual. These 'collectives' (low IDV) societies show tight integration. Hofstede identified highly individualistic countries as the USA, Great Britain and the Netherlands. Collectivist countries were Colombia, Pakistan and Taiwan. The mid-range contains countries such as Japan, India, Austria and Spain.

Power distance

Power distance (PDI) involves the way societies deal with human inequality. People possess unequal physical and intellectual capacities which some societies allow to grow into inequalities in power and wealth. However, some other societies de-emphasise such inequalities. All societies are unequal but some are more unequal than others (Hofstede 1994). The Philippines, India and France score relatively high in power distance. Austria, Israel, Denmark and Sweden show relatively low PDI scores, while the United States ranks slightly below midpoint.

Combining power distance and individualism reveals some interesting relationships (see Figure 3.5). Collectivist countries seem to show large power distance but individualist countries do not necessarily display small power distance. For example, the Latin European countries combine large power distance with high individualism. Other wealthy Western countries combine smaller power distance with high individualism. It is interesting to observe that in Hofstede's sample, almost all developing countries tend to rate high on both collectivism (low individualism) and power distance. Of the countries Hofstede studied, only Costa Rica combined small power distance with high collectivism (low individualism).

Figure 3.5 Power distance/individualism dimensions across cultures

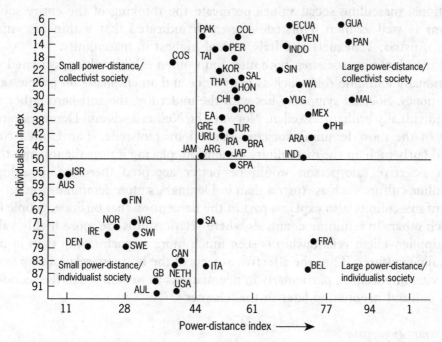

Source: Hofsteade (1980, 1994)

Uncertainty avoidance

Uncertainty Avoidance (UA) reflects how a society deals with uncertainty about the future, a fundamental fact of human existence. At one extreme, weak UA cultures socialise members to accept and handle uncertainty. People in such cultures tend to accept each day as it comes, take risks rather easily, do not work too hard and tolerate opinions and behaviour different from their own. Denmark, Sweden and Hong Kong all rated low in UA. The other extreme – strong UA societies – fosters the need to try to beat the future, resulting in greater nervousness, aggressiveness and emotional stress. Belgium, Japan and France ranked relatively high in uncertainty avoidance while the United States scored somewhat below midpoint.

Masculinity

Masculinity (MAS) deals with the degree to which societies subscribe to the typical stereotypes associated with males and females. Masculine values stress making money and the pursuit of visible achievements. Such societies admire individual brilliance and idolise the successful achiever, the superman. These traditional masculine social values permeate the thinking of the entire society, women as well as men. Hofstede's research indicated that within his sample, Japan, Austria, Venezuela and Italy ranked highest in masculinity.

In more feminine societies, both men and women exhibit values associated with traditionally feminine roles such as endurance and an emphasis on people rather than money. Societal sympathy lies with the underdog, the anti-hero rather than the individually brilliant. Sweden, Norway, the Netherlands and Denmark rank as some of the most feminine societies studied by Hofstede. The United States scored fairly high on the masculinity dimension, placing it near the top one-third.

An assertive salesperson would be better accepted therefore in a highly masculine culture such as Austria than in Denmark's more feminine culture. The level of masculinity also explains part of the perception that business people have of each other. In feminine countries where relationships are more highly valued the supplier–client relationship is seen much more as partnership than in more masculine cultures. Thus the affective aspects of the business relationship is seen as of vital importance, particularly in negotiations as we will see in the section on cross-cultural negotiating later in this chapter.

Confucian dynamism

Later work by Hofstede revealed a fifth dimension, 'Confucian dynamism'. Confucian dynamism assesses cultures to the degree they are universalistic or particularistic. Universalistic cultures believe that what is true and good can be determined and defined and can be applied everywhere. Particularistic cultures evolve where 'unique circumstances and *relationships* are more important considerations in determining what is right and good rather than abstract rules'. Confucian philosophy traditionally pervades Chinese culture. Its major characteristics include a strong bias towards obedience, the importance of rank and hierarchies and the need for smooth social relations. Within Confucian ethics, four relations were basic, between: ruler and those ruled; father and son, husband and wife and friend and friend. Everyone is expected to know where they stand in the hierarchy of human relations and one's place carries with it fixed standards of how one behaves towards others.

Culture/communication typologies

Following on from the research by Hall and Hofstede a number of writers have developed frameworks which can be utilised for cross-cultural analysis. The two we will discuss in this section are the, communication typologies and the learning/diffusion matrix.

Communication typologies

Four verbal communication typologies were suggested by Gudykunst and Ting-Toomey (1988) which can be used as a basis for cross-cultural analysis. These are as follows:

Direct vs Indirect refers to the degree of explicitness of the verbal message of a culture. The Chinese use the indirect style often hiding their real feelings and being concerned more with group harmony and the feelings of others. The use of the indirect style reflects to Hall's high context culture and Hofstede's collective dimension.

Elaborative vs Succinct reflects the quantity of talk that people feel comfortable with in a particular culture. The succinct style is where quantity of talk is relatively low. This reflects high uncertainty avoidance and a high context culture. Elaborative styles may be used more in low context cultures where the spoken language is of greater importance as in the US.

Personal vs Contextual. Contextual style focuses on the role of the speaker and the role of relationships. The role and hierarchical relationship of the parties in conversation will be reflected in the form of address and words that are used. This type of communication reflects high power distance, collectivism and high context cultures such as Japan.

Instrumental vs Affective defines the orientation of the speaker. In the affective verbal style the speaker is process orientated. There is concern that neither the speaker nor the receiver will be put in an uncomfortable position. The speaker also listens to and closely observes the receiver in order to interpret how the message is being taken. This is a reflection of a high context, collective culture such as South East Asia.

Cross cultural/diffusion and learning matrix

The speed of learning and the degree of involvement are essential ingredients of the individual consumer behaviour process. In cross-cultural comparisons, it is possible to analyse the consumer behaviour from this micro perspective.

Wills *et al.* (1991) use the dimensions of diffusion/learning to suggest a cross-cultural analysis model examining the relationships between the context of a culture and the rate of diffusion of new products which varies considerably across cultures. The rate of learning will impact on the rate of diffusion of any new product. By comparing the diffusion rate to whether a culture is high or low context (see Figure 3.6), a firm can gain a much better understanding of the type of strategies to employ to increase the pace of learning and so the rate of diffusion.

Social and cultural influences in business to business marketing

Much of the discussion relating to the influences of social cultural factors on international marketing assumes a market for predominantly fast moving consumer goods where decisions are made on either a family or individual basis. Yet a considerable proportion of exports relates to industrial goods and services where companies are primarily concerned with company to company or business to business marketing and dealing, therefore, with primarily organisational or even government buyers. The question we need now to address is how relevant are the social/cultural factors we have been discussing to these type of markets.

In business to business marketing there are essentially two types of buyers, organisations and governments. In this section we will highlight some of the social/cultural influences on these types of buyers which are particularly relevant to international marketing. Following this we will discuss the impact of culture on cross-cultural negotiating styles and the practice of gift giving in international business relationships.

Figure 3.6 Interrelationship between context and diffusion

Diffusion Rate

High context/Fast diffusion	**High context/Slow diffusion**
South East Asia Japan	India Asia
Low context/Fast diffusion	**Low context/Slow diffusion**
Scandinavia USA Canada	UK Eastern Europe

Source: Wills *et al.* (1991)

Organisational buyers

Business buying decisions are influenced by decisions about technology, the objectives and tasks of the company, the organisational structure of the buying company and the motivations of people in the company. The technology decision is an interesting area. Some companies rely on their own internal capability to produce solutions to problems they need to solve in the areas of the technology and how to manufacture the product. However, Japanese companies have encouraged their suppliers to help them by providing technological improvements. This approach is now influencing business practices across the world. The US adversarial approach of developing a precise buying specification and then challenging supplying firms to win the contract by providing the best deal is now less common.

Culture at the organisational level can play a significant part in the way in which the various roles are enacted. When it come to international encounters, humour for instance can be a double-edged sword. The dangers of a joke backfiring are increased when the parties concerned do not share a common culture. Different cultures have different beliefs and assumptions which determine when humour is considered appropriate. What can be joked about and even who can be joked with. Attitudes to uncertainty, status and the sanctity of business influence the extent to which humour is allowed to intrude on proceedings (see Illustration 3.5).

Welford and Prescott (1994) suggest a number of different corporate cultural characteristics in European countries which influence buyer behaviour. The French have a hierarchical system of management with a strong tendency to centralism. Consequently it is often difficult for sales people to reach the top manager as they may well be buffered behind half a dozen assistants. Spanish and Italian decision making tends to be highly autocratic based on the model of the family, decision making is shared with systems that tend to be informal. The German position is influenced by earned respect for formal qualifications and technical competence. Leadership depends upon respect rather than subservience.

Government buyer behaviour

In many countries the government is the biggest buyer, far larger than any individual consumer or business buyer. Governments buy a wide range of goods and services: roads, education, military, health and welfare. The way in which

Illustration 3.5: The use of humour in international meetings

In cultures where the desire to avoid uncertainty is high, as in Germany, humour with its inherent ambiguity is likely to be restrained. Levity will be welcomed to the extent it contributes to the *Arbeitsklima* (working environment) and supports the highly task-oriented German company.

Status is another important consideration. In some countries people may loosen up as they get promoted but in more hierarchical cultures, such as France, the reverse is more likely to be the case. Seniority is largely determined by intellectual achievement and academic credentials. Consequently, French *cadres* (executives) are keen to avoid being branded lightweight. So whilst clever and sophisticated humour is acceptable, the risk of appearing foolish with the accompanying loss of credibility and intellectual standing, tends to inhibit other forms of humour. Self-mocking humour may be completely misunderstood.

In many Western business cultures teasing is routinely used as a means of social control.

Typically it serves to chastise a late-comer to a meeting or to mark mild displeasure whilst avoiding confrontation. But in certain Asian cultures, making fun of someone may leave managers feeling uncomfortable. In Japan managers use after-hours drinking as a functional equivalent to criticising with humour.

American managers invariably use jokes to warm up speeches and presentation but, once the real business starts, attempts at humour may be met with a frosty silence. Americans have invested heavily in a set of political and economic values embedded in individual liberty and economic opportunity. It follows that business is taken more seriously than in other Anglo-Saxon cultures such as Britain.

International managers have to proceed with caution but humour remains a vital means of bridging cultural differences.

Source: adapted from Barsoux, J.L. (1997) *Financial Times*, 17 February

governments buy is influenced by the extent to which public accountability in the expenditure of public money is thought important.

It has been estimated that 20 per cent of the gross domestic product of the European Union is controlled through the value of purchases and contracts awarded by the public sector. In the US approximately 30 per cent of the gross national product is accounted for by the purchases of US governmental units. For some companies their international business comprises of government buyers in different countries. It is important, therefore, to understand the government buying processes.

Usual forms of buying procedure are the open tender and selective tender. In open bid contracts, tenders are invited against a tight specification, contracts are usually awarded to the lowest price bid. Selective tender contracts are offered to companies who have already demonstrated their ability in the area appropriate to the tender. Only those companies on the selective tender list will be invited to tender. As with open tender, the lowest price is often used to adjudicate the bids.

In the European Union specific rules have been drawn up in an attempt to remove the barriers between potential suppliers of government contracts from different countries of the EU. Suppliers from all EU members states should have an equal opportunity to bid for public authority contracts and public works contracts must be advertised throughout the EU.

The business to business buying process

Various models of the buying process have been developed by different writers. Robinson *et al.* (1979) divide classes of buying into straight re-buy, modified re-buy and new task.

A straight re-buy represents the bulk of the business buying. The buy signal is often triggered through information systems when stock levels reach a predetermined replenishment point. The modified re-buy indicates a certain level of information search and re-evaluation of products/services and supplies before the purchase is made. The new task represents an area of considerable uncertainty in which the company needs to make decisions about what it wants about performance standards and about supplier capabilities. The new task, particularly if the purchase is of major importance to the company, will involve senior management and might take a long time to complete.

The way in which a company manages each of the buy classes will be influenced by cultural factors. Companies with a strong ethnocentric orientation may limit their search for suppliers to suppliers from their own country. For more internationally oriented companies, the country of origin effect will distort information collection and appraisal. The influence of established relationships in cultures in which personal contacts and relationships are important will act as a barrier to companies which operate in a more formal way.

Relationship marketing is very important in business to business marketing where companies may gain competitive advantage not necessarily through the product but through the added value they have built through their relationship. This is especially important in markets such as China. The Chinese rely heavily on personal relationships in business dealings. It is important for foreign companies to understand the dynamics of these relationships (known as *guanxi*). There is a saying in Chinese 'If you do not have a relationship you do not exist!' In the special focus at the end of Part I we examine the entry barriers to the Chinese market and look in particular at the effect of *guanxi* in developing the Chinese market.

Personal selling and negotiation between the buyer and seller as they go through the interaction process in order to build a business relationship which is mutually beneficial is an important part of international marketing. It is in this process of negotiation and relationship building where cultural factors have their greatest impact.

The role of culture in negotiation styles

In a study of Chinese (PRC) and US executives, Tung (1989) concluded that as a determinant of the success or failure of negotiations, culture played an important but dual role. The study showed that although cultural differences in negotiation styles were perceived by executives as major causes of negotiation failure, awareness of cultural differences was not thought to be a major factor in negotiation success.

Druckman (1977) tested bargaining behaviour of subjects from three cultures – India, Argentina and the United States. The studies focused on intracultural bargaining behaviour in an attempt to isolate differences which could be attributed to culture alone. The results indicated that Indian negotiators bargained longer, were more competitive and maximised their gains relative to US and Argentinean negotiators.

Hawrysh and Zaichkowsky (1990) use Graham's (1986) four phase linear model (see Figure 3.7) of the negotiation process to compare US and Japanese negotiating styles and identify at what stage of the negotiation stage cultural factors became most important.

The first stage, *non-task sounding*, describes the process of establishing rapport between members of the negotiation teams. Japanese negotiators would spend considerable time and money entertaining foreign negotiating teams in order to establish a rapport, whereas US executives saw the delays as frustrating and the

Figure 3.7 Linear model of the negotiation process

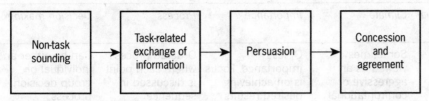

Source: Graham (1986)

money spent wasteful. GEC Alsthon sales executives found Karaoke sessions very useful when negotiating with the North Koreans for a contract for high speed trains between Seoul and Pusan. The firm undertstood from the outset that the first stage of negotiations needed to include a broad range of activities, such as singing, to help establish a rapport on which the relationship could be built.

The *task–related exchange of information stage* describes the exchange of information that defines the participants' needs and expectations. Well over 90 per cent of all large Japanese companies and most of the smaller ones used a decision–making process called *ringi*. The system is based on the principle that decisions are made only when a consensus is reached by the negotiating team. Proposals are circulated amongst the negotiating team and the affected individuals in the main office staff, for each to affix their own personal seal of approval. Without the group's approval, which takes a long time to acquire, no proposal will be accepted. What may appear to US negotiators as stalling tactics is often simply the different process by which the Japanese reach a decision.

The *persuasion stage* for US executives is the one that consumes time, whereas for Japanese negotiators who have previously taken the time to understand each others expectations, it is seen as unnecessary. Japanese negotiators as a result may remain silent. This is not because they do not agree with the proposal but because they are either waiting for more information or that for them, agreement has been reached therefore negotiations are complete.

This often leads to misunderstanding at the *concession and agreement stage*. An extension of the Japanese preference for establishing strong personal relation-ships is their dislike for the formal Western-style contract. A loosely worded statement expressing mutual cooperation and trust developed between negotiat-ing parties is much preferred. The advantage of these agreements is that they allow a great deal of flexibility in the solution of unforeseen problems, whereas Western negotiators may feel the need to bargain to the end and do not see their job as complete until they have actually obtained a signature. Table 3.5 gives an

Table 3.5 Differences in buyer–seller relationships styles

International market	Climate	Importance	Process	Decision making
United States	Sometimes viewed as an aggressive or confrontational climate	Of less importance. Focus is on achieving desired results	Ordered process where each point is discussed in sequence	Can be either an individual or group decision process
Canada	Positive, polite climate. Hard sell will not work here	Of less importance. Focus is on achieving desired results	Ordered process where each point is discussed in sequence	Can be either an individual or group decision process
Latin America	Positive and hospitable climate	Personal, one-on-one relationships very important	Relationship building through socialisation will precede negotiations	Decisions are usually made by a high-level individual
United Kingdom	Traditional, polite climate. Hard sell will not work here	Of less importance. Focus is on achieving desired results	Ordered process where each point is discussed in sequence	Can be either an individual or group decision process
Germany/Austria	Rigid, sober climate	Low, Germans remain aloof until negotiations conclude	Systematic process with emphasis on contractual detail	Even the most routine decisions are made by top-level officials
France/Belgium	Formal, bureaucratic climate Hard sell will not work here	Formal, arm's-length relationships with attention to etiquette	French teams use argument to generate discussion	Usually a group process headed by a senior negotiator
Japan	Formal polite climate with many idiosyncratic nuances	Great importance. Long-term relationships are what matter most	First all general items are agreed on, then details are discussed	A total group process with all levels involved in the final decision
China	Bureaucratic climate with an abundance of 'red tape'	Very important. Traditional, cultural courtesies are expected	Discussions are long and repetitive. Agreements must be in writing	Usually a group process headed by a senior negotiator
Russia	Bureaucratic climate with an abundance of 'red tape'	Low, Russians will remain reserved until negotiations conclude	Cumbersome process due to bureaucratic constraints	Usually a group process headed by a senior negotiator

Source: Lewin and Johnston (1997)

interesting summary of differences in buyer seller negotiating styles in selected countries.

Usiner (1996) suggests a number of ways to minimise cultural impact in negotiations in order to build effective transcultural relationships.

- **Adaptation**. In international business meetings, people who do not appear to feel the need to adapt may be considered indolent: 'Those who adapt are aware of differences, whereas those to whom others adapt remain unaware'.

- **Interpreters**. Be aware that interpreters influence meaning. They may translate better from one language into another than in the opposite direction. The loyalty of interpreters needs to be considered. Are they more in favour of one party than the other? Should you use your own interpreter? Should you use several interpreters to reduce stress errors and bias?

- **Cultural blocks**. Not everything will translate – it is not possible to translate meaning exactly for all elements in an interpretation. Culture-specific elements will block some attempts at translation.

- **The stereotype**. Avoid negative stereotyping which is likely to increase negotiation conflicts and difficulties.

- **Inter-cultural preparation**. Good prior preparation in inter-cultural understanding is a necessary investment to improve international business effectiveness.

Gift giving

An integral part of conducting business internationally is the practice of gift giving. Cross-cultural gift giving is a practice which must be sensitive to cultural, legal and ethical aspects across national borders. Business gift giving, if improperly executed, could stop sensitive negotiations and ruin new and potential business relationships. German and Swiss executives tend to feel uncomfortable accepting gifts as they do not like to feel obliged. However, business gift giving in many cultures is an important part of persuasion. In cultures where a business gift is expected but not given, it is an insult to the host.

Cultures which view business gift giving as imperative seem to belong to Hall's high context category. In such a culture the communication style is more implicit, non-verbal and is more reliant on hidden cues in the context of personal relationships. In Japan for example, a highly developed and affluent society, gift giving practices are widespread in the business culture. Refusing to participate in gift giving in such cultures can cause hard feelings and misunderstandings between business clients.

In high context cultures, gifts are often seen as important steps in bringing a person into the inner circle of a business relationship or to strengthen the relationship between a buyer and a seller.

By contrast, people in low context cultures rely on explicit contracts, communication is more formal and explicit and negotiations based on a more legalistic orientation. Laws applying to business gift giving tend to be very well laid out.

In some cultures, all business gifts will be viewed as illegal bribes, on the other hand other cultures view gifts, pay offs and even bribes merely as a cost of business. Bribery is part of the commercial traditions of many parts of Asia, Africa and the Middle East.

Conclusion

The influence of social and cultural factors in international marketing are complex and often extremely difficult for a firm operating in a foreign market to analyse and understand, especially if the firm is operating across a number of markets and looking for consistent methods of analysing their markets.

In this chapter it is hoped that the reader has obtained some understanding of the components of culture and how these components impact on consumer behaviour and therefore the international marketing strategies of firms, both in consumer and business to business markets.

The reader should also have acquired an awareness of the possible methods that can be used to categorise differences across cultures to enable a cross-cultural analysis to be carried out.

Discussion questions

1 Discuss the view that culture lies at the heart of all problems connected with international marketing.

2 What is culture? Is it important for international markets to take account of it or is globalisation going to make it a thing of the past?

3 In planning domestic marketing the marketer can readily adapt the Self Reference Criterion (SRC) confident in meeting the customers desires.

What are the different issues involved in planning international marketing?

4 How do social and cultural influences impact on international business negotiations? Using examples advise a company preparing for cross-cultural negotiations.

References

Assael, H. (1992) *Consumer behaviour and marketing action*, PWS-Kent Publishing.

Chan, T. S. and Lin, G. (1992) 'An empirical analysis of consumer decision processes in the People's Republic of China', *Journal of International Consumer Marketing*, 4 (4), The Hanworth Press.

Doole, I. and Yaqub, A.C. (1997) *Integrated Communications: the challenge of Saudi Arabia*, Academy of Marketing Conference proceedings, July.

Druckman, D. (1977) *Negotiations, social-psychological perspectives*, Sage.

Engel, J.L., Blackwell, R.D. and Minniard, P.W. (1990) *Consumer Behaviour*, The Dryden Press.

Graham, J.L. (1986) 'Across the negotiating table from the Japanese', *International Marketing Review*, Autumn.

Gudykunst, W.B. and S. Ting-Toomey (1988) *Culture and Interpersonal Communication*, Sage Publications.

Hall, E.T. and Hall, M.R., (1987) *Hidden Differences: doing business with the Japanese*, Anchor Press.

Hawkins, D.I., Best, R.J. and Coney, K.A. (1992) *Consumer Behaviour: Implications for Marketing Strategy*, Library of Congress Catalogue-in-Publication, (5th edn).

Hawrysh, B.M. and Zaichkowsky, J.L. (1990) 'Cultural approaches to negotiations: Understanding the Japanese', *International Marketing Review*, 7 (2).

Hofstede, G. (1980) *Culture's consequences: international differences in work-related values*, Sage.

Hofstede, G. (1994) 'The business of international business is culture', *International Business Review*, 3 (1), –4.

Hofstede, G. (1996) *Cultures and organisations: software of the mind*, McGraw-Hill.

Jeannet, J.-P. and Hennessey, H.O. (1993), *Global Marketing Strategies*, 2nd edn, Houghton Miffin.

Kale, S.H. (1991) 'Culture specific marketing communications: an analytical approach', *International Marketing Review*, 8 (1).

Kotler, P. (1995) *Marketing Management, Analysis, Planning, Implementation and Control*, Prentice Hall.

Lee, J.R. (1966) 'Cultural Analysis in overseas operation', *Harvard Business Review*, March/April.

Lewin, J.E and Johnston, W.L (1997) 'Managing the International Salesforce', *Journal of Business and Industrial Marketing*, 12 (3/4).

Linton, R. (1945) *The Cultural Background of Personality*, Appleton Century.

Maston A. (1970) *Motivation and Personality*, 2nd edn, Harper and Row.

Robinson, P. J., Faris, C.W. and Wind, Y. (1979) *Industrial Buying and Creative Marketing*, Allyn and Bacon.

Terpstra, V. and Sarathy, R. (1997) *International Marketing*, 7th edn, Dryden Press.

Triandis, H. C. (1989) 'The self and social behaviour in differing cultural contexts', *Psychological Review*, 96 (3).

Toyne, B. and Walters, P.G.P. (1993) *Global Marketing Management: A Strategic Perspective*, Allyn and Bacon.

Tung, R.L.(1989) 'A longitudinal study of US–China business negotiations', *China Economic Review*, 1 (1).

Welford, R. and Prescott, K. (1994) *European Business, An Issue Based Approach*, Pitman.

Wills, J.I., Samli, A.C. and Jacobs, L. (1991) 'Developing global products and marketing strategies; a construct and a research agenda', *Journal of the Academy of Marketing Science*, 19 (Winter)1–10.

Usiner, J.C. (1996) *Marketing Across Cultures*, 2nd edn, Prentice Hall.

Chapter 4

International marketing research and opportunity analysis

Introduction

Discussions in previous chapters have illustrated the highly risky and complex environment in which the international marketing manager operates. If a company is to survive in the international marketplace, it is important that it searches for methods to reduce, as far as possible, the risk of making a wrong decision.

This is why marketing research is so fundamentally important to the international marketing process, for whilst it cannot help a manager reduce risk to the point of zero, it can ensure that the starting point for decision making is knowledge, rather than guesswork. Lack of knowledge of foreign markets is one of the first major barriers an international marketing manager has to overcome. An effective marketing research strategy is the first step in overcoming that barrier.

Since 1995 the volume of international marketing research has grown by 32 per cent per annum. Globally, over US$1 billion annually is spent on marketing research; the US accounts for 39 per cent of expenditure, Western Europe 40 per cent and 9 per cent in Japan. Multi-country marketing research is an area that is developing rapidly and taking an increasing strategic role.

The purpose of this chapter is to examine the place of marketing research in international strategy and the contribution it makes to the decision-making process. We shall, therefore, be examining such concepts as the role of marketing research and opportunity analysis in international markets and the building of an international marketing information system. We shall also examine some of the aspects of primary marketing research in international markets and discuss the practicalities and problems in implementing multi-country studies.

The role of marketing research and opportunity analysis

Marketing research can be defined as the systematic gathering, recording, analysis and interpretation of data on problems relating to the marketing of goods and services.

The role of research is primarily to act as an aid to the decision-maker. It is a tool that can help to reduce the risk in decision making caused by the environmental uncertainties and lack of knowledge in international markets. It ensures that the manager bases a decision on the solid foundation of knowledge and focuses strategic thinking on the needs of the marketplace, rather than the product. Such a role is, of course, necessary in all types of marketing.

In international marketing, because of the increased uncertainties and complexities in world markets, the capacity to ensure a systematic planned process in the research and the use of secondary information, prior to field research, is of paramount importance if quality information is to be obtained. The research process (Malhotra *et al.* 1997) consists of six key stages. These steps are the logical process for any research study to go through in its implementation and will be relevant for all research studies:

1 *Defining the problem*. It is important to decide what information is needed and set the objectives of the research ensuring it is both commercially worthwhile and that the objective is feasible and achievable.
2 *Developing the approach to be taken*. The planning phase will concern itself with timescales, resources to carry out the work and the expertise required to meet the objectives. Also the decision as to whether a qualitative or quantitative approach is to be taken.
3 *Designing the research*. In designing the research strategy consideration will be given to the different action steps that need to be taken. Ensuring full use of secondary data sources will be important as will the use of a pilot study to ensure the development of an effective and meaningful questionnaire.
4 *Carrying out the field work*. Decisions as to how the questionnaires will be administered (telephone, mail, personal interviews or focus groups) will be made as well as decisions as to who will do the work and what resources are required.
5 *Analysing the data*. The data analysis stage will need to take full account of the objectives of the research and the clients needs. Many researchers will argue that the methodology to be used should be decided in the first stages of the research planning as it will impact on the questionnaire design and how the interviews are administered.

6 *Preparing the report and presentation.* The report and presentation are the researchers outputs and vital in establishing the credibility of the research methods used and the validity of the findings of the research.

The role of international marketing research

In the new millennium, the ability for research to deliver fast and yet sensitively analysed results across a range of different countries will be crucial. In the past decade, we have seen the development of improved techniques, data availability and research supplier networks in countries where research was in its infancy, especially in such places as India and South East Asia. There has been an increase in the usage of continent-wide or even worldwide surveys which transcend national boundaries, the development of global niche marketing with differing research requirements, and a rapid increase in the rate and spread of product innovation with which research must keep pace. The old days of slow-moving local or national test marketing results are numbered.

There has also been an information explosion. The availability of on-line databases, CD ROMS, the World Wide Web has transformed the nature of international marketing research and the role it plays in the marketing process. The international market research industry has had to develop the ability to meet these challenges.

Research into international market issues can incorporate three major roles:

- cross-cultural research, the conducting of a research project across nation or culture groups;
- foreign research, research conducted in a country other than the country of the commissioning company;
- multi-country research, research conducted in all or important countries where a company is represented (Malhotra *et al.*, 1997).

This does not, however, in any way convey the enormity of the task involved in developing an international market intelligence system which would be sufficient to provide the information necessary to make sound international marketing decisions. Such an information system would not only have to identify and analyse potential markets, but would also have to have the capacity to generate an understanding of the many environmental variables discussed in the previous two chapters. Many levels of environmental factors will affect international marketing decisions from macro level economic factors to political-legal factors, as well as the micro market structures and cultural factors affecting the consumer. However, as Johannson (1972) said:

> In international activities, uncertainty is generally greater and the difficulties in getting information are also greater. It is the lack of market knowledge which is the greatest obstacle to the first foreign venture and it is access to such knowledge which makes it possible for the internationally experienced company to extend their activities to new markets.

As such, the role of the international market researcher is to provide an assessment of market demand globally, an evaluation of potential markets and of the risks and costs involved in market entries, as well as detailed information on which to base effective marketing strategies.

To achieve this the researcher has primarily three functions to carry out:

1 scanning international markets to identify and analyse the opportunities
2 building marketing information systems to monitor environmental trends
3 carrying out primary marketing research studies for input into the development of marketing strategies and to test the feasibility of the possible marketing mix options, both in foreign country markets and across a range of international markets.

In the next three sections we will examine each of these in some detail.

Opportunity identification and analysis

Scanning international markets

There are approximately 200 countries in the world. Even a large multinational corporation would find it difficult to resource market development in all these countries. Thus the first task for the researcher is to scan markets to identify which countries have the potential for growth. International markets are scanned primarily at this stage to identify countries that warrant further research and analysis, thus the researcher will look for countries that meet three qualifying criteria:

1 **Accessibility.** If a company is barred from entering the market, it would be an ineffective use of resources to take research further. The scanning unit would assess such things as tariffs, non-tariff barriers, government regulation and import regulations to assess the accessibility of the market. Japan is seen

as a highly profitable potential market but is viewed by some as inaccessible due to the perception of the difficulties involved in overcoming trade barriers.

2 **Profitability**. At this level the researcher would assess factors that at a macro level could render the market unprofitable – for example, the availability of currency, the existence of exchange regulations, government subsidies to local competition, price controls and substitute products. Eastern European markets including Russia are now accessible, but many companies question the ability of trade partners in those countries to pay. The extra risk of non-payment reduces the profit return calculations of those markets.

3 **Market size**. An assessment is made of the potential market size to evaluate whether future investment is likely to bear fruit.

The specific indicators a company will look for tend to be very product/market specific. Thus a hand tool manufacturer in the north of England specialising in tools for woodworking craftsmen looked for evidence of a hobby market (accessibility) high levels of disposal income (profitability) and large numbers of educated, middle-aged men with leisure time (market size).

At the scanning stage the researcher is attempting to identify countries where marketing opportunities exist. Having identified those opportunities, the researcher will need to make an assessment of their viability for further investigation. In principle, there are three types of market opportunities:

1 **Existing markets**. Here customers needs are already serviced by existing suppliers, therefore, market entry would be difficult unless the company have a superior product or a totally new concept to offer the market.

2 **Latent markets**. In this type of market there are recognised potential customers but no company has yet offered a product to fulfil the latent need. As there is no direct competition, market entry would be easier than in existing markets as long as the company could convey the benefits of its product to the market.

3 **Incipient markets**. Incipient markets are ones that do not exist at present but conditions and trends can be identified that indicate the future emergence of needs that, under present circumstances, would be unfulfilled. It may be, of course, that existing companies in the market are positioning themselves to take advantage of emerging markets but at present there is no direct competition.

The nature of competition can be analysed in a broadly similar way with three distinct product types; competitive products, improved products and breakthrough products. A competitive product is one that has no significant advantages over those already on offer. An improved product is one which, whilst not unique, represents an improvement upon those currently available. A breakthrough product, by way of contrast, represents an innovation and, as such, is likely to have a significant competitive advantage.

The level and nature of competition that a firm will encounter can therefore be analysed by relating the three types of demand to the three types of product. This is illustrated in Figure 4.1 and can be used as a basis for determining first, whether market entry is likely to succeed and second, whether the company possesses any degree of competitive advantage. This, in turn, provides an insight into the nature of the marketing task needed. In saying this, however, it needs to he emphasised that this sort of analysis provides an initial framework for analysis and nothing more. What is then needed is a far more detailed assessment of the degree of competitive advantage that the company possesses.

Obviously the greatest opportunities, together with the greatest risk and potential for profit, are in the identification of *incipient markets*. Researchers,

Figure 4.1 Product/market combinations and the scope for competitive advantage on market entry

		Type of market		
		Existing	Latent	Incipient	
Type of product	Competitive			Existing brands are positioned to take advantage of possible developing needs; no direct competition, but consumers need to be found and then persuaded of the product's value to them. Risk and cost of failure may be high	Low
					Cost and risk of launching the product
	Improved	Superior product offers competitive advantage and eases market entry	Increasingly advanced profile offers greater benefits to the market; no direct competition		
	Breakthrough	Breakthrough product offers self-evident superiority and the competitive advantage is high	Breakthrough product offers significant advantages but markets need to be identified and developed. Little likelihood of competitors in the short and medium term, but consumer resistance may be high		High
		Low	**Cost and risk of opening up the market**		High

Source: Gilligan and Hird (1985)

therefore, use analytical techniques to make sure they recognise incipient markets, thus enabling their companies to develop strategies by which to be first into the market.

In the research techniques used, the basic principle is to compare, contrast or correlate various factors in the market under study with some external variant to identify similarities within the market or with other markets, thus assessing whether the right conditions exist for a market to emerge.

Some of the key techniques used are following.

Demand pattern analysis

In this technique, it is assumed that countries at different levels of economic development have differing patterns of demand and consumption. By comparing the pattern of demand in the country under study with the pattern of demand in an established market when the product was first introduced, a broad estimate of an incipient market can be achieved. An example of how Kodak use econometric indicators is given in Illustration 4.1

Multiple factor indices

This assumes that the demand for a product correlates to demand for other products. By measuring demand for the correlated product, estimates of potential demand can be made. For example, a manufacturer of frozen foods may make an assessment by measuring the number of houses with freezers.

Analogy estimation

Analogy estimation is used where there is a lack of market data in a particular country. Analogies are made with existing markets – perhaps the USA – comparing and contrasting certain ratios to test for market potential. This technique arouses mixed levels of enthusiasm, since experiences with it have been variable. In addition, it is an expensive technique to implement and doubts have been expressed about the accuracy of its forecasts. Those who have used it, typically adopt one of two approaches:

- A cross-section approach, where the product-market size for one country is related to some appropriate gross economic indicator in order to establish a ratio. This ratio is then applied to the specific country under analysis to estimate the potential for the product-market in that country.

- A time-series approach based on the belief that product usage moves through a cycle. Thus one assumes that the country under analysis will follow the

Illustration 4.1: Kodak's use of consumer research to assess global market potential

Consumer research is a key element in the process of assessing the attractiveness of a market because it can provide insight into how consumers in different markets form quality judgements about a product.

In a global organisation, there is more of a focus on econometric research and multi-country benchmarking.

At the corporate level, Kodak wants to pinpoint where to invest finite resources for longer-term pay-offs whether it be in manufacturing or setting up a marketing company or expending large amounts of advertising dollars. Research also provides a common planning framework for the company's different units.

In the global arena, econometric aspects – the economic development mechanisms that produce income for the purchase of both consumer goods and industrial goods – become highly significant. Also important is multi-country benchmarking due to the lack of readily available information and the fact that most products still go through highly specialised channels.

Kodak has been working with the World Bank to develop a framework for improved understanding of the economic engine that drives a country's development.

The analysis began with thirteen primary measures of a country's state of development – industrial infrastructure, disposable income, etc. Multivariate clustering techniques were then applied to these measures to try to give some finite meaning to the notions of developed, developing and undeveloped economies.

It was found that economic parameters were highly interrelated. There is a very long period of time during which money is poured into a country just to develop the support infrastructure – business, roads, education etc. Only in the relatively later stage does the consumer economy seem to develop more fully.

Attitudinal research gives Kodak an understanding or perceptions, preferences and brand images specific to potential target markets. In trying to develop a strategy around cameras for example, Kodak conducted a trade-off exercise involving several broad camera attributes: picture quality, film loading, skill required, size and weight, durability, appearance and range.

The study was conducted in eight countries and resulted in perception maps of basic camera types that were virtually identical across all the countries, with picture quality and weight ranked as the most important camera characteristics.

This information gave Kodak the ability to put together a fairly good global strategic framework for doing camera research.

Source: adapted from *The Economist*, 8 May 1995 and 28 March 1998

same pattern of consumption as a more advanced economy, albeit with a predetermined time-lag.

Regression analysis
This technique is typically used to complement an analogy approach. Regression analysis is particularly useful in enhancing the likely accuracy and eventual confidence that can be placed on cross-sectional studies.

Macrosurvey technique
This method is essentially anthropological in approach and can help companies to establish themselves early in emerging countries with obvious long-term marketing benefits. The technique is based on the notion that as a community grows and develops, more specialised institutions come into being. Thus, one can construct a scale of successively more differentiated institutions against which any particular country can be evaluated to assess its level of development and hence its market potential.

These techniques highlight the importance of comparative research and regular market screening if incipient demand is to be identified at an early stage. However, the value of several of the techniques does rest upon the assumption that all countries and their consumption patterns will develop along broadly common lines. If firms are to make effective use of many of these techniques, the assumption of common economic development patterns must stand. Increasingly however, evidence is emerging to suggest that global commonality does not exist to this degree and there are strong arguments for companies grouping country markets for the purposes of this sort of comparative analysis.

Risk evaluation

As previously stated, incipient markets offer the greatest opportunity for profit potential, but with profit comes risk.

The risk factor in opportunity analysis cannot be over-estimated. Sometimes political risk itself can be the most important determining factor to the success or failure of an international marketing campaign. In the markets where opportunities have been identified, researchers need to make an assessment first as to the type of risk apparent in that market (political, commercial, industrial or financial), and second as to the degree of that risk. Matrices such as the one identified in Figure 4.2 can be useful in carrying out such assessments.

Figure 4.2 The four risk matrix

Country						
Risk level	A	B	C	D	E	F
Risk type	Low	Moderate	Some	Risky	Very risky	Dangerous
Political						
Commercial						
Industrial						
Financial						

Over recent years marketers have developed various indices to help assess the risk factor in the evaluation of potential market opportunities. Two such indices are the Business Environment Risk Index (BERI) and the Goodnow and Hansz (1972) temperature gradient.

BERI

BERI provides country risk forecasts for fifty countries throughout the world and is updated three times a year. This index assesses fifteen environment factors including political stability, balance of payments volatility, inflation, labour productivity, local management skills, bureaucratic delays, etc. Each factor is rated on a scale of 0–4 ranging from unacceptable conditions (0) to superior conditions (4). The key factors are individually weighted to take account of their importance. For example, political stability is weighted by a factor of 2.5. The final score is out of 100 and scores of over 80 would indicate a favourable environment for investors and an advanced economy. Scores of less than 40 would indicate very high risk for companies committing capital.

The Goodnow and Hansz temperature gradient

This classification system rates a country's environmental factors on a temperature gradient whereby environmental factors are defined as being on a scale from hot to moderate to cold. This system examines such factors as political stability, economic development and performance, cultural unity, legal barriers and geo-cultural barriers. Relative positive values on the gradient give degrees of hotness. Relative negative values indicate degrees of coldness. Thus, an advanced economy such as the USA would achieve a relatively hot score whereas a less developed economy such as India would be given a relatively cold score.

The main value of subscribing to such indices is to give companies an appreciation of the risk involved in opportunities identified. There are various publications such as *The Economist* which also publish country risk ratings, so information on risk evaluation is readily available to the researcher.

Major global corporations such as IBM, Honeywell and ICI have specialist political risk analysts, monitoring environmental trends to alert senior managers to changes and developments which may affect their markets.

International marketing segmentation

At the scanning stage, the manager researching international markets is identifying and then analysing opportunities to evaluate which markets to prioritise for further research and development. Some system needs then to be designed to evaluate those opportunities and try to reduce the plethora of countries to a more manageable number. To do this, managers need to divide markets into groups so they can decide which markets to give priority or even to target.

Market segmentation is the strategy by which a firm partitions a market into sub-markets or segments likely to manifest similar responses to marketing inputs. The aim is to identify the markets on which a company can concentrate its resources and efforts so that they can achieve maximum penetration of that market, rather than going for perhaps a market-spreading strategy where they aim to achieve a presence, however small, in as many markets as possible.

The pareto law usually applies to international marketing strategies with its full vigour. The most broad-based and well-established international firms find that 20 per cent of the countries they serve generate at least 80 per cent of the results. Obviously these countries must receive greater managerial attention and allocation of resources. The two main bases for segmenting international markets, are by geographical criteria, (i.e. countries) and transnational criteria (i.e. individual decision-makers.)

Geographical criteria

The traditional practice is to use a country-based classification system as a basis for classifying international markets. The business portfolio matrix (Figure 4.3) is indicative of the approach taken by many companies. In this, they are classified in three categories.

Primary markets
These markets indicate the best opportunities for long-term strategic development. Companies may want to establish a permanent presence and so embark on a thorough research programme.

Secondary markets
These are the markets where opportunities are identified but political or economic risk is perceived as being too high to make long-term irrevocable commitments. These markets would be handled in a more pragmatic way due to potential risks identified. A comprehensive marketing information system would be needed.

Tertiary markets
These are the catch-what-you-can markets. These markets will be perceived as high risk and so the allocation of resources will be minimal. Objectives in such countries would be short term and opportunistic, companies would give no real commitment. No significant research would be carried out.

Figure 4.3 illustrates the business portfolio matrix. The horizontal axis, evaluates the attractiveness of each country on objective and measurable criteria (e.g. size, stability and wealth). The vertical axis evaluates the firm's compatibility with each country on a more subjective and judgemental basis. Primary markets would score high on both axes.

This is a particularly useful device for companies operating in a portfolio of markets to prioritise market opportunity. Ford Tractor carried out such an analysis of key markets. In assessing market attractiveness they explored four basic elements; market size, market growth rate, government regulations and economic and political stability. Competitive strength and compatibility were defined in the international context and such factors as market share, market representation, contribution margin and market support were examined. Using this analysis they identified Kenya, Pakistan and Venezuela as primary markets.

Equally, a company may use the BERI index, Hofstede's cultural dimensions or the Goodnow and Hansz country temperature gradient as a basis for classifying countries. Whatever measurement base is used, once the prime markets have been identified, companies usually then use standard techniques to segment the markets within countries using such variables as demographic/

Figure 4.3 Business portfolio matrix

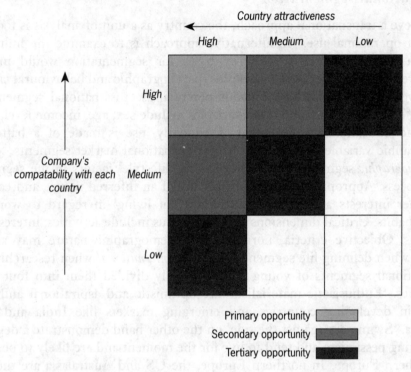

Source: Harrell and Keifer (1993)

economic factors, lifestyles, consumer motivations, geography, buyer behaviour, psychographics, etc.

Thus the primary segmentation base is geographic (by country) and the secondary bases are within countries. The problem here is that depending on the information base, it may be difficult to fully formulate secondary segmentation bases. Furthermore, such an approach can run the risk of leading to a *differentiated* marketing approach which may leave the company with a very fragmented international strategy.

A major drawback with the country based approach is the difficulty in applying the segmentation strategy consistently across markets. If a company is to try and achieve a consistent and controlled marketing strategy across all its international markets, it needs a transnational approach to its segmentation strategy.

Transnational segmentation

To achieve a transnational approach, the country as a unit of analysis is too large to be of operational use. An alternative approach is to examine the individual decision-maker (Walters 1997). Key bases for segmentation would include, therefore, such variables as demographic, psychographic and behavioural criteria.

Demographic variables have obvious potential as cross-national segmentation criteria. The most commonly used variables include sex, age, income level, social class and educational achievement. Frequently, use is made of a battery of demographic variables when delineating transnational market segments.

Psychographic segmentation involves using 'lifestyle' factors in the segmentation process. Appropriate criteria are usually of an inferred nature and concern consumer interests and perceptions of 'way of living' in regard to work and leisure habits. Critical dimensions of lifestyle thus include activities, interests and opinions. Objective criteria, normally of a demographic nature may also be helpful when defining life segments. *Research International* when researching the transnational segments of young adults globally divided them into four broad categories. 'Enthusiastic materialists' are optimistic and aspirational and to be found in developing countries and emerging markets like India and Latin America. 'Swimmers against the tide' on the other hand demonstrate a degree of underlying pessimism and tend to live for the moment and are likely to be found in southern Europe. In northern Europe, the US and Australasia are the 'new realists', looking for a balance between work and leisure with some underlying pessimism in outlook and, finally, the 'complacent materialists' defined as passively optimistic and located in Japan.

Behavioural variables also have a lot of potential as a basis for global market segmentation. In particular, attention to patterns of consumption and loyalty in respect of product category and brand can be useful, along with a focus on the context for usage. Variables such as the benefit sought or the buying motivations may be used. Behaviourally defined segments may be identified in terms of a specific aspect of behaviour which is not broad enough to be defined as a 'lifestyle'. Goodyear have effectively used behavioural characteristics to develop a global segmentation strategy (see Illustration 4.2).

EuroMosaic

One of the trends enabling segmentation, using individualistic characteristics to become a feasible strategy for many companies, is the development of geodemographic databases. One such database is the CCN EuroMosaic. This

Illustration 4.2: Goodyear global segmentation research

Goodyear Tyre and Rubber Company investigated the feasibility of developing a segmentation strategy that could be applied globally to their world markets. The requirement was that the strategy would provide a practical base for an international marketing strategy and prove to be consistent and durable.

After considerable research they identified three decision orientations which could constitute primary attitude segments when buying tyres: brand, outlet and price.

From consumer research they then developed six consumer segments:

1 The *Prestige Buyer* makes the brand decision first and the outlet decision second. This segment is male-dominated, very 'upscale', brand and retailer loyal, does very little information gathering prior to making a purchase and is predisposed to major brands.
2 The *Comfortable Conservative* looks for the outlet first and the brand second. This segment has the same characteristics of the first group but includes more women who are dependent on the retailer for expert advice. These shoppers tend to develop a lasting relationship with a retailer.
3 The *Value Shopper* considers brand first and price second.

This segment is seen as Mr Average. Its members are predisposed to major brands, have a very low retailer loyalty and search for information extensively to educate themselves prior to making the purchase.

4 The *Pretender* wants a major brand but the price ultimately determines the choice. The first decision is price he said, the second is brand. This group has two sub-segments – the aspiring young and emulating old – but all these shoppers exhibit very little loyalty to retailers or brands and do a lot of information searching.
5 The *Trusting Patron* chooses the outlet first and the price second. Montgomery said this group is somewhat 'downscale', heavily female and extremely retailer loyal. The brand is totally unimportant and little searching for information is undertaken.
6 The *Bargain Hunter* shops for price first, outlet second but price is really the only consideration. This group primarily consists of young, 'downscale' people who have low retailer and brand loyalty and who delay the tyre purchase as long as possible.

Source: adapted from *Marketing News*, (1996)

is claimed to be the first pan-European segmentation system allowing the classification of 380 million consumers across the European Union on the basis of the types of neighbourhood in which they live. Ten EuroMosaic types have been identified:

1 Elite suburbs
2 Average areas
3 Luxury flats
4 Low-income inner city
5 High-rise social housing
6 Industrial communities
7 Dynamic families
8 Low-income families
9 Rural agricultural
10 Vacation retirement

The distribution of these typologies can be mapped by country and across Europe. Given the addresses of a company's customers, the system gives the researcher the ability to identify the type of people using certain products and services and to identify at a local level where the similar geodemographic types are, thus acting as an aid to the segmentation of markets and the identification of primary and secondary markets. EuroMosaic will also be of use in identifying the sample in a research survey and for building lists in a direct marketing exercise.

Despite the attractiveness of using individualistic characteristics, it is apparent there is strong potential for significant differences in the patterns of consumer behaviour within global segments derived using this method. Also international similarities in lifestyle and behaviour do tend to be specific, and relevant primarily to specialist products and niche markets.

Hierarchical country – consumer segmentation

To overcome some of the above problems, a compromise approach would be to implement a procedure for global segmentation which integrated features of both processes.

Kale and Sudarshan (1987) have outlined a process to formulate strategically equivalent segments (SES) that transcend national boundaries. On this basis the marketing strategy would follow the premise that world markets consist of both similarities and differences and that the most effective strategies reflect a full recognition of similarities and differences across markets rather than within markets. They argue that companies competing internationally should segment markets on the basis of consumers, not countries. Segmentation by purely geographical factors leads to national stereotyping. It ignores the differences between customers within a nation and ignores similarities across boundaries. Colgate and Palmolive reached such a conclusion when carrying out an analytical review of their own segmentation strategies and use the hierarchical approach.

According to Kale and Sudharsen, to achieve SES, the segmentation process needs to be carried out in stages:

1 Identify the countries that have the infrastructure to support the product and which are accessible to the company.
2 Screen those countries to arrive at a shorter list of countries that meet certain qualifying criteria, e.g. a frozen desert manufacturer may set a qualifying criteria of five million refrigerators per market.
3 Develop within these countries micro-segments, e.g. segment those potential markets by examining such factors as:
   • information search behaviour
   • product characteristics required.

The outcome of this process would be a series of micro-segments within qualified countries.

4 Having disaggregated, the aggregation process then commences by looking for similarities across segments. Factor analysis of the behavioural patterns of these segments would enable managers to understand the characteristics of the demand of each segment as regard marketing mix issues. Each micro-segment would therefore be rated on several strategic factors in terms of potential response.
5 Cluster analysis is then used to identify meaningful cross-national segments, each of which it is thought would evoke a similar response to any marketing mix strategy.

It is argued this approach would enable marketers to design strategies at a cross-national segment level and so take a more consumer-orientated approach to international marketing. In prioritising markets, companies would use consumers as their primary base. Some writers argue that companies still need a secondary segmentation stage to identify the key countries where these transnational segments can be found.

The international marketing information system

Building the information base

Having completed the scanning stage, the researcher will have reduced the number of potential countries to a feasible number requiring further research. The company needs a systematic method for evaluating the markets identified. This is primarily the role of the marketing information system (MIS).

In building any MIS, the objective of the company is to develop a cost effective communication channel between the environment in which the company operates and the decision-makers. As is discussed in Chapter 5, one of the great difficulties in international marketing planning is the long communication lines between headquarters and subsidiaries. This often causes inadequate dataflow which results in misunderstandings and wrong decisions being made.

An effective MIS can contribute to solving these problems and provide a solid base for strategic decisions to be made. Using the 12C environmental analysis model in Table 4.1 we can identify some of the major inputs that an international marketing information system should contain.

The information input into the MIS is used to draw up a market profile analysis as shown in Figure 4.4.

The objective of a market profile analysis is to enable the company to use the environmental information built up in the system to identify opportunities and problems in the potential marketing strategies. For example, the fact that television advertising is prohibited in a country will have major implications for a promotional strategy.

It is this type of detailed assessment that helps companies determine the degree of competitive advantage they may possess and to determine the most appropriate method of market entry. Using consistent frameworks also enables the researcher to make cross-country comparisons much more easily.

Sources of information

In building an MIS, companies would utilise a variety of information services and sources. The starting point for most international researchers in the UK is the Department of Trade and Industry. This government department provides a variety of information services. The majority of Western nations have similar government sponsored organisations helping exporters to develop information on international markets.

Table 4.1 The 12C framework for analysing international markets

Country
- general country information
- basic SLEPT data
- impact of environmental dimensions

Concentration
- structure of the market segments
- geographical spread

Culture/consumer behaviour
- characteristics of the country
- diversity of cultural groupings
- nature of decision-making
- major influences of purchasing behaviour

Choices
- analysis of supply
- international and external competition
- characteristics of competitors
- import analysis
- competitive strengths and weaknesses

Consumption
- demand and end use analysis of economic sectors that use the product
- market share by demand sector
- growth patterns of sectors
- evaluation of the threat of substitute products

Contractual obligations
- business practices
- insurance
- legal obligations

Commitment
- access to market
- trade incentives and barriers
- custom tariffs

Channels
- purchasing behaviour
- capabilities of intermediaries
- coverage of distribution costs
- physical distribution infrastructure
- size and grade of products purchased

Communication
- promotion
- media infrastructure and availability
- which marketing approaches are effective
- cost of promotion
- common selling practices
- media information

Capacity to pay
- pricing
- extrapolation of pricing to examine trends
- culture of pricing
- conditions of payment
- insurance terms

Currency
- stability
- restrictions
- exchange controls

Caveats
- factors to beware of

Some reports have been critical of the deficiencies in the provision of market intelligence by government departments and of firms' abilities to use this information, the main criticisms being:

Figure 4.4 Market profile analysis

	Market entry	Product mix	Promotion mix	Distribution mix	Pricing mix
Social cultural					
Legal factors					
Economic factors					
Political factors					
Technological factors					
Competition					
Trading practices					
Tariff barriers					
Financial					

Source: adapted from Simon Majaro (1992)

- information is non-specific to particular industries
- firms experience problems with the bureaucratic nature of some government services
- data is often in a form which is unsuitable for the company's needs, or too general to be of use
- services have been available only in the capital city
- inadequate publicity about the information and services available.

Other institutions that offer advice and information to companies researching international markets include:

- business libraries
- university libraries
- international chambers of commerce
- International Market Intelligence Centre (DTI)
- business links
- embassies
- banks
- trade associations
- export councils

- overseas distributors
- overseas sales subsidiaries
- foreign brokerage houses
- foreign trade organisations such as JETRO (Japanese Export Trade and Research Organisation).

On-line data sources

One of the main developments in international secondary information over the past five years has been the emergence of a plethora of international on-line and CD ROM databases.

On-line databases are systems which hold computerised information which can be accessed through the telephone network, allowing a wide range of information to be available from an on-line database to a manager in a matter of minutes. By linking a computer terminal via a modem and communications software into the telecommunications network, information can be transmitted from anywhere in the world instantaneously bringing obvious benefits.

There are numerous advantages of using on-line databases. The databases are regularly updated – two or three times per day – and are therefore much more current than traditional printed sources. Retrieving information on-line is much more cost effective than manual searching and is considerably faster. Many on-line databases can be accessed 24 hours a day, seven days a week. You also retrieve and consequently pay for only the information you want.

Table 4.2 gives examples of some of the on-line databases that managers researching international markets may find useful.

Organisations in developing countries are increasingly using on-line computerised databases for their market research work as more of these countries become equipped with telecommunication facilities. The type and volume of trade information available through on-line databases has expanded dramatically over recent years with new databases of interest to business and trade organisations continuously being introduced to the market.

The World Wide Web (WWW)

The use of the Internet for marketing intelligence is one of the most important ways in which connectivity can improve a firm's ability to develop international markets. Buying or commissioning market research reports can be a prohibitively expensive business. For a fraction of the cost and in many cases free of charge, much of the same information can be gathered from the WWW. The volume of

Table 4.2: On-line databases

Company Information

Duns European Marketing Database:	1.8 million companies in 16 countries
European Kompass:	320,000 companies
Datastream:	Financial data on companies worldwide
Extel:	Worldwide company information
McCarthys:	Articles on companies/industries
Predicast:	Worldwide business and industry information

Trade Data

Textline:	Reuters
Comtrade:	UN Foreign trade database
Tradstrat:	Import/export on 22 countries
Croners:	Wide range of data on EC/USA/JAPAN
Eurostar – context:	EU statistical data
IMF/World Bank OECD:	World trade statistics

Market Information

Business International:	Market forecasts worldwide
Euro Monitor:	Covers market reports on 100 consumer markets in Europe and USA
MAID:	Full text market research reports
Informat:	Abstracts from 500 newspapers and trade journals
PTS Prompt:	Abstracts/articles from 1500 trade journals

---

relevant international marketing information available on the Web is too extensive to describe in detail in this chapter but includes numerous on-line newspapers and journals, an extensive list of individual country and industry market research reports, trade lists of suppliers, agents, distributors and government contacts in a large number of countries, details on host country legislation covering imports, agency agreements, joint ventures, etc.

Some of the best sites (Hamill 1997) for undertaking general country screening and export marketing research include:

- International Business Resources on the WWW (http://ciber.bus.msu.edu/ busres.htm),

- State-usa (http://www.Stat-usa.gov/),

- US Department of Commerce, Worldclass Supersite (http://web.idirect.-con/~tiger/supersit.htm),

- Dolphin Marketing (http://merkury.saic.com/dolphin/tradelnk.html),

- The Global Export marketing Information System (http://lcweb2.loc.-gov.8081/glin/x-gem-lk.html), which provides country specific information on new, emerging markets,

- Internet Resources for Exporters (http://www.exportusa.com/resour-ces.html).

All of the sites provide access to a very large number of foreign market research reports and other useful services.

Problems in using secondary data

In carrying out marketing research internationally, problems arise by virtue of the very nature of the number and complexities of the markets being investigated. Whilst the use of secondary data is essential in international marketing research, the reader needs to be aware of its limitations and some of the problems that occur in using secondary data.

Perhaps the most frequently discussed issue is the availability and accessibility of quality secondary information in international markets. The collection of secondary data concerning the economy and the business infrastructure in some countries is still new and, even if the data are available, they may have to be viewed with scepticism. One of the reasons for the distortion of data in some countries is the political considerations of governments.

The International Labour Organisation found the actual unemployment rate in Russia was 10 per cent rather than the officially reported 2 per cent. The Indian government estimates India's middle class numbers 250 million but, according to a recent survey of consumer patterns conducted by the National Council of Applied Economic Research in Delhi, the India middle class probably totals 100 million at best and there is much stratification amongst them.

However, this problem might be solved by obtaining authentic data from international organisations such as the OECD, EU and World Bank, etc. The inconsistencies which can be found in the classification of various types of data in various countries is also a problem when carrying out any comparative analysis across markets.

Terpstra and Sarathy (1997) say that the most important problem associated with the secondary data, especially in developing countries, is its scarcity. Another problem which can be quite misleading is the timeliness of the collected secondary data. The data might have been collected five or even ten years earlier and never updated, therefore outdated information is often used (Czinkota and Ronkainen 1994).

Many countries attempt to attract foreign investment by overstating certain factors that make the economic picture look better. On the other hand, some countries understate certain factors making the economic situation appear worse in order to attract foreign aid.

The Asia-Pacific market is an important market and so obtaining reliable information in this region is of crucial importance for many companies. In a recent survey by INSEAD of one thousand managers of European companies operating in the Asia-Pacific region, it was found that only in Japan and Singapore were companies able to easily access data that were viewed as being of a reliable quality (see Figure 4.5). In China, Taiwan and Vietnam, data were not trusted by researchers. Even though Japanese data were relatively accessible, there were still difficulties due to the fact that the information was over-abundant and so it was difficult to select and interpret the relevant data or to give it any practical application.

None of the limitations discussed above should devalue the importance of secondary data in international marketing research. For many smaller companies lacking the resources to carry out primary research in markets which are geographically distant, it may be the only information where there is relative ease of access.

Primary research in international markets

We have discussed scanning international markets to identify potential market opportunities and the building of market information systems from which the market profile analysis is formulated. So far we have only discussed obtaining information from secondary sources. It is unlikely that a researcher will be able to obtain the information for input into a marketing information system from secondary sources alone. After exhausting these sources the researcher will need to embark on the collecting of primary data to obtain the information required.

Figure 4.5 Perceptions of the quality and accessibility of information in the Asia-Pacific region

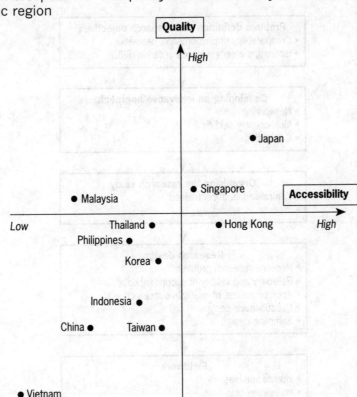

Source: Lassere (1993)

In the following sections we will discuss the issues facing the researcher which should be considered when endeavouring to carry out primary research studies. To do this we use the seven step framework (Malhotra *et al.* 1997) as depicted in Figure 4.6.

Problem definition and establishing objectives

The precise definition of the marketing research problem is more difficult and more important in international marketing research than in domestic marketing research. Unfamiliarity with the cultures and environmental factors of the

Figure 4.6 The international marketing research process

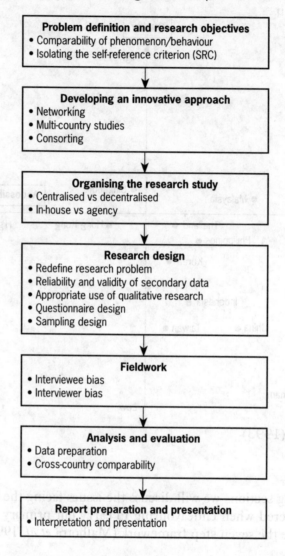

countries where the research is being conducted can greatly increase the difficulty of attaining accurate findings.

On a practical level, the differences in climate and infrastructure create problems. A survey on floor-cleaning products across Europe would have to take account of the fact that Scandinavians have wooden floors, there are lots of tiled and stone floors in the Mediterranean and in the UK many houses have carpets.

Many international marketing efforts fail not because research was not conducted but because the issue of comparability was not adequately addressed in defining the marketing research problem. This is why as we saw in Chapter 3, it is so important to isolate the impact of self-reference criterion (SRC) and the unconscious reference to our own cultural values when defining the problem we are attempting to research in international markets.

Developing an innovative approach

It is important in international marketing research to maintain flexibility in the approach you may have in the initial stages of the research. In the first stage of primary research, companies often use informal means to gather preliminary information and extensive use is made of the network of contacts available to the company both at home and abroad. It is unlikely that a full understanding of the foreign market will be obtained without visiting that market to gain information first hand. The first steps in doing this would be by networking and obtaining information through relatively informal means such as networking consortia or multi-country studies.

Networking
The use of contact networks to build information is vitally important because of the sometimes prohibitive cost of carrying out detailed market research studies overseas. Before any detailed studies are undertaken, trade contacts need to be fully explored.

In order to find solutions to the many international marketing research problems, improvisation in international research is essential.

Most companies will make extensive use of their existing networks to build the market profiles and develop information bases. These could be agents, distributors, licensees, joint venture partners or other companies operating in the country under investigation.

Consortia
Consortia are used by companies as a way of overcoming the difficulties involved in gathering data and establishing contacts in foreign markets. Essentially a group of companies will come together to research a particular market area in which they have a common interest. The advantages are:

- the consortium is more visible in the foreign market
- it is more likely to enjoy the support of the home export promotion organisation
- it achieves economies through the joint use of export facilities both at home and in foreign markets
- it increases the resources available to support the research operation.

However, if a company is to join a consortium, then it has to be prepared to have its autonomy reduced; this fact alone is the major reason most consortia fail. There also has to be a strong reason to join together for the relationship to develop. Nevertheless, by the pooling of resources, consortia are very useful in giving companies the resources needed to acquire knowledge on markets. Often agencies will offer multi-client studies which have much the same benefits (see Illustration 4.3)

Due to the problems and considerations we have discussed above, it may be that detailed research studies will only be carried out in markets where the market viability is seen to be positive and when detailed consumer/market information is required to develop marketing strategy. The cost of primary field research can be high and so it will only be carried out after all other sources have been investigated.

A survey carried out by INSEAD of European companies operating in the Asia-Pacific regions showed that companies perceived the most significant sources of information as being personal contacts of the companies themselves, whether these were customers, other business relationships or their own market surveys (see Figure 4.7).

A second tier of usefulness was then identified as consisting of other direct sources such as government contacts and contracts with competitors or trade associations. Finally, there was a third tier comprising of publicly available information such as newspapers and magazines. This information may be widely read but relatively little weight seems to be given to its strategic value. The importance of directly collected information seems to confirm the view that business in Asia depends more heavily on the creation of a network of relationships than on analysis of hard data collected through published surveys or other published information.

The collection of primary data

The cost and effort of collecting primary data in new markets is far higher than that of collecting such data in the domestic market. This is particularly the case

Illustration 4.3: Use of multi-client studies

Multi-client studies have the advantage of enabling the client to participate in large surveys with quite focused questions at a much smaller expense than would be the case otherwise. A significant growth in this type of field research has been seen in the last few years particularly since the opening up of the Eastern bloc where the practical difficulties in carrying out research are enormous. These studies have specific target audience in specified countries and offer fast analysis. An example of one is as follows:

The East European Omnibus

Guaranteed: to run each and every month in the Czech Republic, Slovania and Hungary 1000 face-to-face interviews per country in respondents' homes.

Genuinely comparable: no subcontracting, using only qualified field force means absolutely identical methods, procedures and quality controls every time in every country.

High quality: all interviewer training, supervision, back-checking and other procedures are to the same high standards. True random pre-selected sample.

Fast: results two weeks after fieldwork.

Other services include: expertly organised focus groups in any part of the region, local telephone centre, hall tests and business research.

in developing countries where no marketing research infrastructure or experience is available. Primary research in these circumstances would entail substantial investment costs in developing basic information relating, for example, to sampling frames or trained qualified interviewers. This, of course, reinforces the importance of secondary data for research purposes and the need for a systematic planning process when embarking on a primary research project.

Organising the research study

There are two major organisational questions which the international marketing manager will need to address:

Figure 4.7 Usefulness of personally collected data in the Asia-Pacific region

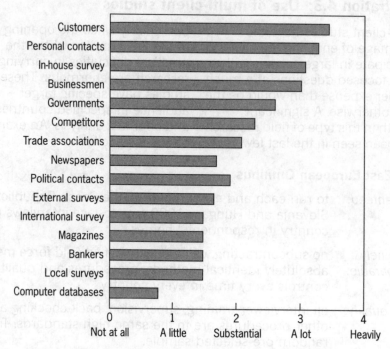

Source: Lassere (1993)

- Should the research be carried out by foreign local subsidiaries or should all marketing research be centralised at headquarters?

- Should the fieldwork be carried out in-house or by an agency?

Centralisation vs decentralisation
If a centralised approach is adopted, then decisions have to be made regarding the specific responsibilities of the operating unit and what managerial arrangements should exist between the unit and headquarters staff. Further to this, decisions have to be taken as to what relationship is to exist between the local research staff who are ultimately responsible to headquarters and the local line management.

If a decentralised approach is chosen, then arrangements have to be made for research findings to be transferred from one operating unit to another. There is also then the question as to who has the overall responsibility for administering and overseeing the market research budget to ensure that resources are not wasted by a possible duplication of research effort.

Such issues are complex and are also related to overall organisational issues which are examined in some depth in Chapter 5. In this chapter we will concentrate our discussion on the decision as to whether the company should carry out international research itself, or should involve independent research agencies.

In-house or agency

Whether the company chooses to do all the research in-house or to use an agency will largely be determined by factors such as company resources, market expertise and product complexity.

If a company operates in a specialist industrial market with highly technological and complex products and has significant experience in the market, it may have no choice but to carry out research itself as it may be difficult to find an agency with the necessary competence.

However, if the company is operating in the consumer field then a different scenario applies. Consumer research may require an established field force and the size of the markets may mean that a research company with field work resources is needed. A priority could well be to obtain an independent objective assessment of a foreign country, this could require specialist interviewing skills which a company alone might not be able to resource and thus would require the services of an agency. If the company is carrying out a multi-country study and needs a consistent research approach across all markets, then an international agency with resources across markets may be much more able to handle the research programme. Often, however, research in foreign markets may require a local firm that can do the field work, gather data and provide some analysis and interpretation. The selection and use of a foreign firm may be extremely important to the success of the whole project.

In choosing an agency, a company has six basic options:

- a local agency in the market under investigation
- a domestic agency with overseas offices
- a domestic agency with overseas associate companies
- a domestic agency which subcontracts field work to an agency in the market under investigation
- a domestic agency with competent foreign staff
- a global agency with offices around the world.

Which solution is best for the researcher will depend on a number of factors; the ease of briefing the agency, supervising and coordinating the project, the probability of language problems arising, the requirements of specialist market knowledge, the standard of competence required and the budget available.

Thus no single option is universally the best to select. It is primarily dependent on the budget available, the requirements of the research and the expertise within the company and, of course, the market under investigation. In a research study in Saudi Arabia the UK agency wished to maintain control and coordination of the project. However, Western interviewers would have had little success in eliciting meaningful information from Saudi businessmen. Therefore it was decided to employ a Cypriot field work agency to translate the questionnaire into Arabic and carry out the required field work. This led to communication and certain control problems but was the only realistic methodology to obtain the required information.

It may often be that in a multi-country study a combination of agencies are used. Hibbert (1993) suggests that a typical multi-country study will go through the following steps:

1 The project is discussed at length with the client.
2 The field work agencies in each country are selected.
3 The questionnaire is designed centrally.
4 The questionnaire is translated locally and the translation is checked centrally.
5 The questionnaire is piloted locally.
6 The questionnaire is finalised centrally.
7 The inteviewers are briefed locally by an executive of the central company.
8 The field work is carried out locally.
9 The coding and editing plan is provided for the local agencies.
10 The edited and coded questionnaires are returned to head office.
11 A coding and editing check is carried out centrally.
12 Computing and analysis are carried out centrally.

Research design

In formulating a research design, considerable effort is needed to ensure that the methods used will ensure comparability of data. In order to handle problems such as cultural bias in research design and interpretation of data, etc., perspectives of researchers from different countries and cultures could be incorporated in the process so that the bias is minimal. However, this method will only work if there are no major problems of communication between researchers from different environments. If this is not the case, there is a possibility that some other kind of unknown bias might be introduced into the research process which could be even more harmful. Therefore a study of the cultural and social values and the method of conducting research in the host country could play an important role in facilitating the process of international marketing research.

One of the first factors to consider in developing a research design is the reliability and validity of the secondary data used. As we have previously discussed, the accuracy of secondary data varies enormously across countries. This means that the database being used to develop primary research may be inaccurate or highly biased or lack the capability to make multi-country comparisons.

Further to this, the research design needs to incorporate methods which will be feasible in the foreign country markets as well as allowing the international researcher to obtain meaningful and relevant findings.

For example, in India, illiteracy affects 64 per cent of the population outside the main areas, there are hundreds of languages and there can be very real fears that the interviewer is a government inspector in disguise. With such a scenario, a researcher would have problems throughout the research process in establishing the basic sample, designing the questionnaire and applying analytical techniques. However, India also has an affluent and educated middle class that in absolute terms is larger in size than the total population of any Western European country.

Social and cultural factors are one of the most important issues which affect the process of international marketing research. Thus in collecting primary data, the researcher needs to consider the issues facing them in evaluating the possible methods under consideration.

In this context, qualitative research, survey methods, questionnaire design and sampling considerations are particularly important.

Qualitative research

Because the researcher is often unfamiliar with the foreign market to be examined, qualitative research is crucial in international marketing research. In the initial stages, qualitative research can provide insights into the problem and help in developing an approach by generating relevant research questions and hypotheses, models and characteristics which influence the research design. Thus, qualitative research may reveal the differences between foreign and domestic markets. It may also help to reduce the psychological distance between the researcher and the respondent. In some cases, the researcher must rely on qualitative research since secondary data may not be available. Goodyear (1982) points out some problems associated with qualitative techniques in developing countries such as accessibility (different concept of time), sampling (extended demographic factors such as religion and tribal membership), shorter span of attention and less familiarity with abstract thinking.

Focus groups can be used in many settings, particularly in industrialised countries. In some cultures though, such as in the Middle or Far East, people are hesitant to discuss their feelings in a group setting. In these cases, in-depth interviews can be used.

The use of projective techniques is sometimes appropriate. Association techniques (word association) completion techniques (sentence completion, story completion) and expressive techniques (role playing, third-person technique) involve the use of verbal cues and so are all good cross-cultural techniques.

Survey methods

There are several issues to consider in evaluating the various interviewing methods available.

Telephone interviewing: in the USA, Canada and Europe, the telephone has achieved almost total penetration of households. In most developing nations, however, only a few households have telephones (e.g. many African countries, India, Brazil). Even in countries like Saudi Arabia, where telephone ownership is extensive, telephone directories tend to be incomplete and out of date.

Therefore, telephone interviews are most useful when employed with relatively upscale consumers who are accustomed to business transactions by phone or consumers who can be reached by phone and can express themselves easily. With the decline of costs for international telephone calls, multi-country studies are now often conducted from a single location.

Mail interviewing: because of low cost, mail interviews continue to be used in most developed countries where literacy is high and the postal system is well developed. In Africa, Asia and South America, however, the use of mail surveys and mail panels is low because of illiteracy and the large proportion of population living in rural areas. Mail surveys are, typically, more effective in industrial international marketing research.

No questionnaire administration method is superior in all situations. Table 4.3 presents a comparative evaluation of the major modes of collecting primary data in the context of international marketing research.

Table 4.3 A comparative evaluation of survey methods for use in marketing international research

Criteria	Telephone	Personal	Mail
High sample control	+	+	−
Difficulty in locating respondents at home	+	−	+
Inaccessibility of homes	+	−	+
Unavailability of a large pool of trained interviewers	+	−	+
Large population in rural areas	−	+	−
Unavailability of current telephone directory	−	+	−
Unavailability of mailing lists	+	+	−
Low penetration of telephones	−	+	+
Lack of an efficient postal system	+	+	−
Low level of literacy	−	+	−
Face-to-face communication culture	−	+	−

Note: + denotes an advantage: − denotes a disadvantage

Source: Malhotra *et al.* (1997)

Questionnaire design

The questionnaire or research instrument should be adapted to the specific cultural environment and should not be biased in terms of any one culture. This requires careful attention to each step of the questionnaire design process. It is important to take into account any differences in underlying consumer behaviour, decision-making processes, psychographics, lifestyles and demographic variables.

The use of unstructured or open-ended questions may be desirable if the researcher lacks knowledge of the possible responses in other cultures. Unstructured questions also reduce cultural bias because they do not impose any response alternatives. However, unstructured questions are more affected by differences in educational levels than structured questions. They should be used with caution in countries with high illiteracy rates.

The questions may have to be translated for administration in different cultures. A set of guidelines has been proposed by Brislin (1990) for writing questionnaires in English so that they can be easily translated. These include:

- use short and simple sentences
- repeat nouns rather than using pronouns
- avoid metaphors
- avoid adverbs and prepositions related to place and time
- avoid possessive forms
- use specific rather than general terms
- avoid vague words
- avoid sentences with two different verbs if the verbs suggest different actions.

The problems of language and translation were discussed in Chapter 3 and equally apply in marketing research. A translation of a questionnaire might be grammatically correct but this does not necessarily mean that it is conveying the appropriate message. For example: value for money is not a common phrase in Spain, the equivalent phrase is 'price for product'. In the Middle East 'payment' is a transactional word, it refers to repaying a debt and so would be inappropriate in the context of purchasing a product.

Another problem is that countries sometimes have more than one official language: a decision has to then be made as to what the most appropriate language is. In Malaysia and Singapore, for instance, consumer surveys regularly employ three languages (English, Malay and Chinese). An interviewer may need a command of several languages or dialects to undertake field work. In Pakistan, the official language is Urdu, but most of the official work in government departments is done in English. However, most local nationals who understand English also usually understand Urdu. There is also a particular segment of social class in the country which prefers English to Urdu in their daily routines. Thus should the researcher use English or Urdu ?

Lodge (1987) argues that the literal translation of a questionnaire can also pose problems. A different language is not just a matter of different spellings but of different linguistic concepts. Choudhry (1986) believes that the back translation into the original language identifies and corrects many of the problems faced in simple translation. He has also suggested the technique of 'decentring' in translation where the material is translated and retranslated each time by a different translator.

Sample frame
The problems of obtaining valid sampling frames tend to be more complicated in researching international markets. It might be difficult or even impossible to

obtain a reliable sampling frame. Due to problems associated with the validity and reliability of secondary data in some countries, experience and judgement need to play an important part in constructing the sample where there is the lack of a reliable database. It may mean that accepted techniques of marketing research in developed countries cannot always be directly transferred even to other developed countries where data might have to be collected through less formalised methods. This applies especially in countries lacking a marketing infrastructure where, unless sufficient care is taken in selecting the sampling frame, the sample chosen will invariably be distorted.

Field work

Interviewee bias

The major problems in field work are errors caused through bias in the interviewing stage of the process which can mean that reliable multi-country studies where results can be compared and contrasted across different countries are sometimes difficult to achieve.

Different cultures will produce a varied response to interviews or questionnaires. For example, purchase intentions for new products frequently peak in Italy because Italians have a propensity to over claim their likelihood to buy, whereas German results are much closer to reality. If Germans say they will buy a product they probably will.

Another problem is that in some countries it is not possible for the female members of a household to respond personally to a survey. In such countries, mail questionnaires for researching the female market might obtain a much better rate of response.

In some countries the rate of response of a particular segment of society might be quite low due to tax evasion problems, respondents being unwilling to provide any information which gives an idea of their economic status (Terpstra and Sarathy 1997). Even within the same country, different social classes of customers could have differing responses to marketing research techniques. In some cultures the respondent may cause bias by attempting to please the interviewer and give the answers they think they want to hear. This happened to BSN in Japan as Illustration 4.4 shows.

The rate of response will also vary depending on how structured the research is. Research by (Mahmoud and Gillian 1988) shows the tendency of managers to use judgemental and unstructured approaches in the research process leads to invalid responses by the respondents.

Illustration 4.4: The Japanese can't say no to yoghurt

The French conglomerate BSN, one of the largest food manufacturing groups in Europe, planned to target Japan as a priority market for its yoghurts and so did a market survey in the country.

The results indicated that the Japanese were becoming much more Westernised in their food and eating habits and that there was a potential market for yoghurts in Japan.

BSN went ahead with the product launch, set up distribution and invested heavily in promotion.

However after two years the sales were disappointing and substantially below expectations.

Follow up research showed that the questions used were too simplistic to elicit accurate responses from the Japanese. The Japanese were far too polite to reply NO to a question. Therefore the responses to yes/no questions were highly misleading. Likewise they did not wish to offend Westerners by criticising the usage of a spoon as an eating implement.

The result had been therefore that a largely fallacious picture of the size, value and potential of the Japanese market had emerged from the original research.

Source: adapted from Hibbert (1993) 'Researching International Markets'

Interviewer bias

Interviewer biases are often due to communication problems between the interviewer and respondents. Several biases have been identified in multi-cultural research including rudeness bias, 'I can answer any question' bias, courtesy bias, sucker bias, hidden premises bias, reticence-loquaciousness bias, social desirability, status difference bias, racial difference bias and individual group opinion bias (Malhotra 1997).

Extensive training and close supervision of the interviewers and other field staff may be required to minimise these biases.

The selection, training, supervision and evaluation of field workers is critical in multi-country research. Local field work agencies are unavailable in many countries. It may be necessary therefore to recruit and train local field workers or import trained foreign workers. The use of local field workers is desirable as they are familiar with the local language and culture. They can thus create an appropriate climate for the interview and be sensitive to the concerns of the respondents.

Data analysis

A number of issues need to be considered at the data analysis stage. First, in preparing data for analysis in multi-country or cross-cultural studies, how do you deal with 'outliers'? These are countries where the data is quite obviously different from the bulk of the data. It may not be a problem at all but, likewise, it could be due to some cultural bias, a problem in the sampling or a problem of translation in the questionnaire.

Second, the issue of how to ensure comparability of data across cultures. Some researchers prefer to standardise data to ensure comparability. In contrast, others prefer statistics based on unstandardised data on the bases that this allows a truer comparative analysis.

Report preparation and presentation

In any research study there is the chance of cultural bias in the research findings. International research often involves researchers from one cultural environment conducting research in another cultural environment or communicating with researchers from another cultural environment. In international research situations, effective communication between the respondents and the researcher is essential to avoid problems of misinterpretation of the data. The phenomenon of culturally self-reference criterion is cited as a possible cause of the misinterpretation of data and can lead to a quite systematic bias in the findings. The reader is referred to the discussion in Chapter 3 and the discussion on the steps that can be taken to remedy self-reference criterion.

Some agencies follow the practice of always ensuring foreign market studies are written in the local language and include interpretation as well as analysis. The nuance can then be discussed with the translator.

Face-to-face debriefings with agencies and researchers are also a good way to synthesise the results from multi-country surveys and form coherent conclusions through open discussions with representatives who have participated in the research across a range of countries.

Continuous research

In this chapter, in order to discuss the relevant issues in a logical manner, we have used the six step research design framework. It is perhaps important to stress however that international market research, whilst expensive, is by no means a 'one-off' activity. In today's dynamic environment where changes occur almost on a daily basis in some rapidly growing markets (e.g. China), it is important that research be on a continuous basis to ensure a company keeps ahead of its competition.

Conclusion

Within this chapter, we have tried to illustrate the strategic importance of opportunity analysis and the contribution that the information system and market research can make to the decision-making process. International research is, in many cases, a complex, expensive and time-consuming task and evidence suggests that for these reasons many international firms fail to research markets to the extent that is really necessary. The consequences of this are significant in terms of both missed opportunities and the failure to meet existing and developing market demand.

The key tasks for the international researcher are to scan markets, to identify and analyse opportunities, building up comprehensive market profiles and carrying out detailed international studies both in foreign country markets and across a range of multi-country markets.

Discussion questions

1 What are the dangers of translating questionnaires that have been designed and used in one country for use in multi-country studies? How would you avoid these dangers?
2 Many companies are looking to emerging markets in their internationalisation programmes. What are the problems in researching these markets? How, if at all, may they be overcome?
3 Identify the principal methods that companies might use in assessing and reviewing opportunities across international markets. Suggest the alternative means by which firms can prioritise and segment international markets.
4 As firms become more global so does their requirement to gather global information. Outline the key categories of a global information system and explain their relevance.

References

Brislin, R.W. (1990) *Applied Cross-cultural psychology*, Sage.
Choudhry, Y.A. (1986) 'Pitfalls in International Marketing Research: Are You Speaking French Like a Spanish Cow?' *Akron Business and Economic Review*, 17 (4).

Czinkota, M.R. and Ronkainen, I.A. (1994) 'Market Research for your Export Operations: Part 1 Using Secondary Sources of Research', *International Trade FORUM*, 3.

De Houd, M. (1982) 'Internationalised Computerised Telephone Research: is it Fiction?' *Marketing Research Society Newsletter*, 190, January: 14–15.

Douglas, C. (1983) *International Marketing Research*, Prentice Hall.

Gilligan, C. and Hird, M. (1985) *International Marketing*, Routledge.

Goodyear, M. (1982) 'Qualitative Research in Developing Countries', *Journal of the Market Research Society*, 24 (2): 86–96.

Gorton, K. and Doole, I. (1989) *Low Cost Marketing Research*, John Wiley.

Hamill, J. (1997) 'Internet and International marketing', *International Marketing Review*, 14 (5), 318–23.

Hammersveld, M.V. (1989) 'Marketing Research, Local, Multi-Domestic or International?' *Marketing and Research Today*, 17.

Harrell, G.D. and Kiefer, R.D. (1993) 'Multinational Market Portfolio in Global Strategy Development', *International Marketing Review*, 10 (1).

Hibbert, E. (1993) 'Researching International Markets. How can we ensure the validity of results?' *Marketing Research Today*, November.

Johannson, J. (1972) *Exportstrategiska problem*, Stockholm Press.

Kale, S.H. and Sudharsan, D.A. (1987), 'A Strategic Approach to International Segmentation', *International Marketing Review*, Summer.

Lassere, P. (1993) 'Gathering and Interpreting Strategic Intelligence in Asia Pacific', *Long Range Planning*, 26 (3).

Lodge, C. (1987) 'International Marketing: Getting to know Foreign Bodies', *Marketing*, 29.

MacFarlane, I. (1991) 'Do it Yourself Marketing Research', *Management Review*, 80 (5).

Mahmoud, H. and Gillian, J. (1988) 'Use of Analytical Techniques in International Marketing', *International Marketing Review*, 5 (3).

Majaro, S. (1992) *International Marketing*, Routledge.

Malhotra, N.K., Agrawal, J. and Peterson, M. (1997) Methodological Issues in Cross Cultural Marketing Research', *International Marketing Review*, 13 (6): 7–43.

Paliwoda, S. (1992) 'Countries Have Failed to Attract Foreign Investment', *International Marketing Review*, 17 (2).

Terpstra, V. and Sarathy, R. (1997) *International Marketing*, Dryden Press, 7th edn.

Walters, P.G.P. (1997) 'Global Market Segmentation: Methodologies and Challenges', *Journal of Marketing Management*, 13, 165–77.

Special focus

Overcoming barriers to entry in China*

Introduction

The Chinese market has attracted foreign investors because of its huge size and market potential. In recent years, more and more foreign investors have endeavoured to introduce new ventures into this market. Market entry barriers are critical factors that influence entry decisions and the firm's performance. Shepherd (1979) states that barriers to entry decrease the likelihood, scope or speed with which potential competitors can come into the markets. In the course of international expansion, the firm encounters new factors such as new government regulations, new legal and financial systems, new cultures, new languages, greater distances, new modes of transportation, currency exchange rates and their vagaries (Czinkota 1996). The most common barriers in international markets are: (1) government policy; (2) cultural barriers; (3) product adoption; and (4) access to distribution channels. In this special focus we will examine each of these in relation to the Chinese market.

Government policies

Generally speaking, China's trade and investment systems lack transparency. Policies and regulations are not readily accessible. Even when central government has clear polices, they are often applied inconsistently and can vary between regions. Both foreign nationals and Chinese officials themselves lack a solid understanding of China's policies (Genzberger *et al*. 1994). The key policies which act as barriers to entry relate to foreign exchange control policies and foreign investment policy.

* By: Lily Lin Qiu, John Hall and Lindsay Turner, Victoria University of Technology, Melbourne, Australia.

1

Foreign exchange control policies: China's central government has pursued a policy of 'centralised control' over foreign exchange. This means that the state is responsible for formulating and promulgating the principles, degrees and regulations for foreign exchange control. The acquisition of foreign exchange is a significant non-tariff barrier to doing business in China. The foreign exchange regulations for foreign invested enterprises (FIEs) required that profits be remitted, imported components or raw materials be purchased, and foreign personnel be compensated in foreign currency rather than in Chinese currency. FIEs for the Chinese domestic market often cite the fact that Chinese currency is not convertible as a serious problem in the conduct of business (Reinganum and Helsell 1994). The Chinese government strongly encourages exporting as a primary means. The other method is selling goods in the domestic economy for foreign exchange, which is unrealistic, because few customers in China have access to foreign currency. Foreign exchange swap centres enable firms to obtain foreign exchange. In theory, foreign exchange is permitted to flow from one swap centre to another to equalise supply and demand, but in practice, local authorities often block the flow of foreign exchange from centres in their jurisdiction. Some centres refuse to sell foreign exchange to companies outside their own area.

Foreign investment policies: there are three major forms of direct foreign investment: equity joint venture, contract joint venture, wholly foreign-owned enterprise. Most legislative attention has been paid to the equity joint venture. During China's economic reform, one of the key foreign investment laws is the Joint Venture Law (JVL), which was promulgated in July 1979 and revised in 1990. JVL created the single investment vehicle of a Sino-foreign equity joint venture with the parties owning shares in a newly created company.

Under the provisions of the original JVL, the management required the president to be a PRC national, with unanimous board of directors approval for major corporate acts and for the fixed duration of the joint venture (Roy 1993). All joint ventures must be approved by the local government affiliate of the Ministry of Foreign Economic Relations and Trade (MOFERT), after the agreement is finalised within one month of gaining the MOFERT's approval. The representatives of the joint venture must register with the local branch office of the State Administration for Industry and Commerce. This agency reviews the joint venture and issues a business license. Wholly foreign-owned ventures have become increasingly numerous since the 1990s. In the 1980s, enterprises with 100 per cent foreign ownership were allowed to set up operations only in the Special Economic Zones, but enactment of the law on enterprises makes it possible to set up a venture of this type in most parts of China. However, the law still requires such a venture to be export oriented and to employ advanced equipment and technology (Genzberger *et al.* 1994).

China encourages foreigners to invest in such capital-intensive industries as energy, transportation and telecommunications, whilst investment in labour-intensive industries is common (Luo 1995). Despite China's ongoing process of trade liberalisation, the complex system of administrative controls and regulations affecting foreign investment and trade still reflects the time when the country was largely closed to the rest of the world.

Cultural differences – *Guanxi*

Chinese culture has influenced the marketing environment. Chinese cultural values are largely formed and created from interpersonal relationships and social orientations. Chinese nations tend to rely heavily on personal relationship (*guanxi*) in business dealings (Chen 1994).

The word *guanxi* is loosely translated into 'special relationship' or 'connections'. In a typical Chinese context, *guanxi* goes deeper than connection. It necessitates very personal interactions with other people and always involves a reciprocal obligation (Stone 1992). *Guanxi* are formed through kinship, schools, institutions and long-term familiarity with business associates. Some findings in the Chinese survey (Chu and Ju 1993) were that the majority (92.4 per cent) affirmed the importance of *guanxi* in their daily lives; 84.5 per cent of Chinese indicated that they do not trust strangers until they have had the opportunity to get to know them better; and 71.7 per cent preferred to use *guanxi* connections over normal bureaucratic channels to advance personal interests and solve problems.

Guanxi is of paramount importance in the initial stages of entering the Chinese market. A survey of foreign companies which included nineteen Hong Kong, United States, Canadian and German companies with business in China (Young and Tung 1996) indicated that the executives consistently considered *guanxi* as a key success factor.

Foreign investors prefer joint ventures because they provide long-term connections and use the *guanxi* of the local partner. The Chinese partner in a joint venture handles dealings with government officials and sells products through the local partner's established marketing channels to penetrate the domestic market. They rely on their *guanxi*, frequently using 'the back door' to get anything done. Small and medium-sized firms tend to place greater emphasis

ß

on *guanxi* than large companies, since large firms can contribute substantially to the local firms sales and other business activities heavily dependent on *guanxi*.

Firms in the tertiary and exporting sectors assigned greater importance to *guanxi* than those engaged in manufacturing and importing. Those in the tertiary and exporting sectors had to frequently broaden their base of operations and search for new suppliers. They had to expand and shift their *guanxi* networks continuously (Young and Tung 1996).

No company in the Chinese business world succeeds unless it benefits from extensive *guanxi*. *Guanxi* bind literally millions of Chinese firms into a social and business network that can be particularly useful for foreign companies with little business experience in China (Luo 1995).

The way of establishing *guanxi* can be to offer immediate rewards, such as gift-giving, social meetings in restaurants, overseas trips and sponsoring the children of Chinese officials at universities abroad. Moreover, introductions into the *guanxi* network can be accomplished through a wide variety of people and organisations, for example, important political figures, well-known business personages who are 'old friends' of China, executives from companies already in China as well as hired intermediaries who act as consultants, agents, representatives and distributors. But doing business in China requires the patient building of a relationship.

For foreign investors who seek to do business in China, to understand the dynamics of *guanxi* can contribute to the success of business. Otherwise, 'if you don't have a relationship in China, you never exist!' (Stone 1992).

Access to the Chinese distribution channels

The Chinese distribution channel was a state-run distribution system, until the mid 1980s. It was established not according to the economic function, but according to political and administrative functions (Qiang and Harris 1990). Production and distribution were all planned by the State Planning Commission. Nearly all the existing distribution channels at that time were state owned. Factories would be allocated a set amount of subsidised raw materials and funds to enable them to achieve state-set production targets.

In the distribution systems, there were classified three-tier distribution centres. The first-tier distribution centre handled products at the state level, such as the three major distribution centres responsible for storing and shipping in Shanghai, Tianjin and Guanzhou. Numerous second and third distribution centres handled products at the local level. Within each of these

4

distribution hierarchies, specific subdivisions handled different types of products. The old system's main flaws were its hierarchy and inefficiency. The wholesale network provided producers little or no contact with product end users, so customer preferences were not considered when production goals were being set. Rather than looking down the chain to the end user and their needs, producers were forced to seek approval from higher administrations. Moreover, the distribution hierarchy absorbed costs and time in each tier, which reflected the inefficiency.

The old distribution channels were narrow for foreign products access. Foreign products entered the country only via state run foreign trade corporations (FTCs), which would purchase and import foreign goods according to central directives. FTCs could also import on behalf of a Chinese end user who had obtained the necessary central provincial and municipal approvals.

The FTC system began to be decentralised in the early 1980s, with some provinces given more authority in foreign trade, and major producers and other entities being allowed to arrange their own deals directly without reference to FTCs. In 1984 China instituted an economic reform that required a clear division between government entities and commercial companies, and mandated that the latter gradually become self-sufficient. In the last years, the Ministry of Foreign Trade and Economic Cooperation (MOFTEC) has further loosened the reins. Recently, any Chinese company that has exported through an FTC US$1 million worth of goods annually for three consecutive years may engage in direct trade (Reinganum and Helsell 1994). In late 1992, the Chinese government published its distribution reform stage with the announcement that foreign businesses could establish joint ventures in the retail sector in several big cities and special economic zones.

Although the Chinese distribution systems have undergone dramatic changes, the barriers to access this system still exist. In the reform, China's distribution system remains unstable. From now on, old style wholesalers at both the local and central levels, new collective and private enterprises and factories, as well as some foreign companies compete to distribute consumer products. Local ministry of commerce wholesalers traditionally served as intermediaries between the producer and retail outlets. Today they still control large warehouses, run fleets of trucks and arrange train transportation. Foreign companies are not permitted to engage in wholesale trade.

The old distribution system left a shaky foundation for the physical movement of goods on China's undeveloped and overcrowded transit system. China's transportation is one of the bottlenecks hampering economic development. Railroad transportation is a common means for long-distance shipping, but the rail system in China is closely controlled. Priority is often given to goods that are still under tight central government control, such as grain and coal. Products bound for export market or those under the care of a shipper who enjoys a good relationship with the local rail officer are usually the competitors for space.

Storage of goods is another problem. Space is limited, and primitive shacks outnumber modern, computerised facilities. Cold-storage facilities are rarely available outside of coastal fish processing areas (Reinganum and Helsell 1994). Foreign firms needing such storage space often work with Chinese firms that own cold-storage facilities.

Product adoption

A strict isolationist policy kept foreign goods and trends out of reach of the average Chinese person. With the door now swung open to international business, numerous foreign products are coming to the Chinese market. Because Chinese consumers have less abundant information and purchasing experience with foreign products, they may rely more heavily on surrogate information cues such as the producing country's image in product evaluation. Japan and the USA are industrialised countries, with a more favourable country image. Some industrialising countries, such as South Korea however, have a less favourable country image compared with the above two industrialised countries (Zheng 1996). For new industrialising countries, in their effort to market their products to Chinese consumers, they may stress and build up a stronger brand image.

Each region in China has differences in economic growth, living standards and education. For foreign products, there are sharp differences between rural and urban attitudes. On a national level, Chinese consumers prefer to buy domestically manufactured products rather than comparable foreign-made goods. However, consumers in big cities are less likely to favour domestic products than are consumers nationally. As more Chinese-made consumer durable products use advanced production techniques, the Chinese population perceives the quality of domestic goods to be comparable to, and the price lower than, that of imported goods.

The average Chinese consumer's purchasing decisions do not significantly hinge on brand names. They prefer to buy inexpensive products with limited features over top rated products with many features. But the consumers in urban areas prefer to pay the higher price for high-quality products than buy inexpensive products, regardless of quality. The urban consumers have a wide recognition of foreign brand names, whilst the most rural consumers recognise only several names (Li and Gullup 1995).

Chinese literacy is different from Western, both in character words and in meaning. Foreign product names translated directly into Chinese, will not be well recognised by Chinese people. Most Chinese consumers recognise Coca-Cola, due to the fact that the translation in Chinese means 'taste good and taste happy'. A symbolically significant name helps sell a product.

Moreover, typical Chinese consumers do not want to be amongst the first to try a new product (Yan 1994). They are reluctant to be pioneers, especially for an expensive, unrecognised (in terms of brand), foreign product.

Implications

The barriers to market entry make China a challenging market for foreign enterprises. However despite the evident difficulties it is perceived by many as perhaps the most important market in which to gain a prescence. The possible modes of entry into the Chinese market include equity joint ventures (EJVs), contractual (or cooperative) joint ventures (CJVs), joint exploration projects (JEPs) and wholly foreign owned enterprises (WFOEs).

The USA and Japan are the third and fourth largest entrants with FDI capital of US$14 253 million (the USA) and US$ 13 980 million (Japan) between 1979 and 1996. In terms of investment, the USA leads all other foreign countries. Japanese firms account for about 20 per cent of investment in manufacturing industries. Amongst these, light industries and textiles rank first, followed by electronics, chemicals, heavy industries, food and construction materials (Cheng 1993).

The UK, Germany and France are also large investors, representing 1.7 per cent of foreign enterprise and 2.7 per cent of FDI capital. In the recent foreign investment boom, they have increased their investment rapidly; for example, the UK with capital of US$1300 million in 1996, increased by 42 per cent over 1995; France with US$423 million in 1995, increased by 47.4 per cent over 1994; Germany with capital of US$518 million, increased by 32.8 per cent. Australia is one of the top ten largest investors in China, with 1269 enterprises and capital of US$953 millon from 1979 to 1996. Recently, Australian investors increased their investment, by US$194 million in 1996, which was fourteen times that of 1985.

7

References

Chen, M. (1994) '*Guanxi* and the Chinese Art of Network Building', *New Asia Review*, Summer: 40–3.

Cheng, C. (1993) 'Strategic Consideration for Foreign Firms operating in China', Working paper, University of Western Sydney, Nepean (9).

Chu, G.C. and Ju, Y. (1993) *The Great Wall in Ruins*, State University of New York Press.

Czinkota, M.R. (1996) Why National Export Promotion, *International Trade Forum*, (2): 10–13.

Genzberger, C.A., *et al.* (1994) *China Business: the Portable Encyclopedia for Doing Business with China*, World Trade Press.

Goodnow, J. and Hansz (1972) 'Environmental Determinants of Overseas Market Entry Strategy', *Journal of International Business Studies*, Spring: 30–50.

Li, D. and Gallup, A.M. (1995) In Search of the Chinese Consumer, *The China Business Review*, September–October: 19–22.

Luo, Y. (1995) 'Business Strategy, Market Structure, and Performance of International Joint Ventures: The Case of Joint Ventures in China', *Management International Review*, 35: 241–64.

Qiang, Z.W. and Harris, P. (1990) 'Retailing Reform and Trends in China', International Journal of Retail and Distribution Management, 18: 31–9.

Reinganum, J. and Helsell, T. (1994) 'To Market, To Market', *The China Business Review*, January–February: 12–17.

Roy, F.G. (1993) 'In Search of Excellence within Chinas Industrial Sector: The Chinese Enterprise and Foreign Technology' *Chinas Economic Dilemmas in The 1990s*, M.E. Sharpe, Inc.: 828–40.

Shepherd, W. (1979) *The Economics of Industrial Organisation*, Prentice Hall.

Stelzer, L., Chunguang, M. and Banthin, J. (1992) 'Gauging Investor Satisfaction', *China Business Review*, June 19: 54–6.

Stone, R. (1992) 'Negotiation in China Is Not Easy', *Hong Kong Business*, November: 64–7.

Yan. R. (1994) 'To Reach Chinas Consumer, Adapt to Guo Qing', *Harvard Business Review*, 72 (5) September–October: 66–74.

Young, I.Y.M. and Tung, R.L. (1996) 'Achieving Business Success in Confusion Societies: The Importance of *Guanxi*', *Organisational Dynamics*, Autumn: 54–65.

Zheng, Y. (1996) 'Chinese Consumers Evaluation of Foreign Products: the Influence of Culture, Product Types and Product Presentation Format', *European Journal of Marketing*, 30(12): 56–68.

Part I Cases

Car security systems in Pakistan

Introduction

Lasman Electronics in Lahore, Pakistan felt that there was a latent demand in Pakistan for electronic car security systems.

The objective of the market research study was to test this perception and carry out an assessment of the market for electronic car security systems in Pakistan and to examine the feasibility of launching the product into that market. At the time of the study, such systems were not available in the Pakistani market.

The project was being administered from the UK and so had all the problems attendant with long and cumbersome communication channels. Furthermore, the project was being carried out in a country which was seen as a researcher's nightmare. There was no recognisable research infrastructure and there were few reliable sources of secondary information, a multiplicity of languages, a mistrust of interviewers and a fierce instinct to protect privacy. The conditions were not seen as being conducive to a successful marketing research exercise.

Whilst wanting to satisfy the client's need for marketing information, the researchers were interested in whether it was possible for a small company to conduct primary research on a limited budget in a country such as Pakistan.

Preliminary research findings

It was found it would be impractical to carry out a full country-wide study of Pakistan. It was assumed there would be difficulties with the sampling plan and it was argued that in such cases the more targeted the consumer segment, the easier it would be to formulate an effective sampling plan.

Preliminary research showed that it was only the affluent consumers who owned reasonably new cars and, therefore, would have an interest in security systems, and that the vast majority of these individuals could be found in the vicinity of the capital city Lahore.

The particular social and cultural problems with carrying out the survey were identified as the following:

- a marked reluctance to talk to strangers and admit strangers to the house even with proper references – this had been further exacerbated by the deteriorating law and order situation
- a need to ensure the privacy and anonymity of respondents
- it would probably be difficult to talk to female respondents
- a lack of trained interviewers
- a high level of illiteracy
- no marketing research culture, meaning there would be a mistrust of interviewers
- less that 1 per cent of the population in Pakistan has telephones and the telephone service in any case was continually breaking down. There was a lack of trained telephone interviewers to administer the survey and record responses.

Another problem to be faced was the lack of an available sampling frame from which to draw an appropriate sample. The Lahore City Vehicle Registration Department held all car registrations but it was impossible to extract information regarding new car registrations over the last five years. Interestingly, this was not because the information was seen as confidential but because the information was too difficult to access. There was no computer database and the information was not stored to enable usage of the data contained in the files.

Discussion questions

1 Fully evaluate the implications for the research study of the problems identified in the preliminary research.
2 Design a research strategy for the study fully explaining how you would implement each stage of the study.

Case comments

This case illustrates the difficulties in researching emerging markets, where there is little infrastructure to support a research strategy. The reader in answering the questions may have to think innovatively as to how they would find a solution to the problem and at the same time ensure the credibility and validity of the findings from such a study.

Derwent Valley Foods

Phileas Fogg is a brand of up-market exotic snackfoods for adults made by Derwent Valley Foods. The company has had *ad hoc* success in a few markets including India, China and Mexico. However, the company stumbled when they tried to launch into continental Europe where the company feel the brand has failed to achieve its potential over the past decade.

The medium-sized company behind the brand is Derwent Valley Foods which has developed impressively since its foundations in 1982, especially in its core market of south-east England. The total revenue for 1998 was £30 million with profits of above £3 million. Yet barely £1 million of its sales are to continental Europe.

The company's top managers were open about their past failings. One of them described their then desultory export efforts as 'a Mickey Mouse operation'. This disarming self-disparagement is typical of the company's style but was not entirely fair for two reasons.

First, its explosive growth in Britain left little management time to cope with the tricky problem of steering Fogg into continental Europe.

Second, the company had encountered the same problems which beset most medium-sized would-be exporters of consumer products within Europe, fragmented and sometimes impenetrable national distribution patterns. In most industries these represent a far greater barrier to the creation of a single market than do national and regional differences in consumer preferences.

Even when national retail patterns seem superficially similar, the reality is often otherwise. France has a growing number of large chains but their buying patterns contrast sharply with those in Britain. They are not only more fragmented but buying groups purchase on behalf of odd combinations of retailers. It is still necessary to sell to individual shops, each of which levies a one-off charge for putting your product on its shelves. The company and its new French partner are spending £200 000 on this in 1998.

In Germany there is a complex mixture of delicatessens and specialist stores plus large retail chains. The latter, unlike their British equivalents, have numerous buying points.

In view of these difficulties, Derwent Valley decided to pause and start a thorough research and planning exercise in order to prepare a real attack on the continent.

The company carried out consumer research. This demonstrated great potential interest in the Phileas Fogg brand but it also showed that the range of flavours would have to be tailored to each market. It uncovered, too, a need not just to do each country's packaging in its own language – at an initial cost of £10 000 a product per country – but also to design a distinctive shape of package to stand out on continental shelves.

By this time a decision had been made to concentrate on four markets with France and Spain the first two main ones. The export drive was still in the hands of the two company founders who were both preoccupied with the domestic market. Hence the move to recruit a 'Mr Europe', an ex-FMCG manager who was operating across Western Europe as international marketing manager for a flavours and essences company.

The new brief involved two key tasks, fine-tuning Derwent Valley's products, looking at packaging, pricing and presentation for each main market and finding strong local partners which, unlike many of the company's previous ones, really knew the country and had expertise and muscle in sales and distribution. They also had to be committed to the brand concept. This strategy contrasted sharply with the company's previous approach of selling the product wherever and through whomever it could.

The groundwork bore fruit with a quick succession of new deals, each with hand-picked but different types of partner, in the Netherlands, France and Spain. These are doing well and have boosted Derwent Valley's exports to continental Europe by half.

That was despite the mishap in Germany. Derwent Valley thought it had broken its long run of bad experiences with German distributors and had just signed up a local tobacco manufacturer which was moving into food brokerage. But, as with other tobacco companies, its sales force failed to break into the food side of supermarkets. The market opportunities in tobacco which arose from East Germany also distracted it in the midst of a Phileas Fogg test marketing exercise and £200 000 of Derwent Valley's investment went down the drain.

On the company's current projections, exports to European countries (including Ireland) will grow from £1.5 million to at least £13 million over the next three years. At best, they could go to almost double that.

Whatever the actual outcome, Phileas Fogg does seem at last to be getting into his continental stride.

Discussion questions

1 Identify the key reasons why Derwent Valley Foods experienced difficulties in getting established in the European market.
2 What are the lessons to be learnt for a company expanding internationally?
3 What recommended changes would you suggest Derwent Valley Foods make to their international marketing strategy?

Case comments

This case illustrates the concept that a company operating successfully in its domestic market can, sometimes, ignore the principles that laid the foundations for that success when it enters new export markets.

You should relate the case information to the marketing process and identify the gaps in the strategic thinking of Derwent Foods when they launched Phileas Fogg into continental Europe.

Amway expands into China

The background

China is on the verge of surpassing all known growth records. To begin with, far from being a slowly emerging economic force, it is already the world's third largest economy trailing only USA and Japan, but not for much longer. By the year 2010 it could be the world's largest. But, of course, size of economy does not equate to standard of living. Within China itself, the major growth is taking place in the coastal regions where roughly one quarter of the population lives, a total of 300 million people, where income is set to grow at 11 per cent a year for the next ten years. To quote Lee Kuan Yew, formerly Prime Minister of Singapore, 'Never in human history have so many grown so rich so fast'.

China, with 1.2 billion people (25 per cent of the world's population), offers the greatest single opportunity and threat for Western products.

Guandong province, neighbouring on Hong Kong, with 60 million people is China's showpiece. Since barriers with Hong Kong ceased in 1978 its GDP has grown 13 per cent per annum and is generally proving to be the springboard for Western products entering the Chinese market. For example, Guandong is Proctor and Gamble's second largest market world-wide for shampoos.

Entering the Chinese market

Patience is a virtue, creativity a must! More open than the Japanese market, nevertheless the careful cultivation of special relationships from influential people down to the everyday consumer is important in doing business. The word for this is *Guanxi* – Chinese for connections. Cultivating connections is part of the culture, with word of mouth counting for more than most of the other forms of marketing communications. Whilst it is true that the market poses challenges to foreign investors, many companies are discovering the key to success is to start at the local level, learn the market, develop trust with Chinese partners, let each experience make the relationship stronger. In other words, the traditional Western approach of marketing as exemplified by the FMCG route requires serious modifications – besides which, the normal tools of marketing communication i.e. advertising etc. are not greatly in evidence.

Amway takes the plunge

Amway, the world's largest direct marketing firm, is gearing itself to enter the Chinese market, focusing on Guandong Province in the short term. Amway operates world-wide via a system of personal sales people each of whom has a number of sales people reporting to them. Much is made of door-to-door selling and what are known as 'party programmes' where groups of potential customers meet in a friend's home. It has already invested £60 million in a new factory in the province. The factory produces products for the Pacific region but these are standard products to meet consumer needs in Japan, Philippines, Taiwan, Singapore, etc. This product range which includes detergents, washing liquids, household cleaners and even cosmetics and vitamins may not be appropriate for China. So whilst Amway has considerable experience in the Far East where sales have been extremely buoyant, the downside is that the Chinese market is not a mirror image of Taiwan, Philippines, etc. where capitalist economies are well established. So it has to start virtually from scratch in marketing the business in China.

Direct marketing has great potential in China. There is a history of trading stretching back hundreds of years, albeit briefly interrupted by Communist rule. The Chinese are natural entrepreneurs. With an underdeveloped retail structure i.e. few supermarkets – a culture of *guanxi* networking already established and a population with rapidly expanding disposable income, the future is rosy. But pitfalls abound. The market is riddled with unscrupulous operators selling substandard goods with poor service, claiming to be legitimate direct marketers. The Chinese are naturally apprehensive – and they ask questions. Door-to-door cold calling is not part of the culture. But the overall portents are good. Avon, a rival direct marketer, has been in China for five years and has racked up impressive sales growth projecting sales of £40 million in 1995. Avon has taken the route of following the culture rather than imposing itself via heavy advertising and price promotion. Indeed, price promotion is virtually unheard of as are discount operators.

Discussion questions

1 Fully assess the SLEPT environmental factors that Amway must consider and assess the implications for Amways strategy in China.

2 Discuss what you consider to be the key strategic marketing concerns facing Amway in the development of the Chinese market.

Case comments

China is a high risk and extremely complex market. It is therefore important that the reader uses a structured approach to their analysis. Some of the conceptual frameworks discussed in Part I may prove useful. The reader should avoid describing the environment. In answering question 1 it is more important to assess the implications of the facts in the case for Amway.

Part II
Development

Introduction

Aims and objectives

Having identified and analysed the opportunities which exist within international markets in the first section of the book, we now turn our attention to the ways in which firms can use international marketing to develop their international business in order to exploit these opportunities profitably. The first chapter in Part II concentrates on helping the reader to gain an understanding of the concepts of international planning. The next two chapters are concerned with the international marketing strategy options available, first, for small and medium-sized firms and, second, for larger firms that are operating within a global context. The final chapter in the section is concerned with the selection of appropriate market entry methods.

Learning outcomes

On the completion of Part II, the reader should be able to:

- evaluate the suitability of different approaches, such as standardisation and adaptation, understand the use of alternative market entry methods as part of the international marketing strategies;
- compare and contrast the strategies for niche marketing, regional and global marketing;
- differentiate between the marketing strategies which are appropriate to developed and emerging economies;
- identify the implications of moving from national to international marketing on the organisation and its managers.

Indicative content

In Chapter 5, we focus upon the international marketing planning process and examine the development of appropriate organisational structures, cultures and capabilities. We also consider the management and control of in-house and external resources and the changing strategic roles of international marketing managers.

Chapter 6 is concerned with smaller firm international niche marketing and includes the different types of firm development, their motivations and barriers, and the success criteria for good international marketers.

In Chapter 7 we discuss the dimensions of globalisation and the implications standardisation and adaptation have for the development of alternative global strategic approaches.

Chapter 8 is concerned with the options available and selection criteria for market entry both in terms of new entry and realignment of existing market presence.

All of the chapters are concerned with the success criteria for the strategies defined and the marketing and financial risks involved.

Chapter 5
International marketing planning and organisation

Introduction

Whilst the majority of companies recognise that planning and control are essential elements of effective management, many managers are unclear or even suspicious about the true purpose of the planning process. In international marketing the very complexity of handling the diverse range of factors that must be considered, make planning and control a difficult activity to carry out satisfactorily. Many companies do not gain the real benefits that should come from a well developed and systematic planning process because the methods used for planning are often incomplete or too fragmented.

For large multi-national companies, the problem becomes one of how to structure the organisation so that its increasingly complex and diverse activities around the world can be planned and managed effectively, its goals can be achieved and its stakeholders' expectations satisfied.

This chapter is concerned, therefore, with first looking at the international marketing planning and control process, the problems that are encountered, and how improvements can be made in order to ensure a satisfactory outcome; second, at how companies organise their diverse operations and, third, how managers must respond to the challenges posed by the need to plan and organise an effective business.

The planning process

The planning process is the method used by the management of the firm to define in detail how it will achieve its current and future strategic aims and objectives. In doing this, it must evaluate the current and future market opportunities, assess its own current and potential capabilities and attempt to forecast how the changes over which it has no control might help or hinder its efforts to reach its objectives.

The international planning process must allow the company to answer the following three marketing questions.

Where is the company now?

Where does it want to go?

How might it get there?

These questions are fundamental for the majority of businesses whether they are large or small, simple or complex, or domestic or international and they emphasise the firm's need to prepare for the future to ensure its own survival and growth within the increasingly competitive business environment. There is an implication in these questions that the future is likely to be significantly different from the past, and so *inevitably planning is about forecasting and implementing change* which determines the very nature and future direction of the organisation. Illustration 5.1 shows how IBM lost its marketing direction, not realising that the market had changed substantially, before Lou Gerstner took over.

As the IBM illustration shows the starting point of the planning process for any company is to set long-term goals and objectives which reflect its overall aspirations. These goals cannot be set in isolation, however, as the company's history and current levels of success in its different country markets are usually major determinants of its future. Other factors too, over which the company has little control in international markets, such as the economic and political situation of the countries in which it is operating, the response of the competition and the diverse background, behaviour and expectations of its customers, all have a major impact upon the company's operations and will have a significant effect on determining whether or not it will meet its goals. Hamel and Prahalad (1994) emphasise that firms must not simply focus on meeting customer needs but must also be aware of and work to their own strengths and capabilities.

Planning should include a control process, which is the mechanism for evaluating the effectiveness of the strategies and the efforts of the staff responsible for their implementation. Control is essentially concerned with monitoring performance, evaluating feedback and taking corrective action if plans are not being followed or if current strategies have become inappropriate.

Too many firms, particularly smaller ones, fail to prepare contingency plans to cope with the unexpected and, in some cases, even the predictable events, and are often surprised and unprepared for success, too. When unexpected events occur,

Illustration 5.1: IBM – finding the right direction once more

In the 1980s IBM lost its direction in marketing, concentrating too much on main frame computers and failing to realise that new competition was emerging particularly in the faster growing personal computing sector. IBM recorded massive losses in 1991–3 and despite restructuring its share price fell by around a quarter.

Lou Gerstner joined in 1993 after spells at American Express and Nabisco. IBM focused on providing solutions for customers rather than computer hardware and Gerstner insisted that the customer should come first – even if the solution meant not providing IBM hardware. Gerstner resisted the temptation to break up IBM but continued to cut costs through restructuring, with the workforce being reduced from just below 400 000 in 1990 to 220 000 in 1994, bureaucracy was reduced and individual SBUs (small business units) were made to focus upon their business priorities and performance.

At the same time Gerstner set the target of regaining global leadership by emphasising again the importance of building relationships with global clients, removing the narrow regional outlook of some SBUs and re-engineering the product development process, allowing it to bring out its new machines ahead of the competition and gain leadership in network computing. By 1997 IBM had increased its workforce from the low point by 25 000 and its share price had reached a new high.

Source: adapted from 'The rebirth of IBM', *The Economist*, 6 June 1998

many companies too easily ignore the plan and then proceed to develop new strategies as they go along. Whilst it may be *possible to survive* in a relatively uncomplicated domestic environment by reacting rapidly to new situations as they arise, it is *impossible to grow significantly in international markets,* as a highly reactive management style is usually wasteful of opportunities and resources.

In international markets, planning and control is essential for both day to day operations and the development of long-term strategies in order to manage the differences of attitudes, standards and values in the extended parts of the organisation and avoid the problems of poor coordination and integration of the diverse activities. The plans which are developed must be sufficiently flexible to cope with the effects of unexpected events too, which affect global companies in one way or another throughout the world on an almost daily basis.

Despite these observations and the high profile which has been given to planning and control by the majority of companies in recent years, only a few could claim to have developed an effective process. For the remainder, planning is still regarded as a time consuming and often unproductive activity which provides few real benefits to the managers in the company. Small companies often develop plans for specific and mainly external purposes, such as to satisfy the demands of the bank, rather than for internal, continuous guidance. There is also considerable evidence of planning and organisational problems, vulnerability to economic down turns and lack of willingness to prepare for market changes in many large companies. For a variety of reasons many firms such as General Motors, IBM and BCCI, all suffered heavy financial losses or failure during the early 1990s.

The benefits of planning in international markets

Many writers have argued that a well-developed planning process is fundamental for the achievement of a coherent approach when attacking international markets. The principal benefits are:

- Planning encourages *proactivity* rather than reactivity so that the company is able to steer its own destiny rather than simply react to events. Firms need to gain competitive advantage by moving into new markets or developing more aggressive strategies in old markets.

- It encourages a *systematic* process of analysis of all the factors involved in decisions, rather than simply those uppermost in the decision-maker's mind at a particular moment.

- Firms are forced to *state objectives and policies clearly and precisely* so that they are not misinterpreted by individual managers who might be quite remote from the point at which decisions are made.

- As the management task becomes more complex in dealing with many different markets it is essential that managers become more *focused in their thinking*.

- As the environment becomes increasingly complex and unstable, planning prepares the company for *reacting quickly and decisively in a coordinated and effective way*.

- It helps the company to *coordinate strategies* in different markets for the benefit of the company as a whole, so that it can out-perform the competition.

- As ease of communication and mobility increases, customers must be able to find *familiar product or service 'offers' in each market*.

- Planning facilitates the development of common *performance and quality standards* which can be used for company-wide control.

- The participation of managers in the planning process *increases ownership* and loyalty and also allows easier intra-company transfer and career development. This is particularly important where there are major cultural differences.

- A better understanding of the requirements of other functions and subsidiaries in different countries *reduces internal company conflict* and encourages the selection of strategies which will be beneficial for the whole company.

- Planning necessitates the development of company-wide *standardised information transfer systems* so that the accessibility and value of information is improved.

- Short-term action and control measures and long-term strategies can be *integrated* through effective planning.

The extent to which individual companies realise these benefits in practice, however, is dependant on a number of largely internal and controllable factors such as the nature and structure of the company, the stage of evolution of the organisation and the managerial philosophy, all of which have a major impact on the culture of the firm. MNEs (multi-national enterprises) are making fundamental decisions about the way that they will operate in future. One example is that German firms: Siemens, Hoechst and Deutsche Telecom have decided that English is easier for communicating complex ideas throughout their diverse organisations and want to see it used even when only Germans are present as they expect that greater Anglicisation will be one of the results of greater globalisation.

The development of planning

As a company moves into international markets, having previously been marketing solely to domestic markets, the processes of planning and control remain largely the same, but the complexity of the process increases dramatically. In a domestic situation misunderstandings between different departmental managers can be relatively quickly sorted out with a face to face discussion, but in the international situation this is much harder and often impractical. More impersonal communications, such as telephone, fax and electronic mail are used and this, along with longer lead times, different cultures and the use of different languages, results in seemingly inconsistent and often negative attitudes in international managers. Research by Arthur Anderson and Batey Research and Information Centre (1997) shows there are some fundamental differences in the styles of management adapted by Western and Eastern managers illustrated in Figure 5.1.

Figure 5.2 illustrates the managers' perceptions of what makes an ideal manager and what measures of success they make.

The research emphasised some similarities in the way that managers perceived the importance of connections, see Figure 5.3 for example, in business relationships and personal friendships but also some marked differences, with local Asian managers and expatriate Western managers regarding government connections, family connections, gifts and favours, and bribes as much more important that Western managers did. These findings add confirmation to the observations made in Chapter 3 on negotiation, networking and offering gifts, and illustrated in the special focus at the end of Part I.

Figure 5.1 Differences in management style

West	East
• Is more open, direct and confrontational	• Puts greater value on seniority, relationships and family ties
• Is more flexible and creative	• Is likely to be paternalistic
• Encourages empowerment of line workers	• Supports lifetime employment and opposes hire-and-fire
• Favours databases and statistics and resists intuition	• Places more emphasis on corporate loyalty
• Is more productivity-oriented than people-oriented	• Is more resistant to women assuming positions of management
• Is characterised more by individual initiative than by group consensus	• Is more likely to stress quantity than quality
• Puts greater importance on short-term profits	

Source: adapted from the *Financial Times* 'From Sunrise to Sunset', 17 January 1997 (Arther Andersen/Batey Research and Information Centre)

Figure 5.2 What makes an ideal manager?

Rank	Western	Asian
1	Offer full support/motivation for staff	Ability to anticipate future trends/changes
2	Ability to anticipate future trends/changes	A role model for co-managers and subordinates
3	Able to identify and recruit talented people	Offer full support/motivation for staff
4	Willing to give subordinates wider responsibilities	Efficient use of resources to meet sales/profit targets
5	Efficient use of resources to meet sales/profit targets	Able to identify and recruit talented people
Measures of success		
	Western	**Asian**
1	Respected by business community	Respected by business community
2	Good salary	Good salary
3	Respected by subordinates	Rapid promotions
4	Rapid promotions	Important job title
5		Respected by subordinates

Source: adapted from the *Financial Times* 'From Sunrise to Sunset', 17 January 1997 (Arther Andersen/Batey Research and Information Centre).

Against the background of differences in management style, the achievement of a consistent corporate culture throughout the MNE is considered in Illustration 5.2. It must reflect the differences in the local country and business culture but also maintain the firm's standards and values.

A number of writers have considered the differences between domestic and international planning and explained that the very nature of international markets, which are geographically dispersed and culturally different means that whilst there may be *greater opportunities for the company there are also greater risks and uncertainties*. It is worth emphasising at this point, however, that because domestic markets are becoming more segmented and more culturally fragmented

Figure 5.3 The importance of connections

% managers	Local Westerners	Expatriate Westerners	Local Asians
Business connections	93	96	90
Government connections	50	81	80
Personal friendships	72	78	73
Family	25	60	65
Gifts or favours	13	48	32
Alumni contacts	25	44	32
Bribes	4	23	24

Source: adapted from *Financial Times*, 17 January 1997 (Arthur Andersen/ Batey Research and Information Centre)

the differences between domestic and international markets are becoming less clear especially as few domestic markets are now unaffected by international competition. The definition of what constitutes the home market is also changing as more countries become part of a trading bloc.

Most companies, as they grow, move gradually into international markets and Gilligan and Hird (1986) identify the major evolutionary stages of planning; the unplanned stage, the budgeting stage, the annual business planning and the strategic planning stage, which equate closely to the evolution of the business.

The unplanned stage
In its early stages of international marketing, the company is likely to be preoccupied with finding new export customers and money to finance its activities. Frequently business is very unpredictable and is consequently unplanned, so that a short-term 'crisis management' culture emerges. Few of the benefits of planning have significant impact upon the business, and if plans are produced, they will probably bear little resemblance to the reactive strategies ultimately adopted and the firm's actual performance. A crisis is likely to occur as delivery times become extended, orders are supplied wrongly and problems of non-payment by international customers arise. One of the difficulties of small firms using the Internet as a means of generating sales is that it is virtually impossible to predict and control the levels of orders generated.

Illustration 5.2: Time is up for the man from head office

The picture of the global company is that of the multi-cultural monster uprooting managers and posting them to different jobs around the world. Sending managers from head office to manage the overseas business units is almost like colonial governors being sent to run overseas possessions. Unilever believe the challenge is to balance local knowledge with global reach but above all to build the corporate culture by maintaining integrity and following the Unilever code of conduct.

Unilever believe that local knowledge is vitally important in the consumer business and, for example, have in the past been concerned that they had too many expatriate managers running their local operating companies. Whereas five years ago three out of four senior managers in Italy were expatriates, they are now all Italian. Consultants McKinsey suggest that managers are still most effective in their own country and, after a short period of placement in an overseas subsidiary, they cannot add more than local managers and therefore simply end up competing with locals but having an in-built disadvantage. Moreover, local managers need to have a career ladder and in practice the family commitments of senior managers make it difficult for them to take up foreign-based appointments for more than four years.

It is still necessary to manage people differently in different countries but Unilever are finding that this is changing as more young people study and travel abroad. However, whilst language does not seem to be so much of a problem there are still differences in management approach which are the result of staff conforming to national stereotypes.

An additional consideration, McKinsey suggest, is that the management style in all but twenty firms worldwide is still dominated by and reflects the home country culture. American firms, for example, believe that globalisation means Americanisation of the world! Young people, no matter what nationality, want to work for MNEs, but after experiencing foreign management styles they soon decide whether or not they fit in. Many do not. Consequently the problem for global MNEs is often retaining a global pool of talent rather than recruiting talent in the first place.

Source: adapted from Jackson, T. (1997) 'The Global Company: Time's up for the man from head office', *Financial Times*, 8 October

The budgeting stage

As the business develops, a system for annual budgeting of sales, costs and cash flow is developed often because of pressure from external stakeholders such as banks. Being largely financial in nature, little account is normally taken of marketing research, product development or the longer term potential of the products. Frequently the information is assembled in an uncoordinated way with little input from marketing, research and development, production and personnel departments. A crisis occurs when the performance of the company deviates substantially from the budget.

Annual business planning

It is frequently as a result of the failures of budgeting, such as significant deviations from the budget and/or a lack of commitment of all staff to achieving the budget, that companies begin to adopt a more formalised annual approach to planning by including the whole of the business in the planning review process. One of three approaches to the process of annual business planning generally emerge at this stage:

Top down planning: this is by far the simplest approach to annual planning with senior managers setting goals and developing quite detailed plans for middle and senior staff to implement. To be successful, this clearly requires the senior managers to be closely in touch with all their international markets and for the business to be relatively uncomplicated in the range of products or services offered. It has the advantage of ensuring that there is little opportunity for misinterpretation by local managers, but the disadvantage of giving little opportunity for local initiative. Most of the strategic decisions at McDonald's and Coca-Cola are taken in the US, and by Sony in Japan.

Bottom up planning: in this approach the different parts of the company prepare their own goals and plans and submit them to top managers for approval. Whilst this encourages local initiative and innovation, it can be difficult to manage as each individual part may have different demands for resources, financial returns and marketing profiles.

Goals down plans up: in an attempt to benefit from the positive elements of the first two approaches, this third approach is based upon senior management assessing the firm's opportunities and needs, setting corporate objectives and developing broad strategies. Financial goals are then set for each part of the company, which then has the responsibility for developing individual strategies and plans to achieve these targets. For this approach to work effectively the senior management generally allows considerable flexibility in the way that the goals are achieved by the component parts of the firm. This approach is adopted particularly by companies such as Hanson, which have a very diverse portfolio of businesses and products.

The strategic planning stage
So far, the stages discussed have been concerned with relatively short-term planning (one to two years), but for many aspects of international marketing such as new market entry, growth strategies and brand management, much longer-term planning is essential. By developing strategies for a five year timescale, it is possible to avoid short-term, highly reactive and frequently contradictory and wasteful activity. The annual plan then becomes a more detailed version of the five year strategic plan which can be rolled forward year on year.

The objective of strategic planning is to create a vision of the company's future for managers who, as a result, will experience less uncertainty about the short-term decisions that they make, and have more freedom to develop their own longer-term contributions.

In practice the five year plan has some potential difficulties. Whilst developing years three to five of the plan, it is only possible to think and plan strategically, whereas in years one to two, there is a tendency to confuse strategic issues with operational tactics and so the early period of the plan often concentrates on detailed short-term tactics rather than starting to make the necessary longer-term strategic changes that have been identified. There is of course, the opposite danger too, that managers can become preoccupied with extensive discussion of long-term strategies during the early years at the expense of managing the day to day activities. This presents particular difficulties of prioritisation for managers in overseas locations who might receive what appear to be conflicting messages from the headquarters.

The obvious *benefits of strategic planning* are that all staff can be better motivated and encouraged to work more effectively by *sharing a vision* of the future. There are, however, potential dangers too. Long-term strategic plans often fail to cope with the consequences of an unexpected event such as the oil crisis in the 1970s and the Gulf War in the early 1990s and the Pacific Rim political and economic crises in the late 1990s, which might occur early in the plan. There is often confusion between managers, too, over what are strategic issues and what are operational tactics. What a manager in a subsidiary might consider to be a strategic issue, such as achieving a substantial market share increase in the country might be regarded as an operational matter by a senior manager at the domestic headquarters, which does not consider success in that particular country a priority for the company.

Attitudes to planning

Individual managers adopt different attitudes to planning, ranging from enthusiasm to reluctance. The *three most common reasons for resistance* to the planning process are, first, planning is time consuming when the time could be better spent on managing the business, second, setting goals and objectives in a volatile environment remote from the HQ is irrelevant, divisive and applies unnecessary constraints and third, planning is purely a process by which senior managers at the domestic HQ can inform themselves and control the international business and is of no benefit for other managers.

The *three most common reasons for supporting* the planning process given by managers are that it first, encourages everyone wherever they might be in the organisation to pull in the same direction, second, avoids waste of time and resources through duplication of work and third, ensures that the company is better prepared for coping with unexpected events and international competition.

The problems of international planning

Of the potential sources of problems of planning in international marketing, it is the relationship between headquarters and local subsidiary staff which is likely to be the largest single factor. Headquarters staff, as guardians of the overall company strategies claim to have a far broader perspective of the company's activities and might expect that subsidiary staff should simply be concerned with implementation of the details of the plan. Subsidiary staff claim that, by being closer to the individual markets, they are in a better position to identify opportunities and should therefore play a large part in developing objectives and strategies. This situation must be resolved if the planning process is to be effective so that all staff have a clear idea of their own role in setting, developing and implementing policy, and understanding how their individual contributions might be integrated into the corporate objectives and strategies.

The difficulties of planning in international markets are further developed by Brandt *et al.* (1980), in a framework of international planning problems, and

Weichmann and Pringle (1979), who identified the key problems experienced by large US and European multi-nationals. Figure 5.4 is a list of problems at head office and in the subsidiary which are the main sources of conflict between headquarters and overseas staff.

Many companies recognise that for strategies to be successful, the managers of all parts of the company must *share ownership* of them through playing an active part in the development and implementation stages of the process itself. With greater emphasis on staff at all levels in the organisation providing increased levels of service to customers it is important to involve all staff in the marketing

Figure 5.4 International planning problems

Headquarters	Overseas subsidiary
Management	*Management*
Unclear allocation of responsibilities and authority	Resistance to planning
Lack of multi-national orientation	Lack of qualified personnel
Unrealistic expectations	Inadequate abilities
Lack of awareness of foreign markets	Misinterpretation of information
Unclear guidelines	Misunderstanding requirements and objectives
Insensitivity to local decisions	Resentment of HQ involvement
Insufficient provision of useful information	Lack of strategic thinking
	Lack of marketing expertise
Processes	*Processes*
Lack of standardised bases for evaluation	Lack of control by HQ
Poor IT systems and support	Incomplete or outdated internal and market information
Poor feedback and control systems	Poorly developed procedures
Excessive bureaucratic control procedures	Too little communication with HQ
Excessive marketing and financial constraints	Inaccurate data returns
Insufficient participation of subsidiaries in process	Insufficient use of multi-national marketing expertise
	Excessive financial and marketing constraints

planning process. This is becoming more difficult as MNEs have ever greater numbers of their workers employed outside the head office country. In 1986 Matsushita Electric had 138 000 employees in Japan and 44 000 abroad but after ten years this has changed to 158 000 in Japan and 108 000 abroad.

As the company grows, therefore, a company-wide planning culture should be developed with the following objectives:

- planning becomes part of the continuous process of management rather than an annual 'event';
- strategic thinking becomes the responsibility of every manager rather than being restricted to a separate strategic planning department;
- the planning process becomes standardised with a format which allows contributions from all parts of the company;
- the plan becomes the working document, updated periodically for all aspects of the company, so allowing performance evaluation to be carried out regularly; and
- the planning process is itself regularly reviewed and refined in order to improve its relevance and effectiveness.

Strategic business units and the roles of different levels of management in the planning process

During the discussion of the stages in the development of the planning process and the attitudes of managers to planning, the need has been identified for both strategic long-term thinking and operational short-term action. It is necessary now to understand how these activities can be related to the structure of the firm and to the roles of the different management levels.

The three management levels

In Figure 5.5 the conceptual framework of a company is illustrated and shows the three management levels, the strategic, management and operational levels. The broad functional areas of the three levels are illustrated in Figure 5.6.

In most companies the strategic level of the firm is typically responsible for formulating the broad aims of the company, setting corporate objectives, identifying resources that can be utilised and selecting broad strategies. These aims, objectives and resources are then broken down into the constituent parts and allocated between the individual subsidiaries or operating units, which are referred to as strategic business units (SBUs).

Figure 5.5 The conceptual framework of a firm

Figure 5.6 Functions of different management levels

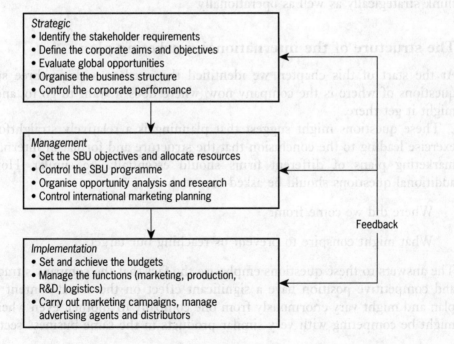

The management level then break down these allocations into departmental objectives, budgets and tasks for which the functional managers (for example in R&D or marketing) at the operational level are responsible.

The performance of the company in implementing the plans is monitored and controlled by operating the process in reverse. The operational level managers are responsible for achieving the objectives set by the management level and the management level is expected to achieve the objectives set by the strategic level.

At an early stage in the company's development, the distinctions between levels are unclear as decisions are made in a largely unplanned, reactive way. As the company develops, the separation of management levels and functions becomes clearer and is reinforced by formalised procedures (reports and meetings) to plan and control the business. Whilst we have indicated three broad levels of management, the number of links in the chain between the chief executive and the customer can vary considerably. The recent trend in many companies has been to remove layers of management in order to have a flatter structure, thus giving individual managers far greater responsibility and authority for their part of the company. This has resulted in less distinction between the management activities, with managers at all levels being required to think strategically as well as operationally.

The structure of the international marketing plan

At the start of this chapter, we identified the need to address three specific questions of where is the company now, where does it want to go to, and how might it get there.

These questions might suggest that planning is a relatively straightforward exercise leading to the conclusion that the structure and format of international marketing plans of different firms should essentially be similar. However, additional questions should be asked too, such as:

Where did we come from?

What might conspire to prevent us reaching our target.

The answers to these questions emphasise the fact that the company's traditions and competitive position have a significant effect on the actual content of the plan and might vary enormously from one company to another, even when they might be competing with very similar products in the same business sector.

A company's traditional activities, identity and values, for example, can play a major role in determining the future plans and strategies. Plans which require owners or managers to break with tradition will often be resisted strongly. Companies which in the past may have had very strong links with the domestic country's traditional trading partners, may find moves to regionalisation and the emergence of new markets a threat to their business.

Similarly, to maintain growth in a mature market some firms are attacking new segments. Mercedes Benz entered the small car market segment as well as maintaining their core 'luxury sector' cars; some argued that the brand could be devalued as a result and this may have been one of the arguments used by the parent company Daimler-Benz in the take-over of Chrysler in 1998.

It is equally necessary to fully evaluate the factors which could prevent the firm's target being met. For example, if a firm embarks on a policy to expand its market share, it is likely to prompt a significant response from competitors. A firm launching a new product must take into account how long it will take for it to be copied by competitors and when even newer technology will supersede it. A number of these situations are discussed later in the book. Sometimes, too, the very traditional ways of operating the business may be a barrier to survival and growth as the Illustration 5.3 of Asea Brown Boveri shows.

Aspects of international marketing planning

There are a number of elements in the international marketing plan. There should be:

- an expression of the stakeholder expectations;
- an audit of the firm's strengths, weaknesses and future potential capabilities;
- an assessment of the likely changes in the external environment and the opportunities and threats which will result;
- a statement of corporate objectives;
- an evaluation of possible strategic options;
- an assessment of likely competitor responses to the strategic options;
- the selection and justification of the appropriate strategy.

However, from the discussions so far in this book, it will have become apparent that international marketing is considerably more complicated, and some of the aspects which make international planning so much more difficult are included in Figure 5.7.

Illustration 5.3: ABB: a new model of global entrepreneurialism

In 1988 Sweden's ASEA and the Swiss company Brown Boveri merged to form ABB the power equipment group which includes amongst its product range power generation and transmission equipment, environmental control systems, factory automation and railway rolling stock. Percy Barnevik as chief executive was faced with merging two companies with different business cultures and operations. He decided to create a fundamentally different model of how a large MNE could be organised and managed. He created the new head office in Zurich to make the merger less like a takeover by the Swedes and started dispersing the two head offices of 6000 staff amongst a number of front-line units. The head office now has 135 staff and manages 1300 companies with 5000 profit centres. He cut 90 per cent of headquarters staff by moving 30 per cent into the SBUs, 30 per cent into free standing service centres concerned with value adding activities and eliminating 30 per cent of the jobs. Similar huge cuts in management were made in the headquarters of the subsidiaries.

The management within the SBUs, which usually have less than 200 employees, have a substantially enhanced role in managing their business but Barnevik, by constantly visiting the operating units and meeting the staff (around 5000 per year), exerts an indirect control by constantly emphasising the vision, standards and values of the company but, above all, the need for entrepreneurialism.

Ghoshall and Bartlett say that Barnevik's obsession is combining the contradictions of big and small, local and global, economies of scale and intimate market knowledge to create a truly global organisation.

A large part of ABB's manufacturing has been moved away from the developed countries to the developing countries, including Eastern Europe where ABB employs 82 000 of its 215 000 staff. Barnevik suggests that by employing people in developing countries ABB is in a position to sell further expertise and services as they build the country's infrastructure.

Barnevik has now taken over chairmanship of Investor, the Wallenberg family's company that controls over 40 per cent of the Swedish stock market and has holdings in drugs (Astra), telecommunications (Ericsson), ball bearings (SKF) media (TV4) and forestry (Stora). Altogether he is chairman, director or lead investor in companies that have in total 2 million employees.

Source: adapted from Caulkin, S. (1998) 'Swede dreams of going truly global', *Observer*, 22 March, and 'Is it a bird? Is it a manager? Percy Barnevik is probably Europe's most successful international manager', *The Economist* (1997) 3 May

Figure 5.7 Aspects of international marketing planning

Stakeholder expectations	Shareholders, customers, host government, employees in each country, pressure groups
Situation analysis	Evaluation of the environment and individual markets
Resources and capabilities	Individual SBU strengths and weaknesses analysis Capability to deal with threats and opportunities
Corporate aims and objectives	Financial, market, area, brand and mix objectives
Marketing strategies	Growth strategies Standardisation and adaptation
Implementation of the plan	Individual SBU and marketing mix plans Regional, global or multi-domestic integration
Control and feedback	Setting relevant standards, measuring performance, correcting deviations

Stakeholder expectations

The development of a company is determined to a large degree by the aims and expectations of the stakeholders, who directly or indirectly provide the resources and support needed to implement the strategies and plans. It is important to clearly identify the different stakeholder groups, understand their expectations and evaluate their power because it is the stakeholders who provide the broad guidelines within which the firm operates. Body Shop the environmentally conscious UK toiletries retailer is always likely to have problems balancing the widely differing pricing and profit expectations and environmental concerns of its franchisees, customers and shareholders.

Whilst the senior management of the firm aim usually to develop and adopt strategies which do not directly oppose these stakeholder expectations, they do, of course frequently widen or alter the firm's activities due to changes in the market and competition. Moreover, a wide range of stakeholders influence what MNEs do by giving greater attention to the political, commercial and ethical behaviour of the organisations as well as taking more interest in the actual operation of the business and the performance and safety of the products. As a result of this, companies need to explain their strategies and plans to shareholders through

Figure 5.8 Some typical stakeholders of multi-national enterprises

```
                    Shareholders
      Expatriate                    Home country
         staff                       government

                                            Individual
    Suppliers                                politicians and
                                             civil servants


  Distributors                                      Host country
  and retailers          The Firm                   government


      Customers                               Local workers
                                              and their
                                              organisations

           Local                       Pressure
           competitors                 groups
                        Competitor
                        MNEs
```

more detailed annual reports, to staff through a variety of briefing methods and to pressure groups and the community in general through various public relations activities, particularly when their activities have an impact on the local environment or economy. In international marketing it is particularly important that the firm addresses the concern of its host country stakeholders, who may be physically and culturally very distant from the headquarters.

Particular attention should be paid to the different expectations of the stakeholders and their power to influence the firm's strategic direction. Given the different expectations of the firm's stakeholders it is inevitable that conflicts will occur as shown in Figure 5.9. For example, shareholders usually want a high return on their investment and may expect the firm to find countries with low production costs, but the workers in these countries want an adequate wage on which to live. It is often the firm's ability to manage these potential conflicts that leads to success or failure in international marketing.

Situation analysis
Situation analysis is the process by which the company develops a clear understanding of each individual market and then evaluates its significance for

Figure 5.9 Stakeholder demands on the firm

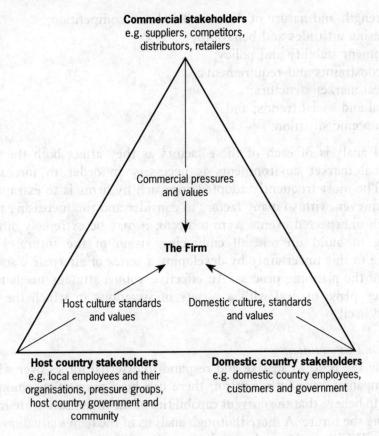

Commercial stakeholders
e.g. suppliers, competitors,
distributors, retailers

Commercial pressures
and values

The Firm

Host culture standards
and values

Domestic culture, standards
and values

Host country stakeholders
e.g. local employees and their
organisations, pressure groups,
host country government and
community

Domestic country stakeholders
e.g. domestic country employees,
customers and government

the company and for other markets in which the business operates. As the international business environment becomes more competitive, dynamic and complex, there is a greater need for individual managers to be aware not simply of their immediate situation, but also of the possible impact of changes taking place in surrounding areas too. Individual national markets can be both surprisingly similar and surprisingly dissimilar in nature, and it is important to understand these linkages and the implications of the changes which take place.

There is a strong argument for adopting a standardised approach to analysing environmental changes, for example, by using the marketing profile analysis discussed in Chapter 4, because this allows comparisons to be made and specific issues to be addressed in a thorough and logical way in order to obtain as precise and complete a picture as possible.

The areas for specific concern in situation analysis include such factors as:

- the strength and nature of direct and indirect competition;
- purchasing attitudes and behaviour;
- government stability and policy;
- legal constraints and requirements;
- the local market structure;
- cultural and social trends; and
- the economic situation.

A detailed analysis of each of these factors as they affect both the local and international market environments is necessary in order to forecast future changes. The most frequently adopted approach by firms is to extrapolate past trends. However, with so many factors to consider and the increasing frequency with which unexpected events seem to occur, it may be extremely difficult and misleading to build up one all embracing vision of the future. Firms are responding to this uncertainty by developing a series of alternative scenarios as the basis of the planning process. An effective, robust strategy needs to contain contingency plans to deal with a variety of situations in which the company might find itself.

Resources and capabilities

In stressing the need to analyse and respond to external forces over which even global companies have little control, there can be a temptation amongst some managers to believe that the current capabilities of the organisation are inadequate when facing the future. A more thorough analysis of the firm's situation is needed and the SWOT framework (analysing the firm's strengths, weaknesses, opportunities and threats) is appropriate for this purpose. It is important therefore to audit not just the most obvious *company weaknesses*, but also the *strengths of the company* which are often taken for granted but which are really its source of competitive advantage. This is particularly important in international markets, as for example, customer and brand loyalty may be much stronger in certain markets than others, and products, which may be at the end of their life in the domestic market may be ideal for less sophisticated markets. SWOT analysis should, therefore, be carried out separately on each area of the business by function, product or market and focus upon what action should be taken to exploit the opportunities and minimise the threats that are identified in the analysis. This will lead to a clearer evaluation of the resources that are available or which must be acquired to ensure the necessary actions are carried out.

As will be discussed later in this chapter the firm's *flexibility, adaptability* and *proactivity* are the attributes necessary for success in a highly competitive and rapidly changing world. It is essential to identify, for example, where the delays in the decision making process might occur, which would prevent a rapid response to a new scenario. These blocks to decision making in an international setting might take the form of excessive bureaucracy or slow transfer of information.

Corporate objectives

Having identified stakeholder expectations, carried out a detailed situation analysis and made an evaluation of the capabilities of the company, the overall goals to be pursued can be set. It is important to stress that there is a need for realism in this, as only too frequently corporate plans are determined more by the desire for short-term credibility with shareholders than with the likelihood that they will be achieved. The objectives must be based on realistic performance expectations rather than on a best case scenario. Consideration must be given too, to developing alternative scenarios so that realistic objectives can be set and accompanied by contingency plans in case the chosen scenario does not materialise.

For smaller businesses operating in a relatively stable market, the sequence of setting company aims, analysing the situation and company capabilities then setting operational objectives can be a linear sequence but for large businesses operating in complex international markets, the process will be more interactive, especially if a goals down, plans up approach is used. The objectives set at management and operational level will reflect the overall aims of the company and the more pragmatic goals of the local strategic business unit as frequently there may well need to be a trade off between the short-term and long-term aims. For example, profitability might be sacrificed for market share, or market share might be sacrificed for a quality, high added value image.

The process adopted for determining long-term and short-term objectives is important and varies significantly depending on the size of the business, the nature of the market and the abilities and motivation of managers in different markets. At an operational level, the national managers need to have an achievable and detailed plan for each country, which will take account of the local situation, explain what is expected and how performance will be measured. Examples of the marketing objectives might be:

- financial performance including return on investment and profitability;
- market penetration including sales (by volume and value), market share by product category;

- customer growth by volume and profitability;
- distribution including strength in supply chain, number of outlets;
- brand awareness and value;
- new product introductions and diffusion; and
- company image including quality and added value service.

Illustration 5.4 shows how Gillette faced the very serious problems of declining financial performance, lack of confidence from stakeholders, low morale amongst staff and the risk of take-over.

Marketing strategies

Having set the objectives for the company, both at corporate level and at the management level the company can develop a detailed programme of activities which will achieve the objectives. There are a number of alternative strategic approaches that can be adopted.

Ansoff identified four growth strategies – product penetration, market development, product development and diversification, and these are shown in Figure 5.10. Following a product penetration strategy is appropriate if a company has an existing portfolio of products and a presence in its target markets which offer considerable potential expansion of sales. The resources available to the company under these circumstances can be best used in concentrating on doing more of what is already being done well.

Diversification, on the other hand is a strategy to be used in international markets in situations where demand for the company's existing products is falling rapidly (for example, in recent years in the defence industry), or where resources are available but would not generate an acceptable return if used on existing activities.

For most companies the most obvious strategic development opportunities are in increasing geographical coverage (market development) which is discussed in Chapter 8 and product development which is discussed in Chapter 9.

As companies move through the stages of the planning process they are faced with making specific decisions. The selection of one of the strategic options available may make it necessary to revise or refine some of the earlier stages such as the initial objectives. For example, Illustration 5.4 shows how Gillette were following two different strategies in Europe and the US, but their decision to select and implement one particular strategy in both markets led them, ultimately, to redefine their objectives and change their organisational structure.

Illustration 5.4: Gillette planning a close shave

In the late 1970s and 1980s the change by many consumers to disposable razors in the US and Europe meant that shaving products appeared to be turning into a commodity market. For Gillette, which had a 65 per cent share of this market, this was extremely serious. Gillette produced its own disposable razor, but consumers did not differentiate between products and so purchased the cheapest. By the mid 1980s the lower margin disposable products had captured 50 per cent of the market, considerably reducing profits and forcing Gillette to cut its advertising spend to a quarter of what it was in 1975, so reducing the power of its brand name. It seemed as though Gillette in the US had almost given up on razors.

In Europe, however, Gillette had taken a different approach, starting to spend on a pan- European campaign featuring the slogan 'Gillette – the best a man can get' to emphasise the name Gillette and the top of the range Contour Plus brand, and this had led both to a gain in market share and an increase in margins of 5 per cent.

Gillette's mission statement over the last twenty five years has been 'There is a better way to shave and we will find it' and Sensor spearheaded Gillette's fight back. Sensor, launched in 1989 had twin blades mounted on tiny springs and was designed to give a closer shave by being able to follow the contours of the face. It had been shown to be significantly better than anything else on the market and user tests showed that 80 per cent of men who tried it kept on using it. Despite some internal opposition Gillette decided to centralise its marketing by combining the European and US sections into one group headed by the previous European head to ensure an effective launch of Sensor under the Gillette umbrella brand. Previously marketing had been carried out by brand managers in each local country.

Since then Sensor has helped Gillette to a 70 per cent share of the world razor market, but recently the double digit sales growth has been flattening signifying the need for a new product. The new product has cost well over $1bn to develop including $750 million on manufacturing systems, $200 million on R&D and $350 on marketing. Gillette has been experimenting on the technology since 1970.

Mach 3 is a three blade system, protected by patents and is designed to give a closer shave. It has a new pivoting system held within a cartridge, thinner blades and automatic deposition onto the skin of moisturiser and vitamin E. Rubber fins stretch the skin and hold the hairs in place for precision cutting. The product will sell at a premium of 25–35 per cent over the price of Sensor. Gillette does not withdraw older products and will retain Sensor within its portfolio. It expects Mach 3 to achieve a market share of between 25–30 per cent by 2000. Gillette expects to roll out Mach 3 to its 100 top countries within a year whereas it took four years to do this for Sensor.

Source: adapted from *The Economist* (1992) 'The Best a Plan Can Get', 15 August and *Financial Times* (1998) 'Gillette Rolls our Mach 3 for Shaving Wars', 15 April and 'At the Cutting Edge', 20 April

Figure 5.10 Ansoff growth matrix

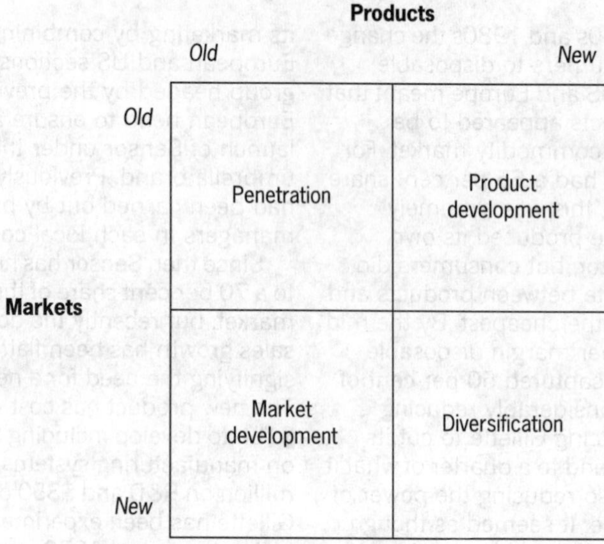

Implementation of the marketing plan

Having agreed the overall marketing strategy, plans for implementation are required at two levels. At a company-wide level the McKinsey 7S framework shown in Figure 5.11 is useful for thinking through the implementation issues.

The first three elements – strategy, structure and systems – are considered to be the hardware of successful management and as such can be implemented across international markets without the need for significant modification. The other four – style, staff, skills and shared values – are the software, and are affected by cultural differences. Often it is the management of these aspects of the business which highlight good management in the best firms and relatively unimpressive management in poorer performing firms. It is quite obvious too that it is these elements of the framework which can vary considerably from country to country.

The characteristics of these four software elements are:

Style: employees share a broadly common way of thinking and behaving. In organisations such as Marks and Spencer and McDonald's, it is the consistency across the world of the management and operational style that is one of the distinguishing features of the companies.

Figure 5.11 McKinsey 7S framework

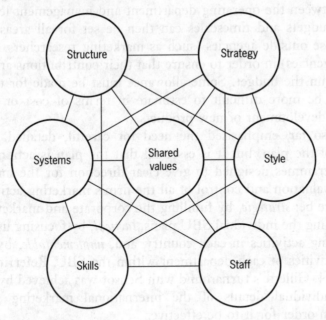

Source: McKinsey and Co

Skills: Because the levels and quality of education vary considerable between countries, employees need to be fully trained in the sorts of skills that are needed to carry out the strategy.

Staff: The people that are recruited around the world need to be capable, well-trained, and given the jobs which will best allow them to make use of their talents. Recognition of the contributions of the staff, the criteria for advancement, acceptance of appraisal and disciplinary processes vary considerably between countries.

Shared values: Despite the fact that staff come from different cultural backgrounds there is a need for employees to share the same values, understand where the organisation is going and what it stands for.

At a local level implementation plans can be developed by the individual SBUs in the form of detailed departmental programmes. Firms usually allocate resources to individual departments on a top down basis, but this needs to be modified to include the special allocations made to enable departments to resource specific market opportunities or difficulties. Agreement is reached through a process of discussion between the operating department and management levels.

Detailed budgets and timescales can then be set for all areas of marketing including those outside agencies (such as marketing researchers, designers and advertising agencies) in order to ensure that their contributions are delivered on time and within the budget. Some allowance must be made for those activities which might be more difficult to estimate in terms of cost or time, such as research and development of new products.

We have, so far, emphasised the need for careful, detailed and thorough preparation of the plan, but it is essential that the plan is action oriented and contains programmes designed to give clear direction for the implementation, continuous evaluation and control of all the firm's marketing activity. The plan must therefore be: *strategic*, by fulfilling the corporate and marketing objectives and coordinating the individual SBU plans, *tactical*, by focusing upon individual SBU marketing activities in each country, and, *implementable*, by detailing the individual activities of each department within the SBU. Referring back to the Illustration 5.4, Gillette's turnaround with Sensor was achieved by ensuring that the many individual details of the international marketing strategy were coordinated in order for it to be effective.

The lessons to be learned from the Gillette strategy are that consumers will buy higher priced products if they are demonstrated to be an improvement over what they are currently using, but only if they can be convinced through a well prepared and implemented plan. It is also quite evident that it takes time to change the strategic direction of a company and obtain a genuine improvement in its performance. A checklist of the essential elements of the international marketing plan are summarised in Figure 5.12.

One of the most significant challenges is to obtain effective coordination between the company's various operating SBUs around the world. The objective is to achieve a high level of effectiveness through the cooperation between managers and staff transfer of knowledge and skills and this is shown in Illustration 5.5.

Gupta and Govindarajan (1998) suggest that a number of methods help:

- An incentive system that links a managers' rewards to multiple performance targets, for example, Proctor and Gamble incentivise international managers both on country and product performance.

- The firm might give high visibility to individuals who achieve results through collaboration.

Figure 5.12 Essential elements of the marketing plan

Does the plan contain:

- assumptions about the world economy and the environmental trends in the principal markets?
- details of historical performance (sales, costs, profitability)?
- forecasts of future performance based on (a) an extrapolation of the past (b) alternative scenarios?
- identified opportunities and threats;
- analysis of the company strengths, weaknesses and future capabilities in comparison with local and international competition?
- long-term aims and objectives and the strategies to achieve them?
- one year marketing objectives and individual strategies (for example, budgets, brand objectives and development of personnel)?
- detailed country by country forecasts and targets?
- detailed country by country plans for all marketing activities and coordination with other functions (for example, manufacturing)?
- an explanation of how country plans will be integrated regionally or globally if appropriate?
- a summary of the critical factors for success?
- an assessment of the likely competitor response?
- a contingency component for when things do not go to plan?
- a control process for feedback, evaluation and taking corrective action?

- Formal rules and procedures such as common terminology, language and routine distribution of reports might be used to enhance communication between managers, and ABB are cited as a good example of this.

- Creation of cross functional teams, such as for brand or category management.

- Use of executive development programmes to bring together managers from many locations.

The control process

The final stage of the planning process is setting up an effective system for obtaining feedback and controlling the business. The importance of control is recognised by Jeanet and Hennesey (1992):

Illustration 5.5: Canon's global R&D strategy

Globalisation is leading a number of firms to rethink their research and development strategy. Canon invented the bubble jet and laser beam computer printers in the late 1970s in Japan but the software that controls them is imported from the US. Canon have noticed that whilst the best ideas are generated in various parts of the world, the growing US venture capital industry is able to snap up the best ideas first and so, over the past decade, Canon has responded to this by devolving significantly more management control to foreign subsidiaries, hired more foreign staff and obtained more ideas from abroad than is usual in Japanese companies.

At about 6–7 per cent of sales over the past decade, research and development is a major expense and commitment. Canon set up five overseas R&D centres a decade ago, now employing 15 per cent of its R&D staff and in 1996 gave its US research unit responsibility for software, a French research unit global telecommunications and in the UK an automated translation centre with a global remit. By contrast Aiwa has 86 per cent of its production abroad but carries out all R&D in Japan.

Canon recognise that the Tokyo headquarters cannot know everything and its responsibilities should include providing low cost capital, moving top management between regions and coming up with investment opportunities. It is setting up regional headquarters each with the responsibility for the development, manufacturing and sales of particular products. Canon has half its staff abroad but of its 40 000 workers outside Japan only 900 are Japanese.

Source: adapted from Dawkins, W. (1996) 'Time to pull back the screen: Japanese multinationals may follow Cannon's example and shift power overseas' *Financial Times*, 18 November

---

Control is the cornerstone of management. Control provides the means to direct, regulate and manage business operations. The importance of a marketing programme requires a significant amount of interaction between the individual areas of marketing (such as product development, advertising and selling) as well as the other functional areas (such as production, research and development).

However, for many firms, control means a separate activity through which senior managers are able to keep a check periodically (weekly, monthly or quarterly) on more junior levels of management who often see this in terms of being called upon to justify their actions. Feedback and control systems should be regarded as an integrated part of the whole planning process, and they are essential in *ensuring that the marketing plans are not only being implemented but are still appropriate for the changing environment*.

There are a number of benefits of an effective strategic control system. It encourages higher standards of performance, forces greater clarity and realism and permits corporate management to intervene when necessary. Moreover, it ensures that the financial objectives do not overwhelm the strategic objectives, encourages clearer definition of responsibilities making decentralisation work more effectively, and so provides more motivation for managers.

There are three essential elements of the control process:

Setting standards: the standards that are set need to be relevant to the corporate goals such as growth and profits, but these are too general in nature. Intermediate goals and individual targets can be set by breaking the plan down into measurable parts, which when successfully completed, will lead to the overall objectives being achieved. The standards must be understandable, achievable and relevant to each local country situation.

Measuring performance against standards: to obtain measurements and ensure rapid feedback of information, firms use a variety of techniques, including reports, meetings and special measurements of specific parts of the marketing programme, such as cost benefit analysis on customers, product lines and territories or marketing audits for a thorough examination of every aspect of marketing in a particular country. They also use *bench marking* which allows comparisons of various aspects of the business, such as efficiency of distribution, customer response times, service levels and complaints, with other companies that are not necessarily from the same business sector.

Correcting deviations from the plan: perhaps the most difficult decisions that must be made are to determine when performance has deviated sufficiently from the plan to require corrective action to be taken either by changing the plan or the management team charged with the responsibility of carrying out the plan.

Evaluation of the performance of a particular management team is particularly difficult in international marketing as the performance of a particular SBU can only be compared with its own plan, a plan determined by the headquarters or with the performance of a 'similar' SBU. There are obvious weaknesses in making any of these comparisons and resulting in considerable difference of opinion between the head office and subsidiary.

Evaluation and improvement of the planning process

In order for the planning process to be effective, it must become part of the culture of the company and so the process needs to be routinely followed on every occasion. This requires continuous consultation and involvement of managers at the management and operational levels so that they are able to feed information into the situation analysis, suggest possible strategic and tactical alternatives and, where possible, set their own objectives. Through greater involvement in the planning process the employees increase their ownership of the plan, and so are likely to be more motivated to overcome the difficulties they will undoubtedly experience in implementing the plan. In order to achieve these aims, the whole planning process must: *be standardised* in order to ensure that full consideration is given by planners to all the identified problems and opportunities and *ensure that each contribution can be consolidated* within the overall corporate plan. It should also be *well defined by agreeing the format* in which the information should be presented and agreeing the firm's interpretation of the actual terms used, such as market size and market share, which might well be otherwise interpreted differently in different countries. The planning process must be *kept within a short and specific timescale* in order that the analysis of different markets is carried out at the same time and that new strategies are implemented without delay and in a coordinated way. There is also the practical point that, whilst accepting that revision to plans is necessary, it does tend to create an endless process in which decisions might be unnecessarily delayed! Finally, *the plan must encourage creativity*, because planning should be concerned with growth and exploiting new opportunities, improved operational effectiveness and bringing about change in attitudes, ideas and methods.

In summary therefore, the marketing plan in its completed form should comprise of the analysis of the current performance and a forecast of the future situation, taking account of likely environmental changes, the company's capabilities and stakeholder expectations. A statement of overall corporate and SBU objectives should be included before the strategies are explained. Finally the tactics and programmes of marketing activity which will be adopted by the SBUs can be detailed.

Organisational structures for international marketing

The process of planning as we have indicated leads to setting overall company aims and objectives, which are then developed into SBU objectives, strategies and tactics. The success of the company in meeting its corporate objectives is dependent not only on the SBUs meeting their targets but also on effectively coordinating and integrating the national operations and plans in order to benefit from economies of scale and the experience effect, and also to minimise the amount of duplicated effort. The firm, therefore, faces a major question about how it should be structured in order to provide the optimum framework of planning, strategy and control mechanisms. Canon has restructured its research and development organisation in order to become more market oriented as Illustration 5.5 shows.

Terpstra and Sarathy (1997) have identified some of the variables which might influence the decision:

- size of the business;
- number of markets in which it operates;
- level and nature of involvement in the markets;
- company objectives;
- company international experience;
- nature of the products;
- width and diversity of the product range; and
- nature of the marketing task.

The organisational structure which a firm develops is ultimately determined by its own operational needs of planning, implementation and control. For a firm starting out in export markets, the decision is relatively simple. Either the international business is integrated within the domestic business or separated as a specialist activity. There are some advantages of setting up a separate activity such as concentrating skills and expertise in one area, avoiding a situation where the international business is 'low priority', recognising the importance of international business and allowing greater independence to look specifically at international marketing opportunities.

There are, however, some disadvantages too as it may be seen as less important by senior managers and could, as a result, create possible conflicts between domestic and international market demands on production. There is also the possibility of creating duplication and ineffective use of company resources.

As the company develops further, it is faced with deciding how its international operations should be organised and there are a number of options for the way in which it might be structured: by area, by product and by function. Figures 5.13 and 5.14 show typical organisational structures for organising along area and product lines. Organisation by function, however, is only really appropriate for companies with relatively simple product ranges.

As the firm grows it may decide to establish control in different ways, for example it may wish to control branding and corporate identity issues centrally through the use of international product managers, but at the same time it might wish to control the profitability of the business by having a chief executive in each individual country. In this way, the firm operates as a matrix structure within which individual managers might be responsible to different senior managers for different activities.

For larger or more complex businesses, Majaro (1991) has identified three basic structures in international organisations, the macropyramid, the umbrella

Figure 5.13 Product structure

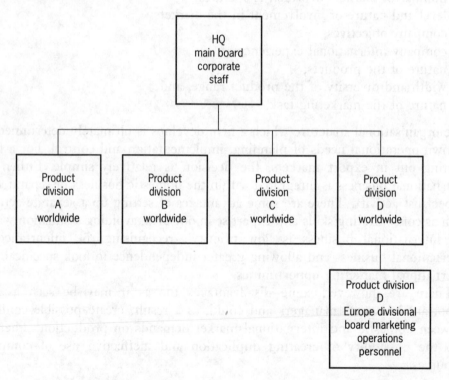

Figure 5.14 Geographic structures

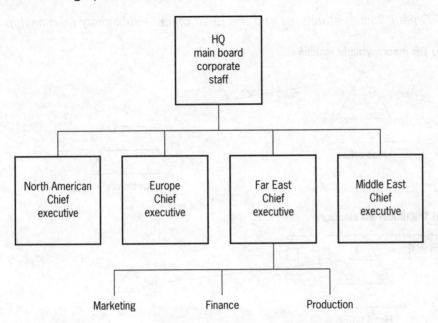

and the interglomerate structures (see Figure 5.15), based on the three levels of management within the organisation identified previously; strategic, management and operational.

The Macropyramid

The macropyramid is found in multi-national organisations which have a strong nerve centre or headquarters. The organisation is usually highly centralised and the foreign SBUs operate at the management or operational levels of the organisation. Examples of this type of company are McDonald's, IBM, Marks and Spencer and Sony. The individual SBUs have relatively little autonomy and their strategies and tactics are largely determined by the strategic level at the centre. The implications of this structure for marketing are that:

- marketing plans are produced centrally;
- all major decisions regarding the marketing mix are taken centrally;
- marketing is standardised as much as possible;
- world markets for their products and services are regarded as largely the same;

Figure 5.15 Development of strategy

Organisational structures and the head office – subsidiary relationship

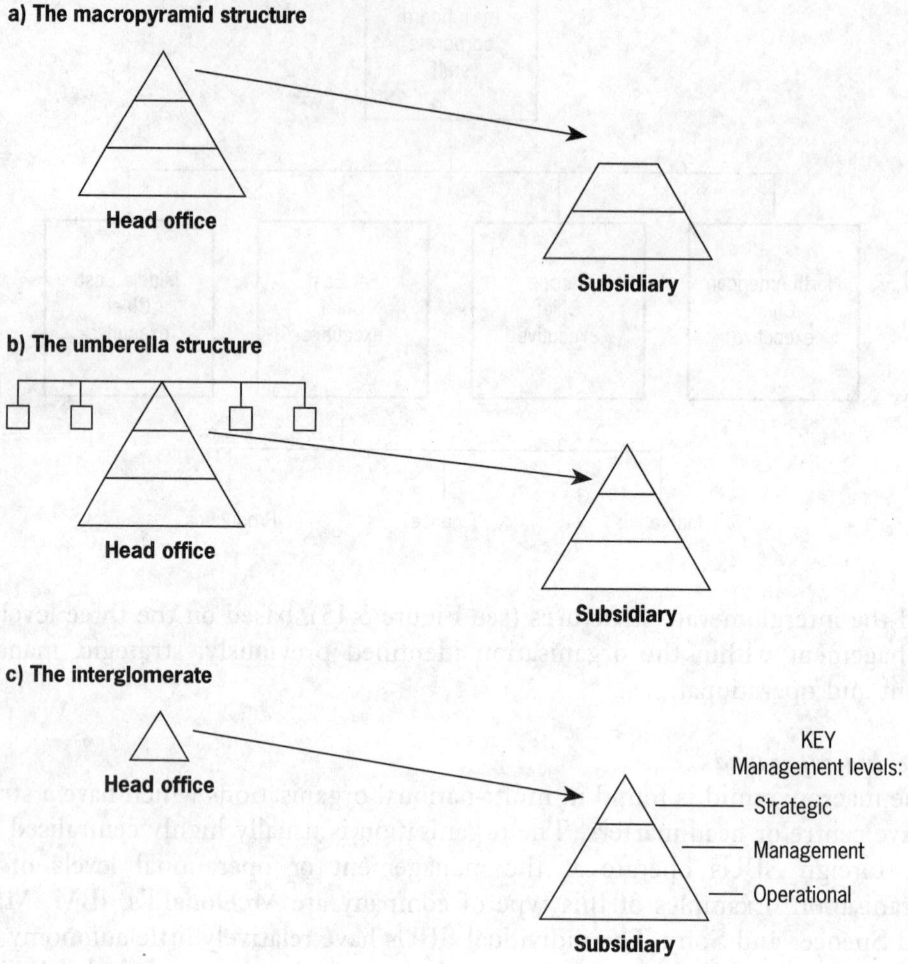

a) The macropyramid structure

Head office

Subsidiary

b) The umberella structure

Head office

Subsidiary

c) The interglomerate

Head office

Subsidiary

KEY
Management levels:
——— Strategic
——— Management
——— Operational

- local creativity is inhibited;
- communication problems occur as a result of difficulty in interpreting instructions from the centre; and
- the lack of local autonomy is a disincentive to good managers who must move to the centre for career advancement.

The umbrella structure

Organisations with the umbrella structure take the opposite view to those with the macropyramid and have fully decentralised planning and control, and give full independence at all levels of management to the foreign subsidiaries. Proctor and Gamble and Unilever in the past have operated such a structure. The centre sets only broad corporate objectives, and will provide advice and support, but essentially, each SBU will develop a plan for their area of responsibility.

The implications for the marketing mix of an umbrella structure are:

- the SBUs can adopt an appropriate marketing mix strategy for the local market;
- an effective local marketing function can develop local marketing plans;
- market planning can respond to local environmental developments and changes;
- different strategies will be followed for each market and there are implications for usually centralised functions, such as R&D, personnel and finance;
- there is little chance of a global strategy; and
- there can be considerable duplication as different SBUs work on similar strategies and tactics.

The interglomerate

The interglomerate embraces multi-markets, multi-products and multi-technologies and so no attempt is made by the centre to develop strategies for the individual SBUs which are likely to be international businesses in their own right. Because of the complexity of the firm the centre takes no significant, active management role, and is concerned purely with financial planning and control.

The implications for international marketing are that:

- interglomerates are finance driven;
- the marketing function will not be represented at the strategic level; and
- corporate and marketing strategies are the sole responsibility of the SBU.

Many Western interglomerates, such as Hanson and BTR have broken up their organisations by demerger and selling off non-core or unprofitable activities. This model is more common in Asian owned businesses which have significantly different patterns of development. The objectives of these Eastern interglomerates must be born in mind when arranging Western–Asian business relationships because they do have potentially serious implications as the Illustration 5.6 shows.

There is a suggestion that some of the Asian conglomerates are reaching the limits of their founding families to manage them and there are suggestions that, in the long term, business methods in Asia will resemble those in the West. Until then Western firms are likely to use the Asian style of networking as a mechanism for working in Asian markets with some degree of commercial security until the Asian markets become more transparent with rules that are written and enforced.

Some Western firms, however, have had enough of networking and it is estimated that very soon a majority of foreign direct investments into China will be wholly foreign owned. For example, Motorola has a wholly owned factory for producing mobile phones and other telecommunications equipment on condition that it agreed to build a chip factory as well. It is operating its sales and marketing operation through a joint venture.

Illustration 5.6: Conflicting Asian–Western business practices

Western businesses do not understand the way networking plays such a huge role in Asian business. Asian companies generally believe relationships come first whereas Western firms prefer to decide the business that interests them and form connections when they are needed. Relationship building is an integral part of Asian business strategy and the opportunities that arise from business connections often result in conglomerates of apparently unrelated business. This system of complex conglomerates seems illogical to Western management where building core competencies is common. As regards Asian–Western relationships, many frustrations emerge because of the differences in business practice. For example, the lack of continuity caused by Western managers moving around from job to job makes it difficult for Asian managers to form the connections necessary for doing business. Moreover, since Asian partners are frequently involved with a number of other firms conflicts of interest arise. Western managers often complain that their Asian counterparts tend to focus on attaining short-term profits to invest in new ventures with new partners rather than the preferred Western method of building brands or expanding market share.

There are a number of trends in the development of organisational structures which have implications for the future of marketing. First, structures are becoming flatter as individual managers have a wider span of control with more subordinates who, in turn, have responsibility for many more activities. Responsibility and authority are, therefore, increasingly pushed down the organisation and increasingly, managers at operational levels are expected to think strategically. Second, whilst the macropyramid structure retains its central identity, the umbrella and interglomerate organisation will increasingly lose theirs as the success of individual units is determined by a much wider variety of factors. It is against this background that the concept of the transnational firms has developed. The Illustration 5.7 shows the evolution of Unilever's

---

Illustration 5.7: Unilever prospering through market development

The founders of Unilever – Unie of Netherlands, Lever in the UK – had both achieved success through a combination of exporting and local production using Dutch and British people to manage local subsidiaries.

Up to the 1960s the management in individual countries were responsible for profit generation with product groups adopting an advisory role. The driving force for the firm's organisation structure at this stage was obtaining raw materials. However, as these became more freely available, emphasis switched to preservation and distribution which became more important. Consequently it became necessary for product groups to take on responsibility for profit, with national managers taking more of a back seat. By the middle of the 1970s, market development was taking a central role – particularly with the advent of convenience and health/low-calorie foods – but this resulted in the existing structure becoming increasingly inappropriate. In the late 1980s, Unilever embarked on further restructuring with the objective of maintaining responsiveness to local markets whilst striving for unity within their complex and diverse activities. In the 1990s, the emphasis is on adding value rather than just profit and sales. They believe that although they are in a mature market position, new opportunities do exist. An example of how they have achieved this is in persuading adults that ice-cream is not simply a children's treat, by introducing the Magnum brand.

organisational structure to the point where it has now become a transnational organisation.

Transnational organisations

The structures outlined, whilst providing some general understanding of alternative methods of organising the management, are for most companies an oversimplification. Bartlett and Ghosal (1987) explain that 'the very act of going international multiplies the firm's organisational complexity'. The domestic organisational variables of product and function are extended by adding the area dimension. In a study of nine firms including ITT, Philips, Proctor and Gamble, they found that the challenge of breaking down biases and building a truly multi-dimensional organisation has proved difficult because there are in-built assumptions within the firm about the roles of the organisational units and the way that they should be managed. The traditional view is that relationships between SBUs should be clear and unambiguous and that the decision making mechanisms should be clearly understood, but in fact the most successful firms have challenged these assumptions and replaced them with new standards. This has implications for the international marketing manager as Bartlett and Ghosal (1992) have concluded. The management of *transnational businesses* requires highly specialised, closely linked groups of global business managers, country or regional managers, and functional managers who work in *networks*. They explain the implications for managers in such transnational organisations. *Global business or product division managers* have the responsibility to further the company's global scale efficiency and competitiveness. They must combine the strategist skills of recognising opportunities and risks across national and functional boundaries, be the architect for worldwide resource and asset utilisation, and the coordinator of activities and capabilities.

The *country manager* must play a pivotal role by sensing local customer needs, but also satisfying the host government's requirements and defend the company's market position. The country manager is likely to have objectives which conflict with the business manager and so must be prepared to negotiate to overcome the differences. The *functional manager* role is the business environment scanner, cross pollinator of ideas and champion of specific aspects of the business which are essential for success. The *global manager* may be required to play a number of roles. The complexity of global operations means that no one person can fulfil the required tasks alone. This manager, therefore, must provide leadership, whilst acting as the talent scout and the developer of the other levels of management.

As a result, patterns of activity in a transnational company will vary considerably in each new situation. Innovations, for example, should be generated at several places and in several ways throughout the world, so that the company is not restricted to making centralised or decentralised decisions. For the last ten to twenty years, firms such as Shell, Philips and Unilever have used an integrated network approach, with resources and capabilities concentrated in various location and accessed through the use of effective free flow of components, products resources and people. By developing these matrix structures, firms can achieve efficiency, responsiveness and the ability to develop and exploit knowledge for success.

As the international operation of firms increase in diversity and *tangible* ties between the activates become strained, so the nature of the formal systems and organisational structures must change too. Training programmes, career path planning, job rotation, company-wide accounting, equitable evaluation and data-processing systems become more important, but the *most important aspect is that the values of the company are shared* between employees in all countries.

So what makes a good international manager?

For many of the most powerful businesses, this is the future scenario, and the most successful will be managed by people who can best embrace and thrive on the ambiguity and complexity of transnational operations. Despite the rapid internationalisation of businesses there are still few really international managers – but the creation of cross-cultural managers with genuinely transferable management skills is the goal for the global companies.

A number of researchers have emphasized the need for managers to be able to handle national differences in business, including cultural divergence on hierarchy, humour, assertiveness and working hours. In France, Germany, Italy and a large part of Asia, for example, performance-related pay is seen negatively as revealing the shortcomings of some members of the work group. Feedback sessions are seen positively in the US but German managers see them as 'enforced admissions of failure'.

The international manager, therefore, must be more culturally aware and show greater sensitivity but, it can be difficult to adapt to the culture and values of a foreign country whilst upholding the culture and values of a parent company. Whilst the only way is to give managers experience overseas the cost of sending people abroad typically costs two and a half times that for a local manager, so firms look for alternatives, such as short-term secondments and exchanges and having multi-cultural project teams.

Wills and Barham (1994) believe that international managers require four sets of attributes. They must:

1 be able to cope with cognitive complexity and be able to understand issues from a variety of complicated perspectives;
2 have cultural empathy, a sense of humility and the power of active listening. Because of their unfamiliarity with different cultural settings international managers cannot be as competent or confident in a foreign environment;
3 have emotional energy and be capable of adding depth and quality to interactions through their emotional self-awareness, emotional resilience, ability to accept risk and be able to rely on the support of the family;
4 demonstrate psychological maturity by having the curiosity to learn, an orientation to time and a fundamental personal morality that will enable them to cope with the diversity of demands made on them.

Ethical challenges for international marketing managers

The fundamental personal morality referred to in point 4 above poses some of the most difficult challenges of all for international marketing managers. Part of the reason for this is that there are no moral absolutes and judgements are made according to the perception of the observer. What is acceptable in one culture may be totally unacceptable in another. The US strongly objects to the employees of US firms, wherever they are in the world, offering or accepting bribes, and yet in Germany bribes are tax deductible. In some South American countries, petty bribery is so institutionalised that it seems that it is virtually impossible to move goods without making payments. Other countries would find the degree of government lobbying in the US as equally morally indefensible as bribery, for example, as public policy and legislation on tobacco and the environment has been unjustifiably influenced by pressure groups.

What cannot be defended, however, are the business practices of the managers and staff of a few MNEs who have vandalised the environment of some countries, banks who have deliberately lent money knowing that it would be expropriated, corrupt politicians and government officials who have stolen money from the country and whose behaviour together has adversely affected the economies of some LDCs often contributing to appalling conditions for local people, who have not had the power to avoid being exploited.

The prospect of successfully implementing worldwide ethical standards is remote but, increasingly, responsible MNEs are beginning to set standards which they expect their staff to adhere to. Part of the reason for this, the cynics would say, is to protect the image of the MNE with its stakeholders. Whilst it is admirable that these firms are setting standards they often do so from the standpoint of Western morality and some of the guidelines set can be offensive to other cultures.

In practice, however, it is individual members of staff on international assignments that are constantly being faced with a wide variety of moral dilemmas which require immediate decisions. Often the alternatives that the managers no doubt feel that they are facing are either to behave ethically and thus fail to meet their performance targets or to behave unethically and meet them. As ethical considerations become increasingly important in the strategic and operational development of MNEs, Lowe (1997) maintains that to be successful in future, international marketing managers must respond by basing their decisions on personal integrity. They must show sensitivity to the culture of the host country and have an appreciation of the country's short- and long-term needs. Only then, when this is common practice will international ethical standards rise.

Conclusion

In this chapter we have discussed the process of planning in which the key elements are thorough analysis of the company's situation, objectives, strategies, capabilities and resources and have explained the sequence and timing of the decisions that make up the process. The differences in the planning process between a first stage exporter and a global marketing company have been highlighted. Whilst we have presented this as a sequential process, we have emphasised its evolving and interactive nature within a complex and dynamic environment.

We have emphasised the need for the plan to be orientated to action and, in order to ensure that this occurs, we have discussed various organisational structures through which the plans can be implemented. Running through in this chapter has not only been the organisational issues of planning but also the importance of recognising the role, capabilities and attitudes of the international manager and the challenges they face. We have emphasised the differences between managing in a company with different levels of commitment to international marketing and the totally different culture and philosophy associated with managing a transnational organisation in which the term home country becomes meaningless.

Discussion questions

1 Evaluate the organisational control and marketing implications of moving from modest international marketing activity to the approach required to achieve the corporate aim of world leadership.

2 In what ways would marketing planning in lesser developed countries (LDCs) differ from planning in more industrially advanced country markets?

3 Show how a multi-national enterprise (MNE) might modify its organisational structure to accommodate various marketing strategies.

4 In which ways is the culture of a company likely to affect its approach to international marketing planning and management?

5 How can the transnational company concept be used to maximise international marketing opportunities and minimise the threats?

References

Bartlett, C.A. and Ghosal, S. (1987) 'Managing Across Borders', *Sloan Management Review*, Fall.

Bartlett, C.A. and Ghosal, S. (1992) 'What Is A Global Manager?' *Harvard Business Review*, September/October .

Brandt, W., Hulbert, J. and Richers, R. (1980) 'Pitfalls in Planning for Multinational Operations', *Long Range Planning*, December.

Caulkin, S. (1998) 'Swede dreams of going truly global', *The Observer*, 22 March.

Dawkins, W. (1996) 'Time to pull back the screen: Japanese multinationals may follow Canon's example and shift power overseas', *Financial Times*, 18 November.

Gilligan, C. and Hird, M. (1986) *International Marketing Strategy and Management*, Croom Helm.

Gupta, A. and Govindarajan, V. (1998) 'Mastering Global Business, Part Two', *Financial Times*, 27 February.

Hamel, G. and Prahalad, C.K. (1994) *Competing for the Future*, Harvard Business School Press.

Jackson, T. (1997) 'The Global Company: Time's up for the man from head office', *Financial Times*, 8 October.

Jeanet, J.P. and Hennesey, H. (1992) *Global Marketing Strategies*, Houghton Mifflin.

Lowe, R. (1997) 'Ethnics and the challenge for international marketing managers', in, I. Doole and R. Lowe, *International Marketing Strategy: Contemporary Readings*, Thomson Business Press.

Majaro, S. (1991) *International Marketing*, Routledge.

Maljers, F.A. (1992) 'Inside Unilever – The Evolving Transnational Company', *Harvard Business Review*, September/October.

Terpstra, V. and Sarathy, R. (1997) *International Marketing*, 7th edn, Dryden.

Weichmann, U.E. and Pringle, L.G. (1979) 'Problems That Plague Multinational Marketers', *Harvard Business Review*, July/August.

Williamson, P.J. (1997) 'Asia's new competitive game', *Harvard Business Review*, September/October.

Wills, S. and Barham, K. (1994) 'Being an international manager' *European Management Journal*, 12 (1).

Chapter 6

International niche marketing strategies for small and medium-sized firms (SMEs)

Introduction

Small and medium sized firms (SMEs) have always been significant creators of wealth and employment in domestic economies, but are a less powerful force outside their home territory usually because of their limited resources. Indeed, many SMEs, despite what may be obvious business capability, never move into international markets at all. However, for reasons which will be explored in this chapter SMEs have the potential to become considerably more important in the future global economy, both in fast growing business sectors, such as new technology and in market niches, where innovation in mature industry sectors can lead to new opportunities. Many SMEs are part of the international supply chains of MNEs as, perhaps, a component supplier, a contract manufacturer or a service provider in business-to-business transactions.

In this chapter we discuss the factors which influence the patterns of international development of small and medium-sized firms, including the strategic options available to them, and the particular problems they face in implementing their strategy.

The traditional model of SME internationalisation is exporting in which goods are manufactured in one country and transferred to buyers in other countries, but many SMEs are involved in a broader range of international marketing activity and it is for this reason we prefer the term niche marketing. For example, small service providers generate revenue from customers in foreign markets either by providing services from the home country which customers can access wherever they are situated (for example, information, and advice supplied via the Internet) or by providing services in the firm's home country, and requiring the customers to visit (for example, tourism, training and education residential courses). The common themes in these approaches, however, are that they all generate foreign currency revenue, have the effect of 'importing' work and jobs for the home country and to be successful require an understanding of the various dimensions of international marketing.

The SME sector and its role within the global economy

A number of definitions of the small and medium-sized firm sector exist but the most commonly used terms relate to the number of employees in the company. The European Union, for example, has recently changed its definition of SMEs from those firms employing less than 500 staff to those employing less than 250. This characterisation, however, effectively includes 99 per cent of all firms in Europe and accounts for roughly 50 per cent of employment and, because it includes sole operators as well as quite sophisticated businesses, is not particularly useful for segmenting the smaller firms sector.

In this chapter, therefore, the review of smaller firm strategies is not restricted to firms with a specific number of employees for the following reasons but instead to issues which apply to businesses in general which think and act like small and medium-sized enterprises. The reason for adopting this stance is that a garment making firm with 250 employees has a very restricted capacity to internationalise, whereas a 250 employee financial services or computer software company could be a significant international player. Many quite large businesses take business decisions within the family group in much the same way that small firms take decisions. Moreover, many of the fastest growing international firms very rapidly grow through the 250 employee ceiling without making significant changes to their international strategic approach. The discussion instead relates to issues affecting firms which could not in any way be described as large MNEs with real global power.

Of the huge number of SMEs only a small percentage, perhaps less than 5 per cent, grow significantly but many of them are likely to be exporters. Indeed, Austrade, the Australian government trade department suggest that successful exporting activity is a major predictor of growth in Australian SMEs. However in a recent study of the 100 fastest growing firms in the UK, Oldfield (1997) reports that more than half do not export at all, less than 15 per cent achieve half their sales from exports and six of the top ten do not export at all.

The SME sector is becoming more important as a creator of wealth and employment because large firms have down-sized during the 1990s, reducing their workforce, and have concentrated on increasingly out-sourcing their non-core components, often from smaller firms. Employment in the public sector has been decreasing during this same period due to the extensive privatisation of public sector owned utilities and agencies, such as gas, electricity, water and telephones, and the increased volume of public sector services, such as cleaning and catering which have been contracted out to private organisations. In many countries this has left the small and medium-sized firms sector as the only significant growing source of wealth and employment. By contrast, SMEs which market their products and services in the domestic economy often grow at the expense of other domestic SMEs because of the relatively limited home market, whereas export markets offer seemingly unlimited scope for SMEs to grow.

As we have seen in the previous chapters the international marketing environment is potentially very hostile. It is a small wonder, therefore, that many companies ignore the export potential of the products and services and concentrate instead on their domestic markets. A study by Barker and Kaynak (1992) for example, found that less than 20 per cent of firms in Texas with export potential actually carried out business in international markets. But although many firms view international markets with trepidation, others still make their decision to go international.

The nature of international marketing in SMEs

In exploiting these opportunities to generate revenue from international markets SMEs have a number of alternative strategies which provide a useful method of categorisation of SME internationalisation.

- **Exporting** is primarily concerned with **selling** domestically developed and produced goods and services abroad.

- **International niche marketing** is concerned with marketing a differentiated product or service overseas using the full range of market entry and marketing mix options available.

- **Domestically delivered or developed niche services** can be marketed or delivered internationally to potential visitors.

- **Direct marketing including electronic commerce** allows firms to market products and services globally from a domestic location.

- **Participation in the international supply chain** of an MNE, can lead to SMEs piggybacking on the MNE's international development. This may involve either domestic production or establishing a facility close to where the MNE's new locations are established in other countries.

Exporting

For many firms exporting is the first significant stage in the internationalisation process as it provides the advantage of considerably expanded market potential with relatively little commitment and limited associated risk. Czinkota (1994) suggests that exporting is essentially marketing expansion and is akin to looking for new customers in the next town, next state or on another coast. Exporting, when defined as the marketing of goods and/or services across national and political boundaries, is not solely the preserve of small and medium-sized businesses, nor for many firms is it a temporary stage in the process of internationalisation. Many firms, both large and small, do not progress beyond the stage of relatively limited involvement in international markets.

Motivation

A number of writers have studied the major motivations for beginning exporting but Katsikeas (1996) notes that the vast majority of this research surveyed firms in the US. Given that considerable differences exist between countries Katsikeas suggests that generalisations can be misleading and that the firm's motivation in its ongoing marketing activities may differ from its initial international involvement.

The research draws the important distinction between whether the motivations to export are principally reactive stimuli or proactive stimuli. Two examples of reactive strategies are as follows: if a product is either stagnant or in decline in the home market, the company may find new foreign markets where the product has not reached the same stage and which therefore offers potential for further growth. It is still appropriate, too, for companies to seek new markets abroad to utilise their production facilities to their full capacity. In these circumstances companies may well embark on marginal pricing and sell at lower prices on the export markets, seeking only a contribution to their overall cost for their home base market.

Katsikeas identifies the following reactive stimuli:

- adverse domestic market conditions
- an opportunity to reduce inventories
- the availability of production capacity
- favourable currency movements
- the opportunity to increase the number of country markets and reduce the market-related risk
- unsolicited orders from overseas customers.

Proactive stimuli for exporting include market diversification. If a company sees only limited growth opportunities in the home market for a proven product it may well see market diversification as a means of expansion. This could mean new market segments within a domestic market but it may well mean geographic expansion in foreign markets. Thus companies try to spread risks and reduce their dependence on any one market. Equally the firm may identify market gaps. The proactive company with a well managed marketing information system may identify foreign market opportunities through its research system. This could, of course, be by undertaking formal structured research or by identifying opportunities through a network of contacts scanning international markets for potential opportunities.

Katsikeas identifies the following proactive stimuli:

- attractive profit and growth opportunities
- the ability to easily modify products for export markets
- public policy programmes for export promotion
- foreign country regulations
- the possession of unique products
- economies resulting from additional orders.

And certain managerial elements including:

- the presence of an export-minded manager
- the opportunity to better utilise management talent and skills
- management beliefs about the value of exporting.

Katsikeas found in researching a group of Cypriot exporters that both proactive stimuli, including having an export-minded manager, attractive growth and profit opportunities and reactive stimuli, including receiving unsolicited orders were particularly important.

Illustration 6.1 is a good example of how the disappearance of an apparently secure and reliable market forced Sure Mining to develop its export activity rapidly and in so doing reinvent the firm.

Barriers to internationalisation

Many companies with export potential never become involved in international marketing, and a series of government export studies have found that it is often a great deal easier to encourage existing exporters to increase their involvement in international markets than to encourage those who are not exporting to begin the

Illustration 6.1: Sure Mining

Sure Mining are manufacturers of hot and cold pressed track components for rail systems. In the 1980s, British Coal was Sure Mining's principal customer accounting for 95 per cent of its turnover. By 1990 the Coal Mine closure programme in the UK had commenced and the company was rapidly losing its traditional customer base. At that time there was a vivid recognition of the fact that if they did not diversify and widen their customer base they would not survive.

As their name suggests, Sure Mining saw themselves as principally serving the mining market. In 1990 they reformulated their company structure and developed a marketing strategy to take the company forward. There were two principal components to this strategy, first a redefinition of their market from mining to 'anywhere there is a tunnel'. Second a decision was made to develop the export markets.

From a zero base in 1990, exports in 1997 accounted for 30 per cent of their turnover, with plans in place to increase this to 50 per cent by the end of the decade.

The strategy put in place has proved successful for three major reasons. First, the top management have a very clear vision as to the type of company they wish to build. The Managing Director demonstrates a great deal of tenacity and resilience in driving his company forward internationally and puts enormous energy into ensuring its success. This has often meant fighting internal battles as well as external.

Second, Sure Mining identified quite clearly two target markets where they could effectively compete, industrial suppliers of railways and the construction industry. Being a small company and without experience they then built a series of strategic alliances involving piggyback operations and other type of partnerships to help them exploit the market opportunities identified.

Third, they made an explicit commitment to a quality policy throughout the company. *'Quality processes are very important to us, it is important to show our international customers we have professional procedures in place. It is no good us acting like market traders, engineers don't want that'.*

Following this strategy has enabled the company to not only survive the collapse of their traditional home market but develop a healthy and diverse customer base in at least a dozen countries which gives a strong foundation for future growth.

process. The reasons given by companies for not exporting are numerous. The biggest barrier to entry into export markets is seen to be a fear by these companies that their products are not marketable overseas, and they consequently become preoccupied with the domestic market.

Barker and Kaynack (1992) listed the most important areas which non-exporters identified as barriers to exporting:

- Too much red tape
- Trade barriers
- Transportation difficulties
- Lack of trained personnel
- Lack of export incentives
- Lack of coordinated assistance
- Unfavourable conditions overseas
- Slow payment by buyers
- Lack of competitive products
- Payment defaults
- Language barriers.

Experienced exporters tend not to highlight issues such as the bureaucracy associated with international markets and trade barriers, which suggests that they have overcome the problems by managerial proactivity, for example, by training staff and seeking expert assistance so that these potential problem areas can be dealt with.

Niche marketing

Having identified the motivations and barriers to exporting it is tempting to conclude that many exporters are characterised by being product oriented – selling abroad the products and services that are successful in the domestic market. Moreover, exporters often seem to throw away their successful domestic marketing strategies in international markets, preferring instead to effectively delegate their marketing to agents and distributors. In doing this they seem to overlook the alternative market entry and marketing mix strategies that are available to them and instead opt for a strategy of least involvement. In many cases this approach may meet the exporting firm's immediate situation and objectives, especially if, for example, they are simply seeking to off-load excess production capacity, but it does not provide them with a sound basis for substantially increasing their international market presence.

By contrast, international niche marketing occurs where firms become a strong force in a narrow specialised market of one or two segments across a number of country markets. Illustration 6.2 of Beatson Clark shows how a traditional manufacturing exporter has redefined its business to become a niche marketer.

Brown and McDonald (1994) explain that the segments must be too small or specialised to attract large competitors and true niche marketing does not include small brands or companies that are minor players in a mass market offering undifferentiated products. For the international niche to be successful the product or service must be distinctive (highly differentiated) and be recognised by consumers and other participants in the international supply chain and have clear positioning.

To sustain and develop the niche the firm must:

- have good information about the segment needs;
- have a clear understanding of the important segmentation criteria;
- understand the value of the product niche to the targeted segment(s);
- provide high levels of service;
- carry out small scale innovations;
- seek cost efficiency in the supply chain;
- maintain a separate focus, perhaps, by being content to remain relatively small;
- concentrate on profit rather than market share; and
- evaluate and apply appropriate market entry and marketing mix strategies to build market share in each country in which they wish to become involved.

The Illustration 6.3 gives two examples of firms which have identified market opportunities but it emphasises that small firms must be very clear about the success criteria in an export niche market and the limits of their ambition.

There are, therefore, significant differences between the traditional view of exporting and international niche marketing and these are summarised in Figure 6.1.

Niche marketing of domestically delivered services

In the past this category of international marketing has largely been dominated by the travel industry with domestic firms such as hotels, tour operators and

Illustration 6.2: Beatson Clark: Defining a niche in a commodity market

Beatson Clark are manufacturers of glass containers for the pharmaceutical, food and drinks industry. They export to over 100 countries worldwide. The global glass container market is highly competitive and virtually all countries have their large indigenous producers who sell the containers as commodity products. This makes it difficult to compete considering the high costs involved in physically distributing large glass containers to overseas markets.

Beatson Clark have developed a very effective niche market strategy by focusing on low volume small items which are not of great interest to the large producers. Their competitive advantage has been developed internationally by building a highly effective customer service operation servicing customers throughout the world.

The company offer a design service for the small items which are too much hassle for their major competitors. In each market the company builds up close relationships with a number of trusted distributors who operate in the packaging market and have a good customer base. The company keeps in regular contact with all their international partners sometimes talking to them 10–15 times a day.

They have then built an effective customer service operation to service all customers wherever they are. This is based on three fundamental principles. First, there is an explicit commitment to quality which is shared throughout the company. All prospective customers throughout the world are sent a signed letter from the MD setting out the commitment to quality procedures and there is an explicit process for translating the company's quality policy into departmental goals.

Second, the company has a team who are dedicated to the effective movement of goods throughout the world and take full responsibility for ensuring safe delivery of all orders to their international destinations, which is no easy task in the glass business!

Third, the company place great emphasis on establishing effective monitoring procedures to measure their performance in customer service as well as their financial performance by customer, order, country etc. to ensure at all times they have full control in their international operations.

This has meant the company has been able to build an international strategy which operates on good margins, is relatively low risk and has achieved a steady rate of growth whilst enabling the company to achieve an element of control in the marketplace.

Illustration 6.3: Enjoying the rich taste of success

Over ten years New Covent Garden Soup Company (UK) has built a market niche with a turnover in 1997 of £20 million selling premium priced chilled soups to up-market delicatessens. It started selling to the USA in 1995 but whereas retailers in the UK have made it easy for specialist manufacturers to get onto the shelves, the US is different. There are benefits in the UK from positioning the company as David against Goliath, but in the US the retailers think the company must be big to even consider exporting. US retailers, therefore, tend to think in terms of very large operations, but whilst the volumes could be massive, the prices would not cover the cost of flying the product in and if the firm tried to compete on price it would fail. The turnover from the US has reached £1 million and the brand has established itself in certain key cities. The key to success is offering a premium product into a market niche. The company is now looking for further market development in the US and is backing a UK expatriate based in San Francisco to set up a factory using manufacturing know-how from the UK.

Halcyon Days is a London West End antiques business which, since 1970, has exported fine enamelled boxes and porcelain for the collectibles market in the US. Recently, it moved from a business selling to tourists to a more proactive and systematic marketing process using mail order catalogues and direct supplies to up-market US retailers. With US sales of £5 million the company works very closely with suppliers in the UK, customers and stockists and a number of US museums to offer designs based on artifacts and exhibits. Halcyon emphasise the criteria for success include recognising the importance of having the right levels and quality of management both in the head office and the US.

Source: adapted from Fazey, H. (1998) 'Enjoying the rich taste of success', *Financial Times Exporter,* March.

leisure attractions which generate foreign earnings for the country by attracting visitors. However, with increased international travel and improved access to worldwide communications a much wider range of services to visiting customers is being offered. Examples include the provision of education, specialised training, healthcare, sports, cultural and leisure events and specialist retailing, for example, luxury goods.

Figure 6.1 The difference between exporting and international niche marketing

	Exporting	International marketing
Marketing strategy	Selling production capacity	Meeting customer needs
Financial objective	To amortise overheads	To add value
Segmentation	Usually by country and customer characteristics	By identifying common international customer benefit
Pricing	Cost based	Market or customer based
Management focus	Efficiency in operations	Meeting market requirements
Distribution	Using existing agents or distributors	Managing the supply chain
Market information	Relying on agent or distributor feedback	Analysing the market situation and customer needs
Customer relationship	Working through intermediary	Building multiple level relationships

Clearly these activities lead to wealth and jobs being generated in the local economy in much the same way as exporting and niche marketing. The international marketing strategy processes and programmes are similar too in that the products and services must meet the requirements of international customer segments. Consequently issues of standardisation and adaptation of the marketing mix elements are equally important. The additional challenge is that the benefits obtained from the service provided must either be unique and superior, and thus outweigh the benefits to the consumer of locally available services as well as the cost of travel that the customers will incur in the course of their purchase.

In addition to the services designed to be offered to individuals in both consumer or business-to-business markets a whole range of additional services which fall into this category of being domestically delivered are concerned with developing solutions for opportunities or problems identified abroad. These might include technology developments, such as research into new drugs, trial and testing facilities, software development and product and packaging design services. One example of this is Verity (UK) which has used its NXT technology to develop flat panel loudspeakers, ideal for public address systems and home audio use. Rather than make the final product it is licensing its portfolio of technology comprising 100 patents and patent applications to manufacturers, such as NEC, Samsung, Fujitsu and Harman International. Given that 2–3 billion speakers are sold in the world each year a royalty of $1 per speaker on 1 per cent of the market would generate considerable revenue for Verity.

Importing and reciprocal trading

Importing is clearly the opposite process to international marketing and as such might be seen by governments as 'exporting' jobs and potential wealth. However, the purpose of raising this issue here is to highlight the nature of international trade as it is today. Rarely do supply chains for products and services involve solely domestic production and delivery. More usually 'exporting' and 'importing' becomes inextricably linked and so the challenge becomes one of adding value to imported components and services, no matter from where they are sourced, so that they can then be re-exported in order to effectively and profitably meet the international customers' needs.

Importing activity can also considerably enhance the company's potential to network, leading ultimately, perhaps, to reciprocal trading in which, as a result, the supplier might take other products or services in return from the customer.

Direct marketing and electronic commerce

A rapidly growing area of international trading is direct marketing and, in particular, electronic commerce. Direct marketing offers the benefits of cutting out other distribution channel members, such as importers, agents, distributors, wholesalers and retailers by using a variety of communications media, including post, telephone, television and networked computers. All these allow borders to be crossed relatively easily and at modest cost without the SME having to face many of the barriers already highlighted in this chapter.

Direct marketing also has a number of disadvantages. Despite the range of media available, communicating can still be problematic and there is always the danger of cultural insensitivity. Because of the need to manage large numbers of customers it is necessary to use databases which must be up to date, accurate and be capable of dealing with foreign languages. Even an incorrect name can be insulting to the recipient.

It is electronic commerce, based on Internet and Intranet trading, which is expected to grow fastest over the next few years. The Internet provides firms with a shop window to the world without a member of staff needing to leave the office. It can provide the means of obtaining payment, organising and tracking shipment and delivery. For some products and services it can provide the means by which market information can be accumulated, new ideas can be collected, developed and modified by customers and other stakeholders.

Electronic commerce has also led firms to redefine their business and it can also be a business in its own right. For example, many electronic commerce services take the form of information transfer and this forms the basis of the product or service itself, for example, specialist advice on personal finance, travel and hobbies.

As well as being a route to market in its own right in the form of direct commerce, Internet as an interactive marketing information provider will have an increasingly important role in each of the above international niche marketing activities.

Hamill (1997) suggests that e-mail has a number of advantages over more traditional forms of communications such as telephone, postal and fax most commonly used by companies. It is more cost-effective over long distances and does not rely on real time presence, which is a particular advantage when different time zones are involved. It is a very reliable and flexible method since graphics, drawings, etc. can be transferred as well as text. Individuals may become more rather than less communicative using e-mail which is best seen as supporting rather than replacing personal, face-to-face relationships. As an increasing number of competitors start to form relationships with international suppliers, partners, agents, etc., supported by electronic communications, SMEs who are not connected face being shut out of the network.

Internet offers the benefits to SMEs of real time communications across distances, and the levelling of the corporate playing field leading to more rapid internationalisation as well as achieving competitive advantage by:

- creating new opportunities;
- erecting barriers to entry;
- making cost savings from on-line communications;
- providing on-line support for inter-firm collaboration, especially in research and development, as an information search and retrieval tool;

- the establishment of company Web sites for marketing and sales promotion; and
- the transmission of any type of data including manuscripts, financial information CAD/CAM (computer aided design, computer aided manufacture) files.

Quelch and Klein (1996) argued that the Internet will revolutionise the dynamics of international commerce and in particular lead to the more rapid internationalisation of SMEs. The World Wide Web will reduce the competitive advantages of small economies in many industries making it easier for small companies to compete on a worldwide basis. The global advertising costs as a barrier to entry will be significantly reduced as the Web makes it possible to reach a global audience more cheaply. Small companies offering specialised niche products will be able to find the critical mass of customers necessary to succeed through the worldwide reach of the Internet. Overall the authors argue that the low cost Internet communications permit firms with limited capital to become global marketers at an early stage in their development. In a survey of Web site and non-Web site owners, Bennett (1997) noted that the Web site owners tended on average to:

- be less experienced at exporting (a quarter had been exporting for less than three years; double the figure for firms without Web sites),
- use fewer foreign agents or other representatives (only 32 per cent of site owners employed foreign representatives compared with 58 per cent for those without Web sites; and
- employ significantly higher proportions of IT-literate staff.

There are some disadvantages, especially the relative ease with which it is possible to become flooded with electronic messages. Moreover, electronic commerce is at early stages of development and many firms are simply trying it to see if it generates sales. Whilst this may be manageable for certain products and services where production volumes can be easily increased or decreased, sales feasts and famines can cause havoc where production capacity is less flexible.

As more firms use electronic commerce it will become more sophisticated, for example, search engines are being designed to find the 'best deal' rather than identify every single offer. The implications of this are that instead of marketing being essentially passive in electronic commerce, the marketing input required in designing Web sites will need to become increasingly sophisticated in promoting the products, providing interactive product design development and safe payment arrangements. Technical and customer service support and initial customer segmentation and targeting will become increasingly important to the delivery of an effective, focused business. Thus, whilst many SMEs have, up until now, seen Internet as a low cost distribution channel, in the future greater competition and more sophisticated versions of electronic-commerce may well make it more difficult for SMEs to compete. The Illustration 6.4 shows how Business Filings are challenging a traditional and powerful competitor. Whilst the Internet may provide Business Filings with the opportunity, future success will be determined by their marketing strategy, supported by innovative development.

Illustration 6.4: David against the incorporation Goliaths

Many businesses offer dull but essential services. An essential part of starting up a business is legal incorporation. Up to now this work has been carried out by old established and traditional firms such as Corporate Agents, an incorporation firm which has been in existence since 1899. It has a well-established reputation and relies on working with law firms, which also usually have a long history. Two 26-year-old law school graduates set up Business Filings in 1995 with $100 000 capital. They read up the incorporation statutes in each state in America and then set up an Internet site.

They provide all that new business start ups need including the corporate seal and will also help with setting up tax accounts. They have a low price guarantee and will even carry out the incorporation work free provided the client signs up for the $99 a year registered agent service. The key to increasing the turnover which was $250 000 in the first year will be using the technology and widening their market development. At the moment typing incorporation into search engines such as Excite, Yahoo and Lycos will result in a banner advert for Business Filings, but at a dollar a time the adverts are not cheap.

The main challenge, however, is to persuade the law firms to deliver repeat business. This could be done by customising software for use on law firm Intranets, allowing lawyers to cut and paste client details without having to retype billing details each time. The other development will be to attack the international markets in London, Tokyo, Zurich and off-shore tax havens.

Source: adapted from Jackson, T. (1997) 'A David amongst incorporation Goliaths', *Financial Times*, 1 April.

The importance of generic strategies for SME internationalisation

Having considered the various categories of SME internationalisation we now turn to the factors which influence the strategic development of SMEs. Before examining the internationalisation of SMEs and discussing the strategic options, it is important first to consider the strategy development process and the broad categories of generic strategies.

Whilst there are an infinite number of individual implementation strategies that an SME might adopt, depending on its particular situation, the principal approach to strategy development follows three stages (normally referred to as segmentation, targeting and positioning (STP marketing):

1 Identification of the various consumer segments that exist within the business sector, using the various segmentation methods which we have discussed earlier in Chapter 4. It is important for SMEs to define cross-border segments with clearly identifiable requirements which it is able to serve.
2 The firm must then target the segments which appear to be most attractive in terms of their size, growth potential, the ease with which they can be reached and their likely purchasing power.
3 In seeking to defend and develop its business the firm needs to position its products or services in a way that will distinguish them from those of its local and international competitors and build up barriers which will prevent those competitors taking its business.

In order to create competitive advantage Porter (1990) suggests that firms should adopt one of the following three generic strategies. However, each poses particular challenges for SMEs:

1 **Cost leadership** requires the firm to establish a lower cost base than its local or international competitors. This strategy has been typically adopted by companies that are located in countries with lower labour costs and who develop business usually as a component or service provider. Because of their limited financial resources, however, SMEs that adopt a low cost strategy spend little on marketing activity and are vulnerable to either local firms or larger multi-nationals temporarily cutting prices to force the firm out of the market. Alternatively changes in currency exchange rates or other instability in the economic climate can result in newer, lower priced competitors emerging.

2 **Focus**, in which the firm concentrates on one or more narrow segments and thus builds up a specialist knowledge of each segment. Such segments in the international marketplace are transnational in nature and companies work to dominate one particular segment across a number of country markets. Typically this strategy necessitates the SME providing high levels of customer and technical service support which can be resource intensive. Moreover, unless the SME has created a highly specialised niche, it may be difficult to defend against local and international competition.

3 **Differentiation**, is achieved through emphasising particular benefits in the product, service, or marketing mix, which customers think are important and a significant improvement over competitive offers, Differentiation typically requires systematic, incremental innovation to continually add customer value. Whilst SMEs are capable of the flexibility, adaptability and responsiveness to customer needs necessary with this strategy, the cost of maintaining high levels of differentiation over competitors in a number of international markets can be demanding of management time and financial resources.

Many SMEs base their international strategy on the generic strategy which has given them competitive advantage in domestic markets and then attempt to apply this same successful strategy in international markets. Of fundamental importance to the development of an effective international strategy for some SMEs is having a very strong position in the home country. US firms have benefited from having a huge potential domestic market. By contrast SMEs from emerging markets and from countries with smaller domestic markets often have to export merely to survive.

The factors which affect the choice of an SME's international marketing strategy

Figure 6.2 indicates a number of the factors which influence the choice and development of an SME's international strategy. Particular issues include environmental trends, the market and industry structure, the customer requirements from different countries, the nature and intensity of local and international competition, and the degree to which the SME can defend its niche. In SMEs, however, specific company factors are particularly important in the decision. These include the resources available, the products and services that have been developed and the firm's attitudes to international development

Figure 6.2 Factors affecting SME internationalisation

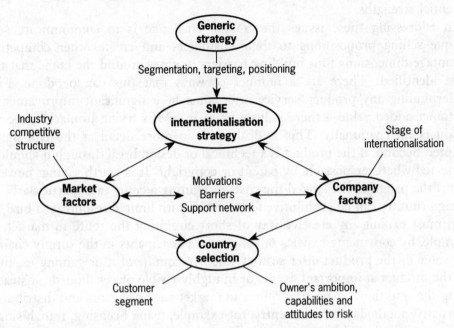

and management of risk. These will result in the firm adopting a specific approach to individual country selection as the strategy develops. Given the potential of SMEs for growth, wealth and job creation governments usually provide considerable resources to SMEs to assist them to develop internationally.

Competition and customer factors

The most significant factor inherent in SMEs is their relatively small size and lack of power in most international markets in which they wish to be active. This puts them at a disadvantage to local competitors and MNEs as they often lack the management resources to spend researching new markets; the contacts necessary to quickly develop effective distribution; sufficient financial resources to enable them to compete with the promotional spend of their competitors necessary to achieve effective diffusion of their products in order to obtain significant market share and to withstand a 'price war'.

The firm's smaller size means that they can offer customers the benefits of a more personal service from the firm's owners or senior managers, faster decision making and, usually, a greater willingness to listen but, of course, the SME must be committed to its international market development and profit from these potential strengths.

In addressing these issues the SMEs' challenge is to communicate some unique selling propositions to their customers and create other competitive advantage dimensions thus building barriers to entry around the niche that they have identified. There are a number of ways that this can be done. First, underpinning any product/service offer must be a significant improvement in customer added value – there is little point in SMEs trying to market 'me-too' products internationally. This is dealt with in more detail at the end of this chapter. Second, if the product is a technical or design breakthrough it should be protected wherever possible by patent or copyright. It is worth saying, however, that if the patent is challenged the costs of fighting a court case, particularly in a foreign country can be prohibitive for an SME with limited resources. Third, the firm must exploit any creative way of short circuiting the route to market, for example, by convincing experts or influential participants in the supply chain of the value of the product offer so they might recommend it or gaining exposure for the product at important events or in highly visible places. Fourth, instead of using the traditional exporting routes to market such as agents and distributors, alternative methods of market entry, for example, using licensing, franchising or joint ventures should be considered. They are relatively rarely used by the vast majority of SMEs and yet these methods are likely to increase the diffusion of the product or service into the market more cost effectively. Finally, in some situations an alternative way of improving the firm's competitive position is to cooperate with another firm – a customer, competitor or a firm engaged in a complementary activity.

Company factors

Given the statistics it is obvious that only a minute proportion of the world's SMEs can be characterised as fast growth organisations likely to become the multi-national enterprises of the future. Therefore, it is important to realise at the outset that the majority of SMEs are developing strategies which will deliver modest growth principally in order to maintain the company's security and viability. The objective of many businesses, such as the corner shop, the market trader, and the car mechanic is to look for sufficient business to provide enough income to survive and they look no further than their domestic market.

Using research in the UK, Storey (1994) estimates that 4 per cent of SMEs contribute 50 per cent of the new jobs created and it is these few firms that are both innovative, in developing new business ideas and marketing methods, and entrepreneurial, in exploiting them commercially; they are the fast growth, international niche marketers.

The very nature of SMEs mean that their smaller size and their entrepreneurial approach usually offers the advantages of flexibility and adaptability to new demands placed on them, speed of response to new opportunities and, usually, very focused management. They suffer from certain disadvantages too, for example, lack of adequate planning skills, being unwilling or unable to devote sufficient time and finances to the research and development of new business opportunities, resulting sometimes in wasted effort and some expensive failures.

Against this background must be set the obvious risk to SMEs of trading in other countries about which they have insufficient knowledge of the culture, market structure and business practices. The response of SMEs to international marketing is affected by their perceptions of this risk. At one extreme the SME will be deterred from becoming involved at all. At the other extreme the risk taking SME will experiment with international marketing, perhaps, with very little preparation believing that the firm will be able to respond quickly enough to deal with any difficulties that emerge. More cautious SMEs will attempt to assess and manage the risks involved by evaluating the market opportunity and planning their use of management operations and financial resources to enable a cost effective internationalisation approach to be developed.

Underlying the diversity in the range of a firm's attitudes to risk are the owners' ambition for the firm and how this fits with the firm's capabilities. To be successful the firm needs a vision of its international future which can be delivered using capabilities and resources that already exist but also can be acquired over a realistic timescale. It is often the case that successful SMEs are those that are able to clearly recognise and correct their weaknesses and build upon their strengths. SMEs that are unsuccessful in internationalising are those that do not understand what new resources and skills are needed or are unwilling to acquire them.

Government support

On a number of occasions in this chapter we have mentioned the benefits of SME international marketing in terms of the contribution it makes to jobs and wealth creation of a country. Recognising this, most national governments offer support to SMEs for their development in general and the encouragement of exporting in particular.

Chapter 7
Globalisation

Introduction

The implications of the phrase 'think global, act local' have preoccupied the major international organisations over the last decade and led them to adopt long-term strategies designed to establish a worldwide presence by introducing, where possible, standardised marketing programmes and processes, but at the same time, adapting certain operational activities to local needs in order to maximise short-term revenue generation. The problem that such firms face is exactly which aspects of their international activity to standardise and which to adapt because the decisions are often context specific and are affected by the particular factors which drive change within their particular industry. This leads to firms adopting different global strategies, from those that are very similar from country to country to those that are substantially different in each country in which the firm operates.

In this chapter the alternative strategic approaches are discussed along with the factors that drive strategic choice. In doing this it is necessary to consider, too, the alternative dimensions of the concept of globalisation. This discussion is then followed by an examination of the strategy implementation issues which MNEs might face in building their global presence, with particular emphasis being placed upon global branding.

Alternative views of globalisation

Globalisation and MNE activity are often considered to be one and the same thing and the public tends to think of global companies dominating international business, influencing the economy of every country and moving their factories from country to country according to which offers the lowest wage rates, with no thought either for those who lose their jobs or the well-being of those who are paid extremely low wages. In practice few companies, even those with the most familiar brand names are truly global as Table 7.1 shows.

Taking an average of these measures provides a picture of what are perhaps the best examples of transnationality (Table 7.2). It is significantly different from Table 7.1.

There is no doubt, however, that the world's largest firms are seeking a worldwide presence and driving this acceleration of global MNE activity appears to be increased competition which Sjobolom (1998) suggests is being brought about by four forces: changes in consumer expectations; technological change; deregulation; and regional forces. An example of how this has affected the telecommunications sector is shown in Illustration 7.1.

In seeking to compete successfully in increasingly globalised markets multinational enterprises realise that a precondition of long-term growth is a worldwide presence.

Table 7.1 The top 15 transnational companies by foreign assets 1995

Company	Industry	Foreign assets as % of total	Foreign sales as % of total	Foreign employment as % of total
Royal Dutch/Shell	Energy	67.8	73.3	77.9
Ford	Automobiles	29.0	30.6	29.8
General Electric	Electronics	30.4	24.4	32.4
Exxon	Energy	73.1	79.6	53.7
General Motors	Automotive	24.9	29.2	33.9
Volkswagen	Automotive	84.8	60.8	44.4
IBM	Computers	51.9	62.7	50.1
Toyota	Automotive	30.5	45.1	23.0
Nestle	Food	86.9	98.2	97.0
Bayer	Chemicals	89.8	63.3	54.6
ABB	Electrical equipment	84.7	87.2	93.9
Nissan	Automotive	42.7	44.2	43.5
Elf Aquitaine	Energy	54.5	65.4	47.5
Mobil	Energy	61.8	65.9	52.2
Daimler Benz	Automotive	39.2	63.2	22.2

Source: 'At a location near you' (1997) *The Economist*, 22 November

Table 7.2 Transnational companies

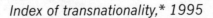

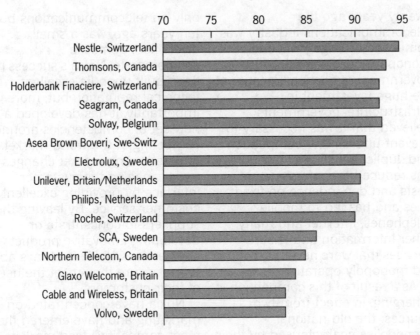

*The average of foreign to total assets, foreign to total sales and foreign to total employment.

Source: UNCTAD (1997) adapted from *The Economist*, 27 September

Over the last two decades a number of writers such as Levitt and Kotler have debated whether or not this will result in globally standardised products and services.

So far, the only examples of product and service offers which have been completely standardised across the world are probably those sold over the Internet. Some of the most widely available products which might be considered to be standardised in fact are substantially adapted with, for example, different recipes (Coca-Cola), menus (McDonald's) and different language options in their service manuals (IBM and Microsoft). The concept of globalisation, therefore, is often characterised by contradictions, such as the need to standardise some elements of the marketing mix whilst, at the same time, accepting the need to respond to local

Illustration 7.1: Competition in the telecommunications industry

Twenty years ago the telecommunications industry was composed of largely national monopolies protected by government regulation. Because of the huge investment in infrastructure, governments believed that it was necessary to prevent undesirable competition and duplication. Digital technology has reduced the infrastructure costs and dependence on fixed lines and has led to mobile telephones, Internet and many other information and leisure services that were never part of the old monopoly operations.

As a result of this competition is emerging, in effect from two sources: the old national monopolies characterised by their high cost structures and poor marketing and the new companies, typically with lower cost structures and excellent marketing skills. The fastest growing companies are those that are focusing upon the new services, such as Nokia, now in the top ten suppliers, who concentrate only on telecommunications but, ten years ago, was a small, diversified, domestic conglomerate. Nokia's success has been built upon its excellent technical reputation but, more importantly, it has developed a new set of competencies around competing in the world market, understanding market changes and managing the customer interface by providing excellent customer service. By leaving their suppliers to concentrate on developing innovative products and services Nokia is always able to make sure they meet the needs of their customers.

Nokia have concentrated on marketing and have entered the most competitive lead markets in Asia and the UK in order to gain a better understanding of the rapidly changing consumer wants and needs.

Source: dapted from Sjobolom, L. (1998) 'Success lies one step ahead of the consumer', *Mastering Global Business, Financial Times*, 6 February

needs and tastes. The true nature of globalisation is encapsulated in the phrase 'think global, act local' in which there is an acknowledgement of the need to balance standardisation and adaptation according to the particular situation.

Against this background the word globalisation is associated in a very imprecise way with many different aspects of the international marketing strategy process. The term 'globalisation' is frequently used by writers in association with:

- market access
- market opportunities
- industry standards
- sourcing
- products and services
- technology
- customer requirements
- competition
- cooperation
- distribution
- communication
- the company's strategy, business programmes and processes.

Globalisation of market access has increased as the number of inaccessible markets has reduced following the political changes that have opened up markets, for example, in central and eastern Europe and China to much greater MNE involvement. Whilst these 'new' markets have become more accessible, firms entering them usually face more difficult problems in viably establishing their global products there because of not only the differences in social and business culture but also, the lack of an infrastructure, legal framework and standards of business practice. As a result many global firms have felt unwilling or unable to 'go it alone' in these markets which are unsophisticated by developed country standards and have found it necessary to form partnerships with local firms or individuals in order to exploit the new opportunities.

Market access is also being improved by the increasing regionalisation, resulting from the growth of trading blocs. Firms are reinforcing this effect by helping to reduce inter-country barriers and thus improve market access by operating more standardised pan-regional marketing programmes and processes such as product development and advertising.

Globalisation of market opportunities has increased with the continued deregulation of certain sectors, such as financial services, where the traditional barriers between the various parts of an industry, such as banking, insurance, pensions, specialist savings and house loan suppliers are being broken down. This has resulted in mergers of specialist firms to form larger and more powerful groups which can offer a complete range of products or services to their customers in the sector. For such MNEs, the power base may be a large domestic or regional market, as is the case for Citigroup (Illustration 9.1) where both companies were from the US. As will be discussed later in this chapter MNEs from different countries, for example, Mercedes Benz (Germany) and Chrysler (USA) merged to create more comprehensive product ranges in their industry sector.

The largest and most powerful firms from one sector are now aggressively attacking other sectors, for example General Motors is offering credit cards and supermarket groups now routinely offer petrol, banking, pensions and savings plans. The privatisation of government owned utilities, such as electricity, gas and telephone is leading to industry restructuring where previously there were monopolies with tight operating restrictions. This is allowing firms to compete in geographic areas and industry sectors from which they have previously been excluded.

Globalisation of industry standards is increasing as technical operating standards, professional rules and guidelines are being adopted more widely primarily due to harmonisation regulations within trading blocks, but more generally around the world as a result of the increased mobility of experts and advisers, and the wider use of quality standards, such as ISO 9000. Despite this there is a long way to go. For example, fifteen adapters are needed to enable a portable computer to be plugged in locally throughout Europe. It is becoming a precondition of supplying major customers that firms operate to certain product and service standards that can be recognised regionally and globally. In addition, the largest MNEs are expected too, to work to ethical standards which cover such diverse areas as employment, environmental protection and unfair competition. As a result, MNEs demand that their staff work to exacting company standards. Professional staff are usually also regulated by country bodies but regional harmonisation is affecting standards of behaviour here too.

Globalisation of sourcing as companies search the world for the best and cheapest materials, components and services rather than rely on local suppliers. The benefits of global sourcing include:

- **Cheaper labour rates**. Fashion and clothing manufacturers obtain supplies from low labour rate countries such as China, Indonesia, Costa Rica, other parts of the Pacific Rim and Latin America. There can, however, be a problem of product quality as purchasers resort to 'island hopping' to the new lower labour rate areas resulting from changes in local country economic development.

- **Better or more uniform quality**. Certain countries and companies have competitive advantage as suppliers over others because of the local availability of materials and skills.

- **Better access to the best technology, innovation and ideas**. Firms search the world to identify a particular research or design centre which might offer the specialist expertise they require. For example, Yip (1996), explains that Kodak, IBM and Hewlett Packard have research facilities in Japan and Nissan and Mazda have design facilities in California. Microsoft have established research facilities close to Cambridge University in the UK.

- **Access to local markets**. Developing stronger links with a country through sourcing can help to generate new business in that country. For example, the aircraft maker Boeing has been able to open up the market in China following its decision to purchase components there.

- **Economies of scale advantages**. Where the location of a manufacturing or distribution operation is convenient to supply a whole region it can lead to significant cost advantages.

- **Lower taxes and duties**. Certain countries may offer tax advantages to manufacturers and low rates of duty when shipping goods to the customer. Caterpillar and Komatsu have located some of their higher added value activities to enable them to spread currency risk.

- **Potentially lower logistics costs**. Global transport and warehousing companies use IT more effectively to control product movement and inventory.

- **More consistent supply**. Some foods would be restricted because of seasonality if steps had not been taken to arrange supplies from countries with different growing seasons.

The major risks in global sourcing are in dealing with countries where there might be political, economic and exchange rate risks. There is also a risk of the supplier using its knowledge and power which results from a strong position in the supply chain to become a competitor. An example of this is shown in Illustration 7.2. What is crucial is that the MNE customer retains the source of competitive advantage and does not outsource to the point where it gives away all its secrets or power in the market. This potential danger needs to be managed by purchasers improving their supplier–purchaser relationships or, perhaps, even

---

Illustration 7.2: Component maker power

The problem with outsourcing of supplies is that eventually the component makers can become a new power in their own right. The strength of the car component makers comes from a wave of consolidations leaving three or four makers of parts, such as brakes, transmissions and suspensions selling to about fifteen worldwide car makers. Suppliers already do three quarters of the engineering for Toyota and Nissan and account for four fifths of the added value. As European and US firms follow this trend it is hardly surprising that the car makers are having to look for profits from distribution, service, leasing, finance and insurance.

Despite the overcapacity in the car industry the component makers have already moved into niche car assembly and could ultimately produce own label products for supermarkets to sell. Finnish parts maker Valmet has started assembling the new Porsche Boxter sports car, Ladas and some Saabs. Steyr Daimler Puch a manufacturer of transmissions in Austria has been assembling Chrysler Jeeps and Voyager minivans and Mercedes off-road vehicle.

Source: adapted from 'Newcomers change the rules', *The Economist* (1998) 21 March

---

forming longer-term strategic alliances. The additional benefit of better supplier–purchaser relationships can be improved communications and the avoidance of some unnecessary supply chain costs resulting from inadequate specifications, misunderstandings about quality and generally poor management.

Using strategic alliances in the supply strategy usually results in a reduction of suppliers and frequently leads to component makers becoming multi-national. For example, Xerox has reduced its suppliers from about 5000 to 400 and its lamps for photocopiers are sourced from a single MNE with plants in Europe, Asia and the US.

Globalisation of core products and services. More and more products are reaching the mature phase of their product life cycle and this is leading to greater commoditisation of products and services. Consumers are able to see very little difference between the offering of many competing suppliers. Also taking into account the increased speed at which new innovations can be copied by other competitors means that core benefits can no longer be a point of differentiation between competitors. MNEs are responding to this and gaining competitive advantage over local competition by differentiating their products through such things as the brand image, higher levels of service, or better technical support.

Globalisation of technology. Technology is converging in and between industries with similar processes and ideas being used, for example, in telecommunications, information technology hardware and software, entertainment and consumer electronics, so that new products and services cross the traditional boundaries between the industry sectors. New technologies are adopted around the world at ever greater speeds and in many industries this is being driven by a small number of global players that have the market power to change the ways of working and sufficient demand from customers to make wider application of the ideas more cost effective. In this way the globalisation of technology is contributing very significantly to the competitive advantage of the MNEs, who are able to market it in a number of industry sectors because they have developed effective distribution channels and international promotion.

Globalisation of customer requirements is resulting from the identification of worldwide customer segments, such as teenagers with similar worldwide tastes in music, fashion and 'junk' food, and managers, who travel extensively meeting their counterparts in other parts of the world and share common expectations of products and services. Equally, with industries becoming more globalised, the demands placed on the business support services such as advertising agencies, accountants, law firms and consultants, is converging too. Customers in both the consumer and business-to-business markets are demanding and getting what they perceive to be better value products and services which better meet their changing needs than those they have been used to receiving from national companies.

Globalisation of competition between industry giants tends to result in the same fight being replicated in each corner of the world with MNEs using largely similar competing product or service offers. Traditional national oligopolies are being outmanoeuvred by aggressive fast growing international competitors who are far better at exploiting technical changes and other globalisation effects. They are also able to cross subsidise their activities in different countries, so helping to make the markets more interdependent.

Mature industries, as well as new technology sectors, are being affected by global competition. For example, whilst the majority of the top ten chemical companies are European, there is increasing competition particularly from Asian companies, which have different cost structures and systems of industry regulation. Success in these industries has traditionally been dependent upon the product portfolio, the customer base and the levels of technical service and support provided, but increasingly the fact that these are components in the supply chain of consumer products means that to succeed suppliers must carry out more effective marketing to members of the supply chain that are closer to the customer.

Globalisation of cooperation. To compete in all the major world markets it is necessary to make available huge financial resources often outside the scope of individual firms. This is leading to the formation of alliances between major MNEs, members of a supply chain, or between firms with complementary activities. The Japanese '*keiretsu*' go further in that they are formal organisations between banks, manufacturers and trading companies with cross-share ownership and have the huge resources necessary to build businesses in the major world markets. They have been prepared and able to make losses over a number of years to establish a dominant long-term market position.

Globalisation of distribution is occurring, first, as the supply chain becomes increasingly concentrated on fewer, more powerful channel distributors, retailers and logistics companies and, second, as technology changes revolutionise the exchange and transfer of data and therefore the whole process of product and service transactions, including methods of product and service selling, ordering, customising, progress chasing, payment arrangement and delivery confirmation.

Globalisation of distribution is particularly important for companies using the Internet for electronic commerce as they must be able to make transaction and logistics arrangements to enable them to provide high levels of service and efficiency to customers wherever they are located.

Globalisation of communication. Major changes in telecommunications and information technology have had two effects. First, global communications, such as satellite and cable TV have made it essential that MNEs develop a consistent worldwide corporate identity and brand image. As consumers travel physically or virtually by way of the media or World Wide Web, they are exposed to communications and advertising from an MNE originating from many parts of the world. Consistency of the communication is vital for reinforcing brand quality and values.

Second, the greatest impact of digital technology is driving both the globalisation and localisation of communications, for example, through local TV channels and through the development of the Internet which goes further than simply improving the accessibility of the traditional one-way communications with customers by adding a two-way dimension to the firms' relationships with their global customers. When IT is coupled with telecommunications, firms are able to customise their product and service offerings to the individual requirements of customers, no matter where in the world they are situated by effectively changing the marketing mix elements, for example, personalising the promotional communications. The interactive nature of the new technologies provides the mechanism to offer complete exchange transactions for products and services globally, allowing customers to order and purchase products on-line.

Globalisation of the company's strategy, business programmes and processes. The result of these globalisation effects is to pose challenges to firms to achieve both improved global operational efficiency and greater global market effectiveness. The global firm's response to managing the complexity of international marketing must include developing an all embracing global strategy supported by effective marketing programmes and processes that will integrate the various disparate activities of the firm's far flung strategic business units.

In considering each of these areas of globalisation in turn it is possible to identify business sector examples in which the globalisation trend is relatively advanced and others in which it is at early stages. For example, until the late 1990s retailing could be regarded as a largely national or, at most, sub-regional activity with few examples of retailers active in more than five or six countries. The challenge for global companies is to lead the development towards globalisation in industry sectors where there is the greatest potential for growth. However, there is no guarantee that by simply being globally active in an industry sector a firm will benefit. Firms must be able to manage the environmental threats and exploit their market opportunities by building global competitive advantage. Even Pepsi Cola failed in its growth objectives in the early 1990s, losing as a result over $0.5 billion from its international operations.

Alternative strategic responses

It is against the background of the trend towards globalisation and the need to build a worldwide presence that firms must develop strategic responses which are appropriate to their situation and are feasible to implement. For MNEs, the question may be how to rationalise their activities to gain greater focus and effectiveness. For firms that have progressed through the early stages of expansion into new country markets, as we discussed in the previous chapter, the next stage is to decide whether or not to progress further and, if so, what strategy they might adopt to enable them to manage their involvement in many countries. Underpinning the growth strategy in either case must be some fundamental

> ## Illustration 7.3: Battered Pepsi licks its wounds
>
> In 1997 Pepsi Cola decided to close down its operations in South Africa. This seemed to draw to an end Pepsi's attempts to challenge Coca-Cola's domination of the international markets at least for the moment. In the US Pepsi was competing well and had a strong share of the market at 31 per cent against Coca-Cola's 43 per cent. Pepsi's parent company had decided to demerge Pizza Hut, Taco Bell and its KFC restaurant division in order to give more focus for the Pepsi operation.
>
> Its international division, however, had lost $500 million as a result of closing down a number of operations. In South Africa it had less than 5 per cent of the market share compared with Coca-Cola's 81 per cent. Its revenues did not even cover its investment. Its strategy of attacking markets where Coca-Cola is dominant seemed to have failed. Adding to the problems were that Pepsi's largest bottler Baesa of Argentina had financial problems and the Venezuelan bottler had defected to Coca-Cola.
>
> Pepsi decided to pull back from markets where they had no chance in favour of using their resources where they could compete aggressively, for example, in India, China, eastern Europe and the Middle East. To stand any chance of developing a viable country operation and, therefore, an effective international strategy, they decided it was essential to attack markets in which they had sufficient market share compared to Coca-Cola that would give them the economies of scale and revenue generation to support the necessary promotion and distribution to compete effectively.
>
> *Source*: adapted from Tomkins, R. (1997) 'Battered PepsiCo licks its wounds', *Financial Times*, 30 May

decisions about, first, how far the firm's marketing activities can and should be standardised and, second, how the firm will develop its product portfolio and geographic coverage.

The level of geographic development and product strength will determine the strategic options available to a company. Gogel and Larreche (1989) argue that the greater competitive threats of global competition will place higher pressures on the effective use of resources. The two main axes for allocating strategic resources are the development of product strength and of geographic coverage. These two axes have to be managed in a balanced way. Focusing too much

Figure 7.1 The international competitive posture mix

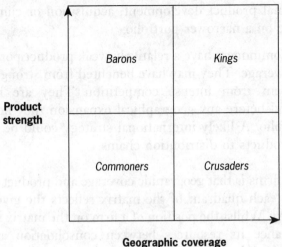

Source: Gogel and Larreche (1989)

attention on product investments at the expense of geographic coverage may result in missed international opportunities. On the other hand, focusing on geographic expansion may result in under investments in products, weakening the competitive position of the firm.

Gogel and Larreche identify four types of competitors along the two dimensions of product range and geographic coverage as displayed in Figure 7.1. The position of a company on the international competitive posture matrix will determine the strategic options.

Kings. These are firms with a wide geographic coverage and strong product portfolio, thus they are in a strong competitive position. They have been able to expand geographically and have not dispersed their resources into weak products. They are in the best position to have an effective global strategy.

Barons. These companies have strong products in a limited number of countries. This makes geographic expansion attractive to them. It also makes them attractive to companies wishing to supplement their own product strength and therefore may be takeover targets.

Crusaders. These have been driven to expand geographically, but they lack strong products. They are vulnerable to an increasing level of global competition. Their challenge is to consolidate their product position which involves internal product development, acquisition or eliminating products to concentrate on a narrower portfolio.

Commoners. Commoners have a relatively weak product portfolio and narrow geographic coverage. They may have benefited from strong mobility barriers protecting them from intense competition They are likely acquisition candidates, and before any geographical expansion they need to build their product portfolio. A likely international strategy could be one of supplying own-brand products to distribution chains.

The key issue for firms is that geographic coverage and product strength compete for resources and each quadrant of the matrix reflects the given trade-offs that have been necessary. Whilst the position of a firm on the matrix reflects how it has been able to balance its resources between consolidation and expansion of geographic coverage and product strength, the decision it has made will have also been based on its chosen attitude and commitment to achieving a global strategy.

The options for strategic development are shown in Figure 7.2.

The challenge facing firms with aspirations to become truly effective global players appears to be turning global presence into global competitive advantage.

Figure 7.2 Alternative worldwide strategies

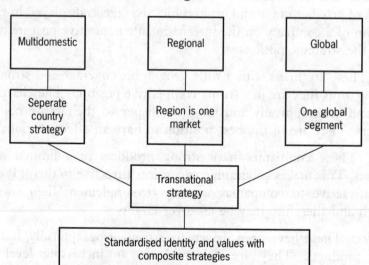

The critical success factor in achieving this is to offer added value for global customers by providing them with benefits which are significantly better than those provided by the competitors, particularly local competitors. At the same time they must aggressively seek cost efficiencies which will enable the firm to offer better value for money than their competitors.

In practice, firms manage this dilemma using strategies which are appropriate to their own situation, and which include different degrees of standardisation or adaptation of the various elements of international marketing.

In general:

- Marketing objectives and strategies are more readily standardised than operational marketing decisions.

- Within the marketing mix, products are most easily standardised, promotion less so and distribution and pricing with difficulty.

- The more operational the decision the more likely it is to be differentiated.

Consequently the elements of marketing management should be seen as being at different points of a continuum of standardisation, where the product and service image is generally easier to standardise than pricing.

Pricing	Differentiation
Distribution	
Sales Force	
Sales Promotion	
Product	
Image	
Objective Strategy	Standardisation

The standardisation/adaptation discussion leads, at one extreme, to the concept of a multi-domestic approach in which the firm has a completely different strategy for every single market and, at the other extreme, a global approach in which everything in the marketing activity is standardised in all countries. In practice firms adopt a combination of standardisation and adaptation of the various elements of the marketing management programmes and processes by globalising some elements and localising others. In broad terms it is possible to categorise a firm's strategic development as multi-domestic, global or regional, a third alternative strategy in which separate, but largely standardised marketing strategies are implemented in different regions of the world.

The largest, most complex companies in the world use a combination of all these strategies. A transnational approach is one in which the firm has a standardised identity and corporate values throughout the firm but delivers its strategic objectives through composite strategies which contain elements of multi-domestic, regional and global strategies.

Global strategy

A company adopting a global strategic orientation makes no distinction between domestic and foreign market opportunities, seeking to serve an essentially identical market appearing in many countries around the world and to develop global strategies to compete with other global competitors. Global marketing can be defined as the focusing of an organisation's resources on the selection and exploitation of global market opportunities consistent with and supportive of its short-term strategic objectives and goals (Toyne and Walters 1989).

Global marketing is the realisation that a firm's foreign marketing activities, in whatever form they take, need to be supportive of some higher objective than just the immediate exploitation of a foreign market opportunity. Other writers have defined global marketing as the selection of a country for its potential contribution to globalisation benefits, even entering an unattractive market which has global strategic significance – for example, the home market of a competitor. Thus an organisation with such a global focus formulates a long-term strategy for the company as a whole and then coordinates the strategies of local subsidiaries to support this.

Many writers, over the last decade have offered views on this issue. For example, Levitt (1983) suggested that in order to be competitive in the world market, firms should shift their emphasis from local customised products to globally standardised products that are advanced, functional, reliable and low priced. Buzzell (1968) argued that product standardisation has the benefits of (a) economies of scale, (b) faster accumulation of learning experience and (c) reduced costs of design modification. Kotabe (1990) concluded that European and Japanese firms which market standardised products have higher levels of product and process innovations and thus the source of competitive advantage than those using product adaptation.

In summarising the forces at work in the standardisation debate Meffet and Bolz (1993) describe the globalisation push and pull factors, shown in Figure 7.3, which are driving marketing standardisation, in terms of both the marketing programmes, such as the product portfolio and the promotion strategy and the marketing processes, for example, how the marketing information system and the planning process can be integrated around the world.

In considering this model, it is important to recognise that the global business environment has changed considerably with many barriers to standardisation being removed or reduced, as has been discussed earlier in this chapter and some of the globalisation effects, such as economies of scale, the experience effect and the high costs of innovation becoming more significant drivers of standardisation.

In practice, however, global firms strike an appropriate balance between the relative advantages of standardisation and adaptation to local tastes. There is little point in standardising programmes for marketing products and services if consumers reject them and only buy the local products and services they are familiar with.

Figure 7.3 Globalisation push and pull factors

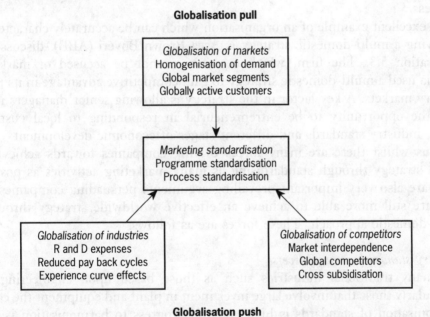

Globalisation pull

Globalisation of markets
Homogenisation of demand
Global market segments
Globally active customers

Marketing standardisation
Programme standardisation
Process standardisation

Globalisation of industries
R and D expenses
Reduced pay back cycles
Experience curve effects

Globalisation of competitors
Market interdependence
Global competitors
Cross subsidisation

Globalisation push

Source: Meffet and Bolz (1993) in Hallibuton and Hunerberg (eds) *European Marketing Readings and Cases,* Addison Wesley

Multi-domestic strategies

The multi-domestic or multi-national market concept focuses on maximising the company's effectiveness and efficiency in exploiting economies of scale, experience and skill in marketing, production and logistics. A company adopting such an orientation assumes that foreign market opportunities are as important as home market opportunities. However, the company takes the view that the differences between its international markets are so acute that adaptation to meet market needs is necessary to retain competitive leverage in local markets. Thus the company essentially follows a differentiated marketing strategy with different marketing mixes in many of their world markets.

Whilst there has been considerable debate amongst writers during the 1980s about the pros and cons of multi-domestic strategies to achieve a worldwide competitive advantage as opposed to the pursuance of a global strategy through the standardisation of marketing activities, it is quite clear that for many major businesses there are few benefits to be obtained from widespread standardisation of their activities and that a well organised and managed multi-domestic strategy is an effective method for the majority of companies for developing a global business.

An excellent example of an organisation which can be accurately characterised as having a multi-domestic strategy is Asea Brown Boveri (ABB), discussed in Illustration 5.3. The firm, which certainly cannot be accused of marketing myopia used a multi-domestic strategy to gain competitive advantage in its target country markets. A key factor in the strategy is allowing senior managers in the firm the opportunity to be entrepreneurial in responding to local customer needs, industry standards and different stages of economic development.

Thus whilst there are many forces driving companies towards achieving a global strategy through standardising as many marketing activities as possible, there are also very important prevailing arguments persuading companies that they are still more able to achieve an effective worldwide strategy through a multi-domestic approach. These forces are as follows.

Industry standards remain diverse

For many traditional industries such as those based upon engineering and particularly those that involve large investment in plant and equipment the cost of harmonisation of standards is high and the progress to harmonisation is slow. The markets for these industries often involve a country's infrastructure, transport and utilities and, consequently, depend on often protracted government spending decisions. Usually in making decision such as these governments will give consideration not simply to market factors, but also the impact on the economy, environment and the electorate's expectations too.

Customers continue to demand locally differentiate products
Cultural heritage and traditions still play a strong role in areas, such as food, drink and shopping. Whilst there are increasing moves to accept cross-border products, there is still resistance in many cultures.

Being an insider remains critically important
The perceived country of origin of goods still has a bearing on take up of products and so local manufacturing of goods is frequently necessary to overcome this scepticism. In business-to-business marketing, there is a definite bias in favour of products sourced from particular areas, such as Silicon Valley in the US and so IT/electronic firms often decide to set up local manufacture there.

Global organisations are difficult to manage
In finding ways to coordinate far flung operations, firms have to decentralise and replace home country loyalties with a system of corporate values and loyalties. For some companies this proves to be problematic and, in some cases, totally unacceptable.

Management myopia
Products and product categories are sometimes candidates for global marketing but managers fail to seize the opportunity. Porter (1985) argues that all global industries have developed from a strong home base. Companies must see the potential for changing the competitive nature of the industry in their favour by triggering a shift from multi-domestic to a global strategy. Because there are no guarantees that a business can succeed, the firm must be willing to risk the heavy investment that a global strategy requires. For some, the resources required and the risks involved are simply too great.

Regional strategy

Perhaps one of the most significant developments in global marketing strategy is how firms respond to the rise of the regional trading blocks. All of the richest industrialised nations belong to regional trading groups. Consequently, even in global industries, companies are being pressured to become more regionally focused. For many companies, regionalisation represents a more manageable compromise between endeavouring to achieve global competitive advantage through building a number of differentiated strategies in multiple domestic markets around the world, and building a global strategy that is as standardised as possible.

For those companies located outside the region there can be significant tariff and non-tariff barriers. By shifting operations and decision making to the region, the company is able to use the benefits of insider advantage. This can take some time, however, as the indigenous manufacturers usually get early warning of new government legislation as they tend to be part of government decision making. Public–private sector committees decide on standards, such as car emissions, safety standards and security. The key to developing effective regional strategies must be in deciding what makes the region distinctive and, in what ways, the marketing strategy for one region should be differentiated from the others. It is only relatively recently that Japanese car manufacturers are beginning to recognise the importance of modifying their styling for regional tastes. Nissan has found that even the shape of the head lights can give away the origins of the design.

A number of companies are taking the opportunity from the formation of regional trading blocks to build on existing or form new trading relationships and are including regional objectives and plans as a significant part of their worldwide strategy. For example, over the last two decades a number of US and Pacific Rim companies have targeted Europe for significant development and now many European and US firms have their sights set on China and Latin America as new growth markets.

The prime motivation in the formation of the regional trading blocks is to enable indigenous companies to build the critical mass of activity within the home region necessary to enable them to compete effectively in global markets. Asian companies have proved to be more effective in developing strategic alliances although now there are some embryo alliances of firms in the European Union that participate in a common supply chain, or offer complementary or competitive products. Where the companies come from different countries, political differences do still arise, particularly if national governments are concerned about the retention of jobs in sensitive industries, such as the defence and airline industry. Airbus is one such consortium and another more recent example is a consortia for producing armoured vehicles as shown in Illustration 7.4.

Illustration 7.4: Defence through alliance

The formation of regional strategic alliances can be initiated by a significant opportunity or threat. Two consortia have been formed to bid for a £4 billion contract for 7000 multiple-role armoured vehicles (MRAVSs) for supply to a number of European countries. Production will start in the year 2004. At the present time the industry sector in Europe is very fragmented, with many national suppliers struggling to survive in the face of huge reductions in defence spending. The way ahead appears to be to form joint ventures that are seen to look after the interests of all the countries but this is sometimes difficult. Eurokonsortium, which includes GKN (UK), Kraso Maffei, Rheinmetall and Wegmann (Germany) and Giat (France) has come up with a modular design for manufacture of MRAVs capable of use in six and eight wheel form which should meet the requirements for all the

participating countries. France wants 100 six-wheel vehicles but is thought likely to withdraw from the project if the rival group, Team International, are not given a realistic opportunity to bid. Team International, which includes Vickers and Alvis (UK), Panhard (France) and Henschel (Germany), devised a six-wheel vehicle with a fixed hull in strict accordance with the specification. The Germans, however, want to go ahead quickly and the Eurokonsortium is their preferred bidder but Team International have a lot to lose and claim they should have the opportunity to produce a new bid. Lorenz suggests this will be one of the most decisive battles of recent years for this European industry as, initially, there will be significant winners and losers.

Source: adapted from Lorenz, A. (1998) 'Land war victory beckons for GKN', *Sunday Times*, 22 February

Transnational strategies

If a firm has sufficient power and resources to exploit all the available opportunities on a worldwide basis, with little need to adapt strategies improve or involve partners to any great extent, then a simple strategy can be developed. However, for many multi-nationals with a wide range of products and services, some of which might be suited to global development and others to multi-domestic development, an approach which involves a number of partners in licensing, joint ventures and strategic alliances might be a much more flexible approach to strategic development.

Transnational companies integrate diverse assets, resources and people into operating units around the world. Through flexible management processes and networks, transnational companies aim to build three strategic capabilities:

- Global scale efficiency and competitiveness.

- National level responsibilities and flexibility.

- Cross-market capacity to leverage learning on a worldwide basis.

In such organisations the ownership of the operations becomes less clear in terms of where any particular product was made, what the domestic nationality of the manufacturing or service provider was, or which firms manufacture and market the product and services.

Ghoshal and Bartlett (1992) argue that the aim of transnational companies is to further the firm's global scale efficiency and competitiveness in its totality. This task means the firm needs the ability to recognise market opportunities and risks across national borders. The overall goal is to achieve global competitiveness through a fully integrated strategy and operations. Thus a transnational approach is not a particular strategy, but a strategic perspective that evolves as firms and the markets in which they operate increase in complexity. IBM is a transnational organisation because certain of its marketing, operations and research and development are centralised and standardised whereas other units operate with a substantial degree of independence. It has a strong corporate identity and some of its promotional themes are common throughout the firm. It has also formed strategic alliances with partners in order to carry out certain research and development activities where it is likely to benefit from the participation of partners. In such organisations the implications for strategic development are significant. Any strategy that is to achieve global competitive advantage needs to accommodate any, or all of the following:

- Simple and complex individual product and market policies, which may be independent or interdependent.

- Customer segments which may be specific and unique to a specific market or transnational and valid across borders.

- Working with firms which are customers, suppliers, competitors and partners at the same time, but simultaneously ensuring that the values of the company are maintained within the organisation and demonstrated to the external stakeholders through establishing clear and unambiguous positioning in all markets by the effective use of the marketing mix variables.

- Maintaining and building relationships in the supply chain.

Implementation issues in building a global presence

So far in this chapter we have identified the changing trends in the business environment which are leading to increasing globalisation and the factors which affect the firms' response to this, particularly in the way they standardise or adapt their marketing programmes and processes. We have shown distinct differences in the way global strategies can be developed to meet individual firm situations. Implementing these global strategies, however, poses considerable problems and it is to these that we now turn.

Building a global presence is hugely expensive and many firms see no value in expanding globally if their home country or region offers sufficient growth prospects without marketing their products and services in what they might perceive to be higher risk areas. US companies have a large domestic market and, despite the rapid growth prospects of other regions of the world, their unfamiliarity often makes them unattractive. However, with growth rates four times as high in Asia as in the rest of the world during the 1990s almost all Fortune 500 companies invested heavily in manufacturing in this area.

Asian firms usually take a longer-term view in the way they develop their business because they usually rely on private capital rather than on shareholders who seek short-term gains. This results in a more conservative, cost conscious and more risk averse approach and this suggests that many, although clearly not all Asian firms, will continue to build their business regionally.

This is especially the case as the predicted medium-term growth rates in the Pacific Rim and particularly in China should provide the strong home market for local Asian companies to build rapidly to become powerful regional players with the prospect of expanding worldwide in the twenty-first century. New competitors have made rapid advances, for example China's Legend group is now number three behind IBM and Compaq in the Chinese computer market, P T Indofood from Indonesia has a major share of the massive instant noodle market and China Ocean Shipping has overtaken Maersk in the container shipping market.

For firms wishing to build a truly global presence, there are a number of challenges and these include:

- achieving truly global reach;
- building global appeal and responding to the changing basis of competitive advantage;
- managing the firm's marketing strategy in less developed countries;
- building the global brand;
- customising the standardised product and service offer to individual customer tastes sometimes called 'global one-to-one marketing'; and
- for service firms globalising presents additional and specific implementation challenges.

International marketing strategies to achieve greater global reach

Few firms have the resources to build a strong presence in all the countries in the world. Few others are prepared to wait until they have built the products and services, image and resources through organic growth within the firm. Instead, they use a wide range of growth, market entry and marketing mix strategies to achieve their objectives in global reach and these are discussed in later chapters. Acquisition and mergers are discussed here because they are being used by MNEs to extend global reach much more quickly and achieve effective marketing worldwide as the Illustration 7.5 of the merger between Grand Metropolitan and Guiness shows.

Mergers of equals

In the past, the rationale for acquisitions and mergers has been that a well-managed company should take over a weaker rival marketer of competing or complimentary products in order to achieve higher growth and savings in operating, management and marketing costs. As market entry methods, acquisition or mergers are used to facilitate access to particular markets. In some business sectors, however, there appears to be the view that it is only by operating on a very large scale on a worldwide basis that customers can receive the level and quality of service that they need. This seems obvious in the case of aircraft manufacture where there are essentially only two players, Boeing and Airbus, but less so in other sectors. For example there are not always scale economies in investment banking and accountancy and smaller firms will continue to thrive in these sectors.

In some sectors, however, there has been a number of *mergers of equals* in which firms of similar market power agree to combine, believing that their future

Illustration 7.5: Drinking to a spirited future

The £23.8 million merger between Grand Metropolitan and Guiness created Diageo, the world's largest spirits and wines businesses. Future growth in the spirits market is likely to be dependant either on drinking spirits suddenly being proved to be an essential part of healthy living (which is unlikely) or the consumption of scotch whisky, tequila, vodka and other spirits and wine rising in the fast growing economies of Asia, Latin America and eastern Europe.

Without the healthy living dream, spirit consumption in the mature markets is forecasted to continue to fall, partly because they are seen as luxury products but also because lower alcohol content drinks, such as wine and beer are perceived to be more healthy. Diageo now has a comprehensive portfolio of world class brands with the potential to provide increased scale economies in the mature markets and the resources to develop new markets in a largely fragmented industry. Before the merger the top four firms had only 20 per cent of the global market.

A greater share of the mature market will depend on Diageo dominating the distribution chain by offering a full range of drinks to wholesalers and retailers, establishing strong brand loyalties using promotion budgets which typically total 15 per cent of sales and, perhaps, eliminating some minor brands.

Distribution will determine the winners in emerging markets. Guinness is strongest in Asia, certain parts of Latin America, especially Venezuela, whereas Grand Met are strongest in central Europe and other parts of Latin America, such as Brazil.

Diageo also believes that it must develop new local products for these markets to win over consumers that will not be able to afford brands such as Johnnie Walker and JB whisky, Smirnoff Vodka, Hennesey cognac and Jose Cuervo tequila. Already in India Kelly's Cream Liqueur is produced to encourage consumers to move towards a Bailey's type product.

Source: adapted from Willman, J. (1997) 'Drinking to a spirited future', *Financial Times*, 17 May

success depends upon achieving comprehensive global reach. Table 7.3 shows some of the world's largest mergers.

Cross-border mergers and acquisitions are becoming increasingly common too. Some recent deals are included in Table 7.4.

Table 7.3 Value of the world's biggest mergers

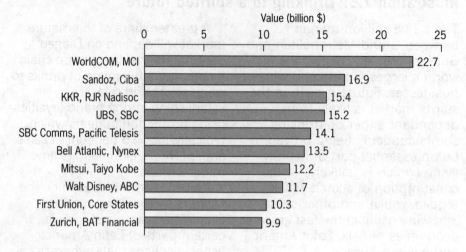

Merger	Value (billion $)
WorldCOM, MCI	22.7
Sandoz, Ciba	16.9
KKR, RJR Nadisoc	15.4
UBS, SBC	15.2
SBC Comms, Pacific Telesis	14.1
Bell Atlantic, Nynex	13.5
Mitsui, Taiyo Kobe	12.2
Walt Disney, ABC	11.7
First Union, Core States	10.3
Zurich, BAT Financial	9.9

Table 7.4 Some recent mergers and acquisitions

Bidder/investor	Target	Sector	Value $
Daimler-Benz (Germany)	Chrysler (USA)	Carmakers	46 bn
Axa-UAP (France)	Royale Belge (Belgium)	Insurance	3.3bn
Cedant (US)	RAC (UK)	Motoring services	743m
Volkswagen (Germany)	Rolls Royce (UK)	Carmakers	710m
Volvo (Swefden)	Unit of Samsung (S Korea)	Heavy equipment	572m

Source: Financial Times, 8 May 1998

The merger between Daimler–Benz and Chrysler has immediately provided a second brand to Mercedes and avoided the need to expand the Mercedes brand into volume products which could result in confused positioning. It also builds upon Mercedes' position as the world's largest makers of trucks. Mercedes has extensive overseas operations especially in Brazil and has opened up its first factory in the US to make its M class sports utility. Chrysler is mainly a US manufacture – its strength is in multi-purpose 'people carriers' and the off-road vehicles under its Jeep brand.

The number of mergers of equals has increased in various business sectors, such the US banking groups Citicorp and Travellers Group discussed in Illustration 9.1 and, in accountancy and consultancy, Coopers and Lybrand and Price Waterhouse.

Such mergers as these clearly lead to oligopolies which are extremely powerful worldwide players but, so far, the regulators have not prevented them from taking place. In the pharmaceutical industry the mergers that have already taken place have been allowed because the regulators have taken the view that the combined research and development resources of worldwide operations might be beneficial in developing new and more effective drugs.

One of the implications of mergers, particularly mergers of equals, is the impact upon branding decisions and whether the merged firm will retain two separate brand identities or whether they will merge them. The decision is taken often against a background of whether the senior management believes the brand is important for their particular company or industry sector. Smith (1998) reports research by McKinsey which suggest that there are three routes to brand consolidation:

- Phasing out over time, when the strategy is to retain loyal customers who will buy as long as it is available.

- Quickly changing which only works well is the firm has control over distribution, advertising and promotion.

- Co-branding to manage the transition, which is the most common approach used for example, when Whirlpool bought Philips domestic appliances.

The pitfalls of mergers and acquisitions

There are serious pitfalls associated with mergers and acquisitions particularly where they involve cross border ownership and cooperation. Finkelstein (1998) refers to a study of 89 US companies acquired by foreign buyers during the period of 1977 and 1990 and found the performance of most of them had not improved within one year. The acquisition of Colombia Pictures by Sony in 1989 is an extreme example of this. Sony's strategy at the time of the acquisition was to develop the ability to market the software of the leisure industry, such as films, videos and CDs to complement their range of hardware, such as TVs, CD players and video recorders. Sony paid a premium for Colombia and left Columbia's established Hollywood executives largely to run their own show, but it was forced to accept a $3.2 billion write down in 1994 after considerable problems had emerged in the way the old management had responded to the new ownership.

As well as the obvious organisational challenges that follow from a merger, such as who will be in charge, whose products and services will be offered (or dropped) and where costs savings should be made, particularly if the merger or acquisition was not entirely harmonious, there are the cross-cultural challenges, such as the different ways of doing business in Europe, the US and Asia. These include issues which have been alluded to earlier in Chapter 5 including different corporate governance, the status and power of different employee and management groups, job security guarantees, government regulations and customer expectations.

Cross-cultural differences are often quite subtle. Upjohn US and Pharmacia merged in 1995 but suffered a number of problems. Upjohn executives scheduled meetings in July when Swedes traditionally take holidays. Their direct, detail oriented style did not fit well with Swedes preference for discussion and a consensus management style. To avoid the fear of domination by one side the new group opened a head office in London but as the two separate parts retained their old corporate offices in the US and Sweden they simply added another layer of management hierarchy.

Finkelstein's (1998) recommend that the integration process should focus on value creation by ensuring employees actually achieve the synergy that is promised before the deal is done; planning in detail how the various cross borders problems will be overcome and developing a clear communication plan to cope with the whole process.

Global appeal and the changing basis of competitive advantage

In the past companies could differentiate their products and services by innovation and developing new core benefits but increasing competition means that this is now only rarely possible. The rapid growth of the Japanese car industry was largely based on value for money criteria, with quality, reliability and performance at a reasonable cost being the basis of the appeal. However, many of their competitors from the emerging economies are now able to offer cheaper and even better value for money cars. Moreover, some of the car makers from the developed countries have substantially improved their quality and reliability and are able to offer designs and brand imagery with better consumer appeal. The focus seems to have moved away from the cheap reliable global car to cars made from global components but with designs and styling which meet the

---

Illustration 7.6: Japanese car makers stall

Of the five major Japanese car makers Toyota, Nissan, Honda, Mitsubishi and Mazda only Toyota and Honda are thriving. Despite reducing their forecasts for the year to the end of March 1998 both will record high net profits. By contrast the others, weakened by declining demand, poor products, bad sales and awful balance sheets, are struggling to survive. Mazda recorded its fifth year of losses and Mitsubishi recorded a loss of Yen 110 billion.

Despite a reduction in sales of Japanese cars from 13.5 million to 11 million cars, Mazda and Toyota have each opened new factories to give a capacity of 14 million in Japan alone.

The weak yen and sales of cars from foreign subsidiaries have helped exports of cars to the US (Honda up 12 per cent and Toyota up 6.5 per cent in 1997) whereas the others experienced a fall in sales. In Europe the problem is also overcapacity with production growing at 4 per cent per annum whilst demand is growing at 1.5 per cent. Toyota and Honda were marginally profitable in Europe whilst Nissan and Mitsubishi were losing money. In Asia car sales have collapsed along with the economies and as most of the firms have a 49 per cent stake in joint ventures, they are under pressure to inject extra equity. Again Toyota and Honda with strong balance sheets have no problem with this but the others, particularly Mitsubishi in Thailand will increasingly find that they are unable to finance a new range of models.

Cost cutting can no longer give the Japanese car makers the edge as their competitors are cutting just as effectively. Mazda is one-third owned by Ford and will increasingly become a niche player and Mitsubishi, owned by the Bank of Tokyo, at the centre of its *keiretsu*, will probably concentrate on trucks and rugged recreational vehicles. Nissan, however, is a global car company with large investments in Europe and the US. It has already closed a factory in Japan and, as a part of the Fuyo group, it has no strong backer and its main bank the Bank of Japan is far from strong.

Source: adapted from 'Japan's car makers stall', *The Economist* (1998) 21 March

requirements of regional customer segments. At a time when some of the Japanese car makers were suffering great competitive pressure, the illustration shows how the problems in the economies of Pacific regional countries have affected the business too.

In the computer industry it is possible to observe similar changes as consumers increasingly expect computer suppliers to offer improved quality and greater reliability as well as becoming more 'user-friendly'. The long-established firms must now offer more intangible benefits, including better styling, higher levels of service support and advice, and more interesting and appealing software.

The implications of appealing to less tangible aspects of service are that these are exactly the elements of the total product offer where there are the greatest cultural differences and the greatest need for adaptations. What constitutes an enjoyable fast-food menu, an attractive car design or more interesting and appealing software is clearly affected by local consumer tastes, values and attitudes. In business-to-business situations whilst the benefits of the product service offer may be standardised it will have to be altered considerably to satisfy local requirements. There is no such thing as a standard power station, advertising agency service or main frame computer.

Global one-to-one marketing

Halliburton (1994) suggests that consumers, too, are increasingly demanding customised solutions for a number of reasons:

- it is no longer possible to classify people into simple and stable segments of customers, now that individuals are part of a complex system of ephemeral tribes;
- it is no longer feasible to consider the individual as a monodimensional customer: now the same person may easily enact a number of lifestyles in a day;
- it is no longer instrumental needs that guide consumption, but 'desires' which are much more difficult to tackle with traditional research;
- the functional and technological attributes of the product or service are balanced by its aesthetics and cultural attributes;
- quality now becomes more subjective, resulting from the object/subject interaction;
- a wide and permanent variety of products is required, rather than old products replacing new ones;
- it is no longer the quest for progress that orientates consumption, but the quest for authenticity.

Figure 7.4 Global one-to-one marketing

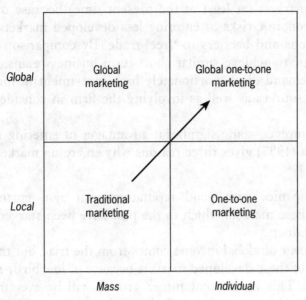

Source: Halliburton, C. W. (1994)

He suggests that the solution is global one-to-one marketing (see Figure 7.4) in which the global marketer appeals to individual people's needs and that the technology is available to do this.

New technology and flexible manufacture allow a new resolution of the variety/cost trade-off due to progress in areas such as:

- just-in-time supply chains
- information and network/system dimensions of lean production
- Computer Aided Design/Computer Aided Manufacture
- computer integrated manufacturing for shorter viable plcs.

This brings rapid changes in product designs and production processes to provide flexibility and fast response to changing market requirements.

Managing the marketing strategy in less developed countries

The implications of pursuing a global strategy are that organisations must continually expand into what are likely to be less attractive markets, perhaps tertiary opportunities from Harrell and Kiefer's model (page 127) or incipient markets in Gilligan and Hird's model (page 120). Typically these will be the less attractive markets (at least at the present time) because of the associated political and economic risks of entering less developed markets, more difficult trading conditions and barriers to 'free' trade. By comparison with the firms' existing markets, to achieve similar short-term business gains, these emerging markets may demand disproportionately high investment in management time and financial resources as well as involving the firm in considerable additional risk.

There are, however, some significant advantages of entering newly emerging markets. Nakata (1997) gives three reasons why emerging markets are becoming attractive:

1 Global companies with good reputations can gain customers relatively quickly in these markets which in the past have been starved of well-known branded products.
2 Eighty per cent of global income comes from the triad but there is increased maturation of these developed markets because of low birth-rates and ageing populations. This means that future growth will be ever more difficult to achieve in developed, operationally less risky markets which are also subject to more intense competition.
3 Typically the average rate of growth of the emerging market economies is much higher than in the industrial nations.

These appear to be exactly the reasons for Kodak's entry into China in Illustration 7.7.

The risks associated with specific emerging country market involvement can be substantial, however, and include some or all of the following:

● financial loss associated with inappropriate investment, such as buying unusable assets, being unable to achieve acceptable levels of performance from the purchased assets, losing the assets by misappropriation to the host country government or to partners;
● damage to the firm's reputation through association with the country, its government and intermediaries, especially where they are seen to be corrupt, engage in unacceptable social or business practices, or have close relation-ships with other countries or organisations which are considered to be corrupt;
● litigation arising from offering an unacceptable product and/or service to the country, or becoming involved in questionable business practices;

Illustration 7.7: Kodak in China: Smile please

In the 1980s Fuji Photo Film developed a strategy attacking the global dominance of Kodak by focusing on the American and European markets. They squeezed Kodak's margins and forced them to cut costs. Kodak's share price went down and there was talk of breaking up the conglomerate. Although Kodak struck back against Fuji in Japan, it has continually lost market share during the 1990s and has been forced to take drastic action.

In 1998 Kodak announced a $1.1 billion deal to take over and modernise three loss-making Chinese film and photographic product companies. The equipment that Kodak has purchased is too old to be of use and so the real value of the purchase is the people, warehouses, distribution system and land. What Kodak has really bought is the entry ticket to a potentially massive market. If Chinese households could be persuaded to double their present film usage from half to a full roll of film each year, Kodak would double its global sales.

The deal which Kodak has arranged gives it considerable competitive advantage. It allows Kodak to avoid the 40 per cent import duty which China applies to film and prevents any other firm, including Fuji, from manufacturing in China for four years. Over the last few years, Kodak have attacked the Chinese market much more aggressively than other markets, offering $2000 financial packages to photoshops that become a Kodak Express on condition they no longer stock rival brands.

Source: adapted from 'Smile Please', *The Economist* (1998) 28 March

- prompting an unexpected international competitor response by attacking a market which it considers to be its home territory;
- initially making arrangements with joint venture partners, distributors, agents or government agencies to secure entry but which become inappropriate in the medium to long term;
- damage to the firm's reputation through insensitivity in its operations in the country, when it might be accused of exploiting local labour, the countries resources or causing environmental damage to the country.

A number of additional dangers in foreign investment are included in Figure 7.5.

Figure 7.5 Unseen dangers in foreign investment

Source: Report by *Export Today* (1997) from Merchant International Group

Entering China and Russia has been particularly problematic and a number of MNEs have had difficulties. Examples are seen in Illustrations 7.7 and 8.6.

Building a global brand

Branding is usually considered within the marketing strategy as part of the product and service policy and we have addressed the use of brands in international marketing there. Global brands, however, are inextricably tied up with achieving a global presence and so we have included a broader based discussion of global branding at this point.

Global brand management

The recession of the early 1990s sparked off the first real challenge to the power of the biggest global brands. Before then, apart from a few exceptions, they had seemed to simply increase their dominant position steadily and consistently over decades. Against the threat of unemployment or reduced incomes, however, many consumers sought to restrict their household spending by becoming more cost conscious. In a number of cases they found that the second or minor brands, and especially supermarket own brands, were often indistinguishable from the premium priced brands in perceived quality and so consumers simply traded down. Marlboro, for example, lost substantial market share in the US to own labels before dramatically cutting prices. As a consequence of this, they suffered profit reductions and turned their attention to less developed countries to make up the shortfall.

Khashani (1995) draws attention to changes in a number of factors which affect the performance of the brands. Customers are better educated, better informed, more sceptical, more willing to experiment, less brand loyal, much more media aware and have higher expectations of the total package. Competition has changed too, with generally higher quality levels. It is more aggressive with more rapid launches of higher quality 'me-too' products.

Retailers have installed better electronic point of sale technology and, as a result, have greater awareness of the performance of brands. In response to better consumer information, they have introduced better quality private labels.

These changes in the brand market environment have been compounded by weaknesses in the management of brands including low investment, inadequate product development, poor consumer communication, an emphasis on quick pay-backs rather than long-term brand building, too little innovation and an emphasis upon small modifications. Khashani criticises brand managers of lazy pricing, insufficient attention to value creation, pricing arrogance, insufficient product differentiation, poor value for money and tolerating high cost bases. He summarises much of the present brand management in terms of complacency and acceptance of a comfortable *status quo*, with little long-term vision, little innovative thinking and insufficient interaction with customers and distributors. Brand management has typically been bureaucratic, risk averse and taken a short-term view. In short he feels that brand managers have lost the killer instinct.

Khashani's solution is to get lean, avoid the temptation to live off past successes, cut costs to improve cost structures and provide a basis for aggressive pricing. He advocates pruning weak brands and reallocating resources, investing and innovating in the product and service and creating more consumer value. It is essential to listen to the market and get closer to customers. He stresses the need to be bold and think creatively setting new market and performance standards and taking risks. The aim must be to think globally, launch products and services sequentially and rapidly across markets and build world brands.

Illustration 7.8 shows how tyre manufacturers are addressing these issues.

Illustration 7.8: Fighting budget brands

The tyre market has traditionally been dominated by high profile and classic brands, including Pirelli, Firestone Michelin and Goodyear. The 1980s were affected seriously by the introduction of budget brands, often introduced by wholesalers and retailers. The early 1990s were difficult for the main brands as they continued to lose share to the low priced competitors and it has prompted a response in four steps: redefine the brand, improve the product, segment the market and cut costs mercilessly.

The main problems was that by the 1980s even budget brands were based on radial tyres, previously the preserve of the premium brands. The main tyre makers had been selling at a loss to the car manufacturers believing that they could make up for this by making profits from increased sales in the retail trade – but this meant they had to increase margins in the retail market. Relatively obscure brands such as Kumho and Hankook of South Korea and east European firms sold at half the price in Europe and quickly built market share. With high fixed overheads and overcapacity and, in 1994, increasing rubber prices, profits disappeared.

Now the major brands are recovering by:

- Redefining brands and products – Pirelli decided to concentrate on the world market for luxury and speed, aiming to have tyres fitted to BMWs and Porsche, increasing sixfold its new products.
- Competing downmarket by introducing second and third tier budget brands such as Michelin with Classic and an agreement with Continental, Goodyear with Kelly-Springfield, Lee and private labels.
- Adapted brand management – Goodyear formed a European division to mange these brands. Continental which used to run nine separate brands now runs them as a portfolio to enable tyres to be matched with market segments.

The tyre makers now claim to have passed on price increases to the car manufacturers and there has been aggressive price cutting – Continental make 25 per cent of its tyres in Portugal and Slovenia compared with, only 1 per cent in 1990, and sales per employee have increased by a third, In two years, Michelin stocks have fallen by 25 per cent as a proportion of sales and Goodyear has cut about 20 000 jobs (20 per cent of its workforce). Michelin's next strategy is the introduction of a new manufacturing process which will considerably improve efficiency.

Source: adapted from 'A bumpy ride' *The Economist* (1996) 17 February

Business-to-business branding

So far the discussion has focused on global consumer branding but branding is important in business-to-business marketing too. The reason for this is that purchasers and users value the commitment of suppliers to the product and service and benefit from the added value from dealing with a firm. For example, buyers talk about suppliers such as IBM or ICI as brands, which lend a sense of authority to the purchasing decision, or users might detail a specific product or service that must be purchased e.g. Hewlett Packard printers.

In some situations there may be benefits which can be gained from association with globally recognised branded components (e.g. Intel microprocessors in computers, Lycra in garments or Teflon for coating materials and cooking utensils). This trend is becoming increasingly important as consumers become more influential in the supply chain and demand products which contain branded components.

In international business-to-business branding firms use different naming strategies with some firms concentrating less on corporate brand endorsement and more on the individual brand in the same way as Procter and Gamble and Unilever do in consumer markets. For example, the product brands Zantac and Tagamet are promoted by Glaxo Welcome and Smith Kline Beecham respectively without any obvious association with the manufacturer.

Ultimately, the rationale for the existence of brands in business-to-business marketing is the same as in consumer goods marketing, to avoid commoditisation of products which leads to decisions being based only on price. As an example of this a study of capital purchasers showed that the success of organisational brands is not price dependent.

Price premiums were paid by purchasers for a number of perceived benefits from globally recognised companies:

- interchangeability of parts
- short delivery time
- working with prestigious suppliers
- full range of spare parts available
- lower operating costs
- lower installation costs
- higher quality materials.

Ethical concerns and brand vulnerability

Of major concern to global brand managers is that their customers' expectations of the standards, quality and integrity of the brand are maintained at all costs and that the MNE owning the brand takes an ethical stance at all times. This can be very difficult when catastrophic accidents occur, such as the Exxon Valdez oil spillage. Following the Zeebrugge ferry disaster Townsend Thoresen stopped using its own name and the company was taken over.

Often it is the mere threat of danger that can be very damaging to the brand. Heinz and Johnson & Johnson have suffered from tampering and contamination by would-be blackmailers and disaffected employees. Sometimes publicity over a trivial factor can be blown out of all proportions. There were suggestions in the US that satanic influences could be seen in Procter and Gamble's corporate logo and claims were made that a new Intel Pentium chip was faulty because it failed to complete a complex mathematical calculation. In fact it was shown that the fault would affect only one commercial user every 2700 years.

The action that companies must take to demonstrate their dedication to achieving quality are very significant indeed. When traces of naturally occurring benzene were detected in Perrier water in Canada in 1990, in quantities which were harmless, the company decided to withdraw all their bottled water worldwide at a cost of $140 million in order to preserve their image of purity.

As soon as ethical issues are raised in respect of the global brand, serious dilemmas arise. The power of ethnocentric brands such as Coca-Cola, McDonald's and Kentucky Fried Chicken is huge in response to their global customer appeal. However, there are suggestions that their success has lead to the imposition of their home country culture in less developed countries, so adversely affecting well-established values and traditions.

In many of these cases global brand managers are not able to resort to adopting a stance based upon what is or is not allowed in law, because this is often seen by stakeholders to be exploiting the inadequate legal system of less developed countries rather than good 'corporate citizenship'. It is against this background that brands must set their own global ethical standards and values.

Service globalisation

Traditionally professional service firms, such as accountants, bankers, insurance, advertising and law firms have developed internationally by following their client firms. The globalisation of some client firms has led to global service contracts, for example, IBM have awarded their advertising contract to Ogilvy and Mather and de Beers to J Walter Thompson. The implications of this are that to win some of the largest contracts it is necessary for service providers to have a truly global presence. This has led to mergers, such as that between Coopers and Lybrand and Price Waterhouse, which are intended to make the best thinking and professional practice experience available to global clients through effective networking.

Matthe and Peras (1994) suggest that for other service providers it is often domestic competition and lack of growth potential which motivates the global development of services. They observe that McDonald's can no longer rely on the US to be the main profit earner and so the number of non-US outlets now considerably exceeds the US outlets with a similar switch in the source of profit generation.

Providing appropriate services depends upon the supplier having a clear understanding of the client's strategy, especially whether they operate a multi-domestic strategy requiring strong independent national offices, a global strategy requiring excellent global coordination or a project by project approach to strategy which requires individual staff members being allocated to contract. Depending on how the client operates, the global service provider must set up the right levels of support services, such as information systems, purchasing and training so that it can cost effectively manage and maintain client relationships.

Mathe and Peras offer a five step process for the global expansion of a service company.

1 Establishing global strategy analysis and design (although they observe that the strategy development of service firms is often reactive).
2 Defining whether the product/service should be transnational or local.
3 Understanding how the firm learns to operate in new markets and globally coordinate the service operations.
4 Expanding reliable international networks and systems for service delivery.
5 Retaining market share and human resources when the products are mature.

Whereas certain service sectors have been successfully gobalised – fast food is the most obvious example – retailing has not. Indeed few retailers had any active international involvement until recently. Consideration of the elements of the McGoldrich and Davies (1995) model in Figure 7.6, which shows the driving forces of internationalisation, goes some way to explaining the reasons for this.

Over the last two decades a number of successful domestic retailers have tried to enter new markets but have had little success. The reason for this may be that

Figure 7.6 Driving forces of internationalisation

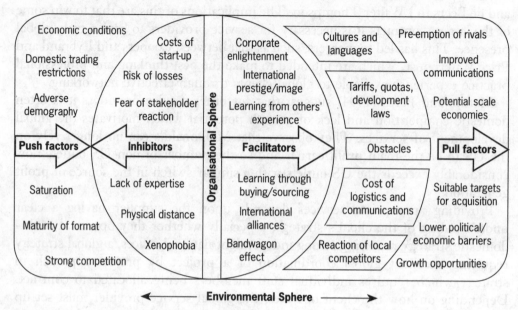

Source: McGoldrich and Davies (1995)

the retail format did not travel well or the firms overestimated the attractiveness of their domestic format to consumers in another market. There are significant problems to face generally in the globalisation of retailing, particularly around the issues of the psychic distance. There are very substantial differences between different cultures both in their frequency of, and attitudes to, shopping, in the product preferences, and their quality standards too. For example, Wal–Mart found that local Brazilian suppliers could not meet their standards for easy to handle packaging and quality control, in China they stocked the wrong merchandise and in Mexico consumers did not find enough US imported products. In some countries the access to suitable locations at an acceptable cost has been limited.

The essential elements of a successful retailing format are attractive stores well recognised for selling distinctive and high quality merchandise and supported by a well-respected brand. To establish a successful format simultaneously in a number of countries, however, can prove to be prohibitively expensive if the facilities are wholly owned. The cost of purchasing land and building suitable stores and undertaking sufficient promotion to establish the brand is likely to limit the rate of expansion of even the most profitable retailer.

It is for these reasons that the use of alternative market entry methods to total ownership, such as franchising and joint ventures has helped to speed up the internationalisation of retailing especially in areas where the foreign country is culturally different or is difficult to enter because of legal controls, for example, local joint venture partners are mandatory in the Philippines.

Ahold has a 50/50 joint venture with Venturtech Investment Corporation in China and is trying to develop its retail brand Tops whilst Otto Versand of Germany are entering China with Shanghai Cheer group, and Japan with the Sumitomo group.

The choice of partner and contract agreement are vital as the objectives of each must be met. The trade-off in the joint venture agreement is that the international partner gets new market access by using the local partner's knowledge and network whilst the local partner gets access to the international retailer's new retail formats, product range and management skills. Often, there are few ideal partners and being the first mover allows the MNE to join up with the best partner. Wal-Mart was able to join up with Cifra the most suitable Mexican retailer but in Brazil, Carrefour from France was able to take first choice.

Joint ventures typically suffer high failure rates. The Mexican joint venture between Auchan, the French hypermarket group and Commercial Mexicana failed in 1997 because of differences in strategy development. Commercial Mexicana retained the hypermarkets that were established and now Auchan will open six hypermarkets by the end of 1998. Wal-Mart and the Thai company Charoen Pokphand had a partnership to enter China and Hong Kong but it broke up after one year because each wanted too much control.

If globalisation of retailing requires an individual retailer to be represented in the majority of the countries in the world then it is likely to be some time before this might be achieved. By using the Internet, virtual global retailing is a much more likely proposition. However, as with other business sectors more innovative international marketing approaches are being used by firms to extend their global reach.

Conclusion

As communications technology improves the speed with which information and knowledge can be accessed and transferred, so the world becomes smaller. This does not mean that we are close to the complete standardisation of marketing strategies, programmes and processes, however. It is for this reason that the word 'globalisation' is used to cover many different issues and firms adopt quite different global strategies.

As a result of this, global firms face a number of challenges which often require solutions which are both innovative and detailed in their response. They must, however, achieve balance in the following areas:

● The desire to globalise but also satisfy local and individual needs.

● The need to compete but also cooperate with other firms.

● The management of the risks of exploiting new market opportunities.

● The need to meet the often conflicting needs of different stakeholders.

● Achievement of balance between cultural empathy, maximising business performance and taking an ethical stance.

● The problems of different perspectives between head office and subsidiary business units.

● The dilemma of organising to optimise product or country market performance.

● The need to lead the business unit with a shared and innovative global vision and yet manage day to day operations cost effectively.

Discussion questions

1 What do you consider to be the definition of globalisation? What forces are driving its development?

2 What are the major differences between a multi-domestic and a global marketing strategy?

3 Identify the reasons why global strategies sometimes fail in their objective to achieve a global marketing advantage.

4 Why is a transnational approach to strategy development important in certain global markets?

5 What are the critical success factors in developing a global brand?

References

Buzzell, R.D. (1968) 'Can you standardise multinational marketing?', *Harvard Business Review*, 46 (6): 101–14.

Davies, R. and Finney, M. (1998) 'Retailers rush to capture new markets', Mastering Global Business Part 7, *Financial Times*, 13 March.

Finkelstein, S. (1998) 'Safe ways to cross the merger minefield', Mastering Global Business Part 4, *Financial Times*, 20 February.

Ghoshal, S. and Bartlett, C.A. (1992) 'What is a Global Manager', *Harvard Business Review*, September–October.

Gogel, R. and Larreche J.C. (1989) 'The battlefield for 1992: Product strength and geograhical coverage', *European Journal of Management*, 17, 289.

Griffith, M.Y. and D.A. (1997) 'Conceptualising the global marketplace: marketing strategy implications', *Marketing Intelligence and Planning*, 15 March.

Halliburton, C.W. (1994) 'Reconciling global marketing and one-to-one marketing – a global individualism response?' *Proceedings of Annual EMAC Conference*, Maastricht.

Khashani, K. (1995) 'A new future for brands', *Financial Times*, 10 November.

Kotabe, M. (1990) 'Corporate Product Policy and Innovative Behaviour of European and Japanese Multinationals: An Empirical Investigation', *Journal of Marketing*, 54: 19–33.

Lemak, D. J. and Arunthanes, W. (1997) 'Global Business strategy: A contingency approach', *Multinational Business Review*, Winter.

Levitt, T. (1983) 'The globalisation of markets', *Harvard Business Review*, May/June.

Lorenz, A. (1998) 'Land war victory beckons for GKN', *Sunday Times*, 22 February.

Matthe and Peras (1994) 'Successful global strategies for service companies', *Long Range Planning*, 27 (1).

McGoldrich, P.J. and Davies, G. (1995) *International Retailing: Trends and Strategies*, Pitman.

Meffet, H. and Bolz, J. (1993) in C. Hallibuton and R. Hunerberg (eds) *European Marketing Readings*, Addison Wesley.

Nakata, C. and Sivakumar, R. (1997) 'Emerging market conditions and their impact on first mover advantages and integrative review', *International Marketing Review*, 14 June.

Porter, M.E. (1985) *Competitive Advantage Creating and Sustaining Superior Performance*, Free Press.

Pyke, D. (1998) 'Strategies for global sourcing', Mastering Global Business, Part 4, *Financial Times*, 20 February.

Sjobolom, L. (1998) 'Success lies one step ahead of the consumer', Mastering Global Management, *Financial Times*, 6 February.

Smith, A. (1998) 'The conundrum of maintaining image', *Financial Times*, 8 May.

The Economist (1998) 'The Japan's car makers stall', 21 March.

The Economist (1998) 'Smile Please', 28 March.

The Economist (1996) 'A bumpy ride', 17 February.

The Economist (1997) 'UNCTAD from the Worldbeater Inc', 22 November.

The Economist (1998) 'Newcomers change the rules', 21 March.

Tomkins, R. (1997) 'Battered PepsiCo licks its wounds', *Financial Times*, 30 May.

Toyne, B. and Walters, P. (1989) *Global Marketing Management: A Strategic Perspective*, Allyn and Bacon.

Willman, J. (1997) 'Drinking to a spirited future', *Financial Times*, 17 May.

Yip, G. (1996) 'Towards a new global strategy', in, I. Doole and R. Lowe, *International Marketing Strategy: Contemporary Readings*, Thomson Business Press.

Chapter 8
Market entry strategies

Introduction

For the majority of the companies, the most significant international marketing decision they are likely to take is how they should enter new markets, as the commitments that they make will affect every aspect of their business for many years ahead. Douglas and Craig (1992) suggest that it signals the firm's intent to key competitors and determines the basis for future battles. Having previously identified potential country, regional and world markets and discussed the development of international marketing strategies, we examine in this chapter, the different market entry options open to firms to enable them to select the most appropriate method for their given situation. For most small and medium-sized businesses, this represents a critical first step, but for established companies, the problem is how to exploit opportunities more effectively within the context of their existing network of international operations and, particularly, how to enter new emerging markets.

There are advantages and disadvantages with each market entry method and critical in the decision-making process are the firm's assessment of the cost and risk associated with each method and the level of involvement the company is allowed by the government, or wishes to have in the market. These factors determine the degree of control which it can exert over the total product and service offer and method of distribution.

There is, however, no ideal market entry strategy and different market entry methods might be adopted by different firms entering the same market and/or by the same firm in different markets.

The alternative market entry methods

The various alternative market entry methods are shown in Figure 8.1, and cover a span of international involvement from virtually zero, when the firm merely makes the products available for others to export but effectively does nothing itself to market its products internationally, to businesses in which only a small proportion of its income is generated in the domestic market.

The market entry decision is taken within the firm and it is determined to a large extent by the firm's objectives and attitudes to international marketing and the confidence in the capability of its managers to operate in foreign countries. In order to select an appropriate and potentially successful market entry method, it is necessary to consider a number of criteria including:

- the company objectives and expectations relating to the size and value of anticipated business;
- the size and financial resources of the company;
- its existing foreign market involvement;
- the skill, abilities and attitudes of the company management towards international marketing;
- the nature and power of the competition with the market;

Figure 8.1 Market entry methods and the levels of involvement in international markets

Levels
of
involvement

Wholly-owned subsidiary
Company acquisition
Assembly operations
Joint venture
Strategic alliance
Licensing
Contract manufacture
Direct marketing
Franchising
Distributors and agents
Sales force
Trading companies
Export management companies
Piggyback operations
Domestic purchasing

- the nature of existing and anticipated tariff and non-tariff barriers;
- the nature of the product itself, particularly any areas of competitive advantage, such as trademark or patent protection; and
- the timing of the move in relation to the market and competitive situation.

This list is not exhaustive as other factors which are very specific to the firm's particular situation might well influence the entry method.

Timing is particularly important in considering entry: emerging markets and the Asian approach of counting time and resources in the expectation of improved trading conditions in the future appears to have paid off as is shown in Illustration 8.1.

Illustration 8.1: Asian first movers

Eastern companies, to a far greater extent than Western companies, recognise the importance of entering new emerging markets at an early stage of development. The rationale for this is the first mover advantage that can be obtained from early entry. They accept that in doing this, mistakes will be made, but they expect to use this experience of customer needs to build a competitive advantage. Competitors who wait to see how others fare before making their move into new markets must select the right entry strategy in order to avoid heavy losses.

Chareon Pokhand (CP) in Bangkok have diversified their business activities from chicken feed, to a range which includes petrochemicals and telecommunications. CP began investing in China in 1970 at a time when it was not seen as an attractive market, but early entry enabled CP to overcome initial difficulties, build expertise and foster long-term relationships with the local authorities before competitors were convinced the environment was stable enough for them to enter.

More recently, Asian firms are again exhibiting a bold approach to investment, focusing on such 'risky' markets as Cambodia and Vietnam.

There is a stark contrast in the attitudes of Western and Eastern managers, with the former assessing the risk associated with every eventuality as opposed to the latter who only tend to consider the probability of surviving the worst case scenario.

Risk and control in market entry

We referred earlier to the fact that one of the most important characteristics of the different market entry methods is the level of involvement of the firm in international operations. The level of involvement has significant implications in terms of levels of control and risk and this is shown diagramatically in Figure 8.2. The cost of resourcing the alternative methods usually equates closely to levels of involvement and risk. The diagram does suggest, however, that associated with higher levels of involvement is not only greater potential for control, but also higher potential risk, usually due to the high cost of investment. Partnerships, in the form of joint ventures and strategic alliances are thought to offer the advantage of achieving higher levels of control at lower levels of risk and cost, provided that there is a higher degree of cooperation between companies and that their individual objectives are not incompatible.

In making a decision on market entry, therefore, the most fundamental questions that the firm must answer are:

- What level of *control* over our international business do we require?

- What level of *risk* are we willing to take?

- What *cost* can we afford to bear?

Figure 8.2 Risk and control in market entry

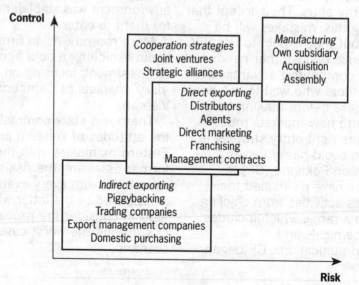

In answering these questions it is important to consider not just the *level* of control, risk and cost, but also the *relative importance* that the firm might place upon the different elements of its marketing activity. For example, lack of control over certain aspects of the marketing process such as after sales servicing may affect the reputation and image of a company or brand because consumers frequently blame the manufacturer rather than a distributor or retailer for the poor quality of after sales service that they have received.

McDonald's decided to franchise its operation in France, but subsequently found that it was difficult to control and standardise the quality of the product offered in the different restaurants. They had no alternative but to take over the franchises and rebuild their damaged image.

Indirect exporting

For firms which have little inclination or few resources for international marketing, the simplest and lowest cost method of market entry is for them to have their products sold overseas by others. The objective of firms which use this method of entry may be to benefit from opportunities which may arise without incurring any expense or simply to sell-off excess capacity into foreign markets with the least possible inconvenience. Firms such as these often withdraw from this activity as soon as their sales into the home market improve. Whilst indirect exporting has the advantage of the least cost and risk of any entry method, it allows the firm little control over how, when, where and by whom the products are sold. In some cases the domestic company may even be unaware that its products are being exported.

There are four main methods of indirect exporting and these are by using:

- domestic purchasing;
- piggyback operations;
- an Export Management Company (EMC) or Export Houses (EH); and
- trading companies.

Domestic purchasing

Some firms or individuals do not realise that their products or services have potential export value until they are approached by the buyer from a foreign organisation, who might make the initial approach, purchase the product at the factory gate and take on the task of exporting, marketing and distributing the product in one or more overseas market. Anita Roddick has used this approach to source naturally occurring ingredients for Body Shop's ranges of toiletries and cosmetics and make domestic purchasing a feature of Body Shop's marketing activity. Taking a moral stance and demonstrating environmental concern, however, can make the firm a target for detractors and suppliers are often difficult to manage.

Whilst for the manufacturer or supplier, domestic purchasing could hardly be called an entry strategy, it does provide the firm with access to and limited knowledge of international markets. However, the supplying organisation is able to exert little control over the choice of markets and the strategies adopted in marketing its products. Small firms find that this is the easiest method of obtaining foreign sales, but being totally dependent on the purchaser, they are unlikely to be aware of a change in consumer behaviour and competitor activity or of the purchasing firm's intention to terminate the arrangement. Ben and Jerry's have taken this approach too in sourcing ingredients for their ice cream from community-based suppliers but they have been criticised when fashions have changed and certain ingredients are no longer popular, leading to supply arrangements being stopped. If a company is intent upon seeking longer-term viability for its export business, it must adapt a more proactive approach which will inevitably involve obtaining a greater understanding of the markets in which their products are sold.

Export management companies (EMCs) or export houses

Export houses or export marketing companies (EMCs) are specialist companies set up to act as the export department for a range of companies. They can help small and medium-sized companies to initiate, develop and maintain their international sales. As well as taking orders from foreign buyers, they provide indirect access to international market information and contacts. By offering ranges of products from various companies they provide a more attractive overall 'sales package' to foreign buyers and by carrying a large range, they can spread selling and administration costs over more products and companies, and reduce transport costs because of the economies of making larger shipments of goods from a number of companies.

EMCs deal with the necessary documentation and their knowledge of local purchasing practices and government regulations are particularly useful in markets which might prove difficult to penetrate. The use of EMCs, therefore, allows individual companies to gain far wider exposure of their products in foreign markets at much lower overall costs than they could achieve on their own, but there are a number of disadvantages too. The export house may specialise by geographical area, product or customer type (retail, industrial or institutional) and this may not coincide with the suppliers' objectives. As a result of this, the *selection of markets may be made on the basis of what is best for the EMC* rather than the manufacturer. As EMCs are paid by commission, they might be tempted to *concentrate upon products with immediate sales potential* rather than those which might require greater customer education and sustained marketing effort to achieve success in the longer term. EMCs may also be tempted to *carry too many product ranges* and as a result the manufacturer's products may not be given the necessary attention from sales people. The EMC may also *carry competitive products* which they may promote preferentially, again to the disadvantage of a particular firm.

Manufacturers should, therefore, take care in selecting a suitable EMC and be prepared to devote resources to managing the relationship and monitoring their performance. The firm must also take the time to learn more about the markets in which their products are being sold in order to ensure that opportunities to sell products into new markets are not being missed by the EMC.

As sales increase, the manufacturer may feel that they could benefit from increased involvement in international markets, by exporting directly themselves. However, the transition may not be very easy. First, the firm is likely to have become very dependant on the export house and unless steps have been taken to build contacts with foreign customers and increase their knowledge of the markets, moving away from using EMCs could prove difficult.

Second, the firm could find it difficult to withdraw from its contractual commitments to the export house. This often happens because when firms are first setting up the arrangement they are unable to predict the kind of relationship they would like to have with the EMC some time in the future. Many agreements, therefore, are based only on the current and short-term situation. Third, the EMC may be able to substitute products from an alternative manufacturer and so use their customer contacts as a basis for introducing new competition against the original manufacturer.

Piggybacking

In piggybacking, an established international distribution network of one manufacturer might be used to carry the products of a second manufacturer. The second manufacturer is able to ride on the back of the existing reputation, contacts and administration of the carrier with little direct investment themselves. Terpstra and Yu (1990) explain that this makes a particularly effective way for firms from developing countries to break into markets in developed countries.

The carrier is either paid by commission and so acts as an agent, or alternatively, buys the product outright and so acts as an independent distributor. There are also advantages of piggybacking for the carrier as they are able to, first, carry a wider product range, and so to present a more attractive sales package to potential buyers and, second, benefit from economies of scale by increasing their revenue without incurring additional costs of marketing, selling administration and distribution.

There can, however, be problems as the terms and conditions of the marketing arrangements are often poorly thought out as, frequently, piggybacking starts on a 'try it and see' basis and so either company might become locked into an arrangement that proves unsatisfactory for them, particularly as a firm's strategic objectives change over a period of time. Decisions about such marketing mix issues as branding might not suit both companies and arrangements for providing technical support and service for products often prove to be a source of disagreement and difficulty.

For smaller firms, piggybacking can work when two products are interdependent, or if the second product provides a service for the first. Larger companies, too, have found it successful, particularly when the rider has experienced some kind of barrier to entering particular markets, or the use of an existing distribution network can provide faster market development.

Trading companies

Trading companies are part of the historical legacy from the colonial days and although different in nature now, they are still important trading forces in Africa and Asia. The United Africa Company, part of Unilever, for example, is claimed to be the largest trader in Africa and the *Sogo Shosha* have traditionally played an important role in Japanese international business although, as Illustration 8.2 shows, different patterns of business activity could result in them becoming less significant in some sectors.

The success of trading companies is the result of building long-term relationships over many years. This is the experience in the US where export trading companies have been permitted only since 1982 and have been slow to get off the ground.

Illustration 8.2: The future of *Sogo Shosha*

In Japan after the war the dominant industrial powers that emerged tended to be the *keiretsu* (industrial groups), which grew out of the pre-war conglomerates, the *zaibatsu* (financial cliques) such as Mitsui, Mitsubishi, Sumimoto and Yasuda. These had evolved from family business empires and government favour and were a key part of the government's expansion abroad. Each *zaibatsu/keiretsu* has its own *Sogo shosha* (trading company) which in the seventeenth century were simple import–export businesses but now have a much wider role, including collecting information. For example, during the Gulf War the Japanese foreign ministry relied on these contacts rather than its own diplomatic sources.

The top five *Sogo Shosha* Mitsubishi, Mitsui, Sumimoto, Itochu and Marabeni had a combined turnover of $720 billion in 1996 but sales are continuing to fall and operating profit margins are only 1.5 per cent. Some estimates suggest that up to 30 per cent of a company's subsidiaries and ventures could be loss-making at any time. Their reputation has also been damaged by the scandal surrounding Sumimoto's $2.6 billion loss as a result of unauthorised copper trading.

The strength of the *Sogo Shosha* has been their ability to take a very long-term view and to reinvent themselves when it has become necessary. They are in such a process at the moment. They have recognised that it is not enough simply to be intermediaries with margins being constantly eroded, and now invest in a whole range of manufacturers, investments and developments of natural resources. Each of the five have around 600 affiliates and joint ventures; investments, equity stakes and related fees now make up nearly 60 per cent of profits.

Most of the *Sogo Shosha* now have venture capital funds. Marubeni, which was originally a textile trader, has expanded into Chinese oil exploration and Burmese steel making, Mitsui is making profits from computer software. Itochu recently helped Japan's Asahi become the biggest brewer in China and is working with Time Warner from the US to build a 2 million household cable network in Japan. The *Soga Shosha* which have grown out of traditional business are particularly focusing on new industries, and their considerable wealth gives them a particular advantage in that it allows them to take greater risks than many of their competitors.

Source: adapted from Bogler, D. (1996) 'Japanese Industry: Survival strategy', *Financial Times*, 5 December

One of the major benefits of using trading houses is that their extensive operations and contacts allow them to operate in more difficult trading areas. One important aspect of their operations is to manage countertrade activities, in which sales into one market are paid for by taking other products from that market in exchange. The essential role of the trading company is to quickly find a buyer for the products that have been taken in exchange.

Indirect exporting is often a small company's first experience of international marketing and has the advantages of being a simple and low-cost method of gaining exposure of products in foreign markets without the company first having to gain the necessary expertise in the various aspects of international trading. However, the company has little control over its international marketing activities and is restricted to simply reacting to new situations and opportunities as they arise. It is extremely difficult to build up international marketing knowledge and expertise by marketing at arms length or to develop any significant long-term product and promotional strategies. Moreover, because of the lack of direct contact between the firm and the market, indirect entry approaches are usually perceived as lacking long-term commitment. As a result, customers and other members of the distribution channels are likely to withhold their full commitment to the firm and its products until the firm becomes more involved in the market, by adopting a more direct approach.

Direct exporting

If a company wishes to secure a more permanent long-term place in international markets, it must become more proactive, through becoming directly involved in the process of exporting. This requires definite commitment from the company and takes the form of investment in the international operation through allocating time and resources to a number of supporting activities. The key components of the export marketing mix are summarised in Figure 8.3.

The benefits of direct over indirect exporting are that the proactive approach makes it easier to exert more influence over international activities resulting in a number of specific advantages for the exporter such as greater control over the selection of markets, greater control over the elements of the marketing mix, improved feedback about the performance of individual products, changing situations in individual markets and competitor activity, and the opportunity to build up expertise in international marketing.

The disadvantages of direct exporting are that the direct investment necessary is considerable because the whole of the marketing, distribution and

Figure 8.3 The components of the export marketing mix

Product:	selection development and sourcing
Pricing:	policy, strategies, discount structures and trading terms
Promotion:	corporate promotions and local selling, trade shows and literature
Distribution:	sales force management, agents, distributors and logistics
Services:	market research, training and sales servicing
Finance and administration:	budgets, order processing, insurance and credit control
Technical:	specifications, testing and product quality

administration costs will now be borne by the company. In taking this decision, the company must be quite sure that the costs can be justified in the light of the market opportunities identified.

There can be significant tariff and non-tariff barriers to exporting including quota systems and additional taxes which are designed to protect domestic manufacturers, as the Illustration 8.3 shows.

For those firms wishing to change from indirect to direct exporting, or to significantly increase their marketing efforts the timing can be critical, as the extra costs involved can often place a huge financial burden on the company. The solution to this is, wherever possible, to make the transition gradually and in a well-planned way.

Mahon and Vachani (1992) analyse the role of establishing beachheads, the first 'landings' in overseas markets, as part of an initial exporting strategy and suggest that companies need to address a series of questions:

- What country or geographic area should be chosen for entry, why and when?

- Should the firm enter the main segment of a given market or a smaller niche?

- By what methods should the beachhead be established?

Establishing a beachhead might take the form of finding a country where there is low psychic distance, of adopting a low profile entry – in retailing, for example, by avoiding main city sites, or in services such as legal, accounting or advertising

Illustration 8.3: Rover seeks to develop the Argentinian market

In the early 1990s Rover Group decided to seek export markets which promised faster growth than the traditional markets in Europe, the US, Japan and Australia. It targeted Asia and Latin America and had an interesting and somewhat surprising success is Argentina, given the animosity following the conflict between Britain and Argentina over the Falklands Islands in 1982.

Rover expected to sell 7500 vehicles in Argentina in 1997, compared to total sales of less than 1500 in 1995, 1500 of which were four wheel drive Land Rovers.

Rover explains that it has succeeded because, first, Argentina still associates British products with quality, second, since 1992 Rover has used a high quality, exclusive importer, Canley SA to do the essential, detailed, local work and, third, Rover has arranged credit insurance for the Argentine business through Trade Indemnity and brokers Sedgwick Group. They regard this as a powerful business tool preferable to letters of credit or bank guarantees, which they regard as expensive and administratively cumbersome. Letters of credit and bank guarantees still need to be used in more risky markets, such as Guatemala, Venezuela and Bolivia.

Argentina, along with Brazil, Paraguay and Uruguay is a member of Mercosur and manages a complex import quota system which severely restricts the sales of products locally manufactured. Rover have been engaged in complex discussions with government officials in order to maximise their volume under the existing quota rules. They recognise that the interpretation of the rules could be different and adversely affect their potential sales volumes in the following year.

Whilst the prospects for growth for four wheel vehicles are attractive in a number of South American countries, such as Columbia, Venezuela and Chile, high car import tariffs or luxury product taxes will continue to make exporting difficult. In response to this a number of car manufacturers are starting to produce in Brazil, the largest market and there is likely soon to be overcapacity in manufacturing. Rover's parent company BMW is already building an engine-making joint venture with Chrysler in Curitaba.

For Rover, Latin America provides a useful contribution to its exporting effort, but perhaps more importantly, it provides useful knowledge about a major potential future growth market.

Source: adapted from Fidler, S. (1997) 'Quality provides the motor', *Financial Times*, 11 December

by merely following existing clients. Komatsu, the Japanese earthmoving equipment manufacturer, for example, initially chose markets for entry where Caterpillar the leading US manufacturer did not have a significant presence. Alternative strategies are to use a specific competitive positioning stance. Ricoh and Nashua offered low price basic products to compete with Xerox in the photocopier market, rather than attack head on. Other firms, however, seek to establish a lead customer, usually a market challenger rather than a leader, in order to test their product before committing themselves to full market presence.

As well as deciding which countries to enter Chryssochoidis (1996) suggests that the selection and subsequent modification of the product portfolio is important and the stages involved in the development of the portfolio are summarised in the adapted model, Figure 8.4.

Factors for success in exporting

A considerable amount of research has been carried out into the barriers and motivations for new exporters and the stages of internationalisation and this was discussed in Chapter 6. Also presented in this chapter were some benchmarks which enable firms to be profiled as being at one of the stages of internationalisation, but Katsikeas *et al.* (1996) explain that the determinants of export performance have not been researched so comprehensively as the barriers, motivations and stages of internationalisation.

In researching Greek exporters, Katsikeas *et al.* concluded that the way exporting performance is assessed is important. The simplest measure is whether firms do or do not export. Measurement of the financial performance of the firm in terms of export sales volume, growth and profitability and the ratio of export to total sales is useful to measure longitudinal firm performance but is less useful for comparing firm performance between industry sectors because the industry sectors may be structured quite differently. Subjective measurements of the performance of the management of the firm are often helpful but pose a problem, too, in their comparability between firms and sectors.

Katsikeas *et al.* did, however, conclude that a number of factors were important in contributing to successful importing:

- commitment of the firms' management
- an exporting approach in the firm which emphasised the importance of augmenting and maintaining skills

Figure 8.4 Initiation and development of export product portfolios

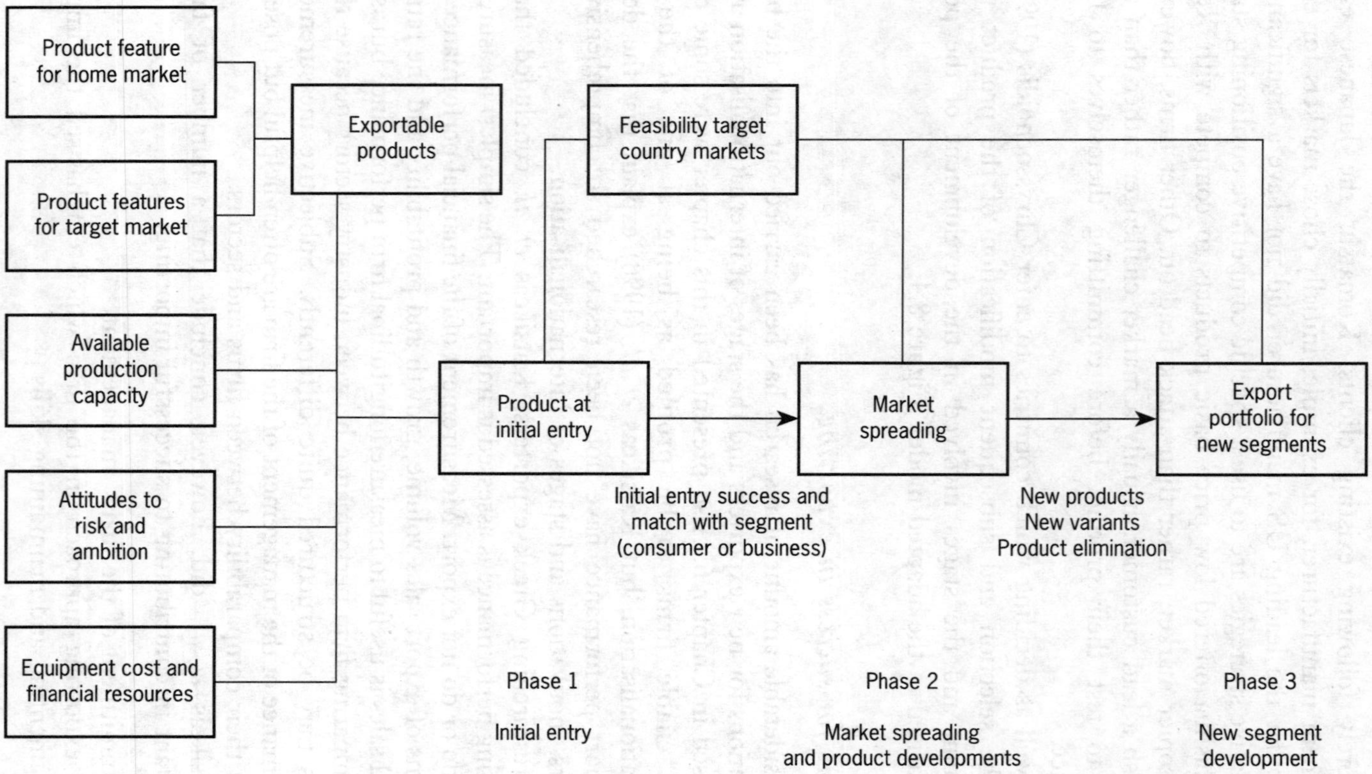
Product feature for home market
Product features for target market
Available production capacity
Attitudes to risk and ambition
Equipment cost and financial resources
Exportable products
Feasibility target country markets
Product at initial entry
Initial entry success and match with segment (consumer or business)
Market spreading
New products
New variants
Product elimination
Export portfolio for new segments
Phase 1
Initial entry
Phase 2
Market spreading and product developments
Phase 3
New segment development

- a good marketing information and communication system
- sufficient production capacity and capability, product superiority and competitive pricing
- effective market research to reduce the psychic distance between the home country and target country market given that it is knowledge that generates business opportunities and drives the international process
- an effective national export policy which provides support at an individual firm level, and emphasises the need for knowledge-based programmes which prioritise market information about foreign market opportunities.

They found that the cost of export planning incurred by the firm did not correlate with export performance and suggested that this might be explained by the fact that a major source of strength in exporting is flexibility and adaptability to export opportunities and the ability to make an immediate strategic response. Moreover, firm size and managers' experience were not critical factors either in export success but they did recognise that these factors may be the source of the export stimuli in the first place, and could be major determinants of the firm's commitment to exporting and its ability to solve problems.

Cavusgil and Naor (1989) concluded that management attitudes and commitment to international expansion are crucial for success. It is generally accepted, therefore, that in small business, attitudes and commitment to international expansion are crucial for success, whereas in larger companies other factors can have a bearing on performance. The size of company can either hinder or encourage international development because of the variations in the capability of the staff for planning, the lack of consistency of information and the degree to which adaptation of the mix is necessary. A number of other factors, such as the types of strategies that are pursued, segmentation, product and pricing can also effect export success.

In most countries or regions, governments actively support export activity through arranging trade missions, seminars and providing information about international markets to stimulate activity particularly amongst smaller businesses. The governments of many developing countries are following the example of Japan and other Asian countries in adopting export promoting strategies. Developing countries, however, find exporting particularly challenging because of the differences in domestic and export market conditions, the adverse competitive positions faced by LDC exporters and the varying motivations for exporting.

Selection of Exporting Method

The choice of the specific individual markets for exporting was discussed in the first section of this book, but it is important to re-emphasise that the more subjective factors, such as a senior executive's existing formal or informal links, particular knowledge of culture or language and specific perceived constraints of markets, may well influence an individual firm's decision.

Once individual markets have been selected and the responsibilities for exporting have been allocated, the decision needs to be taken about precisely how the firm should be represented in the new market. Clearly the nature, size and structure of the market will be significant in determining the method adopted. It may be necessary in a large market, particularly if a high level of market knowledge and customer contact is needed, to have a member of the firm's staff resident in or close to the market, whereas this cannot be justified if the market is small or levels of customer contact need not be so high. Alternatively a home-based sales force may be used to make periodic sales trips in conjunction with follow-up communications by telephone and fax.

Many other factors will affect the cost/benefit analysis of maintaining the company's own staff in foreign markets, such as whether the market is likely to be attractive in the long-term as well as the short-term and whether the high cost of installing a member of the firm's own staff will be offset by the improvements in the quality of contacts, market expertise and communications. The alternative, and usually the first stage in exporting, is to appoint an agent or distributor.

Agents provide the most common form of low cost direct involvement in foreign markets and are independent individuals or firms who are contracted to act on behalf of exporters to obtain orders on a commission basis. They typically represent a number of manufacturers and will handle a number of non-competitive ranges. As part of their contract they would be expected to agree sales targets and contribute substantially to the preparation of forecasts, development of strategies and tactics using their knowledge of the local market.

The selection of suitable agents or distributors can be a problematic process. Moore (1987) has summarised the main factors, and these are identified below. Clearly, the nature of the agreement between the firm and its agent is crucial in ensuring the success of the arrangement, particularly in terms of clarifying what is expected of each party, setting out the basis for the relationships that will be built up and ensuring adequate feedback on the market and product development that is provided.

Sources for finding a suitable agent

- Asking potential customers to suggest a suitable agent.

- Obtaining recommendations from institutions such as trade associations, chambers of commerce and government trade departments.

- Using commercial agencies.

- Using agents for non-competing products.

- Poaching a competitor's agent.

- Advertising in suitable trade papers.

Selection criteria for finding a suitable agent

- The *financial strength* of the agents.

- Their *contacts* with potential customers.

- The nature and extent of *their responsibilities to other organisations*.

- Their *premises, equipment and resources* including sales representatives.

Achieving a satisfactory manufacturer–agent relationship

- Allocate time and resources to finding a suitably qualified agent.

- Ensure that both the manufacturers and agent understand what each expects of the other.

- Ensure that the agent is motivated to improve performance.

- Provide adequate support on a continuing basis including training, joint promotion and developing contacts.

- Ensure that there is sufficient advice and information transfer in both directions.

Distributors

Agents do not take ownership of the goods but work instead on commission, sometimes as low as 2–3 per cent on large volume and orders. This can seriously limit their power and influence on a market. Distributors buy the product from the manufacturer and so take the market risk on unsold products as well as the profit. For this reason, they usually expect to take a higher percentage to cover their costs and risk.

Distributors usually seek exclusive rights for a specific sales territory and generally represent the manufacturer in all aspects of sales and servicing in that area. The exclusivity, therefore, is in return for the substantial capital investment that may be required in handling and selling the products. The capital investment can be particularly high if the product requires special handling equipment or transport and storage equipment in the case of perishable goods, chemicals, materials or components.

The issue of agreeing territories is becoming increasingly important, as in many markets, distributors are becoming fewer in number, larger in size and sometimes more specialised in their activity. The trend to regionalisation is leading distributors increasingly to extend their territories through organic growth, mergers and acquisitions, making it more difficult for firms to appoint different distributors in individual neighbouring markets.

Other direct exporting methods

There are three other modes of exporting which are considered to be direct and these are management contracts, franchising and direct marketing.

Management contracts

Management contracts emphasise the growing importance of services, business skills and management expertise as saleable commodities in international trade. Normally the contracts undertaken are concerned with installing management operating and control systems, and training local staff to take over when the contract is completed. Many construction projects such as the rebuilding of Kuwait following the end of the Gulf War, worth $50 billion, was undertaken in this way.

Other examples of management contracts may be as part of a deal to sell a processing plant as a *turnkey operation*, in which not only is the capital plant supplied, but a management team is also provided by the firm to set up and run the plant for the first few months of operation, and then train the local team to take over. With increased privatisation and outsourcing of facilities management by public and private sector organisations there is a substantial growth in management contracts and in firms providing these services.

Franchising

Franchising is a means of marketing goods and services in which the franchiser grants the legal right to use branding, trademarks and products, and the method of operation is transferred to a third party – the franchisee – in return for a franchise fee. The franchiser provides assistance, training and help with sourcing components, and exercises significant control over the franchisee's method of operation. It is considered to be a relatively less risky business start up for the franchisee but still harnesses the motivation, time and energy of the people who are investing their own capital in the business. For the franchiser it has a number of advantages including the opportunity to build greater market coverage and obtain a steady, predictable stream of income without requiring excessive investment.

Chan (1994) identifies two types of franchise. With product/trade franchises, for example, car dealerships, petrol service stations and soft drinks bottlers, the franchisees are granted the right to distribute a manufacturer's product in a specified territory. Business format franchise is the growing sector and includes many types of businesses including restaurants, convenience stores and hotels. This type of franchise includes the licensing of a trademark and the system for operating the business, and the appearance of the location.

Franchising can take the form of single-unit franchising in which the arrangement is made with a single franchisee or multi-unit in which the franchisee operates more than one unit. The multi-unit franchisee may be given the responsibility for developing a territory and opening a specified number of units alone or, as is common in international markets, operating a master franchise, in which the master franchisee can subfranchise to others. In this case the master franchisee is responsible for collecting the fees, enforcing the agreement and providing the necessary services, such as training and advice.

Franchising has grown rapidly during the late 1980s and 1990s (Welch 1992) due to the strong interest from buyers in a variety of franchise formats. Trading companies have frequently been appointed as master franchisees and, whilst this has helped to accelerate the growth of franchising, it has also influenced the franchiser's internationalisation process. Because of the global power of these trading companies they are able to challenge the franchiser's power in the franchise process and have a considerable say in the strategic development of the business. As competition has increased in franchising so more franchisers, such as Pizza Hut in Australia, have resorted to acquisition of existing chains for conversion to the new franchise.

Welch comments that there is increasing evidence that franchisees, either individually or collectively, are prepared to resort to legal action to control the franchisers' activities when they are considered harmful to their own interests, because they realise that it is not usually in the franchisers' interests to go to court, given the likely adverse publicity. The Arby restaurant chain in the US, Burger King, Benetton the Italian clothing group and Body Shop, the UK toiletries retailer, have all experienced problems with franchisees.

One of the main problems for franchisers is deciding to what extent the franchise format should be modified to take account of local demands and expectations, for example, McDonald's have added spaghetti to the menu to compete more effectively with Jollibee in the Phillipines, Pizza Hut find that corn and not pepperoni sells well in Japan and KFC find that gravy and peas, and pumpkin are popular in Australia.

There are also differences in the way local culture affects franchise operations; for example, Terpstra and Sarathy (1997) explain that Chi-Chi's, a US-based Mexican restaurant operator, faced many problems when they tried to extend their operations into Eastern Europe. They found that there were few entrepreneurs because the current generation had grown up working for the state, were not paid according to performance, and staff were used to treating customers with disdain.

Direct marketing

Direct marketing is concerned with marketing and selling activities which do not depend for success on direct face-to-face contact and include mail order, telephone marketing, television marketing, media marketing, direct mail and electronic commerce using computer networking. There is considerable growth in all these areas largely encouraged by the development of information and communication technology, the changing lifestyles and purchasing behaviour of consumers and the increasing cost of more traditional methods of entering new markets. The critical success factors for direct mail are in the standardisation of the product coupled with the personalisation of the communication. Whilst technical data about the product might be available in one language, often English, the recipients of the direct marketing in international markets expect to receive accurate communications in their domestic language. International direct marketing, therefore, poses considerable challenges, such as the need to build and maintain up to date databases, use sophisticated multilingual data processing and laser personalisation software programs, and develop reliable credit control and secure payment systems.

However, it also offers advantages. Whereas American firms have had trouble breaking into the Japanese market, catalogue firms have been highly successful as they are positioned as good value for money for well-known clothing brands compared to Japanese catalogues which are priced higher for similar quality items.

Direct marketing techniques can also be used to support traditional methods of marketing by providing sales leads, maintaining contact or simply providing improved customer service.

Foreign manufacturing strategies without direct investment

Having so far considered market entry strategies that have been based upon the manufacture and supply of product in the firms' domestic plants, we now turn our attention to strategies which involve production or supply from overseas plants. Before discussing the alternatives available for ownership and control of overseas plants, it is necessary to consider the factors which may lead a firm to start producing in one or more of its international markets.

Reasons for setting up overseas manufacture

The benefits of overseas manufacturing are:

Product. Avoiding problems due to the nature of the product, such as perishability.

Transporting and warehousing. The cost of transporting heavy, bulky components and finished products over long distances is reduced.

Tariff barriers/quotas. Barriers to trade, which make the market inaccessible, are reduced.

Government regulations. Entry to some markets, such as Central and Eastern Europe, are difficult unless accompanied by investment in local operations.

Market. Local manufacture may be viewed more favourably by customers.

Government contacts. Firms are likely to be viewed more favourably if they contribute to the local economy.

Information. A strong local presence improves the quality of market feedback.

International culture. Local manufacture encourages a more international outlook and ensures greater commitment by the firm to international markets.

Delivery. Local manufacture allows faster response and just in time delivery.

Labour costs. Production, distribution and service centres can be moved to lower labour cost markets provided there are appropriate skills and adequate information technology infrastructure to maintain satisfactory quality.

For most companies, the cost of setting up an overseas manufacturing operation is initially much higher than expanding the domestic plant by an equivalent amount as we indicated earlier in this chapter in Figure 8.2. Whilst the equipment costs are likely to be similar, and other costs such as labour, land purchase and building may even be cheaper, it is the cost involved in transferring technology, skills and knowledge which normally proves to be expensive and often underestimated.

For many firms, transferring production from a domestic to an overseas plant also immediately reduces the demand on the home plant which might have traditionally supplied all the firm's overseas markets. In response to this reduced demand on the domestic plant, the firm must plan either to reduce the capacity of the domestic plant quickly or find new business to replace the production that has been transferred, otherwise the viability of the domestic plant might be put at risk. Whereas the expansion of existing plants can be often achieved in an incremental way, setting up new plants overseas involves large cash outflows and can put a significant strain on the firms' finances. Poor planning, underestimation of costs or unforeseen problems associated with setting up a plant overseas have frequently caused businesses to fail or be vulnerable to take over. Moreover, if the overseas plant ultimately fails and the firm finds it necessary to reduce its commitment in the market, it can find that its reputation can be severely damaged.

Whilst the most common reason in the past has related to the nature of the product and been particularly concerned with locating the manufacturing plant close to the market, increasingly it is the costs of manufacture (including labour, raw materials and government support) as well as the costs of transport and being 'close to the market' that are likely to influence the decision about which country location to choose.

Regionalisation is having a significant effect on plant location, for example, the so called 'transplants' of Japanese car manufacturers (Nissan and Toyota) in Europe were not only set up to reduce the cost of transportation, but were also a direct move to avoid the car import quota restrictions of the European Union states. Now the decisions are being based on a variety of factors, such as the participation of the country in monetary union, the different levels of productivity and the need to be closer to the most attractive potential markets.

Having emphasised that a move into overseas manufacture involves high cost and risk, firms can choose between different levels of financial commitment. They can, for example, embark upon foreign manufacturing strategies which do not involve direct investment including: contract manufacture and licensing agreements, or strategies which do involve direct investment albeit at different levels of cost and risk, including: assembly operations, wholly owned subsidiary, company acquisition, joint venture and strategic alliances.

Contract manufacture

A firm which markets and sells products into international markets through its own subsidiary might arrange for a local manufacturer to produce the product for them under contract. The advantage of arranging contract manufacture is that it allows the firm to concentrate upon its sales and marketing activities and, because investment is kept to a minimum, it makes withdrawal relatively easy and less costly if the product proves to be unsuccessful.

Contract manufacture might be necessary in order to overcome trade barriers and sometimes it is the only way to gain entry to a country in which the government attempts to secure local employment by insisting on local production. If political instability makes foreign investment unwise, this may be the best way of achieving a marketing presence without having the risk of a large investment in manufacturing. The disadvantages of contract manufacture as an entry method are that is does not allow the buyer control over the manufacturer's activities as the Illustration 8.4 shows.

Outsourcing from contract manufacturers allows firms, such as Sara Lee, to be very flexible by supplying differentiated products for different regional markets and adjusting costs more quickly when necessary. It also has financial benefits of lower capital employed, but the risk is that the local contractor may not achieve the desired quality levels or may gain the necessary knowledge to market the product themselves and compete directly with the international marketer. The marketing firm has less control over the conditions in the factory (intentionally or unintentionally). Ikea have had problems in Romania and Nike have had bad publicity with the sweatshop conditions plants it has used in Asia. As a result Nike have had to sever contracts with four Indonesian plants which refused to comply with company standards for wage levels and working conditions.

Illustration 8.4: Cadbury faces drinks dilemma

Cadbury Schweppes owns a string of soft drinks brands including Dr Pepper, Canada Dry and Seven-Up but relies on a patchwork of distributors for distribution. Two Midwest independent bottlers and distribution companies worth £500 million have come up for sale.

Cadbury Schweppes relies on a combination of independent bottlers and those controlled by rivals PepsiCo and Coca-Cola as well as those owned by Cadbury Schweppes itself. Independent bottlers have a different set of objectives – they are not in for the long-term and have no real desire to operate for the benefit of the brand.

Cadbury Schweppes is streamlining its European system and expanding in Australia. The Cadbury Schweppes North America managers want to take over the Midwest bottlers, Beverage America of Michigan and Select Beverages of Illinois, but London head office managers are focused on value creation. It would mean yet more money would be needed to support the $2.5 billion acquisition of Dr Pepper in 1995.

The head office of Cadbury has a reported £2 billion to spend on acquisitions but the shareholders would prefer it to be spent on confectionery, especially in new markets such as Russia and China, and on buying up local competitors in other countries, such as the already acquired small companies, Bim Bim in Egypt and La Pie qui Chante in France.

Cadbury has a market value of £6 billion compared to Coca-Cola's £110 billion. Market share in the US market is: Coca-Cola 44 per cent, Pepsi 32 per cent, and Cadbury 15 per cent. With Cola sales falling nearly 1 per cent a year Pepsi and Coke are now focusing on the US non-Cola market in which the Cadbury Schweppes's has a 47 per cent share. For example, Coca-Cola has offered free syrup to McDonald's to persuade them to stop selling Dr Pepper and replace it with Coke brands.

A key to Coca-Cola's success has been distribution. It has its '49 per cent solution' in which it has consolidated dozens of independent bottlers into Coca-Cola Enterprises (CCE) in the mid 1980s to give it far greater control of distribution at a lower cost. Cadbury still needs CCE to ensure effective distribution, but whilst CCE will keep the profitable Dr Pepper brand it is dumping second tier Cadbury brands in favour of Coca-Cola brands. The question for Cadbury Schweppes is how to reduce its reliance on the enemy's distribution system without pouring in vast sums of money.

Source: adapted from Olins, R. (1998) 'Cadbury faces drinks dilemma', *Sunday Times*, 4 January

Licensing

Licensing also requires relatively low levels of investment. Organisations involved in the film, television and sports industries, as diverse as Disney, the Olympic Games Committee and Manchester United Football Club have been particularly successful in licensing the use of brands, characters and themes generating huge sales of licensed products. It is a form of management contract in which the licenser confers to the licensee the right to use one or more of the following: patent rights, trademark rights, copyrights and/or product or process know-how. In some situations, the licenser may continue to sell essential components or services to the licensee as part of the agreement.

There are a number of reasons why licensing is a useful entry method. Financial and management commitments can be kept low, the high cost of setting up a manufacturing or marketing subsidiary can be avoided and tariff and non-tariff barriers can be avoided. It is particularly useful therefore to deal with difficult markets, where direct involvement would not be possible, and where the market segments to be targeted may not be sufficiently large for full involvement.

Licensing usually has a number of benefits for the licenser. The licensee pays for the license normally as a percentage of sales and so as the sales grow so does the revenue to the licenser. Considerable control exists as the licensee uses the rights or know-how in an agreed way and for an agreed quantity of product and the licensee markets and purchases products for an agreed fee.

For the licensee, there are a number of advantages. For a relatively low outlay, it is possible to capitalise on established know-how with little risk and avoid the high research and development cost associated with launching a new product. This is particularly important in the industrial market for example, where licensing of proven technology enables companies to enter markets with products which would be prohibitively expensive to develop.

Problems can occur in licensing if the licenser does not respond to changes in the market or technology, or does not help to develop the market for the licensee. The licensee too, may either be unwilling or unable to develop the market in the way that the licenser would wish. A very capable licensee may have learned so much about the market and product that the licenser is no longer required. These sources of conflict often arise as a result of the environment, competitors and market demand changing over the licensing period.

Terpstra and Sarathy (1997) identify a number of techniques that can be adopted in order to minimise the potential problems of licensing as follows:

- develop a clear policy and plan
- allocate licensing responsibility to a senior manager
- select licences carefully
- draft the agreement carefully to include duration, royalties, trade secrets, quality control and performance measures
- supply the critical ingredients
- obtain equity in the licensee
- limit the product and territorial coverage
- retain patents, trademarks, copyrights
- be an important part of the licences business.

Foreign manufacturing strategies with direct investment

At some point in its international development, a stage is reached when the pressure increases upon a firm to make a much more substantial commitment to an individual market or region. The reasons for investment in local operations are:

- **To gain new business**. Local production demonstrates strong commitment and is the best way to persuade customers to change suppliers, particularly in industrial markets where service and reliability are often the main factors when making purchasing decisions.

- **To defend existing business**. Car imports to a number of countries are subject to restrictions and as their sales increase, so they become more vulnerable.

- **To move with an established customer**. Component suppliers often set up their local subsidiaries in order to retain their existing business, compete with local component makers and benefit from increased sales.

- **To save costs**. By locating production facilities overseas, costs can be saved in a variety of areas such as labour, raw materials and transport.

- **To avoid government restrictions** which might be in force to restrict imports of certain goods.

For most multi-nationals operating a global or multi-domestic strategy, there is a strong requirement to demonstrate that they have a permanent presence in all their major markets. The actual form of their operations in each market is likely to vary considerably from country to country, with the largest multi-national companies operating many variants.

Increasingly multi-nationals are seeking to reduce manufacturing and operations costs through making the supply chain more cost effective. This takes a number of different forms. Some firms, for example, in the shoe and footwear industries obtain component or finished product supplies from the lowest labour cost areas whereas Ford is locating its component suppliers on a manufacturing campus close to its assembly plants.

Assembly

A foreign plant might be set up simply to assemble components manufactured in the domestic market completely knocked down (CKD). It has the advantage of reducing the effect of tariff barriers which are normally lower on components than on finished goods. It is also advantageous if the product is large and transport costs are high, for example, in the case of cars. There are other benefits for the firm too, as retaining component manufacture in the domestic plant, allows development and production skills and investment to be concentrated thus maintaining the benefit from economies of scale. By contrast, the assembly plant can be made a relatively simple activity requiring low levels of local management, engineering skills and development support.

There is an argument that assembly plants do not contribute significantly to the local economy in the long term. In initially attracting Nissan and Toyota assembly plants, the UK government claimed that many jobs would be created at relatively low cost but critics have claimed that the number of jobs created in the assembly plants was not very significant and, unless the components are made locally, little transfer of technology will be achieved and the assembly plants can relatively easily be moved to a new location. Both to counter this threat and also to generate further employment, countries can take steps to develop the component supply business either by interrupting the component supply chain through imposition of import or foreign exchange rate restrictions, or, on the other hand, by supporting local component manufacturers who can supply 'just in time'. The Malaysian government used some of these techniques to protect the Proton car project as explained in the Illustration 8.5. For the international firm, of course, using the assembly option presents an opportunity to move plant from country to country in order to take advantage of lower wage costs and government incentives.

Tait (1997) suggests that one of the considerations of local assembly plants is that costings can be subject to rapid change and global companies investing in them may need to think how quickly they can pull out. Companies typically

Illustration 8.5: Proton cars

Dr Mahathir, the prime minister of Malaysia, launched a national car manufacturing project in 1984. The result was the Proton – the only car produced and built in South East Asia. Following early difficulties, Mitsubishi trading company, and Mitsubishi Motors (both of which belong to the same group) were invited to each take a 15 per cent share of the company, but also to bring in a Japanese management team to set about improving efficiency and quality.

Proton dominated the Malaysian market due to protection, as Toyota, Nissan and Honda had to pay 40 per cent duty on their imported car kits for assembly in Malaysia; of course Mitsubishi did well out of the deal too. In 1997 one of Malaysia's richest tycoons, Yahaya Ahmad, bought most of the Government's controlling interest in the conglomerate Hicom that owns Proton. He cut costs, persuaded Mitsubishi to transfer more technology to Proton, bought Lotus (UK) and formed a joint venture with Peugeot Citroën to make a car in Malaysia based on one of their designs. He planned a factory to treble production to five hundred thousand cars by 2000.

Then things started to go wrong. Mr Yahaya was killed in a helicopter crash and the financial crisis hit Malaysia. Sales dried up as car loans at very favourable interest rates were stopped by the government. Proton, in response to Malaysian sales falling to less than half what they were the year before, were forced to cut overtime and pay rates and do work inside which had previously been contracted out. They have had to delay the new factory so that it may well open in 2002, only a year before the Malaysian market will be opened up to other competitors following pressure from the World Trade Organisation.

Clearly there are some advantages of being able to begin manufacturing in a protected market but other environmental factors can still have a serious effect on the firm's fortunes.

Source: adapted from 'Child of Nippon' (1991) *The Economist*, 11 May and 'Proton bomb' (1998) *The Economist*, 30 May

select a number of regional manufacturing bases which are viewed as longer-term investments useful for testing product innovation, and supplement them with lower skilled assembly plants which can be easily moved between markets. For example Whirlpool have two microwave plants, one acquired when it took control of Philips European domestic appliance businesses in Sweden, which drives product development, and the other added later in China, which manufactures competitively for Asian customers and is used for exporting into developed markets.

Virtually all SGS-Thomson Microelectronics exported from Europe to the US and Canada pass through Africa, Asia or Malta. Whilst 60 per cent of the manufacture is located in Europe testing and assembly is concentrated in low cost areas such as China, Morocco and Malta. It is possible to do this because of the small volume, high value of the products.

Government involvement in foreign direct investment decisions in the early 1990s can be significant. Ford, General Motors, Daewoo, Mercedes, Fiat and Peugeot teamed up with local Indian car makers but were blocked out of the low cost segment by Japan's Suzuki which in collaboration with the government has 80 per cent of the passenger car market. As a result the new entrants launched mid-price cars but these were too highly priced for middle-class India where the average annual per capita purchasing power is $1666 and Ford and GM cars sell for $22 000.

Wholly owned subsidiary

As we indicated in Figure 8.2 at the start of the chapter, for any firm, the most expensive method of market entry is likely to be the development of its own foreign subsidiary as it requires the greatest commitment in terms of management time and resources. It can only be undertaken when demand for the market appears to be assured and success is unlikely to come instantly.

This market entry method indicates that the firm is taking a long-term view especially if full manufacturing facilities are developed rather than simply setting up an assembly plant. Even greater commitment is shown when the R&D facilities are established in local countries too. If the company believes its products have long-term market potential in a relatively politically stable country then only full ownership will provide the level of control necessary to fully meet the firm's strategic objectives. There are considerable risks too, as subsequent withdrawal from the market can be extremely costly, not simply in terms of financial outlay, but also in terms of the firm's reputation in the international and domestic market, particularly with shareholders, customers and staff.

Japanese companies have used this strategy in the past to build a powerful presence in international markets over a long period of time. Their patience has been rewarded with high market shares and substantial profits, but this has not been achieved overnight. They have sometimes spent more than five years gaining an understanding of markets, customers and competition as well as selecting locations for manufacturing, before making a significant move.

Company acquisitions and mergers

In the previous chapters we discussed the role of acquisitions and mergers in achieving globalisation. For many Western companies, particularly those from the UK and USA the considerable pressure to produce short-term profits means that speed of market entry is essential and this can be achieved by acquiring an existing company in the market. Amongst other advantages, acquisition gives immediate access to a trained labour force, existing customer and supplier contacts, recognised brands, an established distribution network and an immediate source of revenue.

The strategy is based upon the assumption that companies for potential acquisition will be available, but if the choice of companies is limited, the decision may be taken on the basis of expediency rather than suitability. The belief that acquisitions will be a time-saving alternative to waiting for organic growth to take effect may not prove to be true in practice. It can take a considerable amount of time to search and evaluate possible acquisition targets, engage in protracted negotiations and then integrate the acquired company into the existing organisation structure.

Acquisition can be an extremely effective method of developing a global business. Between 1984 and 1994, Reuters grew from a turnover of £179 million to £1.5 billion, with a market capitalisation of £8 billion through acquisitions, to become a leading provider of global financial services. The recession and structural changes in the industry, however, has meant that they have had to modify their strategy, as demand for the services reduced and fewer attractive bid targets became available.

Take-over of companies which are regarded as part of the country's heritage can raise considerable national resentment if it seems that they are being taken over by foreign interests. A country looking to develop its own technology and manufacturing is likely to believe that acquisition of a domestic company by an MNE is not as desirable as the MNE setting up a local subsidiary. Moreover, acquisition by a large international firm is often associated with job losses and transfer of production facilities overseas.

Another disadvantage of acquisition is that the acquiring company might take over a demotivated labour force, a poor image and reputation, and out of date products and processes. All of these problems can prove costly and time consuming to improve.

Through the last few years there has been considerable debate about acquisition and mergers as a method of achieving rapid expansion. The rationale that is used for acquisition is that an ineffective company can be purchased by a more effective company, which will be able, first, to reduce costs, second, improve performance through applying better management skills and techniques, and third, build upon the synergy between the two companies and so achieve better results. During the late 1980s many take-overs in the UK and USA were financed by huge bank loans justified on the basis that an improvement in future profits would be used to pay the high interest charges. In practice few companies were able to realise the true benefits of synergy and, as the recession of the early 1990s reduced demand, there were some notable business failures and a return to the core business allowing the peripheral business activities to be sold off to grow independently. The Asian crisis has also freed cash-starved Asian conglomerates to also consider selling off businesses that do not seem to fit.

Joint ventures

There are a number of occasions when a company decides that shared ownership of a specially set up new company for marketing and/or manufacture is the most appropriate method of international market entry. It is usually based on the premise that two or more companies can provide complementary competitive advantages for the new company to exploit. In these situations the intention is that the particular firms should contribute complementary expertise or resources to the joint company.

Table 8.1 shows, for example, what is typically contributed in East-West partnerships.

Whilst contributing complementary expertise might be a significant feature of other entry methods, such as licensing, the difference with joint ventures is that each company takes an equity stake in the newly formed firm. The stake taken by one company might be as low as 10 per cent but this still gives them a voice in the management of the joint venture.

There are a number of reasons given for setting up joint ventures. These include:

- a number of countries, such as the Phillipines, try to restrict foreign ownership

Table 8.1 Who provides what in East–West partnerships

West	East
Marketing systems	Land
Financial management	Buildings and equipment
Forecasting	Distribution networks
Planning	Skills
Technology	Low costs
Information systems	Beneficial wage rates
Capital	Tax relief
Know-how	Political connections
Human resources	Neighbouring markets
Financial incentives	

Source: Florescu, I. and Scibor-Rylski, M. (1993) *Making a success of Joint Ventures in Eastern Europe*, CBI Initiative Eastern Europe, London

- many firms find that partners in the host country can increase the speed of market entry when good business and government contacts are essential for success
- complementary technology or management skills provided by the partners can lead to new opportunities in existing sectors, such as in multimedia, for example, Rupert Murdoch's group, News International, in which information processing, publishing, broadcasting and the printed media are becoming more interdependent
- global operations in R&D and production are prohibitively expensive, but necessary to achieve competitive advantage.

The main advantages to companies entering joint ventures are that, first, they have more direct participation in the local market, and thus gain a better understanding of how it works, second, they should be better able to finance and profit from their activities and third, they are able to exert greater control over the operation of the joint venture.

There are, however, some significant disadvantages of joint ventures as a market entry method. As joint venture companies involve joint ownership, there are often differences in the aims and objectives of the participating companies which can cause disagreements over the strategies adopted by the companies. If ownership is evenly divided between the participant firms, these disagreements can often lead to delays and failure to develop clear policies. In other joint ventures the greater motivation of one partner rather than another, particularly if they have a greater equity stake, can lead to them becoming dominant and the other partner becoming resentful.

Local partners can turn out to be a liability. The German airline, Lufthansa, teamed up with Modi Group in India, which is engaged in a variety of activities with joint venture partners including Walt Disney, Alcatel Rank Xerox and Revlon. Lufthansa signed an agreement with one brother to set up a new domestic private airline in 1993 only to find that the five Modi brothers were engaged in bitter feuds. The airline went bust in 1996 and Lufthansa is now seeking $18.6 million plus the return of three planes whilst Modi has accused Lufthansa of charging too much and delivering defective planes.

The other disadvantages of this form of market entry compared to, for example, licensing or the use of agents is that a substantial commitment of investment of capital and management resources must be made in order to ensure success. Many companies would argue that the demands on management time might be even greater for a joint venture than for a directly owned subsidiary because of the need to educate, negotiate and agree with the partner many of the operational details of the joint venture.

Gomes–Casseres (1989) recommends that a joint venture should be used by companies to *extend their capabilites rather than merely exploit existing advantages* and is not recommended if there are potential conflicts of interest between partners. The role of the government in joint ventures can be particularly influential as it may control access to the domestic market. Moreover, it may be persuaded to adapt government policy if a firm is bringing in advanced technology or is willing to make a major investment. Most of the major multi-nationals have increased their involvement in joint ventures, but the implications of this are that it leads to increasingly *decentralised management and operations*, more closely aligned to transnational operation rather than to global standardisation in which more centralised control is necessary.

It was anticipated that in Central and Eastern Europe, following the collapse of communist regimes, joint ventures would play a significant part in achieving economic regeneration, but this has not, so far, proved to be the case. The reasons for this include the lack of an adequate legal framework to facilitate joint ventures, the scarcity of supplies of raw materials and components and the lack of suitably qualified people to operate the joint venture, particularly in financial control, within these Central and Eastern European countries. There is also the possibility of a conflict of objectives which can occur between the international company, which wishes to develop a new market, whilst the local company and host country wish to develop foreign markets and the chance that international companies have been unable to take out hard currency and have had to take goods in payment instead. Finally, companies from developed countries are unwilling to wait the ten to fifteen years that it is anticipated that these markets will take to develop.

Illustration 8.6 shows the problems faced by Assi-Domain and their success in the Russian joint ventures.

The problems of running joint ventures in China have been equally disastrous for a number of companies, and increasingly US companies are appealing for help from the US government. Kimberly Clark opened up a joint venture in China, only to find that the joint venture manager who worked for its partner Xingha Factory Company had set up a competing factory across the road and was stealing materials.

Although Xingha were not implicated, Kimberly Clark had difficulty getting the local government to take action, and armed security guards were needed to protect the new American manager.

Strategic alliances

In analysing the results of joint ventures in China, Vankonacker (1997) observes that joint ventures are hard to sustain in stable environments and concludes that more direct investment will be wholly owned offering Johnson and Johnson's oral-care, baby and feminine hygiene products business as a success story.

Whilst all market entry methods essentially involve alliances of some kind, during the 1980s the term strategic alliance started to be used without being precisely defined to cover a variety of contractual arrangements which are intended to be strategically beneficial to both parties and which cannot be defined as clearly as licensing or joint ventures. Bronder and Pritzl (1992) have defined strategic alliances in terms of at least two companies combining value chain activities for the purpose of competitive advantage. Perhaps one of the most significant aspects of strategic alliances has been that it has frequently involved cooperation between partners who might in other circumstances be competitors. Some examples of the bases of alliances are:

- technology swaps
- R&D exchanges
- distribution relationships
- marketing relationships

Illustration 8.6: When joint ventures go wrong

The Stockholm-based forestry and packaging group Assi has been a pioneer in moving into former Soviet bloc markets since 1994. The company has built or acquired production facilities in Eastern Europe and, more lately, two in Russia. The Russian market for packaging is growing at 10 per cent a year compared with 4 per cent in Europe.

However they have had mixed fortunes. They have just withdrawn from a paper sack joint venture at Segezhabumprom in the province of Karelia in which it acquired a 57 per cent stake for $45 million in 1996/7. The plant, at 250 000 tonnes, was already Russia's biggest pulp and paper mill and the largest supplier of paper sacks. Assi intended to improve efficiency and quality but this prompted a local campaign to remove the new bosses as workers feared that job losses would result from this initiative. Threats from powerful interests close to the former management team resulted in the Swedish Chief Executive needing a 24-hour armed guard. Corruption was rife and matters came to a head when Karelia's public prosecutor challenged Assi's ownership of the firm and a Moscow court declared that Assi's take-over was illegal and the company's bank accounts were frozen due to back dating of the tax liabilities of the previous owners.

The company suffered payment problems and Assi had to put in working capital to keep the plant running. The joint venture partners, Upack, a Russian paper sack distributor and the Karalenian state property fund, refused to contribute. Assi realised that it had encountered a legal and bureaucratic minefield and the Mafia-style threats against its staff led to it pulling out of its joint venture.

A fortnight earlier, however, the group celebrated the opening of its new $25 million corrugated board plant at Vsevelzhsk outside St Petersburg. It was built in eighteen months received tax concessions form the St Petersburg authorities and has developed a good relationship with the local politicians. The main difference with this plant is that it is Assi's aim to service MNEs, such as Coca-Cola and Proctor and Gamble rather than compete with Russian companies for a share of the existing local market.

Assi suffered in Karelia because it took on many of the problems associated with the factory and, perhaps, it would have been better to take a longer-term view in making the necessary efficiencies.

Source: adapted from McIvor, G. (1998) 'Risk and reward in equal measure', *Financial Times*, 3 March

- manufacturer supplier relationships
- cross-licensing.

There are a number of driving forces for the formation and operation of strategic alliances.

Insufficient resources: the central argument is that no organisation alone has sufficient resources to realise the full global potential of its existing and particularly its new products. Equally if it fails to satisfy all the markets which demand these products, competitors will exploit the opportunities which arise and become stronger. In order to remain competitive, powerful and independent companies need to cooperate.

Pace of innovation and market diffusion: the rate of change of technology and consequent shorter product life cycles mean that new products must be exploited quickly by effective diffusion out into the market. This requires not only effective promotion and efficient physical distribution but also needs good channel management, especially when other members of the channel are powerful, and so, for example the strength of alliances within the recorded music industry including artists, recording labels and retailers has a powerful effect on the success of individual new hardware products such as the Sony compact disc and Philips digital compact cassette.

High research and development costs: as technology becomes more complex and genuinely new products become rarer, so the costs of R&D become higher. For example, Olivetti and Canon set up an alliance to develop copiers and image processors. In order to recover these costs and still remain competitive, companies need to achieve higher sales levels of the product.

The pharmaceutical company Glaxo's success in marketing Zantac, its anti-ulcer drug, was achieved by using a network of alliances the most effective of which was including Roche in the US.

Concentration of firms in mature industries: many industries have used alliances to manage the problem of excess production capacity in mature markets. There have been a number of alliances in the car and airline business, some of which have lead ultimately to full joint ventures or take-overs.

Government cooperation: as the trend towards regionalisation continues, so governments are more prepared to cooperate on high cost projects rather than try to go it alone. There have been a number of alliances in Europe – for example, the European airbus has been developed to challenge Boeing, and the Eurofighter aircraft project has been developed by Britain, Germany, Italy and Spain.

Self-protection: a number of alliances have been formed in the belief that they might afford protection against competition in the form of individual companies or newly formed alliances. This is particularly the case in the emerging global high technology sectors such as information technology, telecommunications, media and entertainment.

Market access: strategic alliances have been used by companies to gain access to difficult markets, for instance, Caterpillar used an alliance with Mitsubishi to enter the Japanese market.

In light of the fact that two thirds of alliances experience severe leadership and financing problems during the first two years, Bronder and Pritzl (1992) emphasise the need to consider carefully the approach adopted for the development of alliances. They have stressed the need to analyse the situation, identify the opportunities for cooperation and evaluate shareholder contributions. Devlin and Blackley (1988) have identified some guidelines for success in forming alliances. There needs to be a clear understanding of whether the alliance has been formed as a short-term stop gap or as a long-term strategy. It is, therefore, important that each understands the other partner's motivations and objectives, as the alliance might expose a weakness in one partner which the other might later exploit. It is apparent that many strategic alliances are a step towards a more permanent relationship, but the consequences of a potential break up must always be borne in mind when setting up the alliance.

Glaxo which was mentioned earlier appears to have changed its strategy resulting in the take-over of Welcome. More recently it announced a proposed merger with Smith Kline Beecham but at the first attempt it failed, apparently because of a clash of personalities of the top executives.

As with all entry strategies, success with strategic alliances depends on: effective management, good planning, adequate research, accountability and monitoring. It is also important to recognise the limitations of this as an entry method. Companies need to be aware of the dangers of becoming drawn into activities for which it is not designed.

Conclusion

We have looked at market entry methods as a series of alternatives and suggested that a firm can make individual decisions based on the factors affecting one specific country. For a firm at the start of internationalisation, this can be regarded as a critical first step, which is vital not only for financial reasons, but also because it will set a pattern of future international involvement. For large established companies that already have extensive involvement in international markets, the market entry decision is taken against the background of an existing and substantial network of operations and within a global strategy. The company's competitive strategy is likely to require simultaneous decisions affecting its arrangements in a number of markets in order to improve its competitive position by entering untapped or emerging markets, or expanding its activities in existing markets. In order to achieve these objectives within a very short time scale, companies increasingly need to use a variety of market entry strategies. This is leading to increasingly complex operations being created in which companies strive to balance the opposing forces of competitiveness and cooperation.

Discussion questions

1 Outline the market entry methods and the levels of involvement associated with the development of a company's globalisation process from initial exporting through to becoming a global corporation. Specify what you consider to be the important criteria in deciding the appropriate entry method.

2 Selecting the market entry strategy is the key decision many companies have to take in expanding into overseas markets because it involves both risk and levels of control. Explain how risk and control is affected by different entry methods.

3 When is it appropriate to use contract manufacturing and foreign assembly within an international marketing strategy?

4 Why is acquisition often the preferred way to establish wholly owned operations abroad, and what are its limitations as an entry method?

5 Under what conditions is the formation of strategic alliances appropriate?

References

Bogler, D. (1996) 'Japanese Industry: Survival strategy', *Financial Times*, 5 December.

Bronder, C. and Pritzl, R. (1992) 'Developing Strategic Alliances: A Conceptual Framework for Successful Co-operation', *European Management Journal*, 10 (4), December.

Cavusgil, S. and Naor, J. (1989) 'Firm and management characteristics as discriminators of export marketing activity', *Journal of Business Research*, 15.

Chan, P.S. (1994) 'Franchising: Key to Global Expansion', *Journal of International Marketing*, 2 (3).

Chryssochoidis, G.M. (1996) 'Successful Exporting: Exploring the Transformation of Export product Portfolios', *Global Marketing*, 10, Part 1: 7–31.

Devlin, G. and Blackley, M. (1988) 'Strategic Alliances – Guidelines for Success', *Long Range Planning*, 21 (5).

Dicle, A. and Dicle, U. (1992) 'Effects of Government Export Policies on Turkish Export Trading Companies', *International Marketing Review*, 9.

Douglas, S.P. and Craig, C.S. (1992) 'Advances in international marketing', *International Journal of Research in Marketing*, 9.

Fidler, S. (1997) 'Quality provides the motor', *Financial Times*, 11 December.

Florescu, I. and Scibor-Rylski, M. (1993) *Making a success of Joint Ventures in Eastern Europe*, CBI Initiative Eastern Europe, London.

Gilligan, C. and Hird, M. (1986) *International Marketing – Strategy and Management*, Croom Helm.

Gomes-Casseres, B. (1989) 'Joint Ventures in the Face of Global Competition' *Sloan Management Review*, Spring.

Katsikeas, C.S., Piercy, N.F. and Ioannidis, C. (1996) 'Determinants of export performance in a European context', *European Journal of Marketing*, 30 (6).

Mahon, J.F. and Vachani, S. (1992) 'Establishing a Beachhead in International Marketing – A Direct or Indirect Approach', *Long Range Planning*, 25 (3).

McIvor, G. (1998) 'Risk and reward in equal measure', *Financial Times*, 3 March.

Moore, R.A. (1987) 'The Selection of Agents and Distributors: A Descriptive Model', *Quarterly Review of Marketing*, Autumn.

Olins, R. (1998) 'Cadbury faces drinks dilemma', *Sunday Times*, 4 January.

Tait, N. (1997) *Financial Times*, 15 October.

Terpstra, V. and Sarathy, R. (1997) *International Marketing*, 7th edn, Dryden Press.

Terpstra, V. and Yu, C.J. (1990) 'Piggybacking: A Quick Road to Internationalisation', *International Marketing Review*, 7 (4).

The Economist (1991) 'Child of Nippon', 11 May.

The Economist (1998) 'Proton bomb', 30 May.

Vankonacker, W. (1997) 'Entering China: An Unconventional Approach', *Harvard Business Review*, March–April.

Welch, L.S. (1992) 'Developments in International Franchising', *Journal of Global Marketing*, 6 (1/2).

Williamson, P.J. (1997) 'Asia's new competitive game', *Harvard Business Review*, September–October.

Special focus

Jollibee, Japan, Johannesburger and Fries

Introduction

Many people probably think that when McDonald's decides to enter a new market, the biggest problem they face is translating 'Enjoy your meal' into the appropriate language. However, even for one of the most global firms with one of the most standardised marketing strategy, market entry can be problematic. McDonald's is increasingly coming under pressure to change its menu to suit local tastes and the Phillipines provides one such challenge. In Japan it was faced not only with pressure to adapt the menu to local tastes but it has also had to deal with significant changes in the Japanese economy during the time that it has been there. It is in South Africa, however, its first entry into the African market, where the problems seemed to have reached a climax.

McDonald's operates 21 000 fast food restaurants in 104 countries and in 1996 was rated by Interbrand as the world's top brand, beating Coca-Cola into second place. During 1994 McDonald's non-US operating income exceeded the US operating income for the first time and by 1996 was around 50 per cent higher as McDonald's increasingly sought new markets to combat the lack of growth in the US market. In new markets McDonald's claim to have successfully adapted the product to local tastes.

Coping with Jollibee in the Phillipines

Jollibee Foods, a family owned chain in the Philippines, has borrowed every trick from McDonald's marketing know-how, but instead of selling a generic burger acceptable to any market in the world, Jollibee caters to a local preference for sweet-and-spicy flavours. 'We've designed our products to suit the Filipino palate', says Mr Bibonia, Jollibee's vice-president of marketing.

The combination of first-class service, matching and sometimes beating McDonald's in delivery of the product in-store, plus the creation of tailored menus, has resulted in Jollibee out-performing McDonald's in the Philippines. Indeed, according to the market researchers A C Neilsen, in ten years Jollibee has grabbed 46 per cent of the market versus McDonald's 16 per cent based on the share of total number of visits. Whereas McDonald's have stabilised the number of stores as a result of a corporate decision taken when the Philippines was undergoing political change in the late 1980s and early 1990s, Jollibee have surged ahead and now has 177 outlets – roughly double McDonald's total of 90, with another 36 added in 1996/97. Jollibee's strategy in distribution has been to locate alongside McDonald's and with their superior store numbers, to 'surround McDonald's'. Additionally, the fact that Jollibee's prices are 5 per cent lower on average than McDonald's doesn't hurt either.

The Jollibee isn't that different from McDonald's. The basic product is broadly similar but the sauce (or spice if you like) is different. 'It's familiar to customers – it's the spice a Filipino mother would cook at home', says Tessa Puno, a consumer analyst. Besides the spicy sauces, Jollibee offers rice and spaghetti as an alternative to french fries, though these are also available.

Just like McDonald's, Jollibee works hard to attract kids with in-store play activities and a line of heavily advertised characters, including a hamburger-headed boxer called Champ and a spaghetti-haired girl named Hetty. Licensed toys, towels and other novelties promoting the characters are on sale in stores. Again, the characters have a local expression and have a Filipino feel to them as does the television advertising. Here again Jollibee feels it has the edge in communicating local values to local customers creating the position of being like McDonald's in broad terms, but being Filipino in the style and manner of delivery.

With sales of £170 million ($250 million US) in 1996, Jollibee is the second largest consumer goods company in the Philippines – but minuscule compared with McDonald's £20 billion ($30 billion US) worldwide sales. But it can see opportunities overseas in niche markets. Already it has pilot ventures in South East Asia as well as in the Gulf states and plans to open a total of 40 restaurants there by the end of 1997. It has already opened in California and thinks Chicago, New York and Miami, with their Asian and Hispanic populations, could offer good prospects. The threat to McDonald's might just get serious.

Jollibee's success has not gone unnoticed although McDonald's subsidiary in Manila has not commented officially and corporate headquarters had little to say. 'We focus on our customers there just as anywhere else' has been the response.

McDonald's may have been handicapped by the fact that government legislation has prohibited foreign companies from owning retail chains, restricting the company therefore to a franchise operation. But this constraint is in the process of being lifted allowing McDonald's to operate its own stores. Furthermore, money is no object. The company could pour in advertising and attempt to overwhelm Jollibee's, reminding other upstart burger-chains around the world of the might of the Golden Arches. Whatever its response McDonald's is unlikely to resist retaliation for long and when it comes it will be serious.

Bucking the trend in Japan

In 1998, the 50/50 joint venture between McDonald's and Fujita in Japan reported record profits despite the gloom in the Japanese economy. Perhaps surprisingly, McDonald's difficulties occurred during Japan's boom period when escalating property prices and high construction costs made it hard to find suitable sites. However, this had the benefit of preventing McDonald's growing too fast. As costs dropped, for example, construction costs halved as stores were designed to be smaller and more simply decorated, McDonald's were able to expand and by 1998 they have over 2500 stores. The firm was receiving requests from developers to participate in new shopping or leisure complexes and from oil companies to open outlets at petrol stations.

McDonald's in Japan was not suffering from the trend of US customers who were defecting to rivals who cook burgers to order. In Japan the two best-sellers were Teriyaki McBurger and Chicken Tasuta, both flavoured with soy sauce to appeal to the Japanese tastes.

Whereas in the US 80 per cent of outlets are franchises, 80 per cent of Japanese outlets were directly owned and run, and so McDonald's suffered less from franchisees complaining of poaching from new stores. Because most of the raw materials were imported – beef from Australia, potatoes from the US – the strong yen in the 1980s had enabled McDonald's to keep prices low and maintain high revenues during difficult economic times. However, as the yen weakened, there was pressure to increase prices and so McDonald's faced the challenge of balancing prices and customer numbers very carefully in order to maintain the healthy profit position in the future.

Johannesburger and fries

When McDonald's attacked its last group of emerging markets in Africa it must have thought that its global brand would make the market entry strategy relatively straightforward. Its first entry point was South Africa.

McDonald's waited for the end of apartheid before it was ready to enter South Africa. During the 1980s there was a strong anti-apartheid lobby in America as well as federal, state and local trade sanctions. Under such pressure US companies which were already trading there, for example, Pepsi Cola left and others waited but made preparations.

McDonald's registered its trademark in South Africa in 1968 and decided to make its first investment in 1993. However, it immediately found that a local trader had applied to use the 'McDonald's' trademark for its own use and to have the American firm's rights to the trademark withdrawn. McDonald's trademark had technically expired because, although it had renewed the mark every five years until 1985, it lost its right to the trademark under South African law if it was unused for five years without a good reason.

McDonald's responded by applying to reregister the trademark and filing a case against the local firm. They did not really expect much trouble with this as McDonald's was, after all, one of the world's most recognised brands selling beef and chicken burgers in many countries around the world and it did not seem unreasonable for the South African court to protect it from obvious copies. McDonald's argued, too, that there were special reasons for the license expiring as trade sanctions against South Africa and the anti-apartheid lobby in the US prevented it from entering the market.

When the case came to the Supreme Court in 1995, three cases were heard at the same time. Two South African traders, Joburgers Drive-Inn Restaurant and Dax Prop, both ran restaurants under the name 'MacDonalds' and wanted to prevent McDonald's having the right to use the name, and the third case was McDonald's suing the other firms for using its brand.

In the end the judgement rested on two questions: First, was McDonald's a well-known mark? If so McDonald's was entitled to protection from local traders who would have to close their operation as a result. Second, could McDonald's claim that special circumstances had prevented it from entering the market?

In defence of the first question McDonald's produced the results of two market research surveys which confirmed that a large majority of respondents had at least heard of the name, over half were aware of the brand and could recognise the logo. However the judge said that as the surveys were conducted in white, affluent suburbs they were unrepresentative of a country whose population was 76 per cent black.

On the second question the judge did not agree that it was 'special circumstances' that had stopped McDonald's entering South Africa but the only reason which explained McDonald's failure to commence business in South Africa was that it was not one of McDonald's market priorities.

Despite losing the case McDonald's were allowed to start opening restaurants pending an appeal. In 1996 the Appeal Court applied a less stringent interpretation of the survey findings, ruling that McDonald's had surveyed its target market and so it was well-known in South Africa and so ruled in favour of McDonald's.

The competing brands

Unlike other developing countries the years of isolation in South Africa had created an unusual market. South Africa was already a sophisticated consumer market isolated from the rest of the world by the shelter of sanctions. With this protection the existing fast food companies had developed a secure market position, established strong brands and a clear understanding of what their loyal customers wanted. Out of the six strongest brands, two were foreign. Kentucky Fried Chicken – now KFC – and Wimpy which together have over 45 per cent of the 1227 fast food outlets.

The others were South African. Nando's are a fast growing Portuguese-style spicy chicken burger chain with 105 restaurants in South Africa as well as 42 abroad, Chicken Licken is a mass-market chain with 275 outlets and Steers is a fast food burger chain with 215 restaurants. In contrast to Brazil, where by 1997 it had 337 stores, McDonalds had only opened 35 restaurants in South Africa, and in two of these in Johannesburg's run-down city centre staff numbers had been cut.

Consumer taste and the restaurant menu

McDonald's is treating the South African market as uniform and decided to introduce its standard worldwide menu in South Africa focusing on a full range of hamburgers supplemented by a few chicken product alternatives, having observed that the competition sells roughly two-thirds chicken and only one-third beef.

In practice, the market is not uniform and the split between chicken and beef is probably more to do with cultural issues than the products offered. In fact most black people prefer chicken, which is cheaper than red meat, and buy their fast food from street hawkers as much as from formal fast food outlets. The McDonald's chicken burger is 30 per cent more expensive than Chicken Licken's equivalent product.

By contrast white people prefer beef, with the weekend barbecue being a ritual – a relic of the Boer hunter past. The white population are more used to Steer's 'man-sized' Big Steer which contains 7oz (200g) of beef and so Interbrand South Africa's Jeremy Sampson says that people laugh at McDonald's biggest burgers, the Big Mac and the quarterpounder which look so small and thin by comparison. Nando's have managed to make the transition between the two cultures by selling spicy chicken burgers to white people by marketing them as an exotic blend of Portuguese and Mozambican cuisine.

McDonald's promotion

McDonald's has a problem in that not only were South Africans isolated from the world brands but they have grown loyal to their own. McDonald's has made some progress in starting to over come the negative image which resulted from the first court case with a television campaign with the slogan 'Its MacTime Now'. It has also begun to establish the idea of service in 90 seconds which the competitors who cook to order cannot do. The McDonald's Happy Meal, complete with plastic toy was a novelty in South Africa. Indeed the first restaurant in a Johannesburg was built with a special children's play area and a sign Playland which was more prominent than the sign McDonald's.

References

CIM (1997) 'International marketing examination case study', June.

Hutton, B. (1998) 'Fast food group blows a McBubble in slow economy', *Financial Times*, 8 May.

The Economist (1997) 'Johannesburger and fries', 27 September.

Part II Cases

TZ Pipes

The executive training room at TZ Pipes was full with young and ambitious managers. The week long training programme was concerned with 'Developing and Improved International Culture at TZ Pipes'. The topic under consideration at the moment was international marketing strategy. One part of the day was concerned with the type of organisation that would be most suitable for TZ. The other part of the day would look at strategic options and their implementation.

The day started with a series of charts giving information about different countries in the world. Some of that information compared country size by population, by gross national product, by past and forecast growth rates. Additionally the charts attempted to compare the amount of cultural difference between the UK and the various countries under discussion.

The distribution of company sales was as follows: UK 28 per cent, other countries in Europe 23 per cent, Middle East 21 per cent, Far East 11 per cent, Africa 8 per cent and South America 9 per cent. The TZ Pipes market in Africa was to the sub-Saharan region and was dependent upon foreign aid and World Bank programmes.

TZ manufacture iron pipes and fittings for the water and gas industries. TZ export pipes to most parts of the world with the exception of North America and to China. Sales in 1995 were in line with the company forecast of £68 million. This was a nine percent increase over 1994.

Until now the company has relied on the sales and marketing efforts of David Jones and the export team of ten people, based at company headquarters just south of London. Direct contact with the market has been achieved through the use of agents and distributors. In order to generate growth for the future David Jones is considering changing to other approaches.

TZ Pipes have to cope with the technical specifications set out by the national organisations responsible for approving the standards of iron pipes for water and gas. Technical standards vary around the world. This is partly because of different climatic conditions, for example to cope with extreme heat in the Middle Eastern countries of Saudi Arabia and Kuwait. It also relates to different views about what are appropriate levels of performance and safety.

TZ Pipes is anxious to expand its international sales considerably. It is one of the larger companies in its field although many companies supply this market when viewed in world terms.

In the role of one of the managers on the training programme, identify options and make recommendations on the following.

Questions

1 How should TZ Pipes investigate market opportunities?

2 What should TZ Pipes do to develop a more international organisation and culture within the company?

Case Comments

TZ Pipes has proved to be an effective exporter with a useful spread of business. The company has used traditional approaches to exporting using agents and distributors. This has enabled them to gain access to the markets and cope with the complexity of the technical specifications which vary from country to country because of the conditions in which they are used.

However, TZ Pipes have a problem with assessing market opportunities because of the lack of detailed information about the specific market for their products and the fact that environmental factors, including the country's economic performance are important in deciding where to focus the marketing effort. The strategy that TZ Pipes adopt must help them get closer to understanding the social and business culture of their international markets.

Harley Davidson

Harley Davidson began manufacturing motorcycles in the USA at the turn of the century. Virtually from the beginning they had a unique design with a powerful, robust engine. Thus, from the outset, Harley had created a style that would become a familiar part of their heritage today.

Steadily, through the first 50 years or so of the company's history, they destroyed domestic competition until, in the early 1960s, they dominated the US market. Then in the early 1960s, the Honda Motor Company of Japan entered the US market. Initially no one, including Harley Davidson, paid any attention to the tiny motorcycles that Honda imported, they were not taken seriously and appeared to pose no threat to Harley's seemingly impregnable position. But the Honda initiative sparked a motorcycle craze and Honda, having established the beachhead with small motorcycles, then started importing larger motorcycles. In less than 10 years, financial problems forced Harley Davidson into a take-over by AMF, an American conglomerate with no motorcycle heritage. However, by the end of the 1970s, after 10 years of ownership, AMF's interest in Harley Davidson waned. For Harley Davidson the picture looked bleak. Japanese competition (for Yamaha, Kawasaki and Suzuki had now entered the US market) accounted for 70 per cent of what was previously Harley Davidson's key market segment – the super heavyweight motorcycle (defined as cycles with over 700cc capacity).

Then, in the early 1980s, Harley Davidson's management managed to buy the company back from AMF, and so began the first stage of the recovery. Throughout the 1980s the company focused on improving quality, cutting costs and monitored closely the relationship between the product and the customer. By 1993, the position had changed with Harley Davidson once again dominating the super heavy motorcycle market sector and proving that the Japanese onslaught could be halted.

1993 Market Share (USA)	
Harley Davidson	63%
Honda	26%
Others	11%

Harley Davidson's strategy

Harley Davidson has focused on its key market sector – the heavyweight motorcycle market. Unlike the Japanese who concentrated on a global standardisation strategy to get economies of scale, Harley concentrated on highly differentiated sub-niches. Based on individual customer needs, Harley produced a range of tailor-made models based on a few basic types, appealing to the older, educated, executive-type customer in the upper-income bracket, prepared to pay a high price for uniqueness.

Harley's market research suggested that its customers did not see 'other motorcycles' as its competition – but products like conservatories, swimming pools and luxury cruises. When buying a Harley Davidson, price was not a factor. Its competitive advantage was 'nostalgia' based on the dream and legendary mystique of owning an American Classic. Customers did not buy a motorcycle but the dream of 'escaping from business' and 'the freedom of the open road'.

International expansion

Harley Davidson has been a long time exporter of its products. Curiously one of the earliest overseas countries to import Harleys was Japan capitalising on American occupation following World War II. However, faced with a deteriorating domestic market position, Harley Davidson virtually abandoned the overseas market. With its recovery in the USA and the retrieval of its position of dominance, coupled with a saturation of demand, the company has in recent years once again focused its attention on overseas markets. With a very limited overseas marketing budget, Harley has seen exports rise steadily and today sales in overseas markets account for around 30 per cent of turnover, caused by the steady growth of the 'executive' sectors in the world market with rising capital income and increased leisure and recreational activities.

The company has recently established a three year goal of overseas sales accounting for 50 per cent of its turnover, with a strong ambition to be represented in the European Union and South East Asia including Japan.

Harley Davidson is a uniquely American company. The heritage, the product, the production facility, the marketing and the dealership network are all handled from corporate headquarters in Milwaukee, USA. It has very little overseas experience. All it knows – via unsolicited enquiries and its emerging very small-scale international distributor network, is that there is a demand. What is not known is the nature of the customer, the degree of competition, state of the development of the market and the role and contribution of marketing. One of the key considerations is whether the company needs to manufacture overseas in order to lower its cost base.

Questions

1 What are the major strategic issues Harley Davidson has to face in planning its three year overseas expansion programme?

2 Select either Europe or South East Asia (including Japan) as your chosen area for overseas development. Do not attempt to write about both. Having identified your chosen area, outline the options Harley Davidson might consider in developing a comprehensive market entry strategy. Make a recommendation which must be justified. Then explain (again in outline) how in marketing and management terms Harley Davidson might implement its strategy.

Electronics and the automobile industry

Throughout its lifetime the automobile industry has been characterised by the application of new advances in technology but, whereas in its early days this was largely the preserve of mechanical engineering, it is now electronics, information technology and communications which are beginning to dominate. As a result much of the future innovation in the automobile industry could be concerned not with design in the core benefits of the car, but with new functions of the car which reflect the changes in the environment and the new expectations of drivers around the world.

Powertrain electronics and other in-vehicle systems

The powertrain systems have been the historical base of electronics in cars and are used increasingly to manage the engine, suspension, vehicle handling and safety systems. In 1994, they accounted for the biggest segment (about one third) of the market and might now be reaching maturity. Other segments, however, are growing rapidly including, for example, safety and comfort, in car entertainment, driver information and car security.

Outside forces are having a substantial effect on the use of electronics in cars. These include insurance companies requiring greater security, government agencies and pressure groups demanding better engine management to reduce pollution and various organisations seeking to reduce deaths on the road.

In response to these demands many new systems are already appearing, for example, electronic steering and suspension, keyless and remote entry systems, and memorised driver seating, mirror and radio positions. These offer many opportunities for technological breakthroughs, for example, silicon sensors which have been pioneered by Motorola.

Cost savings in design, development and production of new vehicles will be possible through the use of standardised hardware. The key change will be that existing systems will be integrated by using modules with standardised interfaces, thus allowing fast configuration for a broad spread of applications. The savings will come because it will be possible to reuse components across the model range and in successive generations of cars.

Car navigation and communication systems

There are a vast range of possible applications of satellite navigation in addition to the obvious route finding, congestion avoidance, car parking direction and so on. Customers could have more in-car features, such as intelligent cruise control, automatic collision avoidance and satellite navigation systems, and many of the office-based communications such as Internet, fax and e-mail could be included as well.

The car manufacturers are becoming increasingly globalised, but at the same time their traditional preserve of mechanical engineering is being challenged by the electronics and computing companies who see substantial new development opportunities in cars.

Questions

1 How is new car innovation likely to be influenced by global business environmental changes (SLEPT factors) and customer demands around the world?

2 As a mass production car manufacturer what marketing strategies would you adopt to exploit the new opportunities internationally?

Case comments

Whilst technology can offer added value benefits, the challenge is to determine when the customers and the environment are ready for its introduction. There are differences between car purchaser requirements around the world, and different infrastructure conditions too. These will ultimately determine what benefits should be offered and, ultimately, what kind of international marketing strategy is appropriate in order to exploit the chosen technological advances.

References

Financial Times (1995) 'Electronics driving forces', 25 May.
Financial Times (1996) 'World Trade: South Koreans to win out in drive by wire', 21 November.

Part III

Approaches to implementation

Introduction

Aims and objectives

The aim of this, the third part of *International Marketing Strategy,* is to examine the implementational issues of international product management, marketing communications, distribution and logistics and pricing. Part III emphasises the importance of selecting appropriate implementation strategies paying attention to the details for the tactical marketing approach adopted and recognising the significance of adaptation and standardisation for international marketing success.

Learning outcomes

- to develop an understanding of the implications of implementing different types of international marketing strategies
- to promote an understanding of those factors that are more likely to lead to success in implementing marketing plans
- to gain a more detailed understanding of international pricing, distribution and logistics, marketing communications and product management
- to understand the ways in which cultural diversity influences successful implementation
- to gain a better understanding of the interrelationship between analysis, the development of strategic plans and their implementation in international markets.

Indicative content

The management of the international product portfolio and the issues of standardisation and differentiation are central to the international marketing managers' task. In Chapter 9, we discuss these issues as well as examining the importance of building added value through customer service, branding and offering flexibility in order to build a competitive advantage internationally.

Whilst the communication process is common to both domestic and international markets, the communication mix appropriate to foreign markets can vary enormously depending on available infrastructure and the cultural diversity across markets. In Chapter 10, we examine these issues and also look at the importance of business-to-business communications, and how firms use communication tools to build corporate identity internationally.

In Chapter 11, we turn to the more operational aspects of the marketing mix. The distribution of goods and services is a high percentage of the sales dollar in international markets. In this Chapter we examine the issues in setting up a distribution system in foreign markets. We also examine how firms manage their supply chain internationally as well as paying particular attention to these issues in physically distributing products. Retailing is for many companies an important stage in their supply chain. We examine the current trends in international retailing and discuss the differing retailing infrastructures around the globe.

Finally, in Chapter 12 we examine the issues of pricing. Pricing is a complex area, especially so when pricing across international markets. Firms face currency risks, transaction risks and the risks of not being paid at all. In this Chapter we examine the problems companies face when pricing across foreign markets and look at some of the tools and techniques used by companies to combat these problems.

Chapter 9
International product management

Introduction

Success in international marketing depends to a large extent upon satisfying the demands of the market and ultimately, on whether the product or service offered is suitable and acceptable for its purpose. More markets are reaching maturity and less and less products can be differentiated by their core benefits. In defining the term 'product', therefore, we include additional elements such as packaging, warranties, after sales service and branding that make up the total product offer for the purchaser. Success also depends on building market awareness and ensuring availability of the product, which can be achieved by the effective use of the other marketing mix elements.

In this chapter we focus upon some of the key aspects and recent trends of international product policy by considering the changes in the nature of the products and services offered individually and within the portfolio, their relationship with the market and how new products and services can be developed. Particularly important is the need to provide customers around the world with a satisfactory experience when using the product or service. To achieve this requires a clear understanding of when to meet the similar needs and wants of transnational customer segments and when to adapt to local tastes and needs.

Products, services and service marketing

The reason that the majority of companies initially develop international markets is to provide a cost effective way of generating new market opportunities and increased demand for a new product, a successful domestic product range or to simply off-load excess capacity. However, the product must be seen as a bundle of satisfactions providing people not just with products but with satisfying experiences in terms of the benefits they provide rather than the functions the products perform. These concepts are particularly important in international marketing, because, for example, the growth of such global consumer products as McDonald's and Coca-Cola cannot be attributable solely to a distinctive taste. Much of their success might be attributed to the aspirations of their international customers to be part of the American way of life, the 'Coca-Cola Culture' by deriving satisfaction from a close association with the product and the brand.

In understanding how products can provide satisfying experiences and benefits for people, it is necessary to clearly identify and understand the motivations of the target consumer and not make assumptions about them. A typical response to Nike sports shoes, reported in *Sky* magazine was: 'It's kind of like, Nike don't give a . . . what you do, they don't care where you come from, and they don't want to hear you talk about it. They just want to see what you can do.'

The term 'product' is used in marketing to refer both to physical goods, such as a can of baked beans or a refrigerator, and services such as insurance or a holiday. Before considering the total product 'offer' in more detail, it is important to consider the specific nature and role of services in international marketing.

Services are characterised by their:

- **Intangibility**: air transportation, insurance and education cannot be touched. Tangible elements of the service, such as food, drink and personal video on airline flights, a written policy and a free gift in insurance and a certificate and a photograph of graduation for success in education, are used as part of the service in order to confirm the benefit provided and enhance its perceived value. However, the physical evidence of the service may be valued very differently from country to country.

- **Perishability**: services cannot be stored – for example, unfilled airline seats are lost once the aircraft takes off. This characteristic causes considerable problems in planning and promotion in order to match supply and demand, for example, at busy and quiet times of the day. Predicting demand and managing capacity in distant and varied locations is particularly difficult.

- **Heterogeneity**: services are rarely the same, because they involve interactions between people. For fast food companies this can cause problems in maintaining consistent quality particularly in international markets where there are quite different attitudes towards customer service.

- **Inseparability**: the service is created at the point of sale. This means that economies of scale and the experience curve benefits can be difficult to achieve and supplying the service in scattered markets can be expensive, particularly in the initial setting up phase. Where the service involves some special expertise, such as a pop music artist, the number of consumers is limited by the size and number of venues that can be visited by the performer. If the fans are in a market which is remote, they are unlikely to see the artist and need other tangible forms of communication in order not to feel too separated from the performer.

The three additional marketing mix elements

These differences between product and service offers have certain implications for the international marketing mix and in addition to the usual four Ps for products (product, price place and promotion) another three Ps for services are added. Because of the importance and nature of service delivery, special emphasis must be placed upon:

- **People**. Consumers must be educated in order for their expectations of the service to be managed and employees must be motivated and well trained in order to ensure that high standards of service and are maintained. However, because of cultural differences the staff and customers in different countries often respond differently not only to training and education but also in their attitudes to the speed of service, punctuality, willingness to queue and so on.

- **Process**. As the success of the service is dependent on the total customer experience a well-designed method of delivery is essential. Customer expectations of process standards vary with different cultures and standardisation is difficult in many varied contexts. Frequently the service process is affected by elements for which the service deliverer may be blamed by frustrated customers but have little control. Sports fans might travel to an event at great expense only to experience delays at an airport, excessive policing or bad weather.

- **Physical aspects**. Many physical reminders including the appearance of the delivery location and the elements provided to make the service more tangible can enhance the experience. Apart from using appropriate artefacts to generate the right atmosphere, constant reminders of the firm's corporate identity help to build customer awareness and loyalty.

There are some specific problems in marketing services internationally. There are particular difficulties in achieving uniformity of standards of these three additional Ps in remote locations where exerting control can be particularly difficult. Pricing, too, can be extremely problematic, because fixed costs can be a very significant part of the total service costs but may vary between locations. As a result the consumer's ability to buy and their perceptions of the service may vary considerably between markets resulting in significantly different prices

---

Illustration 9.1: Citigroup and financial services customer segments

The merger between Citigroup and Travelers Group made Citigroup in the USA the largest financial services provider in the world. Whilst the rationale for the merger is cross-selling extra products to existing customers it is determined not to become a financial supermarket which has been tried in the past by American Express and Sears Roebuck but has failed. Rather than creating a universal institution driven by product sales from a comprehensive range of offerings, Citigroup aims to address the needs of customers holistically across the life cycle through financial needs analysis, backed by the full range of Citicorp and Travelers products and distributed using channels tailored to individual market segments. The key is to package the services under one simplified plan and use one brand.

Younger people are more likely to respond to electronic delivery systems developed by Citicorp whereas the large network of insurance agents and stockbrokers from Travelers might be better adapted to appeal to older, wealthier generations.

Some of these one brand concepts are already successful. San Francisco based Charles Schwab's One Source scheme, uses low cost telephone or Internet channels, and is now the largest discount broker and seller of mutual funds in the US. The Delaware based bank MBNA, although relatively small, is now the second largest credit card issuer in the US. This has been possible by data warehousing, very carefully targeted mail shots at particular market segments and maintaining a low-cost base (no branches). Schwab and MBNA are marketing their concepts internationally.

Source: adapted from Authers, J. (1998) 'Adopting a single brand approach', *Financial Times*, 9 April

being set and profits generated. Increasingly important in service marketing is the need to provide standardised services customised to individual requirements. This clearly poses considerable challenges to international service providers.

There are a number of generalisations that can be made about international marketing of services. Foreign market growth is generally higher and presents greater opportunities for gaining market share and long-term profits, partly because local firms are often less experienced and less competitive on quality. Information technology and communications in service delivery, and the development of expert knowledge networks are the sources of competitive advantage for international service marketers. Due to the high initial cost of financing overseas operations, joint ventures and franchising are rapidly growing entry methods, and frequently, the market entry strategy is based on forming alliances or piggybacking as existing clients move into new markets. Whilst government regulations and attitudes to the protection of local suppliers vary considerably from country to country, more new markets are opening up. Most importantly, however, because of the significance of interpersonal relationships in service marketing, it is often cultural empathy in the way services are developed and delivered that is critical for success.

Whilst it might seem appropriate to categorise physical goods as tangible and services as intangible, marketing increasingly appears to be concerned with blurring this distinction. For example, perfume is not promoted as a complex chemical solution, but instead, as one perfume house executive put it, 'dreams in a bottle'. Many services appear to compete over tangible 'add-ons' as we discussed earlier in this chapter.

The components of the international product offer

In creating a suitable and acceptable product offer for international markets, it is necessary to examine first, what contributes to the 'total' product, and second, decide what might make the product acceptable to the international market. Kotler (1997) suggested three essential aspects of the product offer, which should be considered by marketers in order to meet consumer needs and wants:

- **Product benefits**: the elements that consumers perceive as meeting their needs and providing satisfaction through performance and image.

- **Product attributes**: the elements most closely associated with the core product, such as features, specifications, styling, branding and packaging.

● **The marketing support services**: the additional elements to the core product which contribute to providing satisfaction and include delivery, after sales service and guarantees.

These elements form the augmented product an extended version of which is shown in Figure 9.1. Moving down and to the right of the diagram shows the elements which are relatively more difficult to standardise in different country markets.

Having introduced the concept of the total product offer, it is essential to evaluate each aspect of the product in terms of what benefits the consumer might expect to gain and how the value of the offer will be perceived by consumers by answering the following six questions for each market:

1 For what purpose has the product been developed and how would the product be used in that country?

Figure 9.1 The three elements of the product or service

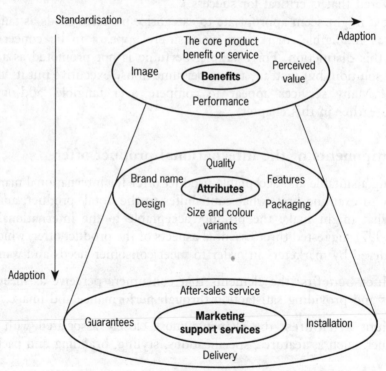

2 What distinctive physical properties does the product have?

3 What benefits is the consumer expected to gain?

4 How is the product positioned and what image do consumers perceive it to have?

5 Which consumer segments of the total market are expected to buy it, on what occasions and for what purposes?

6 How does the product fit into the total market?

The main issue for a company about to commence exporting, is to assess the *suitability of the existing products* for international markets. As a minimum, a purchaser in an overseas market expects to have a clear explanation of how a product should be used, so the instructions on the domestic packaging usually have to be translated for international markets. The question, however, is to what extent the components of the total product offer can and should be adapted for international markets.

In the case of a product where only the packaging needs to be changed, the effect on the overall cost is likely to be minimal, but if more fundamental changes to the product itself are required, because, for example, of differences in use or safety regulations, the higher cost might prove prohibitive for a small company. Such problems can be circumvented by taking an alternative market entry approach such as licensing or franchising, but in making strategic decisions of this type, the company must decide exactly what product or aspect of the augmented product will be most valued by customers in the target market (the core benefit). Put simply, the company needs to decide what business it is actually in. The main source of competitive advantage might be in manufacturing, as in the case of Samsung or in promotion and distribution as in the case of Coca-Cola.

The core benefit or main source of competitive advantage can change. As the market for leisure footwear changed away from white sports shoes Nike's strategy of trying to dominate each sports market by using massive promotional programmes has resulted in considerably reduced margins. In a similar way the clothing retailer, Laura Ashley's designs seem to be locked into a particular fashion phase and both companies could be faulted for taking a very myopic view of their markets and competitive advantage.

Factors affecting international product management

There are a number of factors that affect the international management of products and services and these include:

- the impact on the balance between standardisation and adaptation of:
  - cultural factors
  - usage factors
  - legal factors
- product accessibility and ethical issues
- green environmental issues
- shortening product life cycles
- the effect of different market entry methods
- changes in marketing management.

Towards standardisation

The discussion in Chapter 8 on globalisation leads to the conclusion that for the largest companies in the world the benefits of marketing standardised products are very significant indeed but whilst firms may be prepared to invest heavily to achieve standardisation in practice virtually all products must be adapted to some degree. The issue then becomes to what degree their industrial or consumer product or service should be standardised or adapted to the needs of the local market. Even the most obviously global companies achieve only partial standardisation of products. For example, whilst Coca-Cola adopt a global standardised branding strategy, they modify the product for particular customer segments by offering Diet and Caffeine Free Coca-Cola and altering the sweetness for different national tastes. McDonald's, too, alters its menu in different countries to cater for local tastes.

The issue facing all firms is to identify the benefit or satisfaction that the consumer recognises and will purchase. This benefit must provide the basis upon which the company can differentiate its products from those of its competitors. For a product, such as the Sony Walkman, when it was first introduced, the competitive advantage was a technical breakthrough, the first easily portable music centre, and so *standardisation of the core benefit* was possible. As products are copied so the firm must find a new source of competitive advantage and this leads to *standardisation of non-core elements* of the augmented product. In the case of Coca-Cola, the core benefit of a specific taste produced from a particular combination of ingredients is no longer a significant source of differentiation, although this might be disputed by cola connoisseurs. Instead competitive advantage is achieved by the standardisation of the imagery associated with the brand and sustained by strong advertising messages.

The decision for most companies to standardise or adapt is based on a cost/benefit analysis of what they believe the implications of adaptation or standardisation might be for revenue, profitability and market share. In normal circumstances, the cost of adaptation would be expected to be greater than the cost of successful standardisation, and so it is only if the needs and tastes identified in the target market segment are significantly different to justify product adaptation, and/or the additional business from that segment will off-set the extra cost involved that such adaptation takes place.

Whilst some companies are tempted to adopt a policy of adaptation in order to satisfy immediate demand, others believe that continual exposure to the standardised products will redefine customer needs and ultimately change their tastes, leading to greater market share in the longer term. It is interesting to contrast the strategies of firms of different nations. American companies have traditionally been very unwilling to adapt products because of the dominance of the home market, whereas Japanese companies, being increasingly dependent on exports, have been prepared to adapt products much more readily. Indeed, product differentiation has become a central part of the strategy of Japanese companies and has lead to significant advances, such as production operations being geared to producing small batch sizes and minimum stockholding.

Summarising the advantages of product standardisation the company benefits include more rapid recovery of investment, easier organisation and control of product management and the possibility to reduce costs through economies of scale and the experience effect throughout most of the firm's operations, such as production, advertising and distribution.

Product standardisation is both encouraging and being encouraged by the globalisation trends in markets, which are emerging because of three factors:

1   markets are becoming more homogeneous;
2   and there are more identifiable international consumer segments;
3   there is an increase in the number of firms moving towards globalisation, so forcing greater standardisation throughout industry sectors.

There are some disadvantages of product standardisation too, for example, market opportunities might be lost when it is impossible to match local detailed requirements. Some managers of local subsidiaries who are only expected to implement existing product policies can become de-motivated and miss market opportunities if they are not given the opportunity to innovate.

As we discussed in Chapter 7, whilst product standardisation might be difficult to implement in some countries, there are considerable benefits for the company if excessive adaptation can be avoided.

Greater standardisation of products, however, makes it easier for competitors to follow, leading inevitably to standardisation within a product category so that consumers are unable to differentiate between the core attributes of competing products, with the result that a 'commodity market' is created. To counter this, competition is centring increasingly around the augmented product elements. In the family car market, for example, there is very little to choose between the performance, reliability of the main competitors, including Ford, General Motors, Renault, Toyota, Peugeot and Nissan. Against this background, the promotion of individual cars focuses upon warranties and financing arrangements and rather less on individual performance comparisons.

A more recent trend has been to subdivide particular product categories into smaller niches, such as the Mercedes A Class, the Ford Ka and the new Volkswagen Beetle. The thinking behind this is to appeal to transnational segments whose demands and expectations are more specialised than the mass market. Another recent example of this was the subdivision the 4x4 off-road vehicles into demanding off-road work use and leisure and normal commuting use.

Reasons for adaptation of the product

In some instances, product standardisation may not be possible due to environmental constraints either through mandatory legislation, because of such reasons as differences in electrical systems, language, legal standards, safety requirements or product liability, or because the firm believes that the product appeal can be increased in a particular market by addressing cultural and usage factors.

Cultural factors

Food is a particularly difficult area for standardisation, as the preparation and eating of food are often embedded in the history, religion and/or culture of the country. This presents specific problems for fast food, for example, where the main ingredients of McDonald's and Burger King, beef and pork, prove unacceptable to many potential customers, and the necessary ingredients for fast food, such as the specific type of wheat for pizza bases, suitable chicken and mozzarella cheese are unavailable in certain countries. Indian consumers also prefer a variety of foods and so PepsiCo has Pizza Hut and Kentucky Fried Chicken under one roof in New Delhi.

A potential large market does not guarantee success. In 1994 Kellogg's invested $65 million to launch Corn Flakes in India which has a population of 250 million people but, after initial success, the sales plummeted. Usually Indians eat a bowl of hot vegetables rather than cold cereal. Kellogg's has since introduced other cereals and claims 55 per cent of the cereal market but they have a long way to go before 250 million people are converted.

Whilst the music tastes of older people from different cultures can be distinctly different, music is becoming increasingly standardised amongst young people, who have much more in common with the same age group around the world than with older people in their own country. There are limitations and sometimes a regional strategy is more effective. The Japanese entertainment industry having failed to establish itself in the West, has turned to other south east Asian markets which are believed to be some years behind in developing popular music talent. Whilst older generations in south east Asia remember being forced to learn Japanese in World War II, younger generations see Tokyo in the same way as Western youth sees New York. To the French government, maintaining the traditional culture was politically important, particularly during the GATT discussions (now WTO), and so in 1994 a law was passed that 40 per cent of the output of the music broadcasting stations must be by French musicians.

Changes are taking place in product acceptance, however. For example, fashion is becoming increasingly globalised and the traditional domination of the fashion industry by Western designers is gradually being broken down. Moreover, Levi jeans are now infiltrating countries like India which have hitherto only accepted traditional dress. Some people believe that the erosion of the country's traditional heritage and culture particularly by the media and MNE advertising is unethical and should be resisted but others suggest that larger countries such as India and China simply take those international products which serve a particular need and ignore the rest.

Concern for environmental issues, too, is becoming greater in many countries now and has considerable implications for product policies, but the nature, patterns and strength of interest vary considerably from country to country.

Usage factors

The same product might be used in quite different ways in different markets, partly due to the culture of the country, but also due to the geographical factors of climate and terrain. Unilever and Proctor and Gamble have a large variety of products adapted and branded for different markets because of the different ways products are used. For example, French people wash clothes in scalding hot water, whilst the Australians tend to use cold water. Most Europeans use front loading washing machines, whereas the French use top loaders. Honda found that when they first introduced motorcycles into the US they were unreliable and frequently broke down. Whereas Japanese riders were able only to travel short distances, American riders were used to riding the bikes over longer distances and much rougher terrain. Some years ago General Motors of Canada supplied Chevrolet vehicles to Iraq only to find that they were unsuitable for a hot and dusty climate, which lead to blocked filters and damaged clutches.

Legal standards

Standardisation of products and services can be significantly affected by legislation. Legal standards are often very country specific – often because obscure laws have been left unchanged for decades. There have been considerable problems for the European Union in attempting to harmonise standards during the creation of the single market and it has taken a number of years to achieve agreement on relatively simple products, such as confectionery, jam and sausage.

Lack of precise, reliable, understandable and universally accepted scientific information, for example in the contamination of beef in the UK, serves only to make it more difficult to achieve a satisfactory industry standard. Pharmaceutical companies experience problems in introducing products into different markets, because individual governments have differing standards of public health and approaches to healthcare. Many countries insist that they carry out their own supervised clinical testing on all drugs prior to the products being available on the market. Lax legal standards in some underdeveloped countries can lead to exploitation by unethical MNEs, for example, carrying out new product trials and 'dumping' of out of date drugs which would not be allowed in developed countries.

Product liability

In the US, over the last few years there has been a considerable increase in litigation, with lawyers seeking clients on a no win–no fee basis. For marketers, particularly those selling potentially life-threatening products such as pharmaceuticals and cars this demands much greater caution when introducing standard products based on the home country specification into these markets as litigation can lead in extreme circumstances to huge financial settlements as a result of apparently biased interpretations of the law.

By way of contrast, unscrupulous companies have exploited the different legal controls and lower risks of litigation by sending unchecked lower specification or even hazardous products, such as chemical waste to less developed countries with lower standards. However, this practice is being increasingly challenged by international pressure groups and is backed up in the US courts which have the power to control the actions of US subsidiaries abroad.

Product acceptability and ethical considerations

Consumers generally are becoming much more discerning and have greater expectations of all the elements of the augmented product. The manufacturer must take responsibility for controlling the pre- and post-purchase servicing and warranties provided by independent distributors and retailers. The packaging, branding and trademark decisions are becoming increasingly important as the global village no longer allows mistakes and failures to go unpublicised.

Consumers too, have different perceptions of the value and satisfaction of products and so their acceptability will vary quite considerably from country to country particularly where they differ in the levels of economic development. The product usage and production process may not fit with the culture and environment of the country and the product or service may not be acceptable for its intended use, as was the case with Nestle powdered milk which was sold in LDCs despite the lack of clear water to make up the milk. The technology used in the product may not support the country's development policy and the product and production processes may not make use of local resources.

Green environmental issues

Howard (1998) highlights a number of reasons which are making it necessary for firms to pay more attention to global green environmental concerns. There is:

- greater public awareness following the publicity given to environmental disasters, such as the fires in Indonesia, Thailand and Mexico, deforestation of the rain forest, water pollution, and reduction in biodiversity
- greater national and local regulation of actions which are likely to affect the environment
- greater stakeholder awareness of MNE activity through better global communications

- greater expectations that MNEs will be more responsive because of their need to preserve a good corporate citizenship image
- increasing cross border concerns being shown, with the effect that more powerful countries can exert pressure and influence on MNE activities wherever they are.

Against this background MNEs must respond in an appropriate way to the global and local concerns by taking a more global and comprehensive approach to dealing with environmental issues by anticipating and, where appropriate, initiating changes. They must also evaluate and proactively manage all the effects of the operations on the environment.

A number of companies are setting corporate strategies which address these issues, for example Sony say that by the year 2000, environmental considerations will be incorporated into the planning of every product. Ford is intending to adopt the environmental standard, ISO4001, as a worldwide standard.

The goal is to achieve environmental excellence with firms such as The Body Shop, 3M, British Telecom, Johnson Mathey, Merck, Norsk Hydro and Rank Xerox taking a strategic approach rather than making *ad hoc* decisions. There are many problems in building environmental considerations into corporate strategy, including the uncertainties of the science for example, different views on global warming, the difficulty of deciding on appropriate action because replacement processes or chemicals often give rise to new problems. The problems of adjusting to the scale of the issue have been underestimated as the concerns are increasingly global and cross border. The precise cause of environmental problems, the effect they have and the best solution are often the source of discussion and controversy, for example, there were significant differences in the scientific evidence offered by Shell and Greenpeace for the disposal either at sea or on land of the Brent Spa North Sea drilling rig.

Shortening product life cycles: the merging of markets through increasing globalisation is leading to greater concentration of powerful suppliers who have the resources to rapidly copy a competitor's product or develop their own products to exploit a new market opportunity. The increasing pace of technology means that a technical lead in a product is not likely to be held for very long as competitors catch up. This means that product life cycles are becoming shorter and improvements are introduced more frequently. To this must be added the much higher cost of research, development and commercialisation of new products which places much greater pressures on the firm to distribute the new product throughout world markets as quickly and widely as possible in order to achieve a high return on research and development investment before new products are introduced.

Franchising, joint ventures and alliances: the pressure to exploit new technology and products as quickly and widely as possible has encouraged the rapid expansion of more creative and cost effective ways of achieving cooperation in research, development and distribution, such as franchising, joint ventures and alliances formed between firms to market products. As was discussed in the previous chapter, whilst these market entry methods allow less control than total ownership, they do enable firms to develop a wider sphere of activity than they could do alone.

Marketing management: these trends have led to significant changes in the way that marketing management operates, allowing a more creative approach to be adopted in developing product policy. First, there are a wider range of options available in international marketing management, particularly by using the marketing mix elements which will be discussed later in this book. Second, there have been significant improvements in the tools available for marketing research, performance measurement and planning. Third, there are more accurate and widely available sources of information which allow greater power for global brand management, but it must be pointed out that success in using them depends upon managers being more flexible in redefining niche segments and creative in innovating in all areas of the marketing mix. Fourth, with improved internal and external networking, new product development can become much more effective in being better integrated within the firm's strategies and be capable of more satisfactorily meeting customer needs through the management of customer relationships.

Product policy

Having considered the factors which affect the starting point in developing an international product policy portfolio the next steps are to look first at the suitability of the existing products before embarking on development of new or modified products. The decision about which products should be included in the range to be marketed internationally is determined by several factors:

- the company's overall objectives in terms of growth and profits;
- the experience, philosophies and attitude of the company to international development, and which of the company's financial and managerial resources will be allocated to international marketing;

- the characteristics of the markets, such as the economic development and the barriers to trade of the firm's domestic and host countries;
- the requirements, expectations and attitudes of the consumers in the market;
- the products themselves, their attributes, appeal and perceived values (their positioning), the stage that they are at in the life cycle, economies of scale and the ease of selling them;
- the support the products require from other elements of the marketing mix and after sales services;
- environmental constraints (such as legal or political factors) which must be overcome;
- the level of risk that the company is prepared to take.

Illustration 9.2 shows how Intel is facing just such decisions as the nature of their market has changed very quickly.

Product strategies

Against the background of so many variables, it is inevitable that companies adopt a very wide range of product strategies in international markets. In formulating product policies, Mesdag (1985) has postulated that a company has three basic choices:

SWYG   Sell What You have Got.

SWAB   Sell What people Actually Buy.

GLOB   Sell the same thing GLOBally disregarding national frontiers.

All three strategies have been used for a long time. Heinz, Mars, Heineken and Johnnie Walker have been international brands for decades using global product and brand strategies to enable them to clearly position their products as global brands. The Danes have long dominated the UK bacon market by following a SWAB strategy as have the French in their marketing of cheddar cheese in the UK. The disadvantage of the SWAB strategy is that it is only possible to penetrate one market at time. It may be also difficult to compete with local firms on their own terms. Furthermore, it is sometimes difficult for a foreign company to establish credibility as a supplier of products which have a strong domestic demand, for example, Suntory of Japan made good whisky but could not attempt to market it in the UK and so it acquired Morrison Boxmore Distillers, which produces distinctively Scottish single malt whisky brands.

Illustration 9.2: Intel surprised by the booming cheap PC market and the convergence of computers and consumer electronics.

For the first time in 12 years Intel shed 5 per cent of its 65 000 workers following a 10 per cent dip in profits and the departure of one of its founders Andy Grove. Intel chips are used in 90 per cent of the world's personal computers but its success and profit has come from industrial servers made for example by Sun Microsystems and Hewlett Packard, costing around $250 000.

But rivals, such as AMD and Cyrix are competing strongly against Intel's Celeron chips for more basic PCs. Consumers are no longer prepared to constantly upgrade and have, so far, shown insufficient interest in 'processor hungry' software applications, such as speech recognition, digital imaging and video conferencing. Intel's growth has also been frustrated due to the delays of the telephone companies in bringing into homes and businesses the wide bandwidth that video and graphics rich websites need.

Finally the TV set top boxes for decoding the signals for digital television and providing Internet access are like simple PCs and are expected to sell in many millions but a variety of operating systems and processors have emerged. Already there are more competitors, such as Hitachi, MIPS and ARM. The problems for Intel are first to decide which part of the market it should be in, and particularly whether it should be in the cut-throat part of the market and, second, how can they find a successor to Grove who will supply Intel with the ideas to drive its future success.

Source: adapted from *The Economist* (1998) 'Not good enough? Intel's troubles: The booming market for cheap PCs took Intel by surprise', 4 April

The SWAB approach is the classic differentiated approach, but whilst it is responsive to market needs it does make considerable demands on the firm's development, manufacturing, logistics and financial resources and is often impractical for these reasons. *The Economist* (1997) explains how the first Fiat Palio, launched in Brazil in 1996 was designed specifically for the emerging markets and had already sold 250 000 within 18 months whilst Ford decided to make its Western European Fiesta in Brazil and suffered delays and product recalls and very poor results after launch.

SWYG are the most common form of export strategies, but they are also the most common reason for failure. The key objective for most firms following such strategies is to fill production lines at home rather that meeting a market need, but by concentrating only on a few markets, many companies do successfully implement this kind of strategy. Mesdag argues also that some of the most successful global products started off as domestic products with a SWYG strategy, for example pizza, hamburgers and yoghurt. Success has been the result of the company's ability to meet new international emerging demand for the convenience of fast foods. The products may not necessarily be formulated identically across markets but they appeal to a pan-regional or global need and can therefore be positioned as cross-frontier brands. The success of the strategy has been based on identifying and meeting the needs of transnational customer segments.

Keegan (1989) has highlighted the key aspects of international marketing strategy as a combination of standardisation or adaptation of product and promotion elements of the mix and offers five alternative and more specific approaches to product policy.

One product, one message worldwide

Since the 1920s, Coca-Cola have adopted a global approach, which has allowed them to make enormous cost savings and benefit from continual *reinforcement of the same message*. Whilst a number of writers have argued that this will be the strategy adopted for many products in the future, in practice only handful of products might claim to have achieved this already. A number of firms have tried this and failed. Campbell's soups, for example, found that consumers taste in soup was by no means international.

Product extension, promotion adaptation

Whilst the product stays the same, this strategy allows for the *adaptation of the promotional effort to target either new customer segments* or appeal to the particular tastes of individual countries, for example, Yoplait yoghurt attempts to capture the mood of the country in its various television advertising.

Product adaptation, promotion extension

This strategy is used if a *promotional campaign has achieved international appeal*, but the product needs to be adapted because of the local needs. Many suppliers of capital goods promote the idea of providing technical solutions rather than selling industrial plans and Exxon used the 'tiger in the tank' campaign around the world and IBM have used 'Solutions for a small planet'.

Dual adaptation

By adapting both products and promotion for each market, the firm is adopting a *totally differentiated approach.* This strategy is often adopted by firms when one of the previous three strategies has failed, but particularly if the firm is not in a leadership position and, instead, must react to the market or follow the competitors.

Product invention

Product invention is adopted by firms usually from advanced nations who are supplying products to less well-developed countries. Products are *specifically developed* to meet the needs of the individual markets. After watching a programme about AIDS in Africa at his home on Eel Pie Island in the middle of the Thames in London, Trevor Bayliss invented the clockwork radio to help the news to be spread to areas which did not have electricity and could not afford batteries. Despite rejections by major MNEs, Bayliss persevered and 50 000 radios per month are made by disabled staff by BayGen in South Africa. BayGen is now worth in excess of £100 million.

Managing products across borders

The life cycle concept is used as a model for considering the implications for marketing management of a product passing through the stages of introduction, growth, maturity and decline and can be applied to international marketing. The British popular music industry was outstandingly successful as a major exporter during the 1960s, 1970s and early 1980s, all starting, perhaps, with the era of the Beatles and Rolling Stones, when British artists rapidly gained global recognition. The market share of the industry declined during the early 1990s from 23 per cent to 18 per cent of the world market and this share resulted largely from re-releases and new offerings from ageing rock stars such as Eric Clapton, Elton John and Sting. The mid 1990s saw the emergence of new groups such as the Spice Girls and Oasis, but shortening product life cycles appear to affect this industry too with new stars staying at the top for much shorter periods.

The international product life cycle suggests that products in international markets can have consecutive 'lives' in different countries; this is illustrated in Figure 9.2.

The cycle focuses upon a process in which product saturation in one market is followed by product growth in a less developed country, so that there could be

Figure 9.2 The international product life cycle

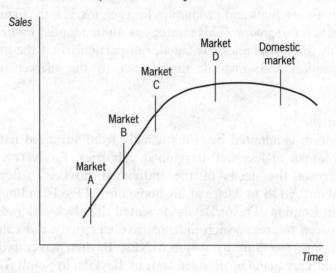

consecutive life cycles for, say, a consumer durable moving progressively from North America to Western Europe, Australasia and finally to South America.

The most significant change for both life cycle models is that the international communication revolution has led to more frequent *simultaneous product introductions,* particularly of consumer products, by global companies into different world markets backed by global branding and promotion, and so the sequential approach to marketing and manufacturing that is encapsulated in the original model applies less frequently. However, as we established earlier, not all companies operating internationally are global corporations, and it is therefore important not to ignore the model altogether. The concept of phases in the life cycle is still useful for a company that is simply exporting from an advanced economy specialist engineering components and tools or agricultural equipment.

On balance, therefore, although the validity of the product life cycle has at various times been attacked by a variety of writers, it does have a role to play for certain types of company insofar as it is a model that provides a framework for thinking in detail about product policy, new product development, product introduction and product elimination. Because life cycles generally are shortening, there is an increased need for a well-developed policy of new product development and differentiation in order to replace or extend the life cycle, as Luxottica have achieved, shown in the Illustration 9.3.

Illustration 9.3: Internationalising in a mature industry sector

Luxottica and Parmalat of Italy have grown rapidly in the last 30 years to become market leaders in essentially mature industry sectors. Luxoticca turned a small venture in making moulds for plastic eyeglass frames into a world leader with 9 per cent of the world market using vertical integration (design, production and distribution) to transform a highly fragmented market.

The key element in the strategy was early recognition of the trend to the use of designer labels. Luxottica manufactures under licence for seven labels including Armani, Yves St Lauren, Bulgari and Valentino, leaving the cheaper glasses to be manufactured by Asian producers. Luxottica also diversified into sunglasses and have recently bought LensCrafter, the largest eyewear retailer in the US.

By contrast with Luxottica's global brand, Parmalat cannot sell fresh products and milk from its home base and instead has adopted a regional approach to globalisation exploiting fragmented markets dominated by small inefficient companies. Parmalat has acquired small companies bringing the new subsidiaries' technology, production and distribution know-how together through a coherent marketing approach and brand. It has focused on fast growing markets such as Eastern Europe and Latin America, which accounts for more than 40 per cent of sales and 50 per cent of profits.

Italian family companies have usually been taken over by multi-nationals when they have outgrown their family structures, and Luxottica and Parmalat are trying to avoid the same fate.

Source: adapted from Betts, P. (1997) 'The global company: Italy's star acquirers aim to defy a trend', *Financial Times,* 22 October

Product portfolio analysis

The use of portfolio approaches in international product management centres around the Boston Consulting Group's growth – Share Matrix, the General Electric/McKinsey Screen, and the Arthur D. Little Business Profile Matrix. They are designed primarily to clarify the *current strategic position* of a company and its competitors, and to help *identify any future strategic options*.

The complexities and dimensions of the analysis increase considerably when applied to the firm's international portfolio, since the competitive positions occupied by a product are likely to differ significantly from one market to another, as indeed will the nature and intensity of competition. Comparing the strength of a portfolio across a variety of markets becomes difficult as the analytical base constantly changes. For these reasons, the BCG matrix, for example, might be based on one product area with the circles in the matrices representing country sales instead of product sales as shown in Figure 9.3. This then provides a basis for analysing the current international product portfolio, assessing competitors' product/market strengths and forecasting the likely development of future portfolios both for itself and its competitors.

Introduction and elimination activities

Whilst the major focus of product policy is upon new product development, the increased pace of the activity has a number of consequences for product management at both ends of the product life cycle. The factors that need to be taken into account in managing the product portfolio are:

Figure 9.3 The portfolio approach to strategic analysis (BCG matrix)

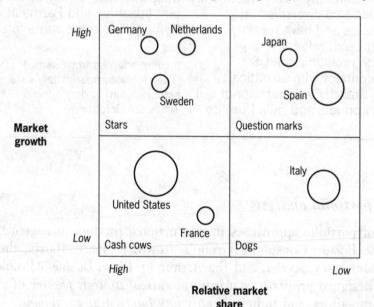

- the firm's objectives;
- the company's existing range of products and degree of overlap in the positioning of products in the range;
- the stage in the life cycle that the products have reached;
- the manufacturing capacity available;
- the likely receptiveness of the market to the new product; and
- the competitive structure of the market.

These factors have a number of implications for the product policy. Too many product introductions, can risk overburdening the firm's marketing system by having too many products. There is a constant need therefore for a regular review of the range and for elimination decisions to be made where a product is either in its decline stage or simply failing to generate sufficient profit. The international perspective, however, means that decision making is more difficult, since a product may be manufactured principally in a plant in the country, be a 'cash cow' in one market and a 'dog' in another. Careful analysis is therefore needed before the product elimination decision is taken. The identification of overlaps or gaps in the product range may necessitate elimination of products if they are in the declining stage of the product life cycle, have been duplicated or have been replaced by a newer product.

The complexity of managing a wide portfolio of products at Nestle is shown in Illustration 9.4 and it raises some fundamental issues about the focus of the business and the scope of its activities.

Image, branding and positioning

Of all the elements of the product or service offer, it is the image of the brand which is the most visible and it is the perceived value which consumers attach to this that is the central factor in positioning the products in the various markets.

The image of products, companies and countries can confer different values to consumers in different countries. Research by a number of writers has shown that products from particular countries have a stereotyped national image for such attributes as quality, price and reliability. Individual corporate brands either benefit from positive country of origin perceptions or must overcome negative perceptions to succeed in international markets.

Illustration 9.4: Nestlé's portfolio

The Swiss-based food manufacturer Nestlé has a vast range of products but just five products account for 35 per cent of its European sales, ten for 50 per cent and 18 for 75 per cent. The remaining 20 other products account for the final 25 per cent. The long tail achieves tiny market shares, geographic coverage and profit. Whilst the company is in a strong cash position, these peripheral products tends to reduce managerial focus – especially as the firm gives individual managers country autonomy, and the minor products do little to assist in achieving the firm's targets of 4 per cent volume growth and 15 per cent return on capital.

Nestlé only identifies processed meat (80 per cent of which is in Herta Germany) as a sell-off candidate, and even then Nestlé would be prepared to sell-off only the simpler processed meats such as sausages and salami preferring to keep the higher margin products. Other strong niche products include Gales honey, Sun Pat peanut butter and Sarsons vinegar in the UK and Buitoni pasta, which had a small unprofitable share of the Italian market but now, with the addition of accompanying sauces, is performing much better.

Nestlé also has an acquisition strategy (they expect two thirds of their overall growth from organic growth and one third from acquisition) and have bought brands including L'Oreal cosmetics, Perrier (France) to develop a mineral water business and Rowntree (UK) to double its confectionery share. Buying Chambourcy in the 1980s gave Nestlé a big yoghurt brand but now it has become a commodity business, except for the higher value products such as chilled desserts and bio-tech yoghurt. Another question for Nestlé is when to keep existing individual product brands and when to use the Nestle brand. Recently they have started moving products from Chambourcy to the Nestlé brand.

Ice cream and pet foods are the top two products and targeted for rapid growth, especially in Europe, but they currently lag behind the market leaders, Unilever in ice cream and Mars in pet foods. Nestlé have reasonable shares in pet foods only in Italy (23 per cent) and France (15 per cent), but a new pan-European management team is in place and Nestlé is likely to make acquisitions in order to increase its share.

Source: adapted from Oram, R. (1996) 'Nestlé portfolio of possibilities', *Financial Times,* 8 August

Country of origin effects

Buyers evaluate the products that they may wish to purchase, based on their assessment of intrinsic cues (taste, design, performance and quality) and extrinsic cues (brand names, packaging and country of origin).

Where the buyers' knowledge about the product is limited, for example because they do not understand the technology, country of origin perceptions influence their buying decisions. The consumers' perceptions of companies are usually based on national stereotypes, for example Japanese products tend to be regarded as high quality, reliable and 'miniaturised'.

By contrast products from developing countries are often seen by Western consumers as low quality, unreliable and usually copies of products from developed countries. This was the perception of Japanese products too some decades ago and shows that it is possible to change consumer attitudes.

There are significant differences between countries in the willingness of consumers to buy locally produced products. Usually this appears to be related to the feeling of nationalism that exists in the country at the particular time the assessment is made. In developing countries, such as China, Ho (1997) found that nationally produced goods are often seen to be inferior to foreign goods.

The country of origin affect does extend further. For example, the stereotyping relates just as much to developed countries. For example, there are strong associations between countries and the products that they are known for, for example Italy and pizza and Germany and machine tools. Agarwal and Sikri (1996) found positive correlations between the best-known product categories from a country and the expectations that buyers have of new products from that country. Overcoming these stereotypes is often the first challenge for international marketers who must prove that their product does not reinforce negative stereotypes.

Increasingly, of course, the MNE's headquarters, the brand's perceived 'home', the location of product design and places of manufacture may all be different countries. Research is being carried out into these effects on consumer purchasing habits, for example, by Haefer (1997) and Thakor and Kohli (1996).

An interesting case is that of British cars such as Jaguar, Rover and Rolls Royce which have not succeeded internationally as well as they might have, perhaps because of negative perceptions and experiences of the cars during the 1960s and 1970s. It will be interesting to see what effect foreign ownership by Ford, BMW and Volkswagen respectively, has on their future.

Product image: as we have already emphasised, product image is one of the most powerful points of differentiation for consumers. The aspirational and achiever groups of purchasers wish to belong to particular worldwide customer segments and are keen to purchase products which are associated with that group. An interesting example of this is that the sales of luxury goods remained buoyant during the recession of the early 1990s due to increased sales to emerging countries as the new rich sought to buy similar products and services to the 'old' rich.

Company image is becoming increasingly important in creating a central theme running through diverse product ranges to demonstrate a vision of the values of the company which can be recognised by employees and customers alike. For this reason many companies have spent considerable effort and resources on controlling and enhancing the corporate identity through consistent style and communications, discussed in more detail in Chapter 10.

Illustration 9.5 shows how a number of country, company and product influences affect the imagery and success of international fashion brands.

Image can be equally important at the other end of the product spectrum to luxury goods. Aldi (Germany), Netto (Denmark) and Lidl (Sweden) use a no frills approach to retailing by reinforcing their message of low prices with simple decor, warehouse-type displays and single colour understated packaging.

The image of a company also plays a vital role in business-to-business marketing, for example, when quoting for international capital projects. Decisions are likely to be made on the grounds of the perceived reputation of the company as, without a strong international presence, it can be quite difficult to break into a small elite circle of international companies, even if very low prices are quoted.

International branding

Closely linked with the image of the product is the issue of branding. The role of branding, important as it is in domestic markets takes on an additional dimension in international markets as it is the most visible of the firm's activities particularly for global companies as we have discussed in Chapter 7. Brands allow customers to identify products or services which will promise specific benefits, such as performance price quality or image. For the firm, brands provide a point of differentiation from their competitors' products and are a way of adding value to the product. For these reasons, brands are extremely valuable in providing access to markets.

Illustration 9.5: Italian fashion influences

The fashion industry is an interesting mixture of global brands, national stereotyping and distinctive brand styles. To the general public, Italy's fashion industry is associated with famous Italian designers such as Giorgio Armani, Gianni Versace, Prada and Valentino and yet the success of the Italian fashion industry has been based on making agreements with local and foreign design talent, such as Jean-Paul Gaultier, Rifat Ozbek and Narcisco Rodriguez. Over the last decade the Italian industry has benefited from its association with a sporty, looser, less formal look whereas the French houses in general have been reluctant to leave behind *haute couture* fashion. The weak lira, too, helped the Italian industry gain ground because of less expensive manufacturing contracts.

At the individual brand level the strategy has been to build up a loyal client-base through a global network of stores. Gucci, following its purchase from the warring Gucci family by the Bahrain-based Investcorp has recovered to become one of the hottest fashion labels of the 1990s largely through better marketing to ensure that the favourable publicity generated by Tom Ford the Texan designer is used for the benefit of all the brands' products.

During the 1980s some inappropriate expansion and brand stretching led to the devaluation of brands such as Gucci and Pierre Cardin in response to relatively unrestrained spending on fashion. The early 1990s saw consumers spending less on fashion and more on the home and so the stores of famous brands, such as Ralf Lauren, Calvin Klein and Mulberry are being used for more thoughtful marketing to encourage clients to purchase a particular brand style not only for fashion but also for interiors too.

Source: adapted from Rawsthorn, A. (1997) 'Survey Italian industry and business: Fashion – the empire strikes back', *Financial Times*, 10 December and van der Post, L. (1996) 'How to spend it: Success on a plate – fashion designers offer total immersion in their labels as they turn to the world of interiors', *Financial Times*, 7 September

In 1988 brand values reached a peak with Kohlberg Kravis Roberts paying $25 billion for RJR Nabisco with the brands valued at $18 billion, and Nestle paying $4.5 billion for Rowntree with the brands valued at $4 billion.

Rather than discuss the definitions of branding, which are covered widely in the business journals it is, perhaps, more useful to consider a different approach which enables a range of consumer and business-to-business brand issues to be considered together. Underpinning the concept of branding is that the company owning the brand and its customers must both obtain benefit. De Chernatony (1989) suggests that there are nine themes which help to define the brand over a wide range of situations:

- a legal instrument
- a differentiating device
- a company
- an identity system
- an image in consumers' minds
- a personality
- a relationship
- added value
- an evolving entity.

These themes suggest that the constituents of the brand can include both tangible benefits, such as quality and reliability and intangible benefits which may bring out a whole range of feelings, such as status, being fashionable or possessing good judgement by purchasing a particular brand. These can be used to improve the relationship between the company and the individual customer, wherever in the world they may be situated.

The brand value equation (Figure 9.4) draws attention to the offer to consumers of the intangible benefits that the brand adds over and above the tangible, functional benefits of a commoditised product or service. The challenge

Figure 9.4 The brand value equation

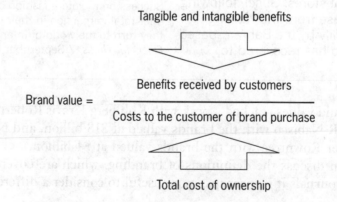

Tangible and intangible benefits

Brand value = $\dfrac{\text{Benefits received by customers}}{\text{Costs to the customer of brand purchase}}$

Total cost of ownership

for international branding, of course, is to what extent the intangible benefits from branded products and services vary between countries, cultures and individuals. During the late 1990s, wearing Nike trainers in some countries was the price of peer pressure, measured in terms of the cost of belonging to a particular reference group, whereas elsewhere it set the wearer apart as the leader of the group, as having status and style to which the other members of the group must aspire. But, of course, Nike trainers in these terms was a fashion item and the test of a truly global brand is its ability to achieve durable brand strength and this will only be established over a period of many years.

These tangible and intangible benefits must also be valued against the background of the total cost of ownership of the branded product by the customer.

The total cost of ownership and the tangible and intangible benefits are accrued over the lifetime of the product. For example, car ownership offers different benefits and costs in different markets especially when considering the longer-term implications of, for example, warranty and servicing costs, car resale value, changing car fashions. Brand strength for cars is, to some extent, determined by the second-hand car values, with car marques such as BMW and Mercedes holding their value exceptionally well and some cars, such as Ferrari even increasing in value.

Brand value

It has been suggested that the strongest brands convey a core value to all their customers by the associations that are made with their name. By adding '-ness' to the brand names consumers instantly associate values which are globally recognised – for example, 'IBMness' is distinguishable from 'Microsoftness'. The great brands (Figure 9.5) have achieved their global status through high levels of investment and consistent management across their country markets of the dimensions used to value the brand over a long period of time. Usually the investment includes a large commitment to advertising but other factors, such as totally consistent quality, reliability and continuous innovation are just as important to achieve widespread customer recommendations.

Brand valuation is to some degree inevitably subjective but the dimensions indicated in Figure 9.6 show that building the brand requires dedicated management across the various markets and there is evidence of this in all the successful brands. Brands can, of course, also decline in value from time to time due, for example, to a failure to understand customer expectations (EuroDisney), to inappropriate brand stretching (a number of the top fashion brands), to a

Figure 9.5 The world's most valuable brands

Brand	Brand value
Coca-Cola	47.99
Marlboro	47.64
IBM	23.70
McDonald's	19.94
Disney	17.07
Sony	14.46
Kodak	14.44
Intel	13.27
Gillette	11.99
Budweiser	11.99
Nike	11.13
Kellogg's	10.67
AT&T	10.39
Nescafe	10.34
GE	10.29
Hewlett-Packard	9.42
Pepsi	9.32
Microsoft	8.99
Frito-Lay	8.99
Levi's	8.17

Source: Financial World (1997) September/October, based on Interbrand formula

Figure 9.6 Brand valuation

The most basic criteria for brand evaluation include:

- title to the brand has to be clear and separately disposable from the rest of the business

- the value has to be substantial and long term, based on separately identifiable earnings that have to be in excess of those achieved by unbranded products

failure to reposition in response to market decline (a number of suppliers) or failure to respond to new competition (Pan Am and many of the European and American car manufacturers at some point in their recent history).

Branding strategies

There are four recognised branding strategies:

Corporate umbrella branding is used by firms such as Heinz, Kellogg's and Cadbury's in which the corporate name is the lead name for all their products, for example, Kellogg's Healthwise, Kellogg's Frosties, Kellogg's Corn Flakes.

Family umbrella names are used to cover a range of products in a variety of markets. For example Marks and Spencer use their St Michael brand for clothing, food, household goods and toiletries.

Range branding is used for a range of products with a particular link in a specific market such as Lean Cuisine for low-calorie foods.

Individual brand names are used with individual products in a particular market, with different weights, colours, flavours and pack sizes. Proctor and Gamble and Unilever use individual brand names such as Daz, Ariel and Omo with no reference to the corporate name.

A further branding strategy, *private branding*, is the practice of supplying products to a third party for sale under their brand name. Ricoh gained a 9 per cent market share for its small plain paper copiers by acting as an *Original Equipment Manufacturer (OEM)* for a number of suppliers including Nashua for Canada and Europe, Kalle of West Germany for Europe and Savin for the US. The two South Korean companies, Samsung and LG, have rapidly developed internationally to the point now where they have high shares of certain product ranges. They have achieved this largely by being an OEM manufacturer but it is interesting to note that these companies over the last few years have increasingly prioritised their own Samsung and Goldstar brands.

Private branding is used widely in retailing and as the major retailers have become more powerful, so the private brand share of the market has increased significantly, especially during the recession. This is because the consumers perceive private brands as providing 'value for money', and this has been encouraged as retailers have continually improved the quality of their own label products.

Quelch and Harding (1996) suggest that supermarket brands increase profits; in the US just over 19 per cent of supermarket volume is from store brands whereas 54 per cent of Sainsbury (UK) and 41 per cent of Tesco (UK) sales are from private labels and they return 5 per cent higher pre-tax profits than the US firms. By being part of a stable oligopoly international retailers have the size and resources to invest in high-quality own label development. Marks and Spencer, for example, supplies only own label.

There are significant implications of these strategies in international markets, and an example of this was Nestle, which was selling Camembert cheese throughout Europe using several different national brands in different styles of packaging. Having redesigned and standardised the packaging, they placed the Nestle brand logo alongside the local brand logo on the packaging and then gradually increased the size of the Nestle brand and reduced the size of the local brand.

Much of what has been said so far about product standardisation and adaptation applies to branding. De Chernatony *et al.* (1995) identify two components of brand planning: the core concept (the essence of what the brand stands for in terms of its added value positioning) and its execution (the detailed implementation through packaging, product contents, tactical promotions and media policy). In a demand–supply model (Figure 9.7) they emphasise the most important considerations to be the extent of customer convergence in the demand side and the cost savings from the supply side.

Brand piracy

One of the most difficult challenges for brand management is the threat of brand piracy. Research suggests that the problem of forgery of famous brand names is increasing and many of the fake products have been found to originate in developing countries and in Asia. It is important to recognise the differences between the ways in which forgery takes place (Kaitiki 1981) identifies:

- Outright piracy in which a product is in the same form and uses the same trademark as the original but is false.

- Reverse engineering in which the original product is stripped down, copied then undersold to the original manufacturer, particularly in the electronics industry.

- Counterfeiting in which the product quality has been altered but the same trademark appears on the label. Benetton, Levi Strauss and LaCoste have all been victims.

Figure 9.7 International branding model

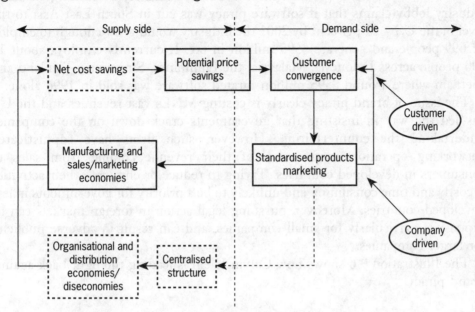

- Passing off involves modifying the product but retaining a trademark which is similar in appearance, phonetic quality or meaning – for example Coalgate for Colgate and Del Mundo for Del Monte.

- Wholesale infringement is the questionable registration of the names of famous brand overseas rather than the introduction of fake products. This might be considered to be brand piracy but is entirely within the law.

There is a vast trade in pirated brands and copied products. It has been estimated that 90 per cent of the software used in India is counterfeit and the problem is likely to be as severe in China. However, some cultures do not accept that individuals should gain from ideas which should benefit everyone and so there can be substantial differences of the perception of the importance of counterfeiting. Others believe that the development of many underdeveloped economies would have been set back considerably if they had paid market rates for software and this raises the ethical question of whether oligopolistic companies such as Microsoft should make fortunes for certain individuals by charging very high prices, whilst effectively excluding customers in under-developed countries who cannot afford to pay.

However, a report by the Business Software Alliance, a Washington-based industry lobby claims that if software piracy was cut in South East Asia to the level in the US – 27 per cent by 2001 the industry would grow enough to employ 22 699 people and generate $595 million in tax. It currently employs about 16 000 people across Indonesia, Malaysia, the Phillipines, Singapore, Thailand and Vietnam where around $595 million pirated software was sold in 1996 alone.

The issue of brand piracy clearly is costing MNEs vast revenues and the US has led the way in insisting that governments crack down on the companies undertaking the counterfeiting. However, such firms have sophisticated networking operations with much of their revenue coming from sales to consumers in developed countries. Trying to reduce or eliminate their activities is costly and time consuming and unlikely to be a priority for governments in less developed countries. Moreover, pursuing legal action in foreign markets can be expensive, particularly for small companies, and can result in adverse publicity for larger companies.

The Illustration 9.6 shows how Calvin Klein is leading the fight back against brand piracy.

Positioning

Closely related to brand strategy and at the heart of the implementation of brand strategy, is positioning. Positioning is largely concerned with how a product or service might be differentiated from the competition. However, it is important to stress that *it is the customers' perceptions of the product or service* offer that will indirectly confirm the positioning and so determine its success. Firms can only seek to establish and confirm the positioning in the consumers' minds through their management of the marketing mix. In countries at different stages of economic development the customer segments that are likely to be able to purchase the product and the occasions on which it is bought may be significantly different. For example, whilst KFC and McDonald's restaurants aim at everyday eating for the mass market in the developed countries, in less developed countries they are perceived as places for special occasion eating, and out of reach of the poorest segments of the population. A Mercedes car may be perceived as a luxury car in many countries but as an 'everyday' taxi in Germany.

Unilever has a different approach. It introduced a new logo for its ice cream, so that whilst the familiar names stay the same, for example, Wall's in the UK and Ola in the Netherlands, the background design and font are being standardised around the world.

Illustration 9.6: Calvin Klein fights the pirates

If you buy a T-shirt with the CK logo of Calvin Klein for $5 it almost certainly will be counterfeit. As well as losing sales, Calvin Klein suffers from the shoddy merchandise affecting the consumers' perception of the quality of the brand.

Whilst Calvin Klein has been regarded as one of the foremost fashion designers in North America since the 1970s, internationally the brand was mainly associated with perfumes, such as Obsession and Eternity. More recently the firm has reached long-term licensing deals for making clothing too.

But, as with other global luxury brands such as Gucci, Chanel and Ralf Lauren, it has become the target of Asian and European counterfeiters. In response the firm has decided to become more proactive, by appointing a new senior vice president at its headquarters to take responsibility for action through a network of hired legal specialists in Europe and Asia, and external specialists, to uncover copyright abuse. They liase with the London and Hong Kong offices of Baker and Mackenzie, an international firm of copyright lawyers, which assembles local teams of lawyers and investigators to work on its behalf.

The network has already seized 370 000 pairs of jeans from 12 factories in the UK, impounded a cargo of 15 487 jeans and 2980 fake shirts manufactured in Bangladesh and bound for Russia.

Source: adapted from Rawsthorn, A. (1997) 'Fashion victim fights back: Calvin Klein is tired of piracy and has started a global offensive against counterfeiters', *Financial Times*, 24 February

The perceptions of the product positioning are likely to vary in some dimensions. However, there appears to be an increasing demand for standardised products particularly in the developed countries, amongst market segments that are mobile and susceptible to influence by the media and through travel, and clearly there is a strongly emerging demand for the same products amongst consumers in the less developed countries. Achieving unique positioning for a product or service must come from the creative dimensions of positioning rather than resorting to simple price positioning.

In confirming the positioning of a product or service in a specific market or region, it is necessary, therefore, to *establish in the consumers' perception exactly what the product stands for and how it differs from existing and potential competition* by designing an identity which will clarify the value of the product. In doing this it is necessary to emphasise the basis of the positioning strategy, which might focus upon one or more element of the total product offer. The differentiation might be based upon price and quality, one or more product or service attributes, a specific application, a target consumer or direct comparison with one competitor.

New product development

A recurring theme of discussions of international marketing issues is the increasing need for companies to have a dynamic and proactive policy for developing new products in order to satisfy the apparently insatiable demand of consumers for new experiences and to reinforce and, where necessary, renew their source of competitive advantage. 3M, for example, sets itself the target that 10 per cent of its sales must come from brand new product introductions and 25 per cent of sales from products less than four years old.

The nature of new product development

It is important to recognise at the outset, however, that few new products are actually revolutionary products. Figure 9.8 shows the various categories of new

Figure 9.8 New product categories

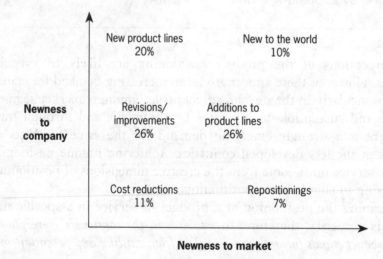

products in terms of their newness to the market and company. The implications of this are that firms need to innovate in every aspect of their business through a process of continual improvement rather than wait for the next breakthrough invention.

Many of the products are largely intended to refresh and reinforce the product range by complementing the existing company and brand image rather than causing a change of direction. In the famous New Coke fiasco, the new recipe, preferred in taste tests and intended to improve the product, was resisted in the US in favour of retaining a traditional image because it was seen to pose a threat to the American culture.

Major invention breakthroughs still occur, although significantly less frequently than before but there are exceptions. Usually developing new technologies is hugely expensive. For example, it is estimated that the cost of developing a new drug is now in excess of $300 million and takes over fifteen years. In order to recover the research and development costs it is necessary to market new ideas simultaneously in all developed countries, as the time taken by competitors to copy or improve products and circumvent patents is shortening. Even the largest companies do not have sufficient resources on their own to achieve rapid distribution of the product into all world markets and so the diffusion of new products into world markets is at least as important a part of the process as the initial idea. This leads to the use of different market entry methods, such as licensing, franchising and strategic alliances to secure cost effective diffusion.

The new product development process

In its simplest form developing products follows a similar process for international markets to that in domestic situations:

- idea generation
- initial screening
- business analysis
- development
- market testing
- commercialisation and launch.

Where the process does differ in international markets, however, is in the level of analysis, coordination and communication that becomes necessary when assessing the new product's suitability for a variety of markets. Particular emphasis must be placed upon the quality of the information system since it is essential that the product or service meets the needs of the customers and is positioned accurately in each market from the outset. With this in mind the international development process should incorporate the following elements.

Idea generation must ensure that ideas worldwide are accessed so that duplication is avoided and synergy is optimised by effectively using all available internal and external resources to generate new ideas, including employees, R&D departments, competitors, sales people, customers, distributors and external experts.

Initial screening involves establishing rigorous international screening criteria, including both production and marketing factors to test the ideas for suitability in all world regions so that opportunities and limitations are not overlooked. Ideas that may, for example, be inappropriate for Western Europe might be appropriate for South America. In doing this an assessment should be made of the degree of adaptation that will be necessary for individual markets.

Business analysis must involve establishing criteria for potential success or failure of the product and linking the criteria with regions and/or markets. It must make provision for contingencies such as environmental and competitive situations and unexpected events which might adversely affect the business case.

Product development must include ensuring that all relevant functions such as production, design, packaging become involved in the process. The most appropriate R&D centres for the development process should be selected with particular attention being paid to such factors as technological expertise and location near prime target and lead markets.

Market testing must involve ensuring the test area is representative in terms of prime target markets, it has an adequate infrastructure in terms of the necessary services such as advertising and market research agencies, and an appropriate distribution network. It should also take account of potential competitor response both in the test market and globally.

The launch must be planned either to be sequential, with an initial concentration upon prime markets or lead markets, or to be a simultaneous launch. Plans should be prepared for aggressive competitive responses as few competitors will give up market share without a fight.

To protect the firm's competitive advantage the company needs to pay particular attention to the ability of competitors to copy a new product and launch it in a separate market. There are a number of actions that companies might take, such as taking strong patent protection, or entering into licensing arrangements to ensure fast, widespread penetration of the world or regional markets.

Timing is perhaps the most critical element of the process, not only in terms of exploiting an opportunity or competitive weakness at the right moment but also minimising the time to market – how long it takes from when the idea was first generated to making it available commercially and the time it takes to achieve the desired level of diffusion.

Lotus Notes (Illustration 9.7) is an interesting example of a development which has taken a different approach to the market needs from the existing competition and demonstrates that development takes time, but the timing for the market must be right.

Approaches to technology transfer and the benefits for marketing

The traditional, sequential and largely internal approach to new product development has considerable disadvantages because of a number of factors including the:

- shortening of product life cycles;
- risk and cost of internal development;
- time, cost and expertise required for testing; and

Illustration 9.7: Raising the profile of Lotus Notes

In 1995, IBM acquired Lotus Notes. Such software company acquisitions are notoriously difficult, but this one was a success, largely because IBM allowed Lotus the space it needed to develop and not become submerged within the company. IBM's main interest was in Lotus Notes groupware which eventually would be the building block for the network computing business. In 3 years, users of Notes increased from 2 million to 22 million.

Initially, Notes was developed for big companies where it is dominant. It was regarded as too expensive (£250) for the mass market of SMEs, but since the merger with IBM, the price of Notes has been reduced to a more reasonable level (£50). In addition, Notes has been developed to be very flexible and powerful, enabling users to edit and process reports from anywhere in the world and use it in conjunction with applications from other suppliers. This development was useful for SMEs who had previously been overwhelmed with information and confused by the restrictions of using competitive products.

● need to have 'non-core' activities such as product and packaging design and process development as part of the in-house development process.

In an attempt to resolve these problems many firms are adopting a more *interactive approach* in which new product developments are carried out jointly between the manufacturer, component maker, designer and technology supplier. A variety of specialist organisations including design companies, R&D companies and universities might be used by the manufacturer to increase the speed and quality of the development. The main benefits of an interactive approach to new product development for the company are the concentration of skills and expertise on core activities, the ability to condense time-scales and access to the best knowledge available on a particular topic. This often leads to a multi-country membership of a project team and with it the difficulties of coordination and management that have already been discussed.

The 707 design for Boeing was developed by engineers, the components put out to competitive tender and then sold to airlines with little customisation.

The initial design for the 777 was created using software that allowed easy access and participation by suppliers from around the world who could make contributions as the design evolved and helped in the process to optimise the design for manufacture, assembly, efficiency, safety and quality. At the same time the airlines could also have an input, from purchasers to baggage handlers, flight attendants and even passengers, as well as Boeing's accountants, assembly workers and marketing experts.

Research and development strategies

No matter which approach is adopted, major international companies must still decide upon the aims of their own R&D, the exact nature of the activities undertaken and where they should be located. They must take decisions on:

● the location of their own internal R&D facilities;
● the extent to which they contract out certain parts of their research and development programme;
● whether or not they might acquire a company which can provide either the required new technology or a new product;
● licensing the technology and process from another company; or
● funding joint ventures or strategic alliances with companies that have complementary technology.

Small companies, with low-key international operations which amount to little more than *ad hoc* exporting, are rarely involved in genuine considerations of international new product development and concentrate their R&D activities in the domestic country, but as they grow, pressures emerge to establish R&D facilities in other locations and it becomes necessary to balance the arguments for and against centralisation. As the operations of transnational companies and the diversity of sources of supply become increasingly complex, different patterns of involvement in R&D investments emerge such as:

- units to transfer technology from the parent company to foreign subsidiaries;
- local technology units to specifically develop new and improved products in the local markets;
- global technology units, not necessarily based at the head office, to develop and launch products simultaneously into the major world markets; and
- corporate technology units, which concentrate upon the generation of new technology of a long-term/exploratory nature.

In general, the R&D activities of international companies tend to follow an evolutionary path, but for many the major question is whether or not they should move away from the dominance of their domestic country R&D location and if so, where should their R&D facilities be located.

R&D location: centralised or decentralised

Many companies still concentrate a large proportion of R&D activity in their country of origin, but as they move increasingly towards transnational operations, so the concept of the 'home country' becomes increasingly meaningless. It is, however, useful to consider the arguments for and against the centralisation of R&D activities and these are shown in Figure 9.9.

Success and failure in new product development

One of the most difficult aspects of NPD is to reduce the risk (and therefore the cost) of new product failure. The classic studies of success and failure of new products in developed countries particularly the US and UK emphasise that for success it is necessary to place greater emphasis upon marketing rather than technical factors. Cooper (1994) suggests that the NPD success factors include the need for a well-defined, unique and superior product; a market driven, customer focused new product development process; the importance of

Figure 9.9 The arguments for and against centralisation of R&D

Arguments for centralisation	Arguments against centralisation
• economies of scale • easier and faster communication • better coordination • greater control over outflow of information with implications for secrecy • greater synergy • avoiding duplication • overcoming problems of ownership	• pressure from subsidiaries • pressure from governments • benefits of public relations • use of wider range of skills and abilities • financial savings • benefits from comparative advantage • greater sensitivity to local tastes • better monitoring of local competitive activity • closeness to possible acquisitions • access new technology wherever it is located

screening, market studies, feasibility studies and preparation of the business case and a cross-functional team approach.

The reasons for the failure of new product developments in international markets include:

- tariff barriers and non-tariff barriers;
- local competitor subsidies;
- cultural insensitivity;
- poor planning;
- poor timing;
- lack of a unique selling proposition in the international market;
- product deficiencies in the market; and
- misguided enthusiasm of top management.

The impact of process development on international marketing

In highlighting the role of research and development, it is important to emphasise not just product development, but also the ways in which process developments have an impact upon international marketing. A good example of this is included in the illustration of Whirlpool (Illustration 9.8).

Illustration 9.8: Whirlpool and the world cooker

Whirlpool (US) are developing the 'world cooker'. Taking an idea from the car industry Whirlpool believe that it can innovate quicker and at lower cost by globalising the development of new products. Its range which includes microwave ovens, air conditioners, dishwashers, laundry products, refrigerators and conventional cookers is manufactured in 35 countries. Whirlpool has 10 per cent of the $85 billion world market.

Although the appliances outwardly differ significantly from market to market when the product engineers from different Whirlpool plants got together they found that the technological differences were much smaller than they had originally thought. The idea is to develop a platform which is the technological heart for each appliance all over the world. The parts of the products which consumers see will then be modified to suit different market requirements.

In the case of a refrigerator the platform includes the casing, compressor, evaporator and sealant system. The features that provide the appearance include the door, the layout of the shelves, the position of the freezing compartment, the controls and the air-blowing system which makes it frost-free. In practice the refrigerators differ significantly, for example, Americans want larger sized, frost-free cabinets, Germans want lots of space for meat, Italians want more vegetable compartments and Indians, with their high proportion of vegetarians within families, want internal compartments sealed to prevent odours circulating.

In this way Whirlpool expects to reduce the current 135 platforms down to 65. To support this Whirlpool have developed a special website with product specifications for its 2000 product engineers worldwide so that, for example, a Brazilian engineer could borrow an idea from elsewhere in the company to solve a new design problem.

Source: adapted from Marsh, P. and Tait, N. (1998) 'Whirlpool's global clean up', *Financial Times*, 24 March

The importance of process development is argued by Kotabe (1990) who points out that, today, product innovations are easily 'reverse engineered', improved upon and invented around by competitors without violating patents and other proprietary protections. In contrast, manufacturing processes are more difficult to copy because they are built on not only tangible machinery but also intangible knowledge and skills hidden away in the firm. Continual improvement of processes is essential as the rate of technological change in the marketplace accelerates and he draws attention to the fact that many US companies that are extensively sourcing products and components externally, could, in the long run, lose touch with technology and lose the ability to manufacture effectively.

Kotabe and Murray (1989) draw attention to the links between process and product innovations, and modes of sourcing in international firms. They found, in a study of European and Japanese firms, that continual process improvements lead to new products, whereas low product or process development activity within the company coupled with high levels of outsourcing tends to equate to lower market performance.

Information technology and communications are central to process development but are also closing the gap between R&D, manufacturing and international marketing.

Computer aided design (CAD) allows engineers and designers to generate new product designs far more quickly and to transfer them from computer to computer via telecommunication, so allowing rapid feedback from distant customers.

Virtual reality allows the design concept to be converted to a three dimensional image of how the product might look and work. It is useful for eliciting ideas and comments from customers and non-design functions in the company.

Flexible manufacturing systems (FMS) are groups of machines that can easily be programmed to switch from manufacturing one product to another.

Computer aided manufacturing (CAM) allows the integration of FMS with design, manufacture and component and resource planning in order to provide *Just In Time (JIT)* manufacturing, a concept which is based upon providing rapid response to orders and minimising stockholding. The major benefit which becomes apparent from this is that the coordination and integration of all operations can be used for competitive advantage in international marketing. JIT as a concept is increasingly being used in retailing, too, through linking *electronic point of sale (EPOS)* sales recording systems into a direct ordering facility.

There is little doubt that the integration of information transfer, communications technology, robotics and computerisation will further enhance product and process development. These same technologies have the capability to intelligently communicate with customers around the world and it is for these reasons that it will be the integration of design, operations and marketing that will be vital in achieving the accuracy and speed of response in product and process development necessary to gain competitive advantage in international product management in the future.

Conclusion

Some significant and far reaching changes, are gaining momentum as a result of the increased globalisation of consumer tastes and the concentration of business activity. These are having a significant effect on the way product management is changing, because of the increasing challenge posed by the increased commoditisation of products.

Whilst the product or service policy is at the centre of international marketing operations, we have emphasised, in this chapter, the extent to which the additional product dimensions, such as branding and new product and process development, have substantial implications for the strategic development of the company and, therefore, for the other aspects of international marketing management.

Discussion questions

1 How do environmental trends affect product portfolio management across international markets?

2 In an ideal world companies would like to manufacture a standardised product. What are the factors that support the case for a standardised product and what are the circumstances that are likely to prevent its implementation?

3 Examine the ways in which a major company operating in many countries around the world can use new product development and commercialisation to enhance its ambitions to become a global company.

4 What justification might there be for keeping an unprofitable product in some international markets?

5 International services marketing is a major growth area. Using as an example one service sector explain what are the main barriers to success and what strategies might be used to overcome them?

References

Agarwal, S. and Sikri, S. (1996) 'Country Image: Consumer evaluation of product category extension', *International Marketing Review*, 13 (4).

Authers, J. (1998) 'Adopting a single brand approach', *Financial Times*, 9 April.

Betts, P. (1997) 'The global company: Italy's star acquirers aim to defy a trend', *Financial Times*, 22 October.

Cooper, R.G. (1994) 'New products: the factors that drive success', *International Marketing Review*, 11 (1).

De Chernatony, L. (1989) *Branding in an era of retailer dominance*, Cranfield School of Management.

De Chernatony, L., Halliburton, C. and Bernath, R. (1995) 'International Branding: demand or supply-drive opportunity?' *Harvard Business Review*, 12 (2): 9–21.

Financial Times (1998) 'Crackdown could bring tax and jobs bonanza', 9 May.

Haefer, S.A. (1997) 'Consumer knowledge of country of origin effects', *European Journal of Marketing*, 31 (1): 56–72.

Halliburton, C. and Bernath, R. (1995) 'International branding: demand or supply driven opportunity', *International Marketing Review*, 12 (2).

Ho, S. (1997) 'The emergence of consumer power in China', *Business Horizons*, September–October.

Howard, E. (1998) 'Keeping ahead of the green regulators' *Mastering Global Management, Part 10, Financial Times*.

Kaitiki, S. (1981) 'How multinationals cope with the international trade mark forgery', *Journal of International Marketing*, 1, (2): 69–80.

Keegan, W.J. (1989) *Multinational Marketing Management*, Prentice Hall.

Kotabe, M. (1990) 'Corporate Product Policy and Innovative Behaviour of European and Japanese Multinationals: An Empriical Investigation', *Journal of Marketing*, 54: 19–33.

Kotabe, M. and Murray, J.Y. (1989) 'Linking product and Process Innovations and Models of International Sourcing in Global Competition: A Case of Foreign Multinational Firms', *Journal of International Business Studies*, Third Quarter: 383–408.

Kotler (1997) *Marketing management: analysis, planning, implementation and control*, 9th edn, Prentice Hall.

Marsh, P. and Tait, N. (1998) 'Whirlpool's global clean up', *Financial Times*, 24 March.

Mesdag, M. van (1985) 'The Frontiers of Choice', *Marketing*, 10 October.

Quelch, J. and Harding, D. (1996) 'Brand versus product labels – fighting to win', *Harvard Business Review*, January–February.

Rawsthorn, A. (1997) 'Fashion victim fights back: Calvin Klein is tired of piracy and has started a global offensive against counterfeiters', *Financial Times*, 24 February.

Rawsthorn, A. (1997) 'Survey Italian industry and business: Fashion – the empire strikes back', *Financial Times*, 10 December.

Roderick, O. (1996) 'Nestle portfolio of possibilities', *Financial Times*, 8 August.

Thakor, M.V. and Kohli, C.S. (1996) 'Brand origin: conceptualisation and review', *Journal of Consumer Marketing*, 13 (3): 27–42.

The Economist (1997) 'A car is born', 13 September.

The Economist (1998) 'Not good enough? Intel's troubles: The booming market for cheap PCs took Intel by surprise', 4 April.

van der Post, L. (1996) 'How to spend it: Success on a plate – fashion designers offer total immersion in their labels as they turn to the world of interiors', *Financial Times*, 7 September.

Chapter 10

International marketing communications

Introduction

The geographical and cultural separation of the company from its marketplaces causes great difficulty in communicating effectively. In this chapter we take a broad view of communications and include not just the traditional promotional mix of personal selling, advertising, sponsorship, sales and public relations but also other methods of communications which have the objective of developing better and more personalised relationships with global customers, such as direct marketing, and the use of the Internet. In our discussions we acknowledge the fact that the target audience extends beyond existing and potential customers and includes other stakeholder groups that have a potential impact on the global development of firms and their international reputation.

In doing this, the development of internal relationships between staff from different strategic business units within the global organisation is vital in influencing overall performance. Some remote strategic business units often appear to have a closer relationship with their customers than they have with the parent organisation and this seems to be particularly important as firms embark on joint ventures and strategic alliances.

Achieving cost effectiveness in communications with all stakeholders, both internal and external, requires the integration of the various communications tools available and success depends upon building good relationships with all these interested parties.

The role of marketing communications

Marketing communications are concerned with presenting and exchanging information with various individuals and organisations to achieve specific results. This means not only that the information must be understood accurately but that, often, elements of persuasion are also required. In a domestic environment the process is difficult enough but the management of international marketing communications is made particularly challenging by a number of factors including the complexity of different market conditions, differences in media availability, languages, cultural sensitivities, regulations controlling advertising and sales promotions, and the challenge of providing adequate resourcing levels.

A variety of approaches have been taken to define and describe the marketing mix area which is concerned with persuasive communications. Some writers refer to the 'communications mix' others to the 'promotional mix' and others, for example, Kotler (1988), use the communications mix and promotions mix to mean the same thing. Communications, embracing as it does the ideas of conveying information, is the most helpful term in implying the need for a two-way process in international marketing. It also implies including internal communications between the organisation's staff and partners especially as organisations become larger, more diverse and complex. In addition, the boundaries are becoming less distinct between organisations participating in alliances and supply chains and so, here too, difficulties are experienced with managing communications.

Figure 10.1 shows the external and internal marketing communication flows and emphasises the need to consider three dimensions, external, internal and interactive or relationship marketing.

The traditional role of international marketing communications was largely concerned with providing a mechanism by which the features and benefits of the product or service could be promoted as inexpensively as possible to existing and potential customers in different countries using the promotion mix (personal selling, advertising, sales promotion and public relations) with the ultimate purpose of persuading customers to buy specific products and services. International marketing communications, however, have now become much more important within the marketing mix and the purposes for which marketing communications might be used externally in international markets are now more diverse. They include the need to communicate with a more diverse range of stakeholders and build higher levels of customer service through interactive or relationship marketing. International marketing communications might now be considered to include the three distinct strategic elements shown in Figure 10.2.

Figure 10.1 External, internal and interactive marketing

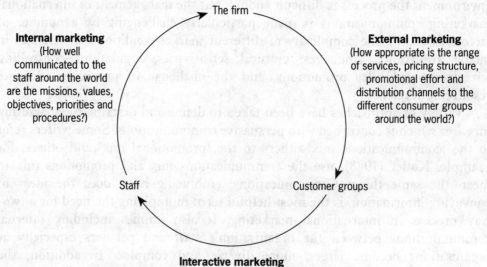

Internal marketing
(How well communicated to the staff around the world are the missions, values, objectives, priorities and procedures?)

The firm

Staff

Customer groups

External marketing
(How appropriate is the range of services, pricing structure, promotional effort and distribution channels to the different consumer groups around the world?)

Interactive marketing
(How effectively – and appropriately – do staff around the world deal with each of the customer or stakeholder groups?)

Figure 10.2 The dimensions of external marketing communications

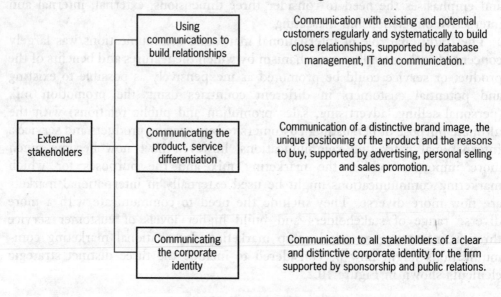

External stakeholders

Using communications to build relationships — Communication with existing and potential customers regularly and systematically to build close relationships, supported by database management, IT and communication.

Communicating the product, service differentiation — Communication of a distinctive brand image, the unique positioning of the product and the reasons to buy, supported by advertising, personal selling and sales promotion.

Communicating the corporate identity — Communication to all stakeholders of a clear and distinctive corporate identity for the firm supported by sponsorship and public relations.

Communicating product and service differentiation

As we have discussed in Chapters 7 and 9, increased competition and the maturation of markets has led to many firms offering largely similar core product and service specifications with the result that, in addition to its traditional role of promoting products and services, international marketing communications is being increasingly used to provide the firm with an important source of differentiation, for example, by providing customers with an easily recognisable and distinctive brand image, and by explaining the unique positioning of the product. Koranteng (1998) suggests that while Nike has relied on sexy, provocative ads of top athletes (see also Illustration 10.3) and Adidas has associated itself with European soccer stars, Reebok has confused the market. It is known as a running shoe in the UK, a fashion statement in the US and more generally as a women's fitness and aerobics shoe, with little consequent appeal for men.

In contrast to this, the Volkswagon Beetle was conceived as the people's car in 1938 to suit the functional needs of the German mass market (Meenagham 1995). By the 1960s it came to represent a particular type of person and lifestyle – not into materialism and status symbols. He or she wanted to make a statement by driving an ugly funky car thereby demonstrating independence – a willingness to go against the grain, irreverence for convention, being young in spirit, admiring a sense of humour and a logical and practical mind. The new Beetle is aiming to build very precisely on those values. It is by no means priced for the 'peoples market', however, but its appeal seems to have worked as it was reported to be immediately oversold at its introduction and commanding even higher immediate resale prices.

However with the vast increase in the range and volume of communications which consumers are exposed to as they go about their normal work and leisure, making one product or service distinctive becomes an increasing challenge. There are a wide variety of promotional tools that might be used to persuade customers to buy the firm's products and services and the newer information and communications technologies are increasing this choice all the time. The challenge for the firm is to use these tools as cost effectively as possible to reach out to consumers wherever they are in the world.

Communicating the corporate identity to international stakeholders

As stakeholders in general have become more aware of how they are affected by international organisations, both good and bad, companies have found it important to justify their international activities by constantly and more widely communicating their core values and standards to their internal and external audience, in order to demonstrate their responsibility to shareholders, trustworthiness to customers and care and concern for the local community, environment and local employees. The methods of communication that are available to them include the use of a clear and distinctive corporate identity, sponsorship and proactive public relations activity. Illustration 10.1 shows the importance of a corporate identity and sponsorship in the international marketing of the host city for the Olympic Games.

Using communications to build relationships

More intense global competition has provided consumers with greater choice of products and services which they perceive to be capable of satisfying their needs and providing new experiences. Given too, perhaps, their feeling that there is less risk of dissatisfaction in switching to alternative products and services customers are becoming less likely to stay loyal to one supplier or brand.

With the increasing cost of marketing communications and need to reach an ever wider international audience, organisations are becoming much more aware of the high costs of winning new customers and the relatively lower costs of retaining existing customers. Attention has been drawn to how much a single customer might purchase of one product over his or her lifetime. Readers might like to calculate how much revenue they contribute to a food retailer, car manufacturer or a travel company if they stay loyal to that supplier for five, ten or twenty years. Food retailers now offer incentives for customer loyalty, such as bonus cards, money-off vouchers for other products and services they offer, such as petrol and banking services. They routinely communicate with consumers using direct mail to inform them of new product offers.

Firms are now much more willing to invest resources to retain existing customers. The concept of relationship marketing has taken on an increased level of significance as improvements in information and communications technology enable firms to use the wide variety of marketing communications to communicate in a much more intelligent way by basing the messages on better knowledge about the characteristics and responses of their existing and potential customers and a better understanding of what they might wish to hear. In this way firms are able to develop better relationships with their customers and other influential stakeholders irrespective of their location in the world.

Illustration 10.1: Corporate identity and the Olympic Games

Arguably the most expensive and prestigious sponsorship event in the world is the Olympic Games. It reaches a huge audience in just about every corner of the world. Some would suggest that the five rings of the Olympic committee is the most recognised symbol (as against company name) in the world. The elite group of sponsors, such as Coca-Cola, McDonald's, Kodak, IBM, Xerox, Samsung and Panasonic pay very large sums to have their logos projected around the world through their association with the Games. For the very short duration of the winter Olympics in Nagano, Japan, in 1998 each paid around $30 million.

To the host city the effectiveness of their international marketing, too, is vital. Montreal's 1976 summer games left the city in debt and the Atlanta 1996 games will be remembered, at least in part, for some poor organisation and questionable commercial activities. By contrast Los Angeles in 1984 was deemed a complete success and the winter games at Lillehammer in Norway and Whistler in Canada have put both venues on the winter sports map. In 1992 Barcelona used the event to rebrand and transform the city by emphasising both the elegance and excitement of the city. A key part of the international marketing of the city is in creating a corporate identity that will live on after the games.

The logos, such as Sam the eagle in LA, Kobi the dog in Barcelona and Izzy the computer character in Atlanta are the source of income through franchising on merchandise, such as stamps, toys, souvenirs and T-shirts. Sydney in 2000 hopes to raise £550 million from its stylised athlete which features Aboriginal boomerang shapes. The challenge for the corporate identity project is to go much further and ensure that all the venues give the games a unique feel which will reflect the distinctiveness of the city and so attract visitors in the future.

Source: adapted from Williams, J. (1998) 'Let the brands begin business', *Financial Times*, 9 February

The fundamental challenges for international marketing communications

All of the forms of international marketing communication have a fundamental purpose which is to ensure that the intended messages (those which are part of the firm's international strategy) are conveyed accurately between the sender and the receiver, and that the impact of unintentional messages (those which are likely to have an adverse effect on the firm's market performance and reputation) are kept to a minimum. The communications process should be two way and the sender should always make provision for feedback to ensure that the receiver has understood the message as it was intended and has responded positively to it.

In practice this apparently simple process poses considerable challenges for firms trying to manage their international marketing communications as can often be seen from the business press which contains many serious but often amusing anecdotes about the failed attempts of major firms to communicate in international markets. Mistakes in the use of language, particularly using messages which do not translate or are mistranslated are a particular problem but more serious is a lack of sensitivity to different cultures amongst international communicators.

Many of the failures of communications are unintentional, of course. Following negotiations with the Council on America–Islamic Relations, Nike had to scrap almost 40 000 pairs of sports shoes because the flame design which was used bore a resemblance to the Arabic for Allah. Two years earlier Nike was forced to withdraw a billboard showing a basketball player above the caption 'They Called him Allah' when it caused an outcry amongst Muslims.

Besides the often highly visible failures which make firms appear to be incompetent and insensitive there are many examples of wasted effort and resources which are not so widely publicised. There are a number of reasons for international marketing communications failure including, for example:

- inconsistency in the messages conveyed to customers by staff at different levels and from different countries and cultures
- different styles of presentation of corporate identity, brand and product image from different departments and country business units which can leave customers confused
- a lack of coordination of messages, such as press releases, advertising campaigns, and changes in product specification or pricing across the various country markets
- failure to appreciate the differences in the fields of perception (the way the message is understood) of the sender and receiver. The field of perception tends to be affected significantly by the self-reference criteria of both parties. This is, perhaps, where the greatest problems arise because, as we have already discussed, avoiding this requires knowledge of different market environments, cultural empathy and the willingness to adapt the communications programmes and processes to local requirements.

Whilst this last area is influenced by knowledge, attitudes and empathy the other three areas of potential communications failure are concerned with the effectiveness of the firm's strategy and planning, and the degree to which the staff within the organisation understand and are involved in the communications planning process. It is almost inevitable that some communication failures occur from time to time and it is vital that firms learn from their mistakes. To ensure success in these areas it is important to have in place an effective control process.

Whilst it can be argued that the majority of these failures are ultimately within the control of the company, a number of situations arise where the firm's communications can be affected by factors which are outside the firm's control or are extremely difficult to control. Examples of these situations are where:

- **counterfeiting** or other infringements of patents or copyright as discussed in Chapter 9 take place. Not only does the firm lose revenue but it may also suffer damage to its image, if consumers believe the low-quality goods supplied by the counterfeiter are genuine;
- **parallel importing**, which is discussed in greater detail in Chapter 12, communicates contradictory messages that do not reflect the image of the brand and thus confuse consumers. This can be particularly problematic if the parallel importer seriously undercuts the prices charged by the official channel; and
- **competitors, governments or pressure groups** attack the standards and values of the MNE by alleging, fairly or unfairly, bad business practice. Perhaps, surprisingly despite their huge resources some of the largest firms are not very effective in responding to allegations from relatively less powerful stakeholders. For example, companies such as Shell, Exxon and McDonald's have suffered following criticism of their lack of concern for the environment.

International marketing communications, standardisation and adaptation

The most obvious tactic for reducing instances of international communications failure might appear to be to adopt a strict policy of standardisation in the implementation of communications plans and firms adopt this principle, for example, in their use of corporate identity and global advertising campaigns. However, given the need also to demonstrate cultural sensitivity and empathy with a wide range of international customers and avoid the type of mistakes referred to earlier it becomes necessary to adapt the international communications to local market needs. In this section therefore we address the factors both inside and outside the control of the firm which affect the degree to which international marketing communications can be standardised or should be adapted.

Towards standardisation

The drivers for standardisation of international marketing communications come, first, from the organisation's desire to improve efficiency. Cost-saving activity in marketing communications includes benefits from economies of scale, for example, in advertising creative work, media buying, more economic use of staff time, and from the experience effect, by replicating successful marketing communications programmes and processes in different countries.

Second, standardisation of communications provides customers with perceived added value, particularly in the intangible elements of the product/service offer. Customers believe that they gain additional benefit and value from a consistent and widely recognised image, for example, teenagers (as well as rather more elderly sports enthusiasts too), gain peer recognition, credibility and prestige from wearing branded sports wear which has a powerful image from its associations with sports stars. A company may use a top international business consultancy or advertising agency just as much for the way that the association is perceived by the company's suppliers and customers as for the cost effectiveness of the work that is carried out.

Consistency in the corporate identity and branding, too, reinforces awareness in stakeholders' minds and provides the familiarity with the company which leads to a feeling of confidence, trust and loyalty. For example, it may be reassuring for a visitor to see the familiar logo and appearance of a fast food outlet, hotel chain or bank in a foreign country that they are visiting.

Over the years changes in the political and economic environment have led to greater prosperity and thus greater buying power at least for some people and a greater acceptance of imported products. Consumers and business-to-business customers often prefer internationally available products, with which they have become familiar through increased travel, radio and television communications and the written media. This familiarity has increased further because of the greater impact of telecommunications and IT. Satellite and cable TV, for example, have assisted considerably in creating worldwide customer segments for many more globally standardised products and services.

The Internet, too, allows customers with personal computers to access products from organisations from very distant locations. Moreover, it not only allows specialist suppliers to make their standard products and services globally available to customers, but also enables smaller companies to compete essentially on equal terms with their much larger counterparts so 'punching above their weight' as Illustration 10.2 shows.

At an operational level advertising standardisation can be used when a number of conditions apply:

- visual messages form the main content of the advertisement
- well-known international film stars, popular celebrities and sports personalities are featured

---

Illustration 10.2: Using new technology to sell heritage

Roger Appleyard is a small antiques dealer whose main overseas markets include Japanese, American and Australian customers. The company's activities involve purchasing a range of items from auction that it feels might be appropriate for one of its key accounts. Prior to using the Internet the firm would photograph or video the pieces and send them via traditional mail for evaluation by the client.

The Internet now offers Appleyard considerable benefits not only because of the reduced time and cost of communication which makes it possible to provide better levels of service but also because of the growth of the Internet which is making it easier to contact a wider range of customers. The company can transfer digital images or video, via e-mail, direct to the offices of distributors and even into the homes of the clients themselves. The effect on customer service and the speed with which transactions might be made has greatly increased – in some cases from weeks to hours.

The use of the Internet by Appleyard illustrates the changes in the way in which new technology can drive the better integration of customer service, improved marketing communications and more rapid transactions and, because of the opportunity to make greater use of visual images of the products and services offered, the communications can allow smaller companies to make better use of targeted marketing in the international environment.

- music is an important part of the communication
- well-known symbols and trademarks are featured. For example, the Grand Canyon in the US can be used to symbolise certain types of outdoor American values.

Even then the real impact of the promotion may be restricted to a particular region. For example, advertisements do not travel well to other countries:

- when the use of spoken and written language form an important part of the communication
- if humour is used – humour is often very specific to certain cultures
- if they use personalities who are well-known in one country but are not known internationally
- if campaigns are used that rely on specific knowledge of previous advertising.

Towards adaptation

The principal drivers of international marketing communications adaptation are the cultural differences that must be managed when communicating with customers in different countries. As we have already seen in this book there are some fundamental differences in the ways that consumers from different cultures respond to different communication approaches. More specifically, however, in a comparison between the US and Chinese responses to advertising Zhang and Neelankavil (1997) observe that, overall, US subjects preferred the individualistic appeal (self-orientation, self-sufficiency and control, the pursuit of individual gains) whereas Chinese subjects favoured the collective appeal (subordination of personal interests to the goals of the group, with emphasis on sharing, cooperation and harmony, and a concern for the group welfare). It is these differences which must be recognised, but there is also likely to be continuing convergence and moves toward standardisation.

Neelankavil *et al.* (1996) studied the contents of advertisements for language, customs and values in local language magazines in Hong Kong, Japan, Korea and Taiwan, countries which they considered to be steeped in ancient Asian culture but also major forces in the global marketplace. They found that the use of Western language and models was affected by the product type, customer countries, countries of origin, use of Western language and countries of manufacture. They observe that with greater liberalisation, there is likely to be a convergence of ideas, cultures, values and even language advertising but they comment that insufficient is known about the effects of benefits of such standardisation.

Advertisers believe that advertising is most effective when it is relevant to the target audience and one area where there are significant differences is in the portrayal of women in advertising.

Siu and Au (1997) report that research studies of advertising suggest that:

- over 80 per cent of voice-overs are male
- women are depicted as housewives, mothers and/or sex objects; and
- females are shown as product users whereas males are shown in the roles of authority.

However, the role of women is changing rapidly with many more women entering the workforce. In research carried out in China and Singapore, they found that sex-role stereotyping was more apparent in China where women were depicted as product users and men as having product authority whereas in Singapore, women appeared as the spokesperson for the product, to have product authority and be the providers of help and advice.

Other environmental factors also make it necessary for the communications strategy to be adapted for local situations. There are political and legal constraints, for example, Wentz (1997) argues, for example, that rather than pricing itself out of the world markets the EU has regulated itself out, restricting promotional activity, offering examples such as the French alcohol ban and a Danish attack on loyalty programmes. Certain countries too prohibit comparative advertising, as well as advertising products for children and alcohol and tobacco.

There are many local reasons why firms may need to adapt their communications strategy. Many companies have to change their brand names because of different meanings they have when they move to new markets. The New Zealand Dairy Board, a large exporter of dairy foods uses the brand name Fern for its butter in Malaysia although Anchor is the flagship brand well known in Western Europe. In Malaysia, Anchor is a widely advertised local beer and Malaysian housewives are unlikely to buy dairy products for their children which they would subconsciously associate with alcohol.

Johnson & Johnson on entering the Hong Kong market used the name zhuang-cheng which means 'an official or lord during feudal times', but this upper-class association was seen as inappropriate for communist China and so the more upbeat modern tone of 'qiang-sheng', meaning 'active life' was used instead to better reflect the drive for modernisation.

The fundamental differences in appeal between Western and Asian communications are more fundamental than simply changing brand names. Chan and Huang (1997) suggest that brands can be enhanced if names and/or symbols of favourite animals and flowers and lucky numbers are used. In Asia written figures may be perceived as potent symbols; thus, as Shufa, Schmitt and Pan (1994) point out, in Asian countries the emphasis may be heavier on the distinctive writing and logo of the brand than on the jingles that Western marketing communications favour.

Firms use a variety of ways of becoming more sensitive to cultural differences. Unilever has set up innovation centres in Asia in order to bring together research, production and marketing staff to speed up developments of international brands which have a local appeal. In Bangkok there are innovation centres responsible for ice-cream, laundry detergents and hair care. Asian Delight is a regional brand of ice-cream – between the Magnum brand and local brands – and uses English and Thai on its packaging in Thailand, English only in Malaysia, Singapore and Indonesia. It is sold from Wall's mobile units and cabinets in convenience stores and supermarkets. The flavours have a local appeal and include coconut milk based ice-cream mixed with fruits and vegetables traditionally used in desserts or chewy strings of green flour, black beans and sago.

International marketing communications strategy

So far in this chapter we have highlighted the need to consider the nature and role of international marketing communications more broadly than was the case in the past, by focusing upon both internal and external communications and a wider range of communications tools. In thinking about developing strategy there are two significant issues to address. First, the need to state clear and precise objectives for the international marketing communications strategy and, second, how the various communications activities might be coordinated to maximise their cost effectiveness.

The promotional objectives (Wilson and Gilligan 1997) can be categorised as sales-related and brand/product communications-related which might be stated in terms of *increasing sales by:*

- increasing in market share at the expense of local and/or international competitors
- identifying new potential customers or obtaining a specific number of responses to a promotional campaign
- reducing the impact of competitors in the market

and brand/product communications related by:

- increasing the value of the corporate brand and product image
- helping to establish the position or to reposition the product or brand
- increasing awareness levels especially in new country markets
- changing consumers perceptions of products, brands or the firm.

The Illustration 10.3 shows that whilst Nike has been extremely effective in using its communications to deliver a number of these objectives it appears to be in danger of losing contact with its target group.

The options that are available for a generic marketing communications strategy centre around the extent to which a push or pull strategy could and should be adopted (Figure 10.3). A push strategy means promoting the product or service to retailers and wholesalers in order to force the product or service down the distribution channel by using promotional methods, such as personal selling, discounts and special deals. A pull strategy means communicating with the final consumer to attract them to the retailer or distributor to purchase the product. In this case mass advertising, sales promotions and point of sales promotions are the most obvious promotional methods. In domestic markets firms realise the need to have a combination of push and pull strategies including both encouraging the intermediaries to stock the products and attracting end users to buy.

In domestic markets the nature of the market structure that already exists may well affect the degree to which push and pull strategies are used, for example, how well the distribution channel is established, how powerful the retailers or distributors are, how well established the competitors are and whether the firm marketing its products or services wishes to, or has the power to challenge the existing 'route to market' by setting up a new channel.

Frequently, the international marketing communications strategy of a firm has to be adapted because of the variation in the market structures and distribution channels from country to country (for example, some are highly fragmented, whilst others are very concentrated). More often than not, however, it is the weakness of the marketing firm in the target country markets that limits its strategic choice. It may well not have sufficient resources to implement a successful domestic strategy in the new market and yet there is a need for quick success. As a result the firm may be forced into making use of and relying heavily upon established intermediaries to do the promotion through existing channels. For this reason it is possible to find organisations that have a pull strategy in their domestic or other established markets and a push strategy in

Illustration 10.3: Nike on the wrong track

Nike's television commercial for the 1998 World Cup featured the Brazilian football team, including stars such as Ronaldo and Roberto Carlos, having a kickabout in an airport lounge whilst waiting to catch a plane. The commercial was typical – the sort Nike have been using for some time: a huge budget, exciting action, humour and the self-confidence which has always been at the heart of Nike's communications. Remember that when Nike used some of the greatest athletics stars in its commercials during the Olympic Games, just about all of them lost or were injured. They produced a final television commercial of the series which demonstrated this humour and confidence with the line 'If you are going to put your foot in it, put it in a Nike'.

In a World Cup year, however, when Nike would expect to get another great improvement in its twenty years of continually amazing business performance, things were a little different. In March 1997, in response to a sudden downturn in business, Nike found it necessary to cut $100 million (15 per cent) from its $850 million global advertising budget. Phil Knight, the founder, who had seen Nike go from nothing to take a third of the market for global branded shoes, believed that Nike's problems resulted from its marketing strategy, and ineffective marketing rather than insufficient marketing. The problems seemed to have started with the introduction in late 1996 of the slogan 'I can'.

Others took a different view, however. Nike had been extremely ambitious, determined to dominate every sport that offered potential, resulting in the production of 150 commercials in 1996 and the introduction of new shoe lines every few months. Nike had wanted to do everything bigger and better than its competitors, hence the sponsorship of the Brazilian football team's kit and the right to use the team in television commercials, at a very high cost. But Nike made its reputation not by working with the establishment, such as the Brazilian football team, but with the irreverent sports fan, the kid hanging out in the street. This could suggest Nike was failing to communicate as effectively with its target audience as they used to. For Wieden and Kennedy from Oregon, US Nike's long-time advertising agency, this must come as bad news. Wieden had expanded around the world piggybacking on Nike's success and were just about to open a new office in London.

Source: adapted from Mills, D. (1998) 'Nike on the wrong track', *Daily Telegraph*, 7 April

Figure 10.3 Push and pull strategies

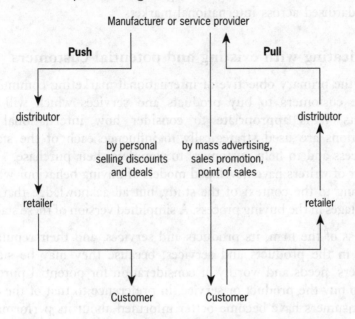

their newer markets. Because of this the firm's promotional and communications mix may be significantly different with a pull strategy appealing directly to the final customer through advertising and promotion used in its domestic markets but then a push strategy through the distribution channel members, such as agents, distributors, wholesalers and retailers, used in international markets with the consequence that the whole communications programme has to be changed.

Having determined the objectives and decided upon the degree to which a push and pull strategy might be used, the following dimensions of the international marketing communications implementation strategy can be defined. These are:

- the message to be communicated
- the target audience to which the message will be directed
- the media that will be used to carry the message
- the ways in which the impact of the communications will be measured.

As we said at the start of this chapter continually evaluating the impact of the communications is vital in not only improving the effectiveness of the communication but also assessing the degree to which each of these dimensions can be standardised across international markets.

Communicating with existing and potential customers

Given that the primary objective of international marketing communications is to persuade customers to buy products and services which will meet their requirements, it is appropriate to consider how international marketing communications are used strategically to influence each of the stages of the buying process and to help customers to complete their purchase.

A number of writers have developed models of buying behaviour which tend to vary according to the context of the study, but all acknowledge that there are a number of stages in the buying process. A simplified version of these stages include:

- awareness of the firm, its products and services, and their reputation
- interest in the products and services, because they may be suited to the consumers' needs and worthy of consideration for potential purchase
- desire to buy the product or service, in preference to that of the competitor, after consumers have become better informed about its performance
- action by the customer in overcoming any remaining reservations or barriers and purchasing the product or service.

Different messages must be prepared and the most appropriate promotional tool selected for each part of the buying process in order to persuade customers to move to the next stage. At each stage in this process the marketing firm faces particular problems in international markets. For example, in fast moving consumer goods marketing, advertising can be used to raise awareness, create interest and encourage consumers to purchase, but only if the messages are sensitive and appealing to the international customers and the customers have access to the media used for advertising. Other tools, such as point of sale promotion can be used to support the strategy provided it is possible for the firm to maintain some level of control over the displays used by local retailers. At the final stage and having been entirely convinced about the firm's offer, customers may still have reservations about buying from a foreign supplier.

There are significant differences between consumer markets and business-to-business and institutional market purchasing. Selling capital equipment usually depends more on personal selling and providing technical service to a buying committee. This would typically be supported by awareness raising in the trade press, using PR and corporate advertising. Here the need for monitoring the consistency of approach and ensuring good communications with the manufacturing operation must be balanced against the need for sensitivity to the way that business is done in that particular country.

Coordination and planning of the international marketing communications strategy

To achieve its objectives, the communications strategy almost certainly will include a variety of promotional tools. The key to success in international promotion is integrating the various promotion elements in a cost-efficient way and adding value through choosing the communications methods which will have the most impact on the customers. The actual mix chosen will depend upon a number of issues surrounding the context of the purchasing situation, including:

- the market area and industry sector
- whether it is consumer, institutional or business-to-business marketing
- the customer segment to be targeted
- the participants in the purchasing process, their requirements and the best methods to reach and influence them
- the country or region, the culture, the communications infrastructure and the preferred methods of communicating
- the resources made available by the organisation and the implications for the level of involvement and control it wishes to exert over the communications process.

Smith *et al.* (1997) suggest that the value of different promotional methods varies according to the context in which the marketing communications are being used and the degree to which they are integrated within a marketing communications strategy shown in Figure 10.4.

The critical issue is to what extent they must be adapted so that they can be effective in international markets. The Illustration 10.4 shows how Shell has encouraged its subsidiaries to use a variety of marketing communications tools within an integrated approach under a similar message by the use of high impact television advertising and a common message.

The marketing communications tools

There are a number of marketing communications tools for the external market and it is to these that we now turn. For convenience we have grouped these tools

Figure 10.4 Internal and external international communications programmes

Marketing programmes influencing communications	International communication aims
Internally focused programmes	
Corporate identity	Consistency in all aspects of company logo, signs and image
Internal marketing communications	Reinforce motivation through telling staff what is happening
Salesforce, dealer and distributor training and development	Training through conferences, manuals and brochures
Retailer merchandising	Point of sale persuasion through displays and shelf facings
First contact customer service	Welcoming first contact through telephonist and receptionist training
After sales service	Customer retention and satisfaction through staff training and brochures
Quality management	Assuring a continuous quality approach in all programmes
Brand management	Achieving common brand satandards and values
Externally focused programmes (marketing mix)	
Product attributes	Offering innovative, high quality products
Distribution channel	Ensuring easy access to products and frequent customer encounters with the products
Price	Messages about quality and status
Product/service promotion	Integration of the marketing mix communications
People	Using staff–customer interactions to reinforce the aims, standards and values of the firm
Customer service process	Providing a statisfactory total experience through the service offer
Physical evidence for the service delivery	All contacts with the facilities reinforce the firm's messages

---

Illustration 10.4: Shell's new image

Shell has designed a high-quality, consistent advertising campaign to offer to local Shell companies around the world at very little cost. The objective is to create a new younger image to replace the now ageing one depicted by the slogan 'You can be sure of Shell'. Through association with Ferrari Formula One and also Lego, their new image is intended to imply power, performance and passion. How Shell companies have utilised the campaigns varies between countries. In Hong Kong, the Ferrari advert has been dropped amidst fears it would damage a locally produced advert. Instead, the local company exploited the Lego promotion successfully, selling the toys, whereas many Shell companies had chosen to give them away. In Singapore, the Ferrari advert links well with the characteristics of the market since, as a consequence of government restrictions aiming to reduce pollution and congestion, cars are young, travel short distances and are kept immaculately. By contrast, fuel is a commodity in Australia and hence convenience is vitally important. Shell Helix is sold at supermarkets and in joint-branding with Burger King. Whilst the promotions fit well with the strategy, the Ferrari ad is considered too expensive for television and will be used at product launches and exhibitions instead.

---

within the three broad categories highlighted at the beginning of this chapter and summarised in Figure 10.2. In practice there is some flexibility in the way the tools are used within a coordinated strategy.

Personal selling and word of mouth

For many companies the first use of the communications mix to promote exports is personal selling. Selling is often used to gain the first few orders in a new market and to persuade distribution channel members, such as agents, distributors or retailers to stock the product as the main component of a push strategy. It is expensive however.

The use of personal selling tends to be limited to situations in which benefits can be derived from two-way information flows and ones in which the revenue from the sale is sufficiently high to justify the costs. This is typically the case with business-to-business marketing and in consumer markets where the purchase price justifies the high cost, for example, for cars, holidays and for consumer durable products. Even this, however, is being challenged as direct marketing, particularly using the Internet is now being used routinely to purchase these products.

In countries where labour costs are very low personal selling is used to a greater extent than in high-cost countries. This ranges from street and market trading to quite sophisticated multi-level distribution chains for business-to-business products. In high labour cost countries personal selling of low unit cost products is used rarely, except for illegal trading, for example, of drugs. It is of course a successful method of selling niche products, such as Avon cosmetics, Tupperware and Amway household products. The basis of the appeal of these products is to make shopping a more social event, by selling to friends or family, and introducing a 'party' atmosphere into the selling process.

Effective selling in international business-to-business and consumer markets involves a wide range of tasks and skills, including product and market knowledge, listening and questioning skills. However, it is in the core selling activities of negotiation and persuasion discussed in Chapter 3 where higher order expertise is required. It is likely that local people will be more effective than home-based representatives in understanding the subtleties of the negotiation process as they apply within the local business culture. They will have fluent language skills and an intimate knowledge of the culture of the country. However, where the negotiations relate to high value contracts they may well require high levels of specialist technical knowledge, an understanding of the processes and systems and strict adherence to the firm's standards and values. For these reasons the company may well prefer to use staff from its head office to ensure that they are well informed about the firm's capabilities and that their activities can be controlled.

This is particularly the case if the opportunities to make a sale are very infrequent (e.g. with capital goods) when high levels of technical skill and an understanding of the company's systems are needed but not easily learnt by new people. For example, Rolls Royce use a complete team of UK-based engineers, accountants, and sales people to sell aero engines to customers in the US. Some of the team will make frequent visits to the US, others will be based in close contact with the customer for a period of many months. The sheer complexity of the contracts mean that only Rolls Royce employees could understand the detail sufficiently to handle the negotiations. The high contract price provides sufficient revenue, if the contract is won, to pay for the costs of the UK-based sales team.

An alternative compromise arrangement to the two extremes of employing local or head-office sales staff, both of which have advantages and disadvantages is to employ expatriates, staff from the domestic country to work for extended periods in the host country in order to bridge the culture and company standards gap.

In practice the expatriate is likely to experience a culture shock, caused by living in a foreign culture, where the familiar symbols, cues and everyday reassurances are missing, often causing feelings of frustration, stress and anxiety. The expatriate can respond to the situation in one of three ways.

At one extreme adjustment is made to the expatriate culture only. In effect the expatriate only adjusts to the way of life of a ready made cultural island within the host country and makes little attempt to adjust to the host culture. At the other extreme the expatriate's first reaction is to completely embrace the host culture and actively minimise contact with the expatriate community and the firm too. Ideally the expatriate adjusts to both the local culture and the expatriate culture. In this way the expatriate retains the home country's and firm's system of values and beliefs, but is considerate and respectful towards the people of his host country and to their culture. It is this last option that is usually most beneficial for the firm's sales effort.

Whichever approach to selling is adopted it is through relevant training that firms aim to manage their sales staff's involvement with the firm and the market, and maintain their enthusiasm for selling. As the cost of personal selling is increasing, so firms are seeking ways of improving their cost effectiveness by using more systematic ways of analysing customer requirements and carrying out the sales role rather than relying on a good firm handshake for closing the deal.

Exhibitions and trade fairs

Exhibitions and trade fairs are an effective method of meeting many existing and potential customers from different countries. The costs of exhibiting at international trade fairs is very high, when the cost of the stand, space rental, sales staff time and travelling expenses are taken into account. It is for this reason that the selection of the most appropriate fairs for the industry is critical. Also important are the creative work for the stand, preparation of sales literature and selection of suitable personnel for the stand bearing in mind the need for cultural and language empathy.

Trade missions

Trade missions are organised visits to a country or region of a group of senior business managers from a number of firms perhaps from the same geographic region or from the same industry. They are often subsidised by national or local government. Discussions with potential customers are arranged in advance in the host country.

Trade missions are usually associated with exporting and may be used both to carry out introductory talks with prospective clients or to negotiate a contract. As with trade fairs, good preparation work before the visit is essential to ensure that meetings are arranged with appropriate customers where there is a genuine possibility of business being generated. Usually the home country's local embassy staff will provide support for trade missions and often, too, depending on the importance of the mission, there will be discussions with the host government civil servants and politicians about how trade between the two countries can be developed.

Advertising

Advertising is one of the most visible forms of communication and is often the most important part of the whole strategy for consumer products in countries with a well-developed media industry. It has disadvantages because it is essentially a one-way method of communication and in international marketing it can be difficult to control in terms of its reach (the geographic area in which consumers are exposed to the messages). The objective is to obtain the maximum exposure of the product or brand and the largest possible target audience. Clearly the opportunities for precise targeting are limited in some advertising media, especially TV and this presents problems in international marketing in terms of targeting specific user segments or even specific countries.

However, cross-border transmission can be problematic too (Hu and Griffith 1997). When Radion was promoted in Germany demand was stimulated in neighbouring Austria through spread of print and commercial television adverts. Although unintended Unilever's advertising reach stretched across national borders. Unilever sold a similar product under another brand (Elinder 1995).

In most business-to-business markets advertising tends to be used as a supporting activity, for example, to increase awareness or interest in the company as a whole or in a new concept such as IBM's focus on electronic business in 1998. In business-to-business markets the number of important customers is often comparatively small and it is essential that advertising is precisely targeted, using appropriate media.

Together with the increased harmonisation of consumer demands for some products and the benefits of standardised products and services to firms, there is a strong move to pan-regional advertising campaigns (Smith 1998).

Advertising agency Young and Rubican say that pan-European campaigns make up 40 per cent of their business, twice the amount of five years ago. Reckitt and Colman, the household goods and pharmaceutical products group find that 90 per cent of media spending is on regional campaigns. Consumers increasingly share common values and characteristics but there are differences as, for example, Central and Eastern European people are still developing their habits as consumers. There are few differences in purchasing between European countries for home and personal-care products, such as deodorants and disinfectants. New products, too, can often use common ad programmes. PepsiCo's Frito-Lay created a single campaign for Doritos, the tortilla chip brand introduced within the last five years, whereas more established snack foods tend to require specific local advertising.

There are considerable differences in the availability and usefulness of other advertising media such as radio, cinema, outdoor and transport posters. These differences make it essential to obtain data about media effectiveness in order to make informed decisions about international media schedules. For instance it might be vital to recognise that in remote regions exposure to certain media is prevented because of the poor transmission output quality from radio stations, the target audience having insufficient disposable income to afford television or radio and low adult literacy levels may prevent significant numbers of adults reading printed advertising.

The opportunity to use mass-communications media to reach the target market is therefore severely limited in some countries. Even in developed countries it may not be possible to reach the majority of the market because of the absence of truly national press or national TV. In these situations it may be necessary to develop a campaign based upon a multitude of individual media activities but this means that the measurement of the cost effectiveness of the campaign is extremely difficult given that individual components of the campaign may produce different effects.

Advertising is shown to work in emerging countries, with increased spending by Coca-Cola leading to them becoming the best-selling soft drink in China and overtaking Pepsi in a number of Central and Eastern European republics. There is also an apparent trend towards advertising amongst conglomerates from emerging countries that appears to recognise the value of moving from product orientation to marketing orientation. In 1996 Daewoo increased ad spending outside the US by 66 per cent, Hyundai by 22 per cent and LG by 29 per cent (Fannin 1997).

In Shanghai, advertising multiplied 16 times between 1990 and 1994 and Soames Hines MD of J Walter Thompson in Shanghai said in 1997 that it was a chaotic outdoor media environment with essentially everything up for sale – every lampost, bus, hoarding, bus shelters and rooftops.

The appeal of advertising in China is based on young people who are not cynical but optimistic – they expect to be better off than their parents, Despite this modernism Chinese traditions still prevail and family values are a powerful selling point even with the young. The Chinese know that foreign brands may be better at the moment but do not like to have this overemphasised. In the past, JWT have used expatriates but some rival agencies believes this cultivates only international clients and deters the growing numbers of Chinese clients. As a consequence JWT have appointed a Taiwanese manager (Harding 1997).

Figure 10.5 shows the top advertising spenders ranked in spending outside the US. This reinforces the suggestions made earlier that there are few truly global players and a number of MNEs are adopting regional strategies.

TV advertising

The main influence on TV advertising expenditure is the size of the economy in gross domestic product per capita, but the regulatory environment also affects spending, particularly TV which tends to be more closely regulated than other media. As a result not all advertisers who wish to use TV advertising are able to gain access. Broadcasting liberalisation has occurred in Europe over the last 15 years. Howard (1997) notes, for example, that following the launch of new commercial TV ad spending increases substantially.

Since 1980 European TV ad spending has increased by 200 per cent in real terms whilst newspapers and magazines have grown by only 53 per cent and 21 per cent respectively. During the period TV's share has almost doubled to just over 31 per cent.

Cable and satellite TV have contributed to a proliferation of TV channels so that viewers can receive a rapidly increasing number of programmes. This means that there is a greater capacity for TV advertising but, of course, there is greater competition for prime TV advertising spots (and much higher costs) if there is likely to be a large audience. Both satellite and cable TV have the potential to cross country borders and attract large audiences for programmes of common international interest, for example, major sporting events.

It is not only overt TV advertising in large amounts that sells. The prominent placing of products on TV shows which are likely to be transmitted in other

Figure 10.5 The top 15 advertising spenders outside the US

1996 rank	Advertiser	HQ country	Spending $m Worldwide	US	Asia	Europe	Latin America
1	Proctor and Gamble	US	5102	2663	501	1664	249
2	Unilever	UK/Netherlands	3304	949	472	1475	362
3	Nestle	Switzerland	1877	403	347	1028	180
4	Toyota	Japan	1789	800	747	210	5
5	Peugeot-Citroën	France	959	0	2	944	12
6	Volkswagen	Germany	1106	172	35	820	67
7	Nissan	Japan	1413	557	550	275	9
8	Coca-Cola	US	1445	612	268	351	188
9	Philip Morris	US	3092	2279	117	598	59
10	General Motors	US	3147	2373	38	553	104
11	Ford	US	1920	1179	129	530	75
12	Mars	US	1289	558	108	597	18
13	Renault	France	644	0	0	633	30
14	Kao	Japan	651	23	619	10	0
15	Fiat	Italy	608	1	0	548	57

Source: unknown

countries can also become an important part of the advertising campaign as the Illustration 10.5 shows.

Shannon (1997) suggests that in future TV will focus more on local targeting. The introduction of digital television technology enables the output to be tailored to the local culture and preferences and provides the opportunity for hundreds of

Illustration 10.5: The power of television

Television is a powerful medium for changing attitudes. It can have a significant effect in preparing the way for international product launches. New television channels using satellite technology are having an effect, on viewing habits and, again, are preparing the way for international brands.

An example of how TV has spread the American culture can be seen in how Israel has absorbed the influence of the US. More than 20 per cent of Jews travel abroad each year and a significant number visit the US, so when US firms enter Israel they usually receive a warm reception. When Dunkin' Donuts were introduced into Israel Steven Esses, the local licensee, found it was not necessary to use the all-encompassing advertising campaign developed with the ad agency because Jews watch US TV shows such as ER in which products are prominently placed and so the awareness levels of Dunkin Donuts was already very high. He has only spent $60 000 on marketing and public relations and yet the first two operating stores have triple the turnover of US stores. Perhaps all the aspects of the American culture have not yet permeated across to Israel because the main difference is that in Israel the customers eat in store whilst in the US they take out.

On the other hand for Palestinians, who number 2.5 million, labelling in Hebrew on the packaging of products is a sign of quality, whereas English labelling is a sign of low quality, largely because inferior quality products with English labelling were supplied in the past from countries like Greece, Turkey and Egypt. The Palestinians, however, do visit Tel Aviv and other big Israeli cities and are exposed to many American brands and are also exposed to dozens of Arabic TV channels via cable and satellite. Palestinians are getting used to American products and already use 'Pampers' as the generic name for disposable nappies.

Source: adapted from Sugarman, M. (1997) 'New Israel embraces cachet of US brands', *Ad Age International*, April

local niche channels to be set up. The established television industry has had to pre-empt this by targeting its output more precisely. MTV has established four European services for the UK, pan-northern, central and southern areas each reflecting distinctive local tastes, Eurosport is now available in 14 languages and CNN has four separate services for different regions of the world.

Press advertising

Media availability and effectiveness are particularly important in deciding the nature of campaigns because they can vary from country to country. High levels of readership of the press in a country is still unusual. The more usual situation is that the press is available but with only token readership outside certain usually urban regions.

In some countries, in Africa and Asia, adult literacy levels might restrict newspaper and magazine sales opportunities but the lack of mass-circulation national titles might cause distribution difficulties, too, as it is easier to distribute quickly in small compact countries than in much larger countries such as France or Spain. Vast countries like the USA are much more likely to develop a distinctive regional press. Newer publishing and printing technology has allowed many more local newspapers and specialist magazines to be introduced to both consumer and business-to-business markets. By their very nature they tend to be highly targeted at specific market segments and can be useful to niche marketers. However, for mass marketers the resulting fragmentation of readership that comes from very localised media titles means that national campaigns are more difficult to coordinate.

The use of agencies and consultancies

Most companies in which marketing communications are an important part of the marketing mix will use agencies and consultancies. The reasons why this is so can be explained by financial considerations, specialist knowledge, creative input and external perspective.

Financial. Advertising agents that are recognised by the media are eligible for a commission based on booked advertising space. The agency can therefore perform the advertising services of creation, media planning and booking more economically than the client.

Agencies and consultancies can use specialist people and resources, such as a database for media planning, with a number of clients. This helps spread costs for both the agency and clients.

Specialist knowledge. By concentrating on one particular area, agencies and consultancies can become experts in specialised techniques, for example, international database marketing or training sales people. Client companies might have an infrequent need for these services and so find it more cost effective to subcontract the work.

Creative input. Creativity is very important in marketing communications. The organisation culture of client companies is unlikely to encourage true creativity in external communications. The challenge of new and different projects for different clients contributes to the creativity of agencies.

External perspective. The external view of agencies reduces some of the myopia of the client company. This might be particularly valuable at times of major transition in international marketing, for example, in moving towards global marketing.

The selection of agencies and consultants is an important business decision. If the agency is going to be involved over a long period and be trusted with large expenditures of time and money the decision process will be significant. An important decision for FMCG global marketers was whether they should select one central agency or many local agencies as the Illustration 10.6 shows.

Sales promotions

Sales promotions can be used in a variety of ways to add value to the sale and are particularly effective if they are part of an integrated communications strategy. Sales promotions can be used within the promotions mix for fast moving consumer goods and business-to-business markets. Consumer goods sales promotions might include coupons or money-off vouchers, 'special offer' price reductions and competitions. As well as these, business-to-business sales promotions might also include database and direct marketing, exhibitions and trade fairs, bundled sales deals, in which extra product features might be added, such as trade-ins on old products, extra warranty and service cover and operative training.

Sales promotions are usually used close to the purchase decision and have the objective of offering better value to the customer at the most influential moment in the purchase process. In some markets there may be no meaningful differences between a number of companies or brands, except for the degree of attractiveness of the sales promotion offer. The customers' perception of the relative value of the alternative promotions depend to a great extent on their cultural values. Citing a recent Turkish craze for collection-based promotions which were not

Illustration 10.6: To centralise advertising or not

The majority of the MNEs with worldwide operations have moved towards using a single global advertising agency. This trend has certainly been favoured by firms, such as IBM, Compaq, Reckitt and Colman and S C Johnson, who can see considerable benefits from having a central global agency. IBM was one of the first to move its £300 million account from 80 agencies in 1994 to one – Ogilvy and Mather. The advantages are seen as helping to create a strong global brand and also making client internal structures more centralised. The driving force is to achieve cost saving, through rationalising both agencies and brands.

The agencies also claim that good advertising ideas cross cultural boundaries. BBH's Levi ads run unchanged in more than 20 markets. If the ad works it does not matter where it was created but if local marketers are forced to use centrally created ads which do not work, they can become frustrated because they are unlikely to be let off their performance targets.

Coca-Cola has been the one company to go against this trend towards centralisation. McCann Erickson had dominated Coca-Cola's account for 30 years when Sergio Zyman took over as chief marketing officer for Coca-Cola. He assembled a group of talented local agencies under the strapline 'Always Coca-Cola' with the intention of developing the think global act local idea. The strategy worked for Coca-Cola because it generated healthy competition in the agencies' creative departments. Zyman is credited with being the major driving force in reinventing the Coca-Cola brand.

In his determination to achieve even better creativity he challenged the ways that agencies thought and worked by setting up a virtual consultancy at CAA, which had until then been better known for managing Hollywood film stars. Whilst this strategy has clearly worked – putting Coca-Cola even further ahead – it has proved to be costly and difficult to manage. When Zyman resigned from Coca-Cola in 1998 the question was, how should they organise their advertising in the future?

Source: adapted from Bentley, S. (1997) 'Big agencies profit from global tactics', *Marketing Week,* 24 January and (1998) 'Will Coke alter Zyman formula', *Marketing Week,* 26 March

replicated in other neighbouring countries, Read (1997) suggests that cultural differences lead to certain types of sales promotion being very successful in one country but failing in another.

Read (1997) notes that legal restrictions also affect the opportunity for firms to standardise sales promotion across country borders. In France the amount of free fill products given away is limited to 7 per cent and in Germany banded offers of three products for the price of two are banned, and cash discounts to customers are limited to 3 per cent. Different legal definitions of the rules for lotteries, too, prevent some competition-based promotions being operated across borders.

Direct marketing

In the past direct marketing has usually taken the form of direct mail or telephone selling and these are still, perhaps, the main routes to the market but the Internet is becoming an important alternative method. The key elements of direct marketing are an accurate up to date database, the ability to purge the database of incorrect data and merge the database with a firm's promotional message. Usually it is important to offer a telephone (toll-free) number and, of course, the customers need to have a telephone if telephone marketing is to be used. Usually firms subcontract direct marketing to specialist agencies which provide the various services, such as list broking, purging and merging. Latin America offers considerable opportunities for direct mailing although the infrastructure in some countries will pose problems as shown in Illustration 10.7.

Cyberspace advertising

Cyberspace advertising is growing rapidly and it represents the first attempts of advertisers on the Internet to take a proactive marketing approach rather than waiting for potential users to discover their site. Herbig and Hale (1997) explain that Cyberspace advertising companies can design a homepage through to an entire advertising campaign at rock bottom prices – as little as $20 per month. For 67 cents a day the target market potential is 30–50 million people, 24 hours a day, seven days a week. An American software company, Management Information Technologies compared conventional and a cyberspace marketing approach. They sent out 120 press releases and received two replies over a seven month period, whereas, within one month of listing the same information on a website, they had received 50 leads and sold ten products. They then set up an electronic mailing list with 800 names and made 40 sales.

There are four emerging types of on-line advertising: banners are static animated poster-style ads, buttons are graphic 'hotlinks' to an advertisers site,

Illustration 10.7: Direct marketing in Latin America

Latin America has a population of 650 million and, given the largely democratic governments, the increasing affluence and its proximity to North America, offers considerable opportunities for direct marketers. The size of the market is impossible to estimate but both consumer and business-to-business markets are expected to grow at 40–50 per cent a year in most countries.

Five to ten years ago companies were predominantly state owned but the privatisation industries, such as telecommunications, transportation, utilities, water, propane distribution, highways and roads are offering the new opportunities. The differences between the markets are considerable:

	Argentina	Brazil	Chile	Peru
Direct marketing agencies	10	72	10	1
Telemarketing firms	25	36	15	3
List brokers	5	16	3	1
Merge/purge companies	2	27	1	0
Toll free service	yes	yes	yes	soon
Phone penetration	65%	n/a	45%	18%

Direct marketing is, therefore, at different stages of development compared to the US with the possible exception of Brazil. However, Latin American countries are likely to catch up fast, but by using a different route – Internet. Direct marketers face some problems in moving forward because different dialects of Spanish are spoken and Portuguese is spoken in Brazil.

Long-distance telephone calls are expensive, so the direct marketers will have to set up local operations. There are few reliable lists of potential customers and few public sources of data. Whilst consumer data is being collected business-to-business marketers usually have to collect their own information.

Source: Adapted from Loro, L. (1998) 'Direct Marketing', *Advertising Age*, January

interjacents are 'commercial breaks' between the lines of display of third party web pages and sponsorship which seeks association with third party web page.

Possibly one of the major problems is measuring current and potential sales through the Internet. World Wide Web sales in 1996 reached half a million dollars. Estimates of the number of Internet users in 1998 ranged from 15–50 million in the US and yet it is clear that there are some substantial differences in individual country growth. For example, in 1997 the Internet market in France declined, partly due to the dominance of the domestic Minitel telecommunications system.

There are some significant marketing challenges facing the future use of Internet.

- Customers from some countries, typically low context countries are likely to embrace Internet much more readily than those in high context cultures, because of the lower emphasis placed on building verbal and non-verbal interactions when building relationships and purchasing products.

- Brand values often depend on a number of communication methods, both explicit and implicit, such as image, reputation, word of mouth and accidental exposure whilst travelling or shopping. It is yet unclear how this will translate to eCommerce.

- By being global, eCommerce favours global players. Consumers expect high quality of performance and image but these can be severely tarnished by a low cost, poorly performing website. One of the most important issues facing Internet advertisers is the degree to which customers will purchase from an international company rather than a domestic company.

- Gordon and Turner (1997), researching US customers of speciality foods made observations on the websites, such as ease of website navigation, company and products information, shipping details and overall rating. If a website had negative ratings the likelihood of purchase from a domestic company was reduced by 42 per cent but from an international company by 87 per cent. For international marketers seeking to use the Internet the design of the website is critical.

- Domestic niche markets can be served by global niche Commerce marketers with the consequence that the barriers to entry must be significant if the defenders of domestic or limited country involvement wish to retain their market share.

- It must be recognised by marketers that the marketing skills to ensure success in eCommerce are different from traditional skills in that success depends on attracting consumers to sites and this is typically more difficult because of the increased media 'noise' which makes access more difficult.

- The major developments in eCommerce are likely to be an increase in intelligent agents which search for specific pieces of information on the International, such as Andersen Consulting Bargain Finder, means that marketers cannot base their business appeal on the traditional dimensions of marketing from the past.

Communicating with the wider range of stakeholders

At the outset we said that the principal objective of the international marketing communications strategy was to sell products and services. However, before messages are communicated with the specific purpose of encouraging consumers to buy it is necessary to make them more broadly aware of the company and its products. In the early stages of the buying process it is the reputation which the international firm has in the wider community which is important. Quite simply customers in a host country are unlikely to even contemplate buying from a foreign firm which is perceived to be exploiting its local workers, bribing government officials, showing little regard to environmental protection issues, offering poor or variable product quality or is likely to pull out from the country at any moment and thus be unable to fulfil its guarantees and obligations. By contrast a foreign firm can build increased loyalty amongst its customers at the expense of local firms if it is perceived to offer better quality and value for money, to be a more reliable supplier, more caring about the local community and, in some cases, through association, to be respected by world personalities.

These objectives can be achieved through the effective use of a number of communications elements under the following general headings:

- Corporate identity
- Sponsorship
- Public relations and lobbying.

Corporate identity

Corporate identity is concerned with consistently communicating not just what business the firm is in and what image it wishes to project in the market, but also how it does its business. It must reflect the standards and values it aims to uphold in its dealings with all its stakeholders. For this reason there are two distinct elements. For many MNEs the focus is upon the image it wishes to create, which is reinforced by consistency in the way the company name and logo is presented and applied to the vast range of physical outputs and assets of the company including a signs, staff uniforms, letterheads, visiting cards, gifts, annual reports, packaging specification and promotional literature.

As we have already discussed, whilst these all can be controlled, in principle, by the firm, there are many challenges applying them consistently in all the countries where the firm operates.

Arguably, of more importance, is the underlying identity of the firm, its beliefs, standards and values which will show through in everything the firm does. These may pose more difficulties to the firm's attempts to achieve consistency and a favourable impact throughout the world because of the different cultural values of its staff and stakeholders in different countries.

Sponsorship

Sponsorship involves a firm (the sponsor) providing finance, resources or other support of an event, activity, firm, person, product or service. In return the sponsor would expect to gain some advantage, such as the exposure of its brand, logo or advertising message. Sponsorship of music, performing arts and sporting events provides opportunities for:

- brand exposure and publicity
- opportunities to entertain customers and employees
- association between brands and events, with the events often reinforcing the brand positioning, for example, Dunhill's golf sponsorship and BMW's sponsorship of classical music concerts in the UK
- improving community relations by supporting community-based projects
- creating the opportunity to promote the brands at the event, either through providing free product or gifts such as T-shirts carrying the brand logo.

Expenditure on global sponsorship has expanded rapidly over the last two decades and it is being used much more for the following reasons identified by Meenahan (1991):

- restrictive government on policies on tobacco and alcohol advertising leaving sponsorship as the most effective way of communicating the brand imagery to a mass market, for example in Formula 1 car racing

- the escalating costs of media advertising
- increased leisure activities and sporting events
- the proven records of sponsorship
- greater media coverage of sponsored events
- the reduced efficiencies of traditional media advertising because of clutter and zapping between television programmes.

There is an increase in the amount of broadcast sponsorship where a television or radio programme is sponsored. This can result in the effect of the event sponsorship being reduced. For example, Heinz sponsored a recent Rugby World Cup only to find that Sony sponsored the national commercial television coverage in the UK resulting in most viewers thinking that Sony had sponsored the whole event.

Public relations

Public relations is concerned with communicating news stories about the firm, its people, products and services through the media without charge in order to develop relationships, goodwill and mutual understanding between the firm and its stakeholders. Because of the wide span of activities covering marketing, finance and human resources management, public relations is not necessarily an exclusively marketing preserve.

Lesly (1991) identifies the purposes as follows:

- helping to foster the prestige and reputation, through the public image of the firm
- raising awareness and creating interest in the firm's products
- dealing with social and environmental issues and opportunities
- improving goodwill with customers through presenting useful information and dealing effectively with complaints
- promoting the sense of identification of employees with the firm through newsletters, social activities and recognition
- discovering and eliminating rumours and other sources of misunderstanding and misconceptions
- building a reputation as a good customer and reliable supplier
- influencing the opinions of public officials and politicians, especially in explaining the responsible operation of the business and the importance of its activities to the community

- dealing promptly, accurately and effectively with unfavourable negative publicity, especially where it is perceived to be a crisis which might damage the firm's reputation
- attracting and keeping good employees.

Public relations is concerned with a wide variety of activities in order to deliver these objectives, for example:

- dealing with press relations
- arranging facility visits
- publishing house journals and newsletters
- preparing videos, audio visual presentations printed reports and publications describing the firm's activities
- training courses
- arranging community projects
- lobbying governments.

From a communications perspective the effect of public relations generated space in the media is different from advertising. The viewer, listener or reader will perceive the information differently. Editorial material in the media is perceived by consumers to be factual and comparatively neutral whereas advertising material is expected to be persuasive and present a positive statement for the advertisers' products. Whereas the firm controls every aspect of advertising, a press release covering a firm's news story will be interpreted by the journalist who writes the story for the press or edits the videotape for TV. Therefore the value of the same amount of media space used in editorial or in advertising is quite different. On occasions a negative story can result from PR designed to enhance the firm's image particularly where language translations and cultural misunderstandings might have shown the foreign firm as having little empathy or understanding of the host country.

Stakeholders

MNEs have a larger number of stakeholders than those firms limited to domestic markets. These stakeholders or target groups have varying degrees of connection with such organisations. Some will be part of the value system of a firm and some will be part of the environment surrounding the firm both domestically and internationally. Some may be supportive, whilst others may have a controlling role.

One of the main roles of international public relations is to try to manage the often substantially different and often conflicting expectations of stakeholders which was illustrated in Chapter 5. Frequently the problem is one of when to disclose information which could prove damaging to the company's image and reputation.

In international marketing one of the most important responsibilities of public relations is to manage unexpected crises which occur from time to time. Over the last few years there have been a number of examples of good and bad practice in managing information when dealing with a crisis within the company. Crises of this type have included environmental pollution, health scares, caused by food contamination, unethical promotion and exploitation of labour. The golden rule is that the firm should be seen to act before the media or government forces it to do so, to show that it is sorry that an incident has occurred, but should neither accept responsibility nor apportion blame until the evidence is investigated and the real cause of the problem identified.

Many MNEs consider government lobbying an essential part of international marketing with the aim of influencing foreign governments both directly and indirectly through asking the home country government to help. The most obvious example of lobbying has been by US firms seeking access to Japanese markets over the last two decades and the main objectives of the strategy have been to convince both governments that allowing market access is in both their interests.

As government lobbying becomes increasingly important it raises issues for the company about how high profile the company should be in pressing its case and how much effort should be expended on persuading the home country government to put pressure on the host country government. There is little doubt that firms are increasingly making lobbying a major responsibility of senior management given the pivotal role of governments in making decisions which might affect the MNE.

Relationship marketing

So far in this chapter we have focused upon the communications strategies that might be used to ensure that the firm's broad base of stakeholders around the world are aware of the company standards and values, the distinctiveness and quality of its brands, products and services and that customers are exposed to the messages that will encourage them to buy the firm's rather than the competitor's products and services. Once customers have been won over, usually at a considerable cost, firms are increasingly realising that it is less costly if they can persuade them to stay loyal to the firm rather than losing them to a competitor and then facing the cost of winning them over again. The potential cost of failing to satisfy customers can be high. For example, Nissan did not produce a successor to its sports coupe which had sales of approximately 40 000 in Europe because the car was not perceived to be a success in Japan and was not worth launching in the US. The calculated loss of potential sales of the replacement was perhaps $1 billion with a considerable number of disappointed customers who were forced to buy from Nissan's competitors.

Keeping customers is particularly important for business-to-business marketing, where the opportunities to win over new customers may be very limited and the loss of a customer could have a very bad effect on the firm.

In response to this the concept of relationship marketing has been introduced. Relationship marketing is concerned with developing and maintaining mutually advantageous relationships between partners in a supply chain and using their resources to deliver the maximum added value for the customer.

There are significant differences between adopting a marketing approach based upon making transactions, the traditional approach to dealing with customers, in which the emphasis is placed on the 4Ps of the product marketing mix and an approach based upon building relationships in which there is an emphasis on the 3 extra Ps of the service mix to which we referred to in Chapter 9. Some of the differences are illustrated in Figure 10.6.

At the core of the concept, therefore, is the idea that rather than simply trying to add customer service on to a predetermined product offer based on a rigid marketing mix, as shown in Figure 10.7, the firm should focus on giving customer satisfaction by being prepared to modify a flexible marketing mix where necessary, as shown in Figure 10.8.

Figure 10.6 The dimensions of transaction and relationship marketing

Transaction	**Relationship**
• Purchaser–marketer interaction	• Team-based, integrated interactions
• Features–benefits offer	• Value added
• Discrete interactions	• Continuous interactions
• Competitive	• Cooperation
• Winning new customers	• Retaining customers
• Top down directives	• Horizontal interactions
• Quality, value and service	• Customer satisfaction

Figure 10.7 Brand value based on customer service

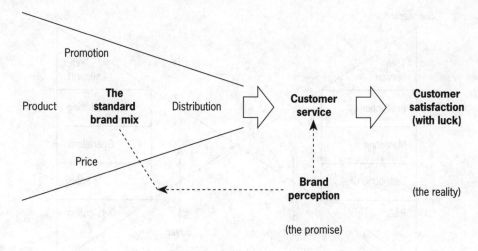

Figure 10.8 Brand value based on customer satisfaction

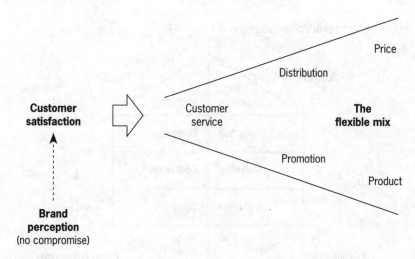

Changing the focus from winning to retaining customers, therefore, has considerable implications for the marketing strategy in general and the communications strategy in particular. Instead of the communications being relatively simple, one direction, with a single point of contact as they are in traditional marketing, shown in Figure 10.9, they become much more complex, with the communications being multilevel and multidirectional as shown in Figure 10.10.

Figure 10.9 Traditional relationship

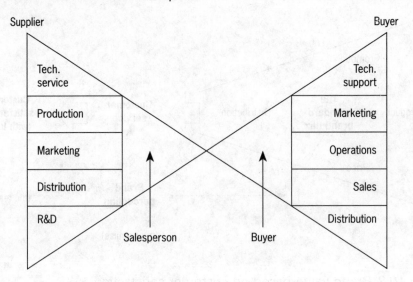

Figure 10.10 Partnership linkages

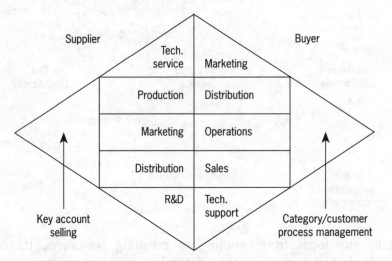

In Figure 10.9 the sales person from the marketing company and the buyer are the only points of contact of the firms, whereas in Figure 10.10 there are many points of contact between the firms.

In international marketing it is clear that managing effective communications between the two sets of staff can be particularly challenging, especially when the various problems of communication, referred to earlier in the chapter are taken into account. It is at this point where effective internal marketing and a good company communication system are needed to ensure that all staff adopt a consistent approach, no matter where they are in the world.

Inevitably relationship marketing requires a different philosophy in the firm and changes in the marketing and communications strategy objectives, budgets and performance measurements. Groonroos (1996) suggests that relationship marketing has two distinct dimensions: strategic relationship marketing and tactical relationship marketing.

The strategic issues of relationship marketing are identified as:

- defining the business as a service business and recognising that the key competitive elements are concerned with services competition (competing with a total service offering, instead of with product alone);
- managing the firm with a process management perspective and not from a functional perspective (the process of creating value for customers rather than managing operations and marketing purely for efficiency); and
- developing partnerships and networks to be able to handle the whole service process, for example, by making close contacts with well-known suppliers and intermediaries.

The tactical or operational issues are concerned within the following:

- seeking direct contacts with customers and other stakeholders;
- building a database covering the necessary information about customers and others stakeholders; and
- developing a customer oriented service system.

The further implications of relationship marketing are that it is necessary to build relationships not only with the final customers but also with those other stakeholders that might influence the final purchase. Payne *et al.* (1995) suggest that typically there are up to six markets, shown in Figure 10.11, that must be targeted for relationship marketing to be used effectively. However, the power and influence of these markets varies considerably around the world.

In thinking about some of the most respected companies around the world, such as Coca-Cola and Marks and Spencer, it is clear that their success has been built on this kind of formula.

Figure 10.11 Focusing on the six markets

> - **Internal markets**. The actions and beliefs of individuals and groups in the organisation determine the style and ethods of its marketing and operational activity.
> - **Referral markets**. Professionals and satisfied customers help the firm to build relationships by encouraging word of mouth recommendations.
> - **Influence markets**. Organisations and individuals influence the marketing environment in which the firm is operating using PR.
> - **Employee markets**. Recruiting and retaining good people makes the firm attractive not only to good potential employees, but also help it gain respect in the wider community.
> - **Supplier markets**. Close and effective relationships improve quality, innovation, lower inventory and faster time to market for the firm.
> - **Customer markets**. The main driver for relationship marketing is to satisfy customers by providing excellence service for external purchasers.

For purchases that matter to them consumers are more prepared to trust those they perceive as friends or 'on the same side' rather than faceless organisations. Richard Branson, the UK entrepreneur, who developed the Virgin Group has adopted the 'man of the people' approach, taking on the establishment and companies such as BA and the financial services industry, which Virgin have portrayed as working against the interests of their customers.

The operational issues of relationship marketing

Whilst it might be argued that relationship marketing has its main impact in business-to-business marketing, increasingly it is being used in consumer markets. For example, Kellogg's build relationships with their existing customers by sending each morning to every person that has registered, an e-mail in the form of a customised newsletter containing the news on their favourite subjects to read whilst they are eating their breakfast.

The key to success in building relationships with many thousands or millions of customers is an effective database. Peppers (1997) suggests that three computer capabilities are needed:

- a database as a powerful base of knowledge about customers, their attitudes and behaviour
- interactivity between customer and supplier, so that there is immediacy in the relationship. This comes, for example, from touch phone, ATM machine, the web membership card swiping
- customisation so that instead of providing products and services for the average person – it is in fact providing what individuals require.

The database can be used to identify those customers with which it is worthwhile developing a good relationship. Hotels, for example, can give a regular customer their favourite room when they book. Many companies have taken the bonus card route to building customer loyalty. Essentially by purchasing more from a company, bonus points are awarded and discounts or free gifts are offered. Marriott Hotels, with 3.5 million on their honoured guest programme, claim to have the most popular incentive programme in the hotel industry. Free gifts or heavily discounted services have a high perceived value to the customer but, for example, offering free or heavily discounted room rates for occupancy when the hotel would otherwise have empty bedrooms costs the hotel very little.

The air miles programme in which frequent flyers collect points until they have enough for a free flight is, perhaps, one of the best known loyalty programmes. Frequent flyer programmes offer customers high perceived added value but are based on the low additional cost of carrying extra passengers in what would otherwise be empty seats.

Customer information stored on a firm's database can be extremely useful not only for giving high added value service to customers but can also be used more fundamentally for targeting. General Motors have developed a database to identify and accurately target their most loyal and creditworthy customers enabling them to offer generous financial rebates for card users. This has resulted in 12 million GM cards being used in the US. Jaya Jusco is one of the main shopping centres in Malaysia which uses loyalty cards to retain customers but also to help its Japanese parent Jusco to adapt and improve its services for the Malaysian market.

Changes in IT, communications and greater awareness of customers to cross-border purchasing means that the opportunities for relationship marketing to offer benefits are increasing. However, Christy *et al.* (1996) suggest that successful establishment of relationship marketing depends on the extent to which each player understands the potential rewards and also the reciprocal duties necessary to make it work. Moreover, Fournier, *et al.* (1998) emphasise that the consumer is not necessarily a willing participant in the relationship mission, and unless this is recognised, relationship marketing will prove to be of limited value.

For relatively low purchase price items there is a danger that the costs of building customer loyalty might out weigh the costs of a more traditional approach to marketing products and services. It is difficult to measure the relative merits of short-term costs against longer-term revenues and few companies are willing to take a long-term view based upon assumptions of what might happen in the future.

Conclusion

In a shrinking world, communications are becoming increasingly important in providing the means of differentiating firms and their products and services from those of their competitors. Equally, however, communications are extremely culturally sensitive and without attention to detail, they can be the source of many problems for firms offering their products throughout the world.

Whilst the methods of communication are changing more rapidly than ever before through the introduction of new technology, they should be regarded as tools in the management of the relationships between the firm and its customers. The international firm must communicate the consistency in its image, standards and values to a diverse range of stakeholders as well as making its direct appeal to existing and potential customers.

Discussion questions

1 Communications are central to effective marketing planning. What are the key issues in planning, executing and controlling an international communications strategy?

2 Critically examine the case for using one advertising agency to create and implement an international advertising campaign.

3 What factors would constrain the use of standardised sales promotion campaigns for a multi-national enterprise in international markets?

4 Select an economic region. Identify the advantages and disadvantages of pan-regional advertising. How would you manage a pan-regional campaign for a product or service of your choice?

5 Direct marketing, through mail, telephone and Internet allows a firm to market its product or service directly to customers around the world. What barriers must the firm overcome and what are the critical factors for success?

References

Bentley, S. (1997) 'Big agencies profit from global tactics', *Marketing Week*, 24 January.

Chan, A. K. and Huang, Y. (1997) 'Brand naming in China: a linguistic approach', *Marketing Intelligence and Planning*, 5 (15): 227–34.

Christy, R., Oliver, G. and Penn, J. (1996) 'Relationship Marketing in Consumer markets', *Journal of Marketing Management*, 12 (1–3).

Elinder, E. (1995) 'How international can European Advertising be?' *Journal of Marketing*, 29, (2).

Fannin, R.A. (1997) 'Top global marketers', *Advertising Age International*, November.

Fournier, S., Dobscha, S. and Divid, G.M. (1998) 'Preventing the Premature Death of Relationship Marketing', *Harvard Business Review*, January–February: 43–51.

Gordon, M.E. and Lima-Turner, K. de (1997) 'Consumer attitudes towards Internet advertising: A social contract perceptive' *International Marketing Review*, 14 (5): 362–75.

Groonroos, C. (1996) 'Relationship marketing strategic and tactical implications', *Management Decision*, 34 (3), MCB University Press.

Harding, J. (1997) 'Consumer revolution: The risks and rewards of marketing western goods in China', *Financial Times*, 14 July.

Herbig, P. and Hale, B. (1997) 'Internet: the marketing challenge of the twentieth century', *Internet Research: Electronic Networking Applications and Policy*, 7 (2): 95–100 MCB.

Howard (1997) 'Survey of European advertising expenditure 1980–1996', *International Journal of Advertising*, 17.

Hu, M. Y. and Griffith, D. (1997) 'Conceptualising the global marketplace: marketing strategy implications', *Marketing Intelligence and Planning*, 15/3.

Koranteng, J. (1998) 'Reebok finds its second wind as it pursues global presence', *Advertising Age International*, January.

Kotler, P. (1988) *Marketing management, analysis, planning, implementation and control*, Prentice Hall.

Lesly, P. (1991) *The handbook of public relations and communications*, McGraw-Hill.

Loro, L. (1998) 'Direct Marketing', *Advertising Age International*, January.

Meenagham, T. (1995) 'The Volkswagen Beetle The role of advertising in brand image development', *Journal of Product and Brand management*, 4 (4).

Meenahan, T. (1991) 'Sponsorship: Legitimising the Medium European', *Journal of Marketing*, 25 (11).

Mills, D. (1998) Nike on the wrong track, *The Daily Telegraph*, April 7

Neelankavil, J.P., Mummalaneni, V. and Sessions, D. (1996) 'Use of foreign language and models in print advertisements in East Asian countries: A logit modelling approach', *European Journal of Management*, 29 (4): 24–38.

Payne, A., Christopher, M., Clark, M. and Peck, H. (1995) *Relationship Marketing for Competitive Advantage*, Butterworth-Heinnemann.

Peppers, D. (1997) 'The man who sold the world', *Direct Response*, March.

Read, D. (1997) 'Country Practice', *Marketing Week*, 3 July.

Schmitt, B.H. and Pan, Y. (1994) 'Managing corporate and brand identities in the Asia Pacific Region', *Californian Business Review*, Summer.

Shannon, J. (1997) 'TV focuses on local targeting', *Marketing Week*, 21 August.

Simms, J. (1998) 'A winning formula', *Marketing Business*, April.

Siu, W. and Au, A.K. (1997) 'Women in advertising: a comparison of television advertisements in China and Singapore', *Marketing Intelligence and Planning*, 15 (5).

Smith, A. (1998) 'Ads across the oceans', *Financial Times*, 24 April.

Smith, P., Berry, C. and Pulford, A. (1997) *Strategic Marketing Communications*, Kogan Page.

Sugarman, M. (1997) 'New Israel embraces cachet of US brands', *Ad Age International*, April.

Wentz, H. (1997) 'A single Europe: reality or mirage', *Advertising Age International*, May.

Williams, J. (1998) 'Let the brands begin business', *Financial Times*, 9 February.

Wilson, R. and Gilligan, C. (1997) *Strategic Marketing Mangement: Planning, Implementation and Control*, Butterworth-Heinemann.

Zhang, Y. and Neelankavil, J.P. (1997) 'The influence of culture on advertising effectiveness in China and the USA: A cross cultural study', *European Journal of Management*, 31 (2): 134–49.

Chapter 11

The management of international distribution and logistics

Introduction

In Chapter 8, we examined strategies for international expansion and the options available for firms entering foreign markets. In this chapter we will build on the issues discussed in Chapter 8 but focus on managing the distribution and logistics within foreign markets.

The management of foreign channels of distribution is a key area in a firm's efforts to gain competitive advantage. As products become more standardised across the world, the ability to compete on customer service becomes more vital. In order to be effective in this area, a firm must have a well-managed supply chain within foreign markets and across international boundaries.

In this chapter, we will examine the strategic issues in managing distribution channels, discuss the issues of selecting intermediaries and how to build long-term effective relationships in international markets. We will also examine the developments in retailing and the differences in retailing across markets at different levels of economic development.

Finally, we will examine the logistics of physically moving goods across national boundaries and the importance of efficient distribution management to minimise costs in international markets.

The challenges in managing an international distribution strategy

Distribution channels are the means by which goods are distributed from the manufacturer to the end user. Some companies own their own means of distribution, some companies only deal directly with the most important customers but many companies rely on other companies to perform distribution services for them. These services include:

- the purchase of goods
- the assembly of an attractive assortment of goods
- holding stocks or inventory
- promoting the sale of goods to the end customer
- the physical movement of goods.

In international marketing, companies usually take advantage of a wide number of different organisations to facilitate the distribution of their products. The large number is explained by considerable differences between countries both in their distribution systems and in the expected level of product sales. The physical movement of goods usually includes several modes of transport – for example, by road to a port, by boat to the country of destination and by road to the customer's premises. The selection of the appropriate distribution strategy is a significant decision. Whilst the marketing mix decisions of product and marketing communications are often more glamorous, they are usually dependent upon the chosen distribution channel. The actual distribution channel decision is a fundamental decision as it affects all aspects of the international marketing strategy.

The key objective in building an effective distribution strategy is to build a supply chain to your markets that is, as Kotler (1996) said, ' a planned and professionally managed vertically integrated marketing system that incorporates both the needs of the manufacturer and the distributors'.

To achieve this across international markets is a daunting task and will mean the international marketing manager has to meet a number of important challenges in order to ensure they develop a distribution strategy which delivers the effective distribution of products and services across international markets. The major areas they will need to consider are as follows:

- *Selection of foreign country intermediaries.* Should the firm use indirect or direct channels? What type of intermediaries will best serve their needs in the marketplace?

- *How to build a relationship with intermediaries.* The management and motivation of intermediaries in foreign country markets is especially important to firms endeavouring to build a long-term presence, competing on offering quality services.

- *How to deal with the varying types of retailing infrastructure across international markets.* Achieving a coordinated strategy across markets where retailing is at varying stages of development and the impact of the growth of retailers themselves globalising are important considerations in the distribution strategies of firms competing in consumer goods markets.

- *How to maximise new and innovative forms of distribution*, particularly opportunities arising through the Internet and electronic forms of distribution.

- *How to manage the logistics of physically distributing products across foreign markets*. Firms need to evaluate the options available and develop a well managed logistics system.

In the following sections of the chapter, we will examine the issues in each of these areas of international distribution and logistics.

Selecting foreign country market intermediaries

A distribution decision is a long-term decision, once established it can be difficult to extract a company from existing agreements. This means that channels chosen have to be appropriate for today and flexible enough to adapt to long-term market developments.

In some instances, difficulties may arise because of legal contracts as in the case of the termination of an agency; in other situations they result from relationships that need to be initiated and then nurtured. For example, the development of sales through wholesalers and distributors might be substantially influenced by the past trading pattern and the expectation of future profitable sales. Therefore a long-term relationship needs to be developed before a firm is willing to invest significantly in an intermediary.

The long-term nature of distribution decisions forces a careful analysis of future developments in the distribution channel. If new forms of distribution are emerging (for example, mass merchandise retailing or Internet retailing), this has to be considered early in the planning stage of the distribution channel.

Another important challenge is the comparative inexperience of managers in the channel selection process in international markets. In domestic marketing, most marketing managers develop marketing plans which will usually be implemented within the existing arrangement of the company's distribution channels. This is quite a different proposition to the pioneering process of establishing a distribution channel in the first place and then achieving a well-supported availability through channel members in different country markets.

Furthermore, if foreign market channels are being managed from the home market, there maybe preconceived notions and preferences that home market systems can operate elsewhere. Because they are unfamiliar with the market, managers may underestimate the barriers to entry erected by local competitors and even government regulations. For instance, in both France and Japan there are restrictive laws which inhibit the growth of large retailers. In Japan no one can open a store larger than 5382 square feet without the permission from the community store owners. Thus it can take eight to ten years for a store to win approval.

Indirect and direct channels

One of the first decisions to make in selecting intermediaries for international markets is, should the product be distributed indirectly? In other words, using outside sales agents and distributors in the country or should the product be distributed directly, using the company's sales force, company owned distribution channel or other intermediaries in a foreign country? The former option is an independent channel which is non-integrated and provides very little or no control over its international distribution and virtually affords no links with the end users. On the other hand, direct distribution, which is an integrated channel, generally affords the manufacturer more control and, at the same time, brings responsibility, commitment and attendant risks. As we have discussed distribution decisions are difficult to change and so it is important for firms to consider the alternatives available and the differing degrees of commitment and risk, evaluate the alternatives and select the most appropriate type of distribution.

Integrated (direct) channels of distribution are seen to be beneficial when a firm's marketing strategy requires a high level of service before or after the sale. Integrated channels will be more helpful than independent channels in ensuring that high levels of customer service will be achieved.

Indirect channels on the other hand require less investment both in terms of money and management time. Indirect channels also are seen to be beneficial in overcoming freight rate, negotiating disadvantages, lowering the cost of exporting and allowing higher margins and profits for the manufacturer. An independent channel, therefore, allows the international firm to tap the benefits of a distribution specialist within a foreign market such as economies of scale and pooling the demand for the distribution services of several manufacturers.

The advantages and disadvantages of indirect exporting were discussed in Chapter 8. In this section we will focus on issues facing firms who have made the decision to involve themselves with intermediaries in foreign country markets, either through the use of agents, distributors or using their own company-owned sales force. These intermediaries offer a wide range of services which are as follows:

- **Export distributors** – usually perform a variety of functions including: stock inventories, handle promotion, extend customer credit, process orders, arrange shipping, product maintenance and repair.

- **Export agents** – responsibilities often include: buyer/seller introductions, host market information, trade fair exhibitions, general promotional activities.

- **Cooperative organisations** – carry on exporting activities on behalf of several producers and are partly under their administrative control (often used by producers of primary products – e.g. bananas, coffee, sugar).

A company-owned sales force may be one of three types:

1 **Travelling export sales representatives**. The company can begin by sending home-based sales people abroad to gather important information, to

Figure 11.1 Distribution channels for business goods

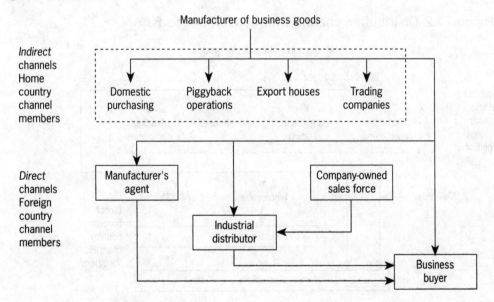

make the necessary customer contacts and to conduct the negotiating and selling process.

2 **Domestic-based export department or division**. An export sales manager carries on the actual selling and draws on market assistance as needed. It might evolve into a self-contained export department performing all the activities in export and operating as a profit centre.

3 **Foreign-based sales branch or subsidiary**. A foreign-based sales branch allows the company to achieve greater presence and programme control in the foreign market. The sales branch handles sales and distribution and may also handle warehousing and promotion. It often serves as a display centre and customer service centre as well.

The choices available to a firm may well be determined by whether they are operating in the business-to-business or consumer goods sector. Figure 11.1 illustrates the choices for a manufacturer of business goods.

The main channels for business goods, therefore, tend to be agents, distributors and companies wholly owned sales force. The main distribution channels for consumer goods are shown in Figure 11.2.

Over the past few years there have been considerable developments in retailing across national boundaries. In a later section in this chapter, we will examine

Figure 11.2 Distribution channels for consumer goods

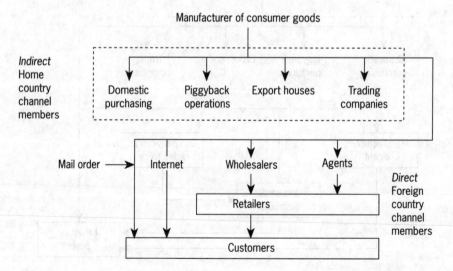

these trends and other new forms of retailing. First, however, we will look at the factors to consider in selecting channels of distribution and then building effective relationships with intermediaries.

Channel selection

In selecting appropriate channel intermediaries, a firm has to consider many factors. Czinkota and Ronkainen (1993) suggested the *11c model* to explain the factors a firm should consider in their selection process. The eleven elements to consider are:

1 Customer Characteristics
2 Culture
3 Competition
4 Company objectives
5 Character of the market
6 Cost
7 Capital required
8 Coverage needed
9 Control issues
10 Continuity provided
11 Communication effectiveness

Customer characteristics and culture

Channels of distribution have usually developed through the cultural traditions of the country and so there are great disparities across nations making the development of any standardised approach difficult.

The distribution system of a country can vary enormously. In Finland, there are four centralised wholesalers covering the whole market for most product categories. In Japan there are over 300 000 wholesalers and over 1.6 million retailers. The entire distribution system is based on networks with lots of wholesalers selling to other wholesalers. Because the price of land is so high in Japan, many wholesalers cannot carry stock in the traditional sense, so may order on a daily basis. This means that there are many layers between the foreign company and the final consumer as depicted in Figure 11.3.

The Japanese system centres on distributor linkages to *dainyo* manufacturers, where the distributor accepts a subservient social status in return for the economic security. From this interaction emerges the *ryatsu-keiretsuka*, a political

Figure 11.3 The typical distribution system in Japan

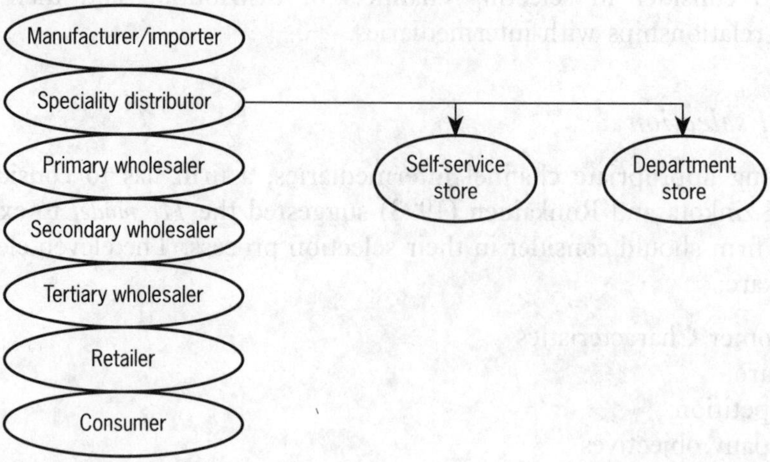

hierarchy in which units are arrayed in hierarchical layers and power resides at the 'commanding heights' of large *keiretsus.*

Distributors at 'lower' layers in the vertical structure are tied to the *keiretsu* system by bonds of loyalty, mutual obligation, trust and power that extend throughout existing distribution structures. Whilst this arrangement guarantees members some degree of security it also deprives them of economic freedom. Thus, distributors that choose to deal with firms outside of the established group risk severing their ties with the group.

Whilst distributors lack the freedom to transact with whomever they wish, they are also relieved of many costs associated with being independent – for example, smaller distributors in the system need not shoulder the risk of carrying inventories of products that will not sell and can depend on reliable delivery and financial help where necessary. A number of companies have tried to circumvent the system as can be seen in Illustration 11.1

Thus the characteristics of the customer and the cultural traditions of the country have a major impact on the choices available to a firm. A Belgian shopper may buy groceries from huge hypermarkets, concentrating on purchases which have long shelf lives and are easy to store in their spacious apartments and houses. The Japanese customers on the other hand can be characterised by their logistical imperatives, confined living space makes storage of goods very difficult. Therefore, customers make frequent visits to shops and rely on stores to keep their inventories. Moreover, Japan's narrow roads and lack

---

Illustration 11.1: Changing the Japanese distribution system

Japan has traditionally had a multi-tiered distribution system but, marketers are now looking to innovative new methods which avoid the existing channels. Discounters are a relatively new breed of retailer that operate outside of the *ruyutsu-keiretsuku* hierarchy. Toys 'R' Us, the American toy retailing giant, was the first large US discount store to open in Japan. The company teamed up with McDonald's Japan to operate toy stores and fast food outlets on the same site. By purchasing directly from manufacturers with low-cost, direct supply contracts, the multiple layers of wholesalers are eliminated. The inflow of foreign retailers is being aided by the Japanese government's push for deregulation in retail markets, but is proving to be a huge threat to traditional, small family-owned stores which have previously been protected by the rigid relationships in the distribution system.

---

of parking space (except for suburbs) predispose most of its population to do its shopping on foot.

Company objectives and competitive activity

The channel choice will also be determined by the company's objectives and what the firm's competitors are doing in a particular market. The distribution policy is part of a firm's international direction. Therefore, the distribution system developed will depend on the company's objective, i.e. whether their strategic objective is long term or short term and how quickly they need to realise their investment.

Most firms operating in international markets will endeavour to maintain a cost-effective balance between direct and indirect channels of distribution. Firms will use direct channels, perhaps their own sales force, in foreign country markets where their company's objective is to deliver high value solutions to buying problems in order to maximise customer satisfaction. Thus, the firm is practising 'interaction' marketing as opposed to 'transaction' marketing. A firm whose objective is to build long-term, stable relationships with its foreign customers will have quite different objectives in the building of relationships throughout the supply chain than a firm who has relatively short-term objectives in foreign country markets and purely wishes to complete the transaction before moving on to the next customer.

Character of the market

The characteristics of the market will also determine the choice available. Products often are introduced later into international markets than to the home domestic market, the company's image and awareness is normally lower, in many cases much lower, than in the domestic market and the market share attainable in the market is lower, at least initially. This makes it a much less profitable business proposition for distribution channel intermediaries. Furthermore, distribution channels are already being used by other companies who will have built up relationships with the intermediaries. This provides less space and opportunity for firms newly entering the market.

Developing countries are characterised by distribution systems consisting of a myriad of intermediaries and retail outlets. Such fragmentation results in cost inefficiencies as large volumes of product cannot be centralised and moved quickly from manufacturers to wholesalers to retailers.

Fragmented and circuitous channels also diminish possible competitive advantage by reducing the abilities of firms to get their products and services quickly and efficiently to masses of buyers. This is particularly the case for time-sensitive products. For example, overnight package couriers in some markets have failed in some cases to live up to delivery promises due to flight cancellations, poor road conditions and insufficient phone lines (Nakata and Sivakumar 1997).

Often in emerging markets, the problems of fragmented distribution are compounded by legal restrictions as to which channels of distribution can be used by foreign imported products.

The World Trade Organisation is working towards the opening up of participation in distribution systems by foreign firms in a number of countries. Recently, Indonesia has eased restrictions as is discussed in Illustration 11.2.

Capital required and costings

In assessing the financial implications of channel selection, a firm needs to assess the relative cost of each channel, the consequences on cash flow and the capital required.

The relative costs of each channel. It is generally considered that it may be cheaper to use agents than setting up a firms own sales force in international markets. However the firm has little control and may have little commitment from the agent. Also, if the company has long-term objectives in the market, then as sales develop the use of agents may be more expensive than employing the company's own sales force. A break-even analysis is necessary to evaluate the relative cost of each channel alternative over time.

Illustration 11.2: Jakarta eases distribution restrictions

In 1998, Indonesia cut trade tariffs and opened up its distribution and wholesale sector for foreign investors. Foreign companies will now be allowed to set up their own distribution and wholesale companies and will be allowed to retail as well by the year 2003.

The ban of foreign participation in distribution set up to defend traditional marketplaces and small shop owners, has kept out many producers of consumer goods and limited profits of existing projects.

Previously foreign companies were forced to rely on well-connected but often inefficient wholesale and retail agents, often little more than front companies to market their goods.

Hopefully, this will make it much easier for international marketers to develop more sophisticated distribution strategies in this emerging market.

Source: adapted from Thoener, S. (1997) *Financial Times*, 4 November

---

Consequences on cashflow. If a firm uses wholesalers or distributors then traditionally they take ownership of the goods and the risks. This has a positive impact on cash flow.

If the firm wishes to circumvent such channels and deal direct with the retailer or even the consumer, it means they have to be prepared to take on some of the traditional wholesaler services e.g. offering of credit, breaking bulk, small orders. This means the firm will have capital and resources tied up in managing the distribution chain rather than developing the market.

Capital required. Direct distribution systems need capital injected to establish them. Non-recurring capital costs, as well as the recurring running costs when evaluating expected return in the long term, have to be taken into account.

A company also needs to evaluate whether it can raise the finance locally or whether borrowing restrictions are placed on foreign companies. What grants are available and what the regulations on earnings capital repatriation will be.

The coverage needed

Required coverage will also be a determining factor. In some markets to get 100 per cent coverage of a market, the costs of using the company's own sales force may be too high and so indirect channels are more appropriate, especially in countries which are characterised by large rural populations. However, firms who rely on sparse retail outlets can maximise the opportunities that fragmented distribution channels afford. Avon has recruited and groomed armies of sales representatives to sell its cosmetics directly to millions in all reaches of Brazil, Mexico, Poland, China and Argentina. Altogether Avon is successfully operating in 26 emerging economies and targeting more (e.g. India, South Africa and Vietnam).

Control, continuity and communication

If a firm is building an international competitive advantage in providing a quality service throughout the world then channels that enable the firm to achieve rapid response in foreign markets will be important as will the development of a distribution system which gives them total control in the marketplace and effective direct communication to their customer.

It is the drive to achieve high levels of quality of service that, to some extent, has led to the breakdown of conventional barriers between manufacturers, agents, distributors and retailers, as firms strive to develop effective vertical marketing systems. To achieve this, some manufacturers have bought themselves into retailing and other parts of the supply chain. Whilst others, such as Benneton have pursued similar results by franchising.

Such firms will be selecting intermediaries which will enable them to be solution oriented service providers operating on high margins across a multitude of international markets.

The selection and contracting process

Having evaluated the criteria discussed above a firm must select intermediaries capable of helping the firm achieve its goals and objectives. The intermediaries chosen must provide the geographic coverage needed and the services required in the particular international market(s). It is often desirable to select intermediaries that are native to the country where they will be doing business as this will enhance their ability to build and maintain customer relationships.

The selection process for channel members will be based upon an assessment of their sales volume potential, geographic and customer coverage, financial strength (which will be checked through credit rating services and references), managerial capabilities and the size and quality of the sales force and any marketing communications services and the nature and reputation of the business. In some countries, religious or ethnic differences might make an agent suitable for part of the market coverage but unsuitable in another. This can result in more channel members being required to give an adequate market coverage.

Before final contractual arrangements are made, it is thought wise to make personal visits to the prospective channel member. The long-term commitment involved in distribution channels can become particularly difficult if the contract between the company and the channel member is not carefully drafted. It is normal to prescribe a time limit and a minimum sales level to be achieved in addition to the particular responsibilities for each party. If this is not carried out satisfactorily, the company may be stuck with a weak performer that either cannot be removed or is very costly to buy out from their contract.

Building relationships in foreign market channels

Management of sales activities and business relationships across international boundaries is a particularly complex and often overwhelming task. The combination of diverse languages, dissimilar cultural heritages and remote geographic locations can create strong barriers to building and maintaining effective buyer–seller relationships. Further, in international settings, communications are often complicated by a lack of trust – a critical dimension in any business relationship. Non-verbal cues, product origin biases, sales force nationality issues and differences in inter-cultural negotiation styles add even more complexity to the international business environment. Added to the traditional responsibilities of a sales manager, these factors make managing international relationships in distribution channels a unique and challenging task. Thus it is crucial for firms and their sales managers to both understand and be able to work within various international markets throughout the world (Lewin and Johnston 1997).

Motivating international marketing intermediaries

International marketing intermediaries can pick and choose the products they will promote to their customers. Therefore, they need to be motivated to emphasise the firm's products. But as difficult as it is for manufacturers to motivate their domestic distributors or dealers, it is even more difficult in the international arena. The environment, culture and customs affecting seller–intermediary relationships can be complicating factors for the uninitiated.

Motivation, whether in the context of domestic or international channels, is the process through which the manufacturer seeks to gain the support of the marketing intermediary in carrying out the manufacturer's marketing objectives. Three basic elements are involved in this process (Rosenbloom 1990):

1 finding out the needs and problems of marketing intermediaries
2 offering support that is consistent with their needs and problems
3 building continuing relationships.

First the needs and problems of international marketing intermediaries can be dramatically different from those at home. One of the most common differences is in the size of the intermediary. This is particularly true in some of the less-developed countries in Asia, Africa, Latin America and Eastern Europe. However, it also holds even for some highly developed countries such as Japan and Italy. Many of these dealers have little desire to grow larger. Thus, they may not aggressively promote a manufacturer's product.

Second, although the specific support programme provided by the manufacturer to its international intermediaries should be based on a careful analysis of their needs and problems, recent research in international marketing stresses four factors that are often crucial in many countries around the world (Rosenbloom 1990). These factors are:

- the adequacy of the profit margins available
- the guarantee of exclusive territories
- the adequacy and availability of advertising assistance
- the offer of needed financial assistance.

In light of the cost structures faced by many foreign distributors and dealers, the need to provide them with good margin potentials on the foreign products they handle is even more important. Doing so, however, may force manufacturers to change their ideas of what constitutes a 'fair' or 'reasonable' margin for foreign distributors.

Territorial protection or even the guarantee of exclusive territories sought by many distributors in the domestic market can be even more desirable in foreign markets. Overseas distributors, many of whom have quite limited financial resources, will not want to assume the risk of handling and promoting the manufacturer's product line if other distributors will be competing in the same territory for the same customers.

Advertising assistance for foreign distributors and dealers is another vital form of support. A foreign manufacturer, especially a large one, can have an advantage over indigenous firms in providing advertising support because of its often greater financial resources and experience in the use of advertising. For example, firms such as Johnson Wax (with extensive distribution in Europe) and 3M (in Asia) have used their considerable resources and advertising expertise to support distributors to very good advantage in those markets.

Financial assistance in countries where intermediaries are small and fragmented is essential. Levi-Strauss found in Russia they needed to give a six month credit period to persuade intermediaries to stock their products. Their usual credit period was 30 to 60 days. Such constraints do not mean that manufacturers selling through international intermediaries cannot build strong relationships with them, it is certainly possible to do so. However, the approach used may have to be quite different from that taken with domestic intermediaries. For example, for thousands of years agents and distributors in the Middle East have been influenced by bazaar trading. Marketing to them means to 'sit on the product' and wait for the customer to come to them. A common attitude amongst merchants is that they do not sell, but people buy. The 'carrot and stick' philosophy of motivating distributors in the US and Europe fails in the Middle East. Financial incentives may not motivate them to push the product aggressively if the process is complex and long. If they are making money today, they are not particularly motivated by making more (Stern and El-Ansary 1992).

It is important to keep in regular contact with intermediaries. A consistent flow of all relevant types of communications will stimulate interest and sales performance. The cultural interface between the company and the channel member is the essence of corporate rapport. Business people from low context cultures may be thought to be insensitive and disrespectful by agents in high context culture countries. The problem can be compounded if sales performance is discussed too personally. According to Usunier (1996) precise measurement of sales people's performance, for example of the agent or the distributors, may be considered as almost evil in some countries. 'In South East Asia the ethics of non-confrontation clearly clashes with an objective to review performance'. Various types of motivation need to be considered. In some cultures, intrinsic and group-related rewards work best. In the US, a country in which individualism and rationalism are the foundations of its society, individual and extrinsic rewards work best.

Controlling intermediaries in international markets

The process of control is difficult. Control problems are substantially reduced if channel members are selected carefully, have appropriately drafted contracts which have been mutually understood and agreed and are motivated in a culturally empathetic way.

Control attempts are often exercised through other companies and sometimes through several layers of distribution intermediaries. Control should be sought through the development of written plans with clearly expressed performance objectives. These performance objectives would include some of the following: sales turnover per year, number of accounts, market share, growth rate, introduction of new products, price charged and marketing communications support. Control should be exercised through a regular report programme and periodic personal meetings.

Evaluation of performance and control against agreed plans has to be interpreted against the changing environment. In some situations, economic recession or fierce competition activity prevent the possibility of objectives being met. However, if poor performance is established, the contract between the company and the channel member will have to be reconsidered and, perhaps, terminated. In an age in which relationship marketing is becoming more important in the Western world, the long-term building of suitable distribution relationships provides something of the Eastern flavour of obligation and working together.

Channel updating

In managing distribution channels, firms need to ensure that as they increase their involvement in the market, they are able to adapt and update their channel strategy accordingly. Thus, the management monitoring and control mechanisms a firm puts in place should give them the ability to develop their presence in the marketplace. In China, Kodak (see Illustration 11.3) ensured this capability was in place in their early negotiations.

Developing a company-owned international salesforce

Firms with expansion plans and an interest in becoming more involved in global markets will eventually take control of implementing their own marketing strategies and establish and manage their own international salesforce. Generally, the firms begin to gradually move from indirect exporting to direct exporting via marketing intermediaries to a company-owned sales force (Kotler 1996). The company can do this in several ways, including: travelling export sales reps, domestic-based export department or division and foreign-based sales branch or subsidiary.

The advantages of using a company-owned sales force include:

- it provides far greater control over the sales and marketing effort since the sales force is now directly employed by the company
- it facilitates formation of closer manufacturer–customer relationships
- once established, the company-owned sales force can be helpful in identifying and exploiting new international marketing opportunities.

Illustration 11.3: Kodak's distribution strategy in China

In 1998 Kodak invested $1.1 billion to take over and modernise three loss making Chinese film and photographic product companies and will pay $380 million for the assets. The deal not only trounces Fuji, it sets a new pattern in big foreign involvement in China.

Kodak's executive vice-president reckons the main assets of value he has bought are people, warehouses, a distribution system and land.

Beyond the sheer size of the market, Kodak is keen on China because it is the one place in the world where it is clearly trouncing Fuji. By manufacturing and distributing locally, Kodak hopes to turn the battle into a rout. As part of the deal, no other foreign film company will be allowed to manufacture in China for four years.

Three years ago China was solid Fuji territory. The Japanese film maker had been an early and energetic entrant to the market. Its green banners could be seen above photo shops everywhere. But Kodak attacked with force.

Offering help including 'marketing assistance' of $2000 or more to corner shops in exchange for becoming a Kodak Express and evicting competing film brands, Kodak expanded its Chinese sales by 30 per cent a year. They now amount to 7 per cent of the firm's global business.

Last year, Kodak says it overtook Fuji to become the market leader in China for film and film products. (Fuji claims it still has a lead of a few percentage points for film itself). Kodak now has 3700 stores to Fuji's 2000. Between them the two companies have more than 90 per cent of the $800 million market, the world's third largest.

Source: adapted from *The Economist* (1998) 'Kodak in China', 28 March

---

The disadvantages of developing a company-owned sales force include:

- a relatively larger resource commitment
- somewhat higher exit costs should the firm decide to no longer serve a particular market
- increased exposure to unexpected changes in the political/social environment of the host country.

One common strategy is to begin export operations by establishing a domestic-based export department and/or using home-based travelling salespeople. Then, as sales reach a certain volume in the new market, the decision is made to set up a foreign-based sales branch or subsidiary in the country.

The new unit may be strictly a marketing/sales arm or may also involve a production or warehouse facility. In either event, the firm must make a commitment of resources to develop its own direct sales force to sell the firm's offerings and build relationships with the firm's customers in that market.

It may well be that a firm uses its own sales force for key accounts and agents and distributors for small accounts. Equally, its own sales force may work in conjunction with international intermediaries. Building links directly with customers but always with and through the intermediaries. This has the advantage of enabling the firm to build relationships with the customer and the intermediaries whilst not having to make the capital investment required to run a wholly owned subsidiary.

Trends in retailing in international markets

Retailing structures differ across countries, reflecting their different histories, geography and politics. Retailing varies across the different levels of economic development and is influenced by cultural variations. The cultural importance attached to food in France provides the opportunity for small specialist food retailers to survive and prosper. In other developed countries, for example the US, the trend is towards very large superstores which incorporate a wide range of speciality foods. The French approach relies on small-scale production by the retail proprietor. The US approach encourages mass production, branding and sophisticated distribution systems to handle inventory and freshness issues.

In this section, our discussion will be concerned with three important issues for international marketers. First, the differences in the patterns of retailing around the world with particular reference to emerging markets and developing countries. Second, the internationalisation of retailers and its impact on distribution channel structures and, third, the emergence of new forms of retailing which are particularly relevant to firms competing on international markets.

The differing patterns of retailing around the world

The concentration of the retailing industry varies significantly between markets. Low concentration ratios of retailer ownership gives more power to the manufacturer. A 'no' decision from any one retailer does not make a big impact on total sales. Whilst the low concentration ratios to be found in Japan and Italy and in many lesser developed countries increase the relative power of the manufacturer, there are problems. First, low concentration ratios in retailers might be counterbalanced by powerful wholesalers. Second, the costs of the sales force in calling on a multiplicity of very small retailers and the logistics of delivering products to them can reduce the manufacturer's profitability. If economies are sought by using wholesalers, the power balance might tilt away from the manufacturer to the wholesaler.

The main differences between traditional retailing structures found in lesser developed countries and the advanced retailing structures in more developed economies are illustrated in Table 11.1.

Retailing in developing countries is characterised by low levels of capital investment. The large size, purpose-built retail outlet, full of specialist display shelving and electronic point of sale equipment is rarely found in LDCs. The more likely picture is of a very small space with goods sold by the counter service method and technology limited to a cash register or a pocket calculator.

Retail stores are often managed by the owner/proprietor and staffed by the extended family. The lack of capital input is partially offset by large quantities of low-cost labour. The management style is usually based on limiting risks. The retailer will seek to stock goods with a proven demand pattern. In addition, the retailer will try to obtain interest-free credit from the interface channel partners: the wholesaler and the manufacturer.

Distribution channels in developing countries depend on manufacturers and wholesalers for their sales promotion ideas and materials. In developed countries retailers often take the initiative regarding sales promotions and will develop their own sales promotions. The opportunities for the manufacturer to influence the retailer in advanced countries are becoming fewer and fewer.

Small-scale retailing limits the opportunities to follow own-label strategies. The minimum economies of scale cannot be reached by the small urban and rural retailer in developing countries. The balance of power lies with the manufacturer to innovate and adapt products.

The proliferation of very many small–scale retailers means that the retail market is widely dispersed. The levels of concentration of ownership are much lower than are found in mature economies with relatively structured levels of retailing.

Illustration 11.4 compares the retailing patterns of three very culturally and geographically dispersed countries, Greece, India and New Zealand but all of whom exhibit a similar traditional retailing structure.

Table 11.1 Retailers – typical differences between developing and developed countries

Retailing issues	Traditional retailers in developing countries	Advanced retailing structures in mature economies
Concentration of retail power	Low	Often high
Site selection and retail location	Limited to the immediate locality	Very important, often sophisticated techniques to pin-point the most valuable sites
Size of outlet	Limited	Large and tending to get larger
Retailer initiation of product assortment	Limited to the buy/no buy decision	Wide range of stock possible. Use of own-label and store-specific sales promotions
Retail concepts, images and corporate identity	Rarely used	Very important – examples: Toys 'R' Us, Laura Ashley, Boots, Benneton
Retailer-initiated sales promotion	Rarely used. Reliance on manufacturer and wholesaler-developed sales promotion and point of sale material	Very important
Use of retail technology	Limited	Vital e.g. EDI, EPOS
Service	Mainly counter-service	Efficient customer response systems

These differences give rise to principally four stages of retailing around the world: traditional, intermediary, structured and advanced (McGoldrick and Davies 1995).

Traditional retailing
'Traditional retailers' are typically found in Southern Europe, Latin America and Japan. The concentration of operators is weak, segmentation is non-existent and the level of integration of new technology is very low. These are often small-scale family retailing businesses employing few people and with a low turnover.

Illustration 11.4: Comparative retailing traditions

In India, most retail stores are family owned and are much smaller in size. With the exception of a few (small) super bazaars, consumers are not allowed to walk freely inside the stores, examine and compare labels of different brands before making the selection. Instead, consumers approach shops with a predetermined list of items to purchase which are then pulled out of the bins by the salesperson. There are some regional shopping chains that carry tailored clothes or uncut fabric in different designs and fashions. However, Indian consumers, on average, do not have as much disposable income as they do in the Western countries. A relatively small percentage of people in India carry credit cards and most purchases are made with cash, even though purchases of some durables can be made by paying for them in monthly installments. As a result, shopping for clothes is generally done during the Indian festival and wedding seasons but not throughout the year.

Moreover, in clothing stores the shopper specifies the range of price he/she is interested in spending and the salesperson brings the selection of clothing to the customer. Browsing for merchandise cannot be done so easily as a result.

Greece reflects a society in transition where the traditional way of life coexists with modernisation. The overall economic and social situation in Greece is reflected in the retail environment. The majority of stores are family owned and small in size and shopping for pleasure is less popular. Most purchases are made in cash although credit cards are becoming more popular.

In New Zealand, stores close at 5.30 pm except for one night each week when they are open until 9.00 pm. Stores are also closed on Sundays and many are closed on Saturday afternoons. With a population of only 3.3 million, competition among retailers is not as intense. Hence consumers have less choice. Brand consciousness is at an early state of development compared with the USA.

Source: adapted from Lysonski, Durrasula and Zotas (1996) *European Journal of Marketing*, 30 (12)

Intermediary retailing

Retailing in Italy, Spain and Eastern Europe is in the process of transformation, being both modern and traditional and so examples of intermediary retailing. Most businesses are independent with a turnover lower than the European average. However, there is a marked tendency towards concentration, particularly in the food sector, where the number of food retailing outlets per 1000 people is dropping. The importance of wholesalers and voluntary chains is still very strong, particularly in Italy (192 000 wholesale businesses).

In the major cities of China there have been huge developments in the retail structure of the country taking retailing in the major cities to intermediary status.

One of the most aggressive foreign investors has been Yaohan, a Japanese retailer which plans to open more than 1000 supermarkets and stores there by 2005. To show its zeal, Yaohan even moved its group headquarters to Shanghai where it now operates one of the world's largest department stores. But it has found it harder to set up shop in China than it expected. Faced with mounting debts, it has put further expansion on hold. The problem, in a nutshell, is that most of the Chinese trooping through its smart new stores are only window shopping!

Countries with intermediary retailing structures have been attractive locations for retailers expanding internationally. Spain and Central European countries have been attractive markets for retail expansion. The level of economic development, the intermediary structure of retailing has meant that these countries are not host to large domestic retailers making entry into the market relatively easy.

Over the course of the last five years, the entry of foreign operators into areas like Latin America has altered the retailing landscape. There are now hypermarkets, variety stores and non-food specialists which have stimulated competition and greatly modernised retailing as can be seen in Illustration 11.5.

Structured retailing

Retailing in the north of Europe tends to be fairly structured reflecting the level of economic development. Denmark, Luxembourg, the Netherlands and France have enterprises larger in size, have a higher level of concentration and a greater level of productivity per employee than Southern European retailers.

In these markets, retail competition is fairly well developed and there is a mature relationship between suppliers and retailers.

Retailers also have introduced fairly sophisticated technologies facilitating more elaborate competitive strategies. They are also, themselves, finding growth through opportunities overseas and new retailing formats.

Illustration 11.5: Retailing in South America

Frustrated by saturated markets and planning controls at home, some of the world's leading retailers have been pouring money into the Latin American region.

In most Latin American countries retailing has always been much less protected than manufacturing. France's Carrefour, a hypermarket operator, set up in Brazil and Argentina in the 1970s, it now has $7 billion of sales in the region. The more recent entrants include Auchan, another French hypermarket firm and Wal-Mart, America's and the world's largest retailer which recently announced that it was paying $1.2 billion for a controlling stake in Cifra, its partner in Mexico, where the two operate 145 stores. Since 1995, Wal-Mart has opened five stores in Brazil and six in Argentina. It plans more in both countries.

The chief advantage of the invaders is size. Latin America's family-owned corner shops and small supermarkets have found it hard to match the low unit-costs of the foreign giants and the bargaining power they wield over suppliers. Carrefour's Brazilian operation extracts net-profit margins of close to 4 per cent compared with only around 1 per cent in France.

Self-service retail floorspace in Latin America is growing by 12 per cent a year with almost half of that coming from foreign operators.

Inevitably, domestic firms have found it rough going but now some Latin American chains are beginning to fight back, making use of their local knowledge.

A sharp drop in the cost of retailing technology has also helped the native chains. They can now afford to install the stock-control and logistics computers that have contributed so much to the giants' efficiency.

Two retailers that are successfully defending their turf are Brazil's Companhia Brasileira de Distribuicao, better known as Pao de Azucar, the name under which its supermarkets trade and Argentian's Disco. Like so many other Latin American businesses, both are family firms.

Pao de Azucar is Brazil's second largest retailer with 155 supermarkets, 10 hypermarkets and 11 discount food stores, plus a chain of electrical shops. Pao de Acuzar is spending around half of its annual investment budget of almost $250 million on new stores but the rest is aimed at increasing the productivity of existing shops. That has meant investing in information technology and in doubling the size of its central warehouse in São Paulo.

Disco is thriving by not trying to imitate the hypermarkets. Its 59 small neighbourhood supermarkets in the richer parts of Buenos Aires and Argentina's provincial cities emphasise quality and freshness, half the sales are of perishables, and services such as home delivery, telephone ordering and Argentina's first customer-loyalty card which has attracted 750 members in a year are core components of their fight back strategy.

Source: adapted from *The Economist* (1997) 'Retailing in South America', 10 July

Advanced retailing

The US, Germany and the UK are all examples of countries in which retailing is the most advanced in terms of concentration, segmentation, capitalisation and integration. In Germany and the UK there are about 60 retailing businesses per 10 000 inhabitants, 98 being the European average. Retailer strategies in these advanced countries are becoming much more marketing focused and generally incorporate five important dimensions.

Interactive customer marketing. Targeting of customers as individuals, developing strategies to improve retention and increase sales per shop visit.

Mass customisation. Retailers are looking for improved margins through higher volumes, reduced costs and achieving low levels of returns.

Data mining. Retailers are using technology and electronic point of sale (EPOS) information to improve knowledge of customers, ensure the ability to make targeted offers which are timely and clearly differentiated. Data mining is beginning to be used by retailers in emerging and developing markets where there has been little reliable data on which to previously base decisions.

Category management. Retailers are aiming to achieve improved levels of customer satisfaction through reducing costs, reducing mark downs and optimising product assortment.

Effective consumer response. Retailers are establishing permanent links with manufacturers, establishing electronic data interchange (EDI) systems for efficient inventory replenishment and ensuring a continuous just in time delivery of supplies.

In these markets the balance of power in the supply chain, for the present at least, seems to lay firmly with these large retailers who are increasingly dictating the trends in their home markets and as these reach maturity are seeking growth opportunities by expanding internationally.

The internationalisation of retailing

Up to the 1970s few retailers had any involvement in markets outside their own domestic terrain. Now many retailers are beginning to accelerate their moves into global or regional development. The 1980s were characterised by 'border hopping'.

The French hypermarket groups Auchan, Carrefour and Promodes, the German discount food retailers Aldi, Lidl and Swartz have moved into other European countries. The US retailer Wal-Mart and specialists Toys 'R' Us, Home Depot and Staples have expanded throughout the world. Hong Kong retailers A S Watson and Dairy Farm entered neighbouring countries with supermarkets and pharmaceutical chains and Japanese department stores Takashimaya and Isetan have established outlets in Singapore.

More recently this trend has accelerated with German retailers Metro, Rewe and Tengelmann expanding into the Czech Republic, Hungary and Poland often using joint ventures with former socialist cooperatives. Three Western European retailers, Tengelmann (Germany), Ahold (Netherlands) and Delhaizae Le Lion (Belgium), now generate more sales and profit from their foreign activities which include the US, Central Europe and Asia. Tesco have also recently announced plans to move into Asia.

Towards the end of the 1980s and the start of the 1990s retailers such as Benneton, Body Shop and Marks and Spencer started franchising. Their internationalisation is being built around their brands clearly with the intention of eventually developing world brands. Marks and Spencer is using four methods of market entry: acquisitions, e.g. Brook Brothers in the US, joint ventures with Cortofiel in Spain, organic growth in France and franchising in the Far East.

The expansion of international activity of retailers around the world has given rise to four different types of international retailers developing: the hypermarket, the power retailers, the niche retailer and the designer brand retailer. Examples of these are given in Table 11.2.

Besides the growing sophistication of the industry, and the opening up of new markets around the world, Horovitz and Kumar (1998) ascribe the increase in retailer internationalisation to a number of 'pull' and 'push' factors:

The 'push' factors are:

- saturation of the home market or over-competition
- economic recession or limited growth in spending
- a declining or aging population
- strict planning policies on store development
- high operating costs – labour, rents, taxation
- shareholder pressure to maintain profit growth
- the 'me too' syndrome in retailing.

The 'pull' factors are:

- the underdevelopment of some markets or weak competition
- strong economic growth or rising standards of living
- high population growth or a high concentration of young adults
- a relaxed regulatory framework
- favourable operating costs – labour, rents, taxation

Table 11.2 Global retailer categories

Category	Companies	Countries entered
Hypermarkets	Carrefour	15
	Promodes	11
	Auchan	8
	Metro	17
	Ahold	12
Power retailers	Ikea	28
	Toys 'R' Us	27
	Wal-Mart	8
Niche retailers	Body Shop	46
	Tie Rack	30
	HMV	9
Designer brand companies	Donna Karan	(large flagship stores in
	Ralf Lauren	capital cities)

Source: Davies and Finney (1998)

- the geographical spread of trading risks
- the opportunity to innovate under new market conditions.

Marketing implications for development of international distribution strategies

The internationalisation of retailing has meant a new era of distribution is developing. This new competitive landscape in distribution has a number of implications for the development of the distribution strategies of international firms. The most important of these are:

- power shifts in supply chains towards retailers
- intense concentrated competition with significant buyer power across country markets
- rapidly advancing technology facilitating global sourcing and global electronic transactions
- unrelenting performance measures being demanded of suppliers by international retailers
- smart demanding consumers expecting high levels of customer service.

Thus power in many international markets is moving from the supplier down the supply chain to the consumer. This means effective management is critical to suppliers competing in international markets. It again highlights the importance of ensuring the distribution strategy across international markets is driven by an understanding of the target market segments both within each foreign country market and across national market boundaries.

This intensive growth in the size and power of retailers in countries with advanced retailing structures and retailers internationalising means there is now tremendous pressure on suppliers to improve the quality of service to them. Retailers are demanding:

- stream-lined and flexible supply chains
- suppliers who can guarantee quality and reliability across global markets
- the ability to supply high volumes and often intensive relationships with intermediaries in the supply chain
- suppliers who can meet the global sourcing requirements of large-scale retailers who wish to buy centrally across the globe.

It could mean, therefore, that the firms who are successful are the firms who develop the capability to compete effectively in the supply chain activities compared to their international competitors. It is for this reason that the distribution strategy of the international company has taken on such an important dimension in recent times.

International electronic forms of retailing

Multi-media technology has provided a number of opportunities for interactive shopping which offer particular opportunities in international markets. Tele-shopping and the Internet offer suppliers the retailing opportunities for direct contact with consumers throughout the globe without the problems and expense of having to establish infrastructures in foreign country markets.

For example, Amazon.com is a bookshop which sells purely over the Internet. It carries no books as they are directly shipped from the publishers' or distributors' warehouses and so Amazon have few inventory or real estate costs. They offer 2.5 million titles including every English language book in print whereas even the largest bookstore would only stock 170 000.

The diffusion of the Internet and with it electronic commerce, increasingly is challenging the traditional channels of distribution as the World Wide Web (WWW) brings together buyers and sellers through the creation of an on-line marketplace.

Klein and Quelch (1997) identify three types of markets developing on the Internet which are impacting on the way the traditional channels of distribution carry out business transactions:

Auctions. On-line marketplaces where negotiations of price between independent buyers and sellers is implemented through a standard auction open to all participants (e.g. On Sale).

Single buyer markets. Where a large buyer establishes an on-line market for its own suppliers (e.g. GE Trade Web).

Pure exchanges. Where individual buyers and sellers are matched according to product offers and needs.

The most promising products are often those where existing intermediaries do not perform many of the traditional 'wholesaler' functions for a broad market owing to the high cost of servicing small diverse and geographically or functionally dispersed players (Stern and El-Ansary 1992). Klein and Quelch (1997) identify several market characteristics which favour the development of electronic channels of distribution:

- *Inefficiencies in traditional distribution channels.* Buyers cannot find all possible sellers or vice versa.

- *Market fragmentation.* Markets with many geographically dispersed buyers and sellers across the globe.

- *Minimum scale barriers.* In traditional markets, smaller manufacturers may be boxed out of regular channels by larger players who reap economies of scale and exploit distribution relationships.

- *Commodity-type products.* Products with well-known technical specifications, or manufacturer brands that can easily be price-compared and those products that do not require substantial after-sales service.

- *Short life-cycle products.* Product-markets with short life cycles create large quantities of obsolete and discontinued items. Customers may experience difficulty finding spare parts or compatible accessories for earlier generations of product.

- *Trade association involvement.* Industries where trade associations play an active role in organising members, e.g. TRADEex's partnership with the Australian Chamber of Manufacturers.

The management of the physical distribution of goods

Physical distribution management (PDM) is concerned with the planning, implementing and control of physical flows of materials and final goods from points of origin to points of use to meet customer needs at a profit (Kotler 1997).

In international physical distribution of goods the total distribution costs will be higher than domestic distribution. The extra activities, increased time taken and the need to adapt to special country requirements will all increase costs. The extra costs centre around three areas:

Increased distance; this means in terms of costs increased transport time, inventory, cash flow and insurance.

New variables to consider; new modes of transport (air, sea, rail, road), new types of documentation, packaging for long transit times.

Greater market complexity; language differences requires the translation of documents, the extra costs of bureaucracy and longer lines of communication.

It is important for the firm to take full account of all these extra costs when evaluating alternative distribution strategies. In taking the total distribution cost approach firms will include the costs of transport, warehousing, inventory, order-processing, documentation, packaging and the total cost of lost sales if delays occur. Companies find that changes to one element of distribution influence the performance and the costs of other elements.

The logistics approach to physical distribution

Many writers on physical distribution use logistics and physical distribution as terms meaning the same thing. Kotler makes the distinction between physical distribution as a more traditional activity and logistics as being more market-oriented. In this way, physical distribution thinking starts with the finished product at the end of the production line and then attempts to find low–cost solutions to get the product to the customer. Logistics thinking, on the other hand, considers the customer and then works back to the factory. In this section we will use the market-oriented view. We will use the term logistics to mean an integrated view of physical distribution management in which customer demand influences are at least as important as cost-cutting forces. More and more companies are integrating their physical distribution strategies and linking their operations in different countries with more common processes and so rationalising their manufacturing and distribution infrastructure to make more effective use of business resources and so taking a logistical view of their distribution operations.

In Europe 75 per cent of businesses operating across European markets have a pan-European logistics or distribution strategy in place. The logistics function is having an increasing influence in many parts of the business, especially in inventory planning, information technology, purchasing and manufacturing.

There are a number of factors influencing this change:

- Customers demanding improved levels of customer service.

- Electronic Data Interchange (EDI) becoming the all pervading technology for firms to build links with customers, suppliers and distribution providers.

- Companies restructuring their physical distribution operations in response to the formation of regional trading blocs.

In the following sections, we will briefly examine the developments in each of the above areas.

Customer service

The main elements of customer service will revolve around:

- order to delivery time
- consistency and reliability of delivery
- inventory availability
- order, size constraints
- ordering convenience
- delivery time and flexibility
- invoicing procedures, documentation and accuracy
- claims procedure
- condition of goods
- salesperson's visits
- order status information
- after-sales support.

In developing customer service levels it is essential to use the elements of service that the customer regards as important. Delivery reliability might be more important than a quick order to delivery time that is unreliable in meeting delivery schedules. Understanding the way in which the international customer perceives service is important. There will be considerable differences. Customers who are distant might be more concerned about the guarantees of reliable rapid availability than customers much closer to the production source. The ability and corporate capability to meet widely differing customer requirements in different countries needs to be managed.

In all countries, customers are becoming increasingly demanding. Partnership arrangements are becoming significant in many sectors as supply chains become more integrated. These developments are usually customer-led demands for improved service.

Consumers are demanding ever quicker delivery and ever more added value from their products that increasingly require 'just-in-time' distribution. The product cycle from manufacture to payment is becoming shorter, a trend that is likely to accelerate.

Information technology

Developments in information technology are critical. It is forecast that more than three in four companies actively involved in international markets will have introduced multi-national computer systems for logistics processes and international electronic data interchange (EDI) by the year 2000.

The 'old silk road' has been replaced by the 'new silc road' with optical fibre systems making direct links between Europe, East Asia and Australia. Much of the new SDH-based silc road (SDH or syndchronoms digital hierarchy which is an enabling technology that increases the speed and volume of traffic using optical fibre networks) has been laid. The network stretches 2500 miles across the former Soviet Union into China through countries such as Uzbekistan, re-generating their economies.

Optic fibre cables are being routed through Japan, South East Asia and through to Australia. Thus there are significant developments in electronic links between companies and distributors and producers around the world.

In regional trading blocs, such as the European Union and NAFTA, we are seeing the developments of common systems for customer order processing, demand forecasting and inventory planning.

Foreign companies are increasingly using the internet to track the progress of products through the distribution system. DHL have websites which allow customers to track the progress of their packages and is attracting 400 000 hits a day. The other major area of IT involvement is in stock control and buying. Despite having 600 stores in 14 countries and using 12 different own labels, C&A is still able to deliver nine times a day to its stores due to its efficient centralised buying operation for menswear and childrenswear in Brussels, womenswear in Dusseldorf.

The restructuring of physical distribution operations

In mature trading regions such as the US and Europe, a large number of firms have restructured their distribution networks in response to changes in the trading structures in the region. Cross-border deliveries have increased and the number of factories and warehouses have decreased. The number of distribution centres serving more than one country have increased whereas there has been a decrease in the number of warehouses dedicated to within country movements.

Lucent Technology, dispatches all its products from its factory in Spain to a test and assembly centre in Singapore before final delivery. It might go back to a customer sitting 10 kilometres away from the factory in Spain but it will still go to Singapore. The company gives a 48 hour delivery guarantee to customers anywhere in the world, posing demanding logistical challenges.

The physical movement of goods is a high-cost activity. Companies often incur 10 to 35 per cent of their expenditure on physical distribution. Because distribution is such a high-cost activity, it is now receiving close attention from general management and from marketing management.

The logistics approach is to analyse customer requirements and to review what competitors are providing. Customers are interested in a number of things: deliveries to meet agreed time schedules, zero defect delivery, supplier willingness to meet emergency needs, supplier willingness to replace damaged goods quickly and supplier willingness to engage in just in time (JIT) delivery and inventory holding.

If a company is to achieve a logistically effective system of distribution it will become involved in a highly complex and sophisticated system and would, therefore, need to:

- clearly define areas of responsibility across foreign country markets
- have a highly developed planning system
- have an up to date and comprehensive information support system
- develop expertise in distribution management
- have a centralised planning body to coordinate activities and exercise overall control.

Thus, a logistical system helps the company not only pay attention to inventory levels but think through market relationships to minimise costs of stock out and maximise distribution efficiency across a large number of markets.

In developing an efficient logistical system of physical distribution across international markets there are a number of important considerations:

- what modes of transportation should be used
- how can the firm make effective use of export processing zones
- what documentation is required
- how can intermediaries such as freight forwarders enhance our service
- what are the packaging requirements for transit and the market
- how should the export sales contract be organised.

In the following sections, we will briefly discuss some of the important issues in each of these areas.

Transportation

The physical handling and movement of goods over long distances will practically always have to be performed by third parties.

Transportation is the most visible part of the physical distribution strategy. The main options are:

- **Ocean transport**: capacity for large loads of differentiated products, raw materials, semi-finished goods, finished goods. Handling of goods in bulk, in packaged or unitised form, pallets, containers.

- **Inland waterway transport**: heavy and bulk products. Growing container transport. Restrictions because of need for suitable loading/unloading terminals.

- **Air transport**: urgent shipments, perishables, low-density light/heavy value, relatively small shipments.

- **Road transport**: most flexible door-to-door transport for all kinds of products but mostly finished goods. Container transport.

- **Rail transport**: long distance heavy and bulk products. Container transport.

Ocean and inland waterways
Sea and inland waterways provide a very low-cost way to transport bulky, low value or non-perishable products such as coal and oil. Water transport is slow and is subject to difficulties caused by the weather, for example, some ports are

iced over for part of the winter. Water transport usually needs to be used with other modes of transport to achieve door-to-door delivery.

One of the policies used to encourage growth in South Korea, a newly industrialised country, has been the stimulation of its shipping and shipbuilding industry.

Ocean shipping can be *open market*, i.e. *free ocean* where there are very few restrictions or it can be organised in *conferences* which are essentially cartels that regulate rates and capacities available on routes.

As in other areas of distribution, the containerisation of ports and the impact of information technology has meant sea transport has become a capital intensive industry where there is high pressure to achieve full capacity utilisation.

The cost of ocean freight, as a result, have declined over the past decade and so it is still the most cost effective method of transporting goods to distant markets.

The average cost for a 6 metre dry cargo container to be shipped from the UK to Shanghai in China will be between £750–£950 and the approximate transit time would be 30–35 days.

However, a number of hidden costs can arise in overseas shipping:

- overseas warehousing costs due to having to send large inventories in container loads
- inventory losses from handling spoilage, theft, obsolescence and exchange rate charges in manual time
- cost of time in transit
- lost sales from late arrival.

Inland waterways are very important in countries with poor infrastructures. In Vietnam the most popular mode of transportation is by water. A dense network of waterways exists although even this system will suffer the vagaries of both flood and drought conditions.

Air

Air freight is considerably more expensive per tonne/kilometre than the other modes of transport. Air freight is particularly appropriate for the movement of high-value low-bulk and perishable items. For example, diamonds, computer software, specialist component parts and cut flowers use air freight. Air freight is extending its market through promoting its advantages. The higher freight charges can often be off-set. Packing costs and insurance rates are significantly less by air. Storage en route, overseas warehousing, inventory losses may all be less by air as will the actual cost of the time in transit. In addition, the development of larger and more flexible aeroplanes for air freight has helped reduce costs.

Road

Very flexible in route and time. Schedules can deliver direct to customers' premises. Very efficient for short hauls of high-value goods. Restrictions at border controls can be time-consuming however and long distances and the need for sea crossings reduce the attractiveness of freight transport by road. In some parts of the world, particularly in LDCs, road surfaces are poor and the distribution infrastructure poor. In Vietnam, an attractive emerging market for many international firms, the majority of the road network is beaten track which, in periods of dense rain (six months of the year), make transporting anything by road very difficult.

Rail

Rail services provide a very good method of transporting bulky goods over long land distances. The increasing use of containers provides a flexible means to use rail and road modes with minimal load transfer times and costs.

In Europe, we are seeing the development of the use of 'Bloc Trains' as a highly efficient means of rail transport. In the US they use 'Double Bloc' trains to transport goods across the vast plains. In a number of markets, rail transport is fraught with difficulties. In China, a shipment from Shanghai to Guangzhou, a distance of approximately 2000 kilometres can take 25 days. Across the interior it is even slower. Shanghai to Xian 1500 kilometres can take 45 days. Much of the rail capacity is antiquated and many of the rail lines are old, leading to frequent derailments.

The final decision on transport

The decision concerning which transport mode to use is discussed by Branch (1990). He identifies four factors as decisive in choosing transport: the terms of the export contract, the commodity specification, freight and overall transit time.

In the terms of the export contract, the customer can specify the mode(s) of transport and can insist on the country's national shipping line or airline being used. In considering different modes of transport, the specification of the commodity will have a strong influence on modal choice. For example, transport of fresh food will have requirements to prevent spoilage and contamination. The cost of transport is of major importance. It creates extra costs above the normal domestic cost. It is important, therefore, that transport options are researched thoroughly so that the best value arrangements can be made for both the buyer and the supplier.

Export processing zones

The principle of export processing zones (EPZs) started with the opening of the world's first EPZ at Shannon in the Republic of Ireland. Since then there has been a proliferation in the establishment of EPZs worldwide, with notable examples being Jebel Ali, at Dubai in the UAE and Subic Bay in the Philippines. The principle of the EPZ has been embraced as a worldwide instrument for national economic development by the United Nations.

The concept of the EPZ concerns the duty-free and tax-free manufacture or processing of products for export purposes within a customs-controlled ('off-shore') environment. Components may be imported into the zone duty-free and tax-free to be processed or manufactured into the finished product or stored for onward distribution and are then re-exported without any liability of import duties or other taxes. The purpose of the EPZ is to ensure that at least 70 per cent of the zone-produced articles are re-exported. Although the remaining percentage of items produced within the zone may be imported into domestic territory upon payment of the appropriate import duty and tax for the finished article.

Companies trading from within the export processing zone can be wholly owned by foreign-based enterprises and, in most cases, all profits may be repatriated to the home country. Foreign direct investment by overseas-based companies is encouraged in zone operations, since normal national rules regarding profits or ownership do not apply. It is also possible for locally based companies to engage in zone operations as long as they are involved in import and export operations.

It is also likely that the workforce used will cost the zone company less than for home-based operations, since the majority of the EPZs are located in developing countries, especially East and South East Asia and Central America.

The advantages for companies in taking advantage of EPZs are:

- All goods entering the EPZ are exempted from customs duties and import permits.

- Firms can use foreign currency to settle transactions.

- EPZs can be used for assembly of products and so help reduce transportation costs.

- EPZs give a company much more flexibility and helps avoid unwanted bureaucracy of customs and excise.

China in the 1990s has developed a number of export processing zones in the coastal regions and in the interior of China special economic zones (SEZs) to help develop export sea trade. Examples of EPZs in China are Hong Kong, Shenzen, Shanghai and Tianjin.

Documentation

A number of different documents are required in cross-border marketing. These include invoices, consignment notes and customs documents. SITRO, the Simpler Trade Procedures Board, has been involved in developing simpler documentation and export procedures with the aim of encouraging international trade. Electronic data interchange (EDI) is expanding and now providing a fast integrated system which is reducing documentation preparation time and errors.

The process of documentation has more importance than its rather mechanistic and bureaucratic nature would suggest. Errors made in documents can result in laws being broken, customs regulations being violated or, in financial institutions, refusing to honour demands for payment. Country variations are considerable with regard to export documentation procedures. Different documents are required in different formats. Figure 11.4 shows a typical export order process.

Documentation problems have five main causes: complexity, culture, change, cost and error. Complexity arises from the number of different parties requiring precise documents delivered at the correct time. In addition to the customer, banks, chambers of commerce, consulates, international carriers, domestic carriers, customs, port/terminal/customs clearance areas, insurance companies and the exporting company or freight forwarding company are being used by the exporter.

Different countries require different numbers of copies of documents, sometimes in their own language and, sometimes open to official scrutiny that is strongly influenced by the culture of that country. Document clearance can, therefore, be slow and subject to bureaucratic delays.

Errors in documentation can have serious consequences. The definition of an 'error' is open to interpretation. Errors can result in goods being held in customs or in a port. Clearance delays cause failure to meet customer service objectives. In extreme cases, errors result in goods being confiscated or not being paid for.

The development of regional trading blocs is reducing some the complexity of documentation. Previous to the single European market, a firm transporting

Figure 11.4 The export order and physical distribution

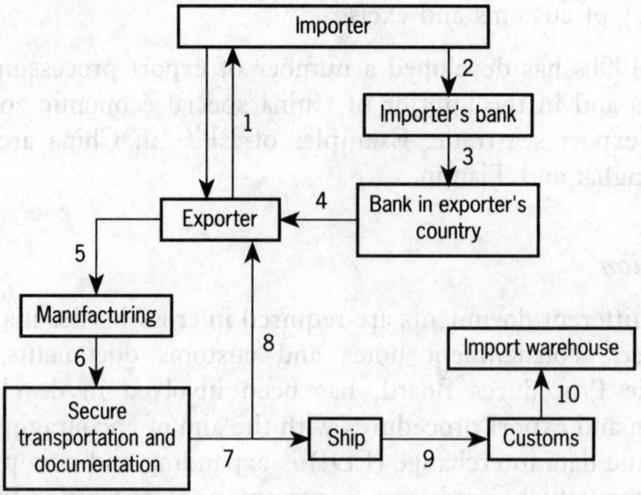

Note: 1 Importer makes enquiry to potential supplier; Exporter sends catalogues and price list; Importer requests samples; Importer requests pro-forma invoice (price quote); Exporter sends pro-forma invoice; Importer sends purchase order; Exporter receives purchase order. 2 Importer arranges financing through his bank. 3 Importer's bank sends letter of credit (most frequently used form of payment). 4 Exporter's bank notifies exporter that letter of credit is received. 5 Exporter produces or acquires goods.
6 Exporter arranges transportation and documentation (obtained by exporter or through freight forwarding company). Space reserved on ship or aircraft. Documents acquired or produced, as required: Exporter's licence; Shipper's export declaration; Commercial invoice; Bills of lading; Marine insurance certificate; Consular invoice; Certificate of origin; Inspection certificates; Dock receipts. 7 Exporter ships goods to importer.
8 Exporter presents documents to bank for payment. 9 Importer has goods cleared through customs and delivered to his warehouse.

goods from Manchester (UK) to Milan (Italy) would require 38 different documents. Now, theoretically, none are required! Some companies seek to minimise their exposure to documentation problems by using freight forwarders to handle freight and documentation. Other companies develop their own expertise and handle documentation in-house.

The use of intermediaries

Traditionally freight companies simply offered transportation by land, sea and air. They then developed a more integrated customer oriented approach as the importance of logistics gained ground. Most freight forwarders will offer services such as, preparation and processing of international transport documents, coordination of transport services and the provision of warehousing. However many of the larger firms will now offer a whole range of functions beyond this.

There have been two driving forces for this. First, global competition has meant a downward pressure on costs. This has spawned the phenomenon that began in the logistics sector with out-sourcing but has extended to the whole range of other services now regarded as legitimate logistics tasks. Indeed, many of the multi-national logistics companies such as DHL, Fedex, UPS and TNT, the so called integrators, themselves out-source the functions they take on to small specialist suppliers.

Second, the technological advances discussed earlier means that logistics specialists are able to offer increasingly sophisticated services to exporters that firms cannot provide in-house. For example, a firm's products might once have passed from factory to national warehouse and then on to a foreign regional warehouse, then to a local depot, before delivery to the end consumer: a wasteful process in terms of time and cost. Today, using state-of-the-art systems, a logistics specialist taking responsibility for the warehouse function will deliver to the customer direct from the main warehouse, cutting out three of four links in the chain.

At the more advanced end of the logistics services spectrum, companies are handing control of more and more roles to their logistics partners. This is partly driven by the sheer geographical complexity of many exporters' operations where, for example, head office, factory and customer may be separated by thousands of miles.

As more companies attempt to develop the newly opened emerging markets where they have little knowledge or understanding of the distribution system, third party help will be essential. The Russian distribution system is still in its formative stage and so inside knowledge is vital (see Illustration 11.6).

Packaging

Packaging for international markets needs to reflect climatic, geographical, economic, cultural and distribution channel considerations. In this section we will concentrate on the specific requirements that particularly relate to transport and warehousing.

The main packaging issues of interest for the exporter are: loss, damage and the provision of handling points to cope with the range of transport modes and the levels of handling sophistication and types of equipment used throughout the entire transit.

Illustration 11.6: Russia's fledgling distribution industry

The distribution of consumer goods in Russia, a country of almost 150 million people, is still in its formative stages. Distribution has improved since Soviet times but not nearly enough. The main constraint on growth is finance. Borrowing money in Russia is difficult and expensive. Soyuzkontrakt's, a major distribution firm in St Petersburg, was reported to be trying to pay back bank loans with frozen chicken.

Soyuzkontrakt concentrate on Western-style branded goods, the familiar stock of the supermarket shelf such as confectionery and washing powders. The mass-market demand for such things in Russia which used to be confined to the biggest cities, has trickled down in the past year or two to provincial cities of 500 000 people or so. Soon it will trickle further down to the towns of 100 000 places where, for the moment, shopping still means browsing among a dozen near-identical grimy and thinly stocked grocery stores for a slab of fatty sausage. Soyuzkontrakt did roughly 20 per cent of its business in branded goods last year, that figure may soon rise to 100 per cent.

There are other changes in the pattern of supply of the distribution. More and more of the goods, though 'Western' in style are produced or packaged in Russia, perhaps 60 per cent of them against just 10 per cent two years ago.

Foreign firms have also been investing in local production. Russian firms have been learning to compete. That makes importing a much less significant part of the distribution business, the more so since many foreign firms without local production have learnt to do their own importing and warehousing and use Russian distributors to reach remote regions.

The main worry for Russian distributors is how long they can have the market to themselves. In principle, there is nothing much to stop big and brave Western firms moving in. They might lack local knowledge but they would probably have access to cheaper financing and so be able to win market share by offering easier credit terms.

Source: adapted from 'Palletable' (1998) *The Economist* 14 February

---

- **Loss**. The main concerns of loss of goods relate to misdirection and to theft (pilferage). The use of containers has reduced some of the opportunities for theft. Misdirection can be minimised by the appropriate use of shipping marks and labelling. High-value consignments need to be marked in such a way as to avoid drawing them to the attention of potential thieves. Marking needs to be simple, security-conscious and readily understandable by different people in different countries

- **Damage**. The length of transit and variations in climate and physical movement give rise to many opportunities for damage to occur. Goods stowed in large ships might be contaminated by chemical odours or corroding machinery. Goods might be left out in the open air in equatorial or severe winter conditions. Wal-Mart found that local Brazillian suppliers could not meet their standards for packaging and quality control.

A good balance needs to be achieved between the high costs of the substantial export packing required to eliminate all or almost all damage and the price and profit implications that this has for the customer and the exporter.

Over the years, export packaging has been modified from wooden crates and straw, etc., towards fibreboard and cardboard cartons. Different countries have different regulations about what materials are acceptable. In addition, export packaging influences customer satisfaction through its appearance and in its appropriateness to minimise handling costs for the customer.

The export sales contract

The export sales contract covers important terms for the delivery of products in international trade. There are three main areas of uncertainty in international trade contracts which Branch (1990) identifies as:

- uncertainty about which legal system will be used to adjudicate the contract
- difficulties resulting from inadequate and unreliable information
- differences in the interpretation of different trade terms.

The International Chamber of Commerce (ICC) has formulated a set of internationally recognised trade terms called *Incoterms*. The use of Incoterms will reduce these uncertainties. However, because there are many different ways in which the customer and the supplier could contract for the international delivery of products, the possibility of ambiguity can exist unless care is taken.

At one extreme the customer could buy the product at the factory gate, taking all the responsibility for permits, arrangements and costs of transport and insurance. At the other extreme the supplier can arrange and pay for all costs to the point where the product is delivered to the customer's premises. There are a variety of different steps between manufacture and delivery to the customer, Keegan (1989) identifies nine steps:

- obtaining an export permit, if required. For example, for the sale of armaments
- obtaining a currency permit, if required
- packing the goods for export
- transporting the goods to the place of departure. This is usually road transport to a seaport or to an airport. For some countries, for example, within continental Europe transport could be entirely by road transport
- preparing a bill of lading
- completing necessary customs export papers
- preparing customs or consular invoices as required in the country of destination
- arranging for ocean freight and preparation
- obtaining marine insurance and certificate of the policy.

There are many Incoterms specifying many variations of responsibility for the required steps in the delivery process. The main terms are defined below:

- **Ex-works (EXW).** In this contract the exporter makes goods available at a specified time at the exporter's factory or warehouse. The advantage to the buyer in this arrangement is that of obtaining the goods at the lowest possible price.

- **Free on board (FOB).** In this contract the exporter is responsible for the costs and risks of moving the goods up to the point of passing them over the ship's rail. The FOB contract will specify that name of the ship and the name of the port. The benefit to the buyer in this arrangement is that the goods can be transported in the national shipping line of the buyer and can be insured using a national insurance company. In this way the amount of foreign currency needed to finance the contract is reduced.

- **Cost, insurance, freight (CIF).** This contract specifies that the exporter is responsible for all costs and risks to a specified destination port indicated by the buyer. The buyer benefits from receiving the goods in the home country and is, therefore, spared the costs, risks and management of the goods in transit. The exporter can benefit from a higher price for the contract. Whether the contract is more profitable will depend on the extra total

Companies can decide on the basis of their knowledge, objectives and situation to take either a cost, market or competition-oriented approach.

Cost-oriented approaches are intended to achieve either:

- a specific return on investment; or
- ensure an early cash recovery.

Market-oriented pricing approaches give the company the opportunity to:

- stabilise competitive positions within the market
- skim the most profitable business; or
- penetrate the market by adopting an aggressive strategy to increase market share.

Competition-oriented approaches are designed to:
- maintain and improve market position
- meet and follow competition
- reflect differences in the perceived value and performance of competitive products; or
- prevent or discourage new entrants in the market.

No matter which of these broad strategies are adopted, the process for determining export pricing is essentially the same

- determine export market potential
- estimate the price range and target price
- calculate sales potential at the target price
- evaluate tariff and non-tariff barriers
- select suitable pricing strategy in line with company objectives
- consider likely competitor response
- select pricing tactics, set distributor and end-user prices
- monitor performance and take necessary corrective action.

Problems of pricing

There are a number of specific problems which arise in setting and managing prices in international markets. Problems arise in four main areas:

> *Problems in multi-national pricing.* Companies find difficulty in coordinating and controlling prices across their activities sufficiently to enable them to achieve effective financial performance and their desired price positioning:

- How can prices be coordinated by the company across the various markets?
- How can a company retain uniform price positioning in different market situations?
- At what price should a company transfer products or services from a subsidiary in one country to a subsidiary in another?
- How can a firm deal with importation and sale of its products by an unauthorised dealer?

Problems in managing foreign currency and economic conditions. Considerable problems arise in foreign transactions because of the need to buy and sell products in different currencies:
- In what currency should a company price its products in international markets?
- How should the company deal with fluctuating exchange rates?
- What strategies are available for a company to deal with high inflation rates?

Problems of obtaining suitable payment in less developed countries. Obtaining payment promptly and in a suitable currency from the less developed countries can cause expense and additional difficulties:
- How might/should a company deal with selling to countries where there is a risk of non-payment?
- How should a company approach selling to countries which have a shortage of hard currency?

Administrative problems of cross-border transfer of goods. Problems of bureaucracy and delays arise as a result of simply moving goods physically across borders:
- At what point should an exporter release control and responsibility for goods?
- What steps can be taken in the export order process to minimise delays?

Problems in multi-national pricing

Coordination of prices across markets

The pressure on companies to market truly global products backed by globally standardised advertising campaigns is caused by three major trends; the homogenisation of customer demand, the lowering of trade barriers and the emergence of international competitors. At the same time these largely undifferentiated global products can be sold at very different prices in different countries, based on factors such as purchasing power, exchange rate changes and competition and consumer preferences.

Until recently this has been a perfectly acceptable practice. However in the past decade it has become increasingly difficult for companies to maintain a differentiated pricing strategy across international markets when they are marketing similar if not standardised products. Readily available information on worldwide prices through modern data transfer, and advances in telecommunications systems have greatly reduced international transaction costs. Global companies who obviously follow differentiated pricing policies are often threatened, first from an erosion of consumer confidence as customers learn of the more attractive pricing policies in other markets and second by *grey marketing* which can result in the cannibalisation of sales in countries with relatively high prices and damaging relationships with authorised distributors.

The issue of achieving price coordination across markets has become particularly pertinent in the European Union (EU) since the inauguration of the European Monetary Union and the launch of the Euro in 1999.

National price levels across the EU are far from uniform. Amongst the inaugural group of countries joining the EMU, Austria and Finland are significantly high-priced markets, France, Belgium, Portugal and Germany are seen as average and Spain as the bargain basement of Europe. In Denmark, which has not joined the EMU, price levels are on average 40 per cent higher than Spain.

Differences in taxation, excise duties as well as disparities in production costs and wage levels lead to price differentials. Firms in the past have tended to adapt their prices to the buying power, income levels and consumer preferences of national markets. Despite the formation of the Single European Market these differences have been largely concealed from the European consumer. The formation of the EMU and the introduction of the Euro has changed all that.

Now prices are no longer distorted by fluctuating exchange rates. This means companies competing on the European market need to consider the implications of the transparent *euro* dominated prices that are now emerging across Europe. Many firms are now operating a euro pricing policy (see Illustration 12.4).

The on-set of price transparency will impact on firms in different ways. Highly specialised products with few direct rivals could be largely immune to the risk of price transparency generating more intense competition. However companies marketing goods that are supplied direct to the consumer could come under pressure from retailers to reduce margins if retailers themselves have had to cut prices to meet new price points set in euros. Furthermore, as more

---

Illustration 12.4: Suppliers to the European market need to use the euro

Firms who are unwilling or unable to quote for business in euros from 1999 and who fail to prepare for the euro will lose out as they will be unable to compete for business on an equal basis with companies who can, according to the Chief Executive of Siemans.

Siemans itself adopted the Euro as its house currency, replacing the Deustchmark in 1999.

Suppliers using the Euro as opposed to sterling or the US dollar have a competitive advantage because it offers extra benefits to the customer, including, reduced costs of handling transactions and reduced currency risks. Whether in the European Monetary Union or not, companies not quoting in euros will lose out to competitors who do.

Siemans believe that customers will begin to expect the cost savings associated with the wider use of the euro to be passed on. They will demand these to be reflected in prices, whether or not the suppliers in question are capable of achieving these cost savings.

Source: adapted from 'Business warned to use euros' (1998) *Financial Times*, 16 January

---

retailers and businesses move to a policy of European wide sourcing it will soon become impossible for companies to operate on the European market without a sophisticated strategy to effectively coordinate prices across the EU. As a result of this a number of firms have revamped their European marketing strategies (see Illustration 12.5).

Firms who fail to meet this challenge will be leaving themselves open to the threat of grey market goods cannibalising their sales in high-priced national markets.

What is grey marketing?

Assmus and Wiess (1995) define grey market goods as 'brand name products sold through unauthorized channels'. Typically grey market goods are international brands with high price differentials and low costs of arbitrage. The costs connected with the arbitrage are transportation costs, tariffs, taxes and the costs of modifying the product, i.e. changing the language of instructions. It is perhaps important to point out that there is nothing illegal about grey market goods, it is

---

Illustration 12.5: ICI rethink brand strategy for EMU

Imperial Chemical Industries (ICI) is launching pan-European paint brands in place of products aimed at national markets in response to the European Monetary Union (EMU).

ICI sees preparing for the EMU as primarily a commercial rather than information technology project. Key issues to resolve are price coordination across Europe, supply chain management, manufacturing location, packaging, distribution and training.

ICI feel it is crucial for the company to have the correct commercial strategies in place so they mitigate any threats out of EMU and seize any opportunities. The on-set of price transparency through the use of the euro will impact on all their product ranges.

ICI view it as unacceptably expensive for ICI to aim products purely at different national markets. It is necessary therefore to offer products in standard pan-European format and sizes. This has meant adjusting the price of the products and re-educating the consumer.

On the purchasing side, ICI are reformulating their strategy to take advantage of the improved access to the single market created by the euro to buy from a wider pool of suppliers.

Source: adapted from *Financial Times* (1998) 22 January

---

purely the practice of buying a product in one market and selling it in other markets in order to benefit from the prevailing price differential. Grey markets tend to develop in markets where information on prices for basically the same product in different countries is cheap and easy to obtain (e.g. cars, designer goods, consumer durables).

There are three types of grey markets (see Figure 12.1).

Parallel importing. When the product is priced lower in the home market where it is produced than the export market. The grey marketer in the export market will parallel import directly from the home market rather than source from within their own country, for example there is a strong parallel import trade in Levi jeans between the USA and Germany.

Re-importing. When the product is priced cheaper in an export market than in the home market where it was produced, re-importation in this case can be profitable to the grey marketer.

Figure 12.1 Three types of grey market

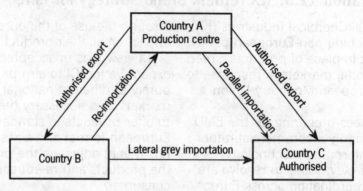

Note: Price in Country B < price in Country C
Source: Assmus and Weiss (1995)

Lateral importing. When there is a price difference between export markets, products are sold from one country to another through unauthorised channels.

Price coordination strategies

Typically firms try to defend themselves against grey market activities by calling for government intervention or legal protection. They may resort to imposing restrictions or even threats to retailers. Retailers such as Wal-Mart in the US and Tesco in the UK have sourced products through grey markets and suffered the resultant threats from firms such as Adidas and Levi jeans. Other reactive measures have included the refusal to issue warranties in certain markets or even buying out the grey marketer.

Companies competing in international markets who wish to develop strategies to deal with the problem of price coordination across increasingly interdependent markets and the threat of grey market goods more effectively have four options open to them.

Economic measures. The company can influence the country manager's pricing decision by controlling the input into those decisions. A multi-national can do this through *transfer pricing* (see later section in this chapter). By raising the price by which it transfers products to the low priced country the headquarters essentially impose a tax on that market. Closely related to transfer pricing is *rationing* the product quantities allocated to each country or region and so limiting the number of units sold in the diverting country.

Centralisation. The company can move towards more centralisation in the setting of prices. Traditionally many multi-national companies have given country managers a high degree of decision-making autonomy. Usually they are in the best position to assess consumer response to any given pricing decisions and they are able to react swiftly to competitor activity. A centralised approach, however, could overcome difficulties with grey market goods although it does usually result in dissatisfaction amongst country managers. A compromise approach is to shift the decision-making authority in pricing from a country to a regional level, however increasingly grey market goods are becoming a global issue.

Formalisation. The company can standardise the process of planning and implementing of pricing decisions. Thus the company influences prices at the local level by prescribing a process that is followed by country managers when establishing pricing policy.

Informal coordination. A number of companies have moved towards a more informal system of coordination without either a high degree of centralisation or normalisation. This thinking is usual in the transnational company where international subsidiaries make differentiated and innovative contributions to an integrated worldwide operation. Whilst this approach may incorporate a variety of techniques the essential asset is that there are common shared business values across the subsidiaries that are backed by compatible incentive systems.

In a proactive approach to coordinating its pricing decision across international markets, a company has to select the appropriate strategy which will in effect be determined first, by the level of local resources available, and then by the level of environmental complexity, as illustrated in Figure 12.2.

Transfer pricing in international markets

Transfer pricing is an area that has created complications for many international marketing firms. It is concerned with the pricing of goods sold within a corporate family, when the transactions involved are from division to division, to a foreign subsidiary, or to a partner in a joint venture agreement. Whilst these transfer prices are internal to the company, they are important externally because goods being transferred from country to country must have a value for cross-border taxation purposes.

Figure 12.2 A framework for selecting a coordination method

Environmental complexity

	Low	High
Low	Centralisation	Formalisation
High	Economic measures	Informal coordination

Level of local resources

Source: Assmus and Weiss (1995)

The objective of the corporation in this situation is to ensure that the transfer price paid optimises corporate rather than divisional objectives. This can prove difficult when a company internationally is organised into profit centres. For profit centres to work effectively, a price must be set for everything that is transferred, be it working materials, components, finished goods or services. A high transfer price, for example, from the domestic division to a foreign subsidiary, is reflected in an apparently poor performance by the foreign subsidiary, whereas a low price would not be acceptable to the domestic division providing the goods. This issue alone can be the cause of much mistrust between subsidiaries – at best leading to fierce arguments, and at worst leading to loss of business through overpricing.

There tend to be three bases for transfer pricing:

Transfer at cost, in which the transfer price is set at the level of the production cost, and the international division is credited with the entire profit that the firm makes. This means that the production centre is evaluated on efficiency parameters rather than profitability.

Transfer at arm's length, when the international division is charged the same as any buyer outside the firm. Problems occur if the overseas division is allowed to buy elsewhere when the price is uncompetitive or the product quality is inferior, and further difficulties arise if there are no external buyers, making it difficult to establish a relevant price.

Transfer at cost plus is the usual compromise, where profits are split between the production and international divisions. The actual formula used for assessing the transfer price can vary, but usually it is this method which has the greatest chance of minimising executive time spent on transfer price disagreements, optimising corporate profits and motivating the home and international divisions. Often a senior executive is appointed to rule on disputes.

However, the real interest of transfer pricing is how it is used strategically by companies either to act as a barrier to entry, or to marshal resources around the world.

To create barriers to entry
Most oil companies are vertically integrated, from oil exploration right through to selling petrol at the pumps, and use transfer pricing as part of their strategy to maintain barriers to entry. The major cost for oil companies is at the exploration and refining stage and so, by charging high transfer prices for crude oil, profits are generated at the refining stage of the process, rather than in distribution, where it is relatively easy to enter the market. Oil companies therefore attempt by the use of transfer pricing to make petrol distribution unattractive to potential competitors. Supermarkets and hypermarkets, however, with their huge purchasing power, are increasingly challenging the dominance of the oil companies by using low-priced petrol as a loss leader to entice customers to stores.

To avoid domestic tax liabilities
When countries have different levels of taxation on corporate profits, firms try to ensure that profits are accumulated at the most advantageous point. Companies operating in countries with high corporation tax may be tempted to sell at low transfer prices to their subsidiaries in countries with lower corporate taxation.

To avoid foreign tax
Foreign tax authorities wish to maximise the taxable income within their jurisdiction, and there are a number of strategies a company might use to avoid tax – for example, by charging lower transfer prices if there is high customs duty on goods. The impact of such avoidance strategies is diminishing, as customs authorities become more aware of this practice. However, it can be argued that as the general level of import duties is reducing as international trade agreements come into effect, so the need to take avoiding action is declining.

To manage the level of involvement in markets
If a firm has both a fully owned subsidiary and a joint venture in a particular country, it will wish to sell at a higher price to a company with which it has a joint venture than one that is a fully owned subsidiary. Selling at a low price to foreign partnerships or licensees has the effect of sharing more of the profit with the partner.

Transfer pricing is an area where profit objectives, managerial motivations and government regulation interact and so the expertise of many people – accountants, legal counsel, tax advisors and division managers – is needed to achieve an agreement. The international marketing manager's contribution is primarily concerned with two aspects of the problem:

- achieving an effective distribution of goods to world markets
- ensuring that the impact of the transfer price does not affect foreign market opportunities.

Problems in managing foreign currency transactions

Currency issues
Perhaps the most critical issue for managers is how to deal with the various problems involved in managing transactions which involve currency exchange; a second difficulty is what action to take when selling to countries where there is high inflation.

What currency should the price be quoted in?
In any international marketing transaction, the exporter has the option of quoting in either the domestic or the local currency. If the exporter quotes in the domestic currency, then not only is it administratively much easier, but also the risks associated with changes in the exchange rate are borne by the customer, whereas by quoting prices in the foreign currency the exporter bears the exchange rate risk. However, there are benefits to the exporter in quoting in foreign currency:

- it could provide access to finance abroad at lower interest rates
- good currency management may be a means of gaining additional profits
- quoting in foreign currency could be a condition of the contract
- customers normally prefer to be quoted in their own currency in order to be able to make competitive comparisons and to know exactly what the eventual price will be.

Furthermore customers in export markets often prefer quotations in their own currency to enable them to more easily compare the tenders of competitors from a range of countries.

Often the choice of currency for the price quotation depends partly on the trade practices in the export market and the industry concerned. Suppliers competing for business in the oil industry, wherever in the world they may be supplying may well find they are asked to quote in US dollars.

In 1998 the international markets experienced tremendous turbulence in the foreign exchange markets through what has become known as the 'Asian crisis'. Currencies such as the Malaysian ringit, the Indonesian rupiah and the Thai bhat saw their values halved in a matter of weeks. UK exporters meanwhile experienced a very strong pound sterling, reducing their competitiveness on international markets and subjecting them to price-cutting pressures from overseas customers.

Thus as well as the decision as to what currency to quote in, the main worry for both suppliers and customers on international markets are fluctuating exchange rates and how to deal with them.

The introduction of the euro will effectively eliminate exchange rate risk in the countries that enter the European Monetary Union. Even countries like the UK, who have initially decided to delay their decision to enter the EMU until 2002, may increasingly find that companies selling goods into Europe will be pressurised to quote prices in the euro.

Should prices be raised/lowered as exchange rates fluctuate?
One of the most difficult problems that exporters face is caused by fluctuating exchange rates. The major trading nations appear to have differing strategies to deal with exchange rate appreciation – for example, UK, French and Canadian firms all tend to increase their prices by more than the exchange rate appreciation, whereas Japanese firms only pass on about half the appreciation of the yen in the form of a price rise. Japanese exporters have, therefore, preferred to retain market share by absorbing some of the impact of yen appreciation, at the expense of short-term profits.

Terpstra and Sarathy (1997) identified three types of risk affecting firms, arising from exchange rate fluctuations:

1 **Transaction risk** occurs when the exporter quotes in a foreign currency, which then appreciate, diminishing the financial return to the firm. US hoteliers in Hawaii experienced a very noticeable decline in Japanese

tourism when the dollar rose in value from Yen 90 to Yen 120 in just over a year.

2 **Competitive risk** arises because the geographic pattern of a firm's manufacturing and sales puts them at a disadvantage compared to their competition. If, for instance, the firm is manufacturing in a country with an appreciating currency but trying to compete in a marketplace where currencies are depreciating, it could lose out to a local manufacturer.

3 **Market portfolio risk** occurs because a company with a narrow market portfolio will be influenced to a much greater extent by changes in exchange rates than a diversified firm that is better able to balance charges in exchange rates through operating in many countries.

Various tactics can be adopted to deal with currency fluctuations. When the domestic currency is weak, the firm should:

- compete on price
- introduce new products with additional features
- source and manufacture in the domestic country
- fully exploit export opportunities
- obtain payment in cash
- use full-cost approach for existing markets, but use marginal costs for new more competitive markets
- repatriate foreign-earned income quickly
- reduce expenditure and buy services (advertising, transport etc.) locally
- minimise overseas borrowing
- invoice in domestic currency

When the domestic currency is strong, the firm should:

- compete on non-price factors (quality, delivery, service)
- improve productivity and reduce costs
- prioritise strong currency countries for exports
- use counter-trade for weak currency countries
- reduce profit margins and use marginal costs for pricing
- keep the foreign-earned income in the local country
- maximise expenditures in local country currency
- buy services abroad in local currencies
- borrow money for expansion in local markets
- invoice foreign customers in their own currency.

Forward buying of currency
Where companies are engaged in continual trade transactions between countries which involve substantial amounts of foreign currency exchange, it is usual to attempt to forecast the likely movements of the currencies. Depending on whether a currency is expected to rise or fall, a company might purchase, in advance, the currency it will need to finance its future transactions, at a current advantageous rate.

Problems of obtaining payment in less developed countries
In dealing with less developed countries, companies are sometimes taking additional risks due to the greater political and economic instability. For a company exporting goods there is a considerable risk of non-payment, for a variety of reasons, such as:

- the buyer failing or refusing to pay for the goods
- insolvency of the buyer
- a general moratorium on external debt by the government of the buyer's country
- political and legal decisions
- war
- failure to fulfil the conditions of the contract.

Many governments accept that these disincentives discourage exporting but attempt to reduce these risks by providing low-cost protection against default by the buyer. In situations of high-risk firms use other strategies to ensure payment. Generally counter-trading and leasing methods are common techniques.

Leasing and counter-trade

So far in this chapter we have focused upon largely conventional approaches to international pricing; however, over the last two decades there has been a dramatic increase in the use of leasing and counter-trade deals, which are used as a response to the lack of hard currency, particularly amongst less developed countries.

Leasing
Leasing is used as an alternative to outright purchase in countries where there is a shortage of capital available to purchase high-priced capital and industrial goods. Usually the rental fee will cover servicing and the cost of spares too, and

so the problem of poor levels of maintenance which is often associated with high technology and capital equipment in LDCs can be overcome. Leasing arrangements can be attractive, too, in countries where investment grants and tax incentives are offered for new plant and machinery, in which case the lessor can take advantage of the tax provisions in a way that the lessee cannot, and share some of the savings. It is estimated that leased aircraft account for about 20 per cent of the world's aircraft fleet.

Counter-trade

Ancient forms of trading such as barter are continuing to play a significant role in international business, to address a number of problems that are faced by international companies. Counter-trade covers various forms of trading arrangements where part or all of the payment for goods is in the form of other goods or services, and price-setting and financing are dealt with together in one transaction. The original and simple barter system has been developed in order to accommodate modern trading situations.

Estimates of counter-trade activity range from 20 to 30 per cent of world trade, and it is predicted to grow further due to its ability, first, to overcome market imperfections and, second, to provide opportunities for extraordinary profits to be made.

Counter-trade is much more prevalent in less developed countries. Neale *et al.* (1997) identify the following reasons why it has grown:

- Emerging markets have limited access to hard foreign currency.

- The rise in protectionism can be counteracted by linking imports and exports, so that there is no net loss of jobs, and occasionally jobs might be created.

- Since the opening up of Central and Eastern Europe in 1989 there have been further significant developments in counter-trade as former communist countries fight to develop their economies by encouraging deals with Western companies.

Forms of counter-trade

There are many variants of counter-trade, resulting from the need to adapt arrangements to meet the needs of individual transactions. The following are the basic forms, but Neale *et al.* (1997) and Aggarwal (1989) provide more comprehensive studies.

- **Barter** is a single exchange of goods with no direct use of money, and does not require intermediaries. It is the simplest form, but has become unpopular because, first, if the goods are not exchange simultaneously then one participant is effectively financing the other, and second, one of the parties may well receive unwanted goods as part of the deal.

- **Compensation trading** involves an agreement in which payment for goods is accepted in a combination of goods and cash.

- **Counter-purchase** involves the negotiation of two contracts. In the first, the international marketer agrees to sell the product at an established price in local currency. In the second, simultaneous, contract the international firm buys goods or services for an equivalent or proportionate cash payment from another local supplier.

- **Off-set** is similar to counter-purchase, but in this case national governments become involved in supporting the deal. In this way the international firm is able to obtain more saleable goods from the country in exchange. For example, Boeing sold AWACS aircraft to the British Ministry of Defence on the basis that the purchase price would be spent on British goods (see Illustration 12.6).

Illustration 12.6: Countertrade deals for GEC

GEC – the Marconi electronics subsidiary – became involved in 3 'off-set' counter-trade deals to entitle them to trade in the Middle East. The contribution to the local economy in the form of investment in a furniture factory in Abu Dhabi, was made in return for an arms contract. In the deal, local craftsmen assemble furniture and fittings for palaces, hotels etc. in UAE. GEC is in partnership with local sheikhs and a Birmingham company for the venture, who agreed to export at least 50 per cent of the output to Europe and the Far East.

Other off-set counter-trade projects include the formation of a local company to charter ships for an Emirate group and a joint venture to provide geological and topographical information to help evaluate water, oil and gas and other natural resources.

- **Switch deals** involve a third party (usually a merchant house) which specialises in barter trading, disposing of the goods. For example, if an Eastern European company importing Western products can only provide in return heavily discounted relatively low-quality products, which may not be saleable in the West, a third country will need to be found in order that a switch deal can be set up in which these lower-quality goods can be exchanged for other products that are more suitable for the original Western markets.

- **Buyback** is an arrangement whereby part or all of the cost of purchase of capital equipment might be paid for in the form of production from the equipment supplied. Illustration 12.7 shows how Ikea are using this strategy to improve their supplier base.

In studies of counter-trade in Indonesia and Japan, Palia (1992 and 1993) concluded that compensation and off-set were the most frequently used forms of counter-trade in developed countries, and barter and counter-purchase were most common in less developed countries.

Illustration 12.7: Buyback by Ikea

Ikea, the Swedish furniture and furnishings retailing group, is continually searching out new sources of supply, increasing its product range and striving to reduce costs. It sees suppliers in Eastern European as playing a key role in its strategy. An essential part of the process is buyback – one form of counter-trade in which machinery and equipment for increasing and upgrading production is leased to Eastern European companies in exchange for an export contract. In this way the suppliers are able to meet Ikea's high quality standards and specifications. The repayment period is between three to five years, and in return, Ikea usually buys three to four times the value of the equipment supplied.

Drilling and planing equipment worth £300 000 has been supplied to a Polish joint venture for producing lacquered wooden lamps, and £500 000 of sewing machines and leather and fabric cutting machines has been supplied to a firm in the Czech Republic, both on a buyback agreement.

Source: adapted from 'A Useful Instrument – Bartering and Other forms of Countertrade Are a Key To Eastern Europe', *Financial Times*, 29 June 1993, FT Exporter (22).

So far, the examples of counter-trade have involved deals of products, but in future, many other less tangible elements such as know-how, software and information will be included in agreements. Many of the deals that have been set up have been extremely complicated and in some cases covered a period of years because the purchaser was unable to provide in exchange saleable goods which would allow straightforward barter.

Advantages and limitations of counter-trade

Neale *et al.* (1997) and Aggarwal (1989) have identified various advantages of counter-trade:

- New markets can be developed for a country's products, as marketing and quality control skills are often 'imported' with the deal, and it can lead to gaining experience in Western markets.

- Surplus and poorer quality products can be sold through counter-trade whereas they could not be sold for cash. Moreover, dumping and heavy discounting can be disguised.

- Counter-trade through bilateral and multilateral trade agreement can strengthen political ties.

- Counter-trade and contract manufacture can be used to enter high-risk areas.

- Counter-trade can provide extraordinary profits as it allows companies to circumvent government restrictions.

However, there are disadvantages and limitations in using counter-trade:

- There is a lack of flexibility, as the transactions are often dependent on product availability, and counter-traded products are often of poor quality, overpriced or are available due to a surplus.

- Products taken in exchange may not fit with the firm's trading objectives, or may be difficult to sell.

- Dealing with companies and government organisations may be difficult, particularly in locating and organising counter-trade products.

- Negotiations may be difficult, as there are no guide market prices.

- Counter-trade deals are difficult to evaluate in terms of profitability and companies can, through counter-trade, create new competition.

It is likely that in the future, counter-trading will develop further in the form of longer-term rather than shorter-term partnerships as multi-nationals seek permanent foreign sources for incorporation in their global sourcing strategy. LDCs offer the benefits of low-cost labour and materials, as well as relatively untapped markets for goods. This has resulted in multi-nationals reversing the traditional counter-trade process by first seeking opportunities, and then identifying potential counter-trade partners with which to exploit the opportunities.

Administrative problems resulting from the cross-border transfer of goods

For many companies, particularly those that are infrequent exporters or that have insufficient resources for effective export administration, the process of ensuring that goods reach their ultimate destination is beset with difficulties: goods held in customs warehouses without apparent reason, confusing paper-work, high and apparently arbitrary duties, levies and surcharges, and the need to make exorbitant payments to expedite the release of goods. The UN Conference on Trade and Development (UNCTAD) believe these additional costs to world trade could be as much as 10 per cent of the US$ 5 trillion taken a year in total world trade. UNCTAD also believes that those costs could be cut by US$ 100 billion. By customs computerisation. It is unlikely, however, that such changes as these will happen quickly, and so companies face a series of decisions about how to manage their own risks and costs, whilst still providing an effective service to their customers.

Deciding at what stage of the export sales process the price should be quoted

Export price quotations are important, because they spell out the legal and cost responsibilities of the buyer and seller. Sellers, as previously mentioned, favour a quote that gives them the least liability and responsibility, such as FOB (free on board), or ex-works, which means the exporter's liability finishes when the goods are loaded on to the buyer's carrier. Buyers, on the other hand, would prefer either franco domicile, where responsibility is borne by the supplier all the way to the customer's warehouse, or CIF port of discharge, which means the buyer's responsibility begins only when the goods are in their own country.

Generally, the more market-oriented pricing policies are based on CIF, which indicates a strong commitment to the market. By pricing ex-works, an exporter is not taking any steps to build relations with the market and so may be indicating only short-term commitment. The major stages at which export prices might be quoted are as follows:

Ex (point of origin), such as ex-factory, ex-mine, ex-warehouse.

FOB: free on board.

FAS: free alongside.
FAS vessel (named port of shipment).

C. & F. cost and freight.

CIF: cost, insurance freight:

DDP: direct to destination point.

The export order process
To further emphasise the complexity of managing international pricing, a major task of the marketer is to choose payment terms that will satisfy importers and at the same time safeguard the interests of the exporter. The export process for handling transactions is illustrated in Figure 12.3.

In the process, the customer agrees to payment by a confirmed letter of credit. The customer begins the process (1) by sending an enquiry for the goods. The price and terms are confirmed by a pro-forma invoice (2) by the supplier, so that the customer knows for what amount (3) to instruct its bank (the issuing bank) to open a letter of credit (L/C)(4). The L/C is confirmed by a bank (5) in the supplier's country.

When the goods are shipped (6) the shipping documents are returned to the supplier (7), so that shipment is confirmed by their presentation (8) together with the L/C and all other stipulated documents and certificates for payment (9). The moneys are automatically transmitted from the customer's account via the issuing bank. The customer may only collect the goods (10) when all the documents have been returned to them.

Whilst letters of credit and drafts are the most common payment method, there are also several other methods:

- **A draft**. Drawn by the exporter on the importer, who makes it into a **trade acceptance** by writing on it the word 'accepted'.

Figure 12.3 The export order process

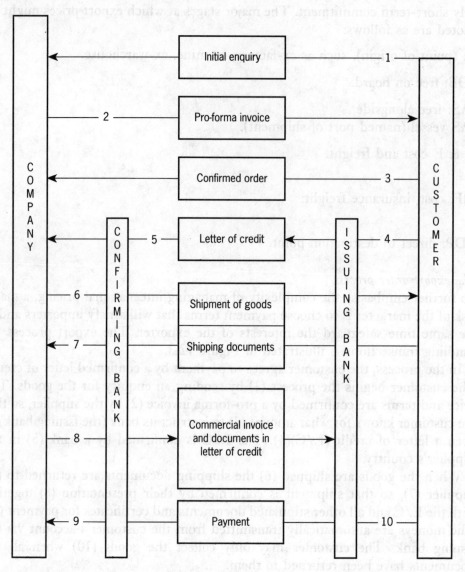

- **A letter of credit.** Similar to a draft, except it is drawn on the bank and becomes a bank acceptance rather than a trade acceptance. There is greater assurance of payment, as an unconditional undertaking is given by the bank that the debts of the buyer will be paid to the seller.

- **Open account**. Sales terms are agreed between buyer and seller, but without documents specifying clearly the importer's payment obligations. There is less paperwork but greater risk of non-payment, so it is only used when a trusting relationship has been developed between the trading parties. In countries where foreign exchange is difficult to obtain, drafts and letters of credit will be given priority in any currency allocation.

- **Consignment**. The exporter retains title of the goods until the importer sells them. Exporters own the goods longer in this method than any other, and so the financial burden and risks are at their greatest. In addition, the recovery of either goods or debt could be very difficult, and so it is for this reason that consignments tend to be limited to companies trading with their subsidiaries.

- **Bill of exchange**. An unconditional order in writing is signed by one person and requires the person to whom it is addressed to pay a certain sum of money on instruction at a specified time.

The credit terms given are also important in determining the final price to the buyer. When products from international competitors are perceived to be similar, the purchaser may choose the supplier that offers the best credit terms, in order to effect a greater discount. In effect the supplier is offering a source of finance to the buyer, and in some countries – for example, Brazil – government support is given to firms to help them gain a competitive advantage through this method. There has been a variety of international agreements to try and stop such practices, but it is still quite prevalent in some countries.

Conclusion

In this chapter we have discussed the many factors and problems that contribute to making effective pricing management one of the most difficult aspects of international marketing to achieve. What becomes quite clear in developing international pricing is that there is a need not only to use pricing in a key role in achieving a company's financial objectives, but also as part of an integrated strategy to respond positively to the opportunities and threats of the various markets in which it operates. In addition to this strategic role, there are a number of issues relating to the detailed operational management of international transactions, in which pricing can contribute significantly.

Discussion questions

1 What are the arguments for and against using price and non-price factors when competing in international markets?

2 What pricing problems might a multi-national company face in marketing to less developed countries, and how might they be overcome?

3 How can exporting companies reduce financial risk?

4 Why should a domestic supplier invoice export goods in a foreign currency? What are the advantages and disadvantages of foreign currency invoicing?

5 Examine the ways in which costs influence export pricing decisions.

References

Abell, D.F. and Hammond, J.S. (1979) *Strategic Market Planning: Problems and Analytical Approaches*, Prentice-Hall.

Aggarwal, R. (1989) 'International Business Through Barter and Countertrade', *Long Range Planning*, 22 (3).

Assmos and Wiesse (1997), 'How to address the gray market threat using price coordination', in I. Doole and R. Lowe, *International Marketing Strategy*: *contemporary readings*, Thomson Business Press.

Buzzell, R.D. and Gale, B.T. (1987) *The PIMS Principles: Linking Strategy to Performance*, Free Press.

Carter, J. and Gagne, J. (1988) 'The Do's and Don'ts of International Countertrade', *Sloan Management Review*, Spring: 31–38.

Cavusgil, S. and Sikora, E. (1988) 'How Multinationals Can Counter Grey Market Imports', *Columbian Journal of World Business*, 23 (4), Winter: 75–87.

Davidson, J.H. (1987) *Offensive Marketing or How to Make your Competitors Followers*, 2nd edn, Penguin.

Duhan, D. and Sheffet, M. (1988) 'Gray Markets and the Legal Status of Parallel Importation', *Journal of Marketing*, 52 (July): 75–83.

Hermann, S. and Eckhard, K. (1992) 'The European Pricing Time Bomb – and How to Cope With It', *European Management Journal* 10 (2).

Huszagh, S.M. and Huszagh, F.W. (1986) 'International Barter and Counter-trade', *International Marketing Review*, Summer.

Keegan, W.J. (1989) *Global Marketing Management*, Prentice-Hall.

Mueller, B. and Cavusgil, S.T. (1996) 'Unraveling the Mystique of Export Pricing', *Business Horizons*, 31 (3).

Nagle, T.T. (1987) *The Strategies and Tactics of Pricing*, Prentice-Hall.

Neale, C.W., Akis, Y.Y. and Pass, C.L. (1997) 'The Life Cycle pattern of East West countertrade', *International Marketing Review*, 14 (4).

Palia, A.P. (1993) 'Countertrade Practices in Japan', *Industrial Marketing Management*, 22 (2), May.

Samiee, S. (1987) 'Pricing in Marketing Strategies of US and Foreign Based Companies', *Journal of Business Research*, 15.

Terpstra, V. and Sarathy, R. (1997) *International Marketing*, Dryden Press.

If the locals won't roll over, Molly Malone will deal with them

Introduction

There is an assumption amongst many MNEs that if they approach emerging
markets with the formula that made them successful in developed markets, there
will be sufficient affluent customers ready to buy the products and, very quickly,
the local suppliers will just give in and leave the MNE to it. The beer market is
not like that. Whilst there may be a transnational segment that will buy the well-
known international brands, there is also a very traditional segment that prefers
the local brew. As the emerging markets offer the best prospects for growth this
is leading to the most effective local brewers becoming stronger and forcing
international brewers, such as Guinness to respond by being rather more
creative. Guinness' response has been to export the experience as well as the
beer.

When the customers prefer the local brew

All the growth in the beer industry is forecast to occur in Asia, Africa, Latin
America and Eastern Europe, where beer is increasingly preferred over other
alcoholic drinks by young people. These markets are developing as a result of
rising incomes and further deregulation and they are becoming the target of the
large international brewery groups. These international brewers have generally
used joint ventures with local companies as the only way to enter these markets
which were usually protected from foreign involvement. Carlsberg (Denmark)
and Guineas (UK), for example, share 95 per cent of the Malaysian beer market
through two competing joint ventures.

When the local brewers fight back

A report by investment bankers Flemings suggests that local firms are in a good position to succeed as major forces with their emerging region. Castle of South African breweries is the fastest growing international beer brand with sales up 17 per cent per year from 1990–96. The group has 98 per cent of its home market, has rapidly entered into the rest of Southern and East Africa and now several Eastern European markets to become the world's fourth largest brewer. Companhia Cervejaria Brahma, the Brazilian drinks group, has half the huge Brazilian beer market and has expanded into Argentina and Venezuela and is not only the world's fifth largest brewer but is also one of the three most profitable in merging markets, when measured in profit/litre. These firms are beginning to export successfully too. For Grupo Modela of Mexico, which brews Corona, exporting accounts for 14 per cent of production and 21 per cent of sales.

China is likely to become the world's biggest beer drinking country in the world by the year 2000. Tougher economic criteria are having the effect of consolidation in the number of breweries which have reduced by a third to 600 over the two years up to 1998. Because the Chinese economy is growing at between 7–10 per cent per year with the urban centres growing at 12 per cent per year, the average consumer's income is set to double every six years.

Here too, however, many of the MNEs have underestimated the difficulties of doing business, especially when using joint ventures as a method of market entry, and they have often been caught out by sudden and arbitrary taxation decisions by the government, and did not foresee how hard the locals would fight back. *The Economist* (1997) has wondered whether the huge levels of foreign investment in China have resulted in the investors actually making any profit. For example, the Australian brewer Fosters and Singapore's Asia Pacific Breweries, which make Tiger beer, are both losing money. Whilst some Chinese have started buying the premium international brands the majority of Chinese drinkers still prefer local beers.

Whilst Guinness sees a market of some 300 million people, they face the problem that the Chinese drink lager and converting them to a dark beer will be difficult. Moreover, in Asia where consumers drink beer they drink it with food.

Will Molly Malone's be good for Guinness

It is against this background that Guinness are developing their strategy to compete internationally. However, a short time ago Guinness had an even bigger problem. They were concerned that their customers were dying. Not because of the Guinness, of course – indeed some of their loyal customers believe that it prolongs life – but rather more because the average age of its customers was increasing year by year. But how things have changed. Guinness is a classic example of repositioning a product so that it now appeals to a new, younger customer segment as well as its lifelong devotees of advancing years. Now Guinness have added another dimension – they are not simply selling beer, they are selling the whole Irish experience.

Molly Malone's is all an Irish pub should be: packed with red faced, laughing, story-telling drinkers downing their Guinness and whiskey chasers. The heavy atmosphere is thick with cigarette smoke and condensation is running down the windows. The noise of Irish fiddles and stamping to the music fills every corner of the bar. The sawdust on the floor, the beer barrels, stone jars and bric-a-brac tell you that this must be the village pub in Ballykissangel or possibly a back street in Dublin. But this little piece of genuine Irish heritage came as a £500 000 flat-packed self-assembly bar shipped from Dublin and was erected at the chichi Boat Quay, a new development reclaimed from Singapore harbour in 1996.

A further look reveals that the drinkers are fashionable diners eating American-style burgers, curries and local seafood by the water's edge and, of course, they are drinking Guinness.

The Guinness Irish Pub Concept was an inspired international marketing tool which provides direct access to customers who might be persuaded to try the black beer with the white foam head. It was established in 1992 and by 1998 there were 1584 Irish pubs in over 35 countries around the world with a further 368 planned for the following year. Volumes of Guinness have increased 20–30 per cent in markets where Irish pubs have been established.

The challenge for Guinness is to use this novel distribution channel to cut through the barriers to entry in the Asia Pacific region where, including Australia, by 1988 it had only 52 pubs. In Irish pubs in the Asia Pacific region consumption of Guinness is 15 times higher than in non-Irish pubs.

Originally expatriate colonials took Guinness with them to Indonesia almost a century ago and its distribution expanded at the same rate as the colonies. Indeed it became the fashionable drink for plantation owners in Malaysia in the 1930s. The beer was carbonated stout rather the smooth beer of today. It had twice the alcohol content of normal beers in order to combat the germs which it might have encountered on its trip from the brewery in Dublin. The dark, bitter, viscous Foreign Extra Stout was sold in medical halls as a tonic for the health-conscious Chinese in Singapore, Malaysia and Hong Kong. The locals believed it was good for them, helping to give protection against disease and balancing their yin and yang.

Guinness's proposition that 'Guinness in good for you' held for several decades, and although consumption levels per capita were low it was very profitable because of the premium pricing and huge market. As the economies grew and became more affluent and urbanised, consumption increased and other competitors appeared. Now there are 20 beer brands in Asia.

The challenge for Guinness was to make the brand proposition relevant to a changing market, which accounts for half the worlds population and includes very varied markets from Australia and New Zealand, through Japan, Indonesia and Malaysia to China. Some of these are only just opening up to investment and Guinness must decide whether the same product and brand proposition will appeal in Jakarta, Peking and Bondi Beach.

The fact that a number of vast markets are emerging provides considerable potential. In the past the success has depended on finding a suitable local brewer as a partner but now Guinness can look strategically at the opportunities that these markets now offer and decide which of the markets it should enter and then focus its efforts in the target market. Moreover, with the opening up of more markets Guinness can take a pan-regional approach to its branding strategy and seize the opportunity to standardise its products, packaging and brand with the considerable benefits this offers, and making it easier to break into new markets.

Guinness is particularly aware, however, that these markets are changing rapidly and it is necessary to carry out rigorous and continuous research to collect useful data and keep abreast of consumer needs, particularly in China, where there are considerable differences in tastes and purchasing habits even within the same family. They believe, however, that there is increasing convergence of consumers. They have found that men go through different life stages and beer plays a part at each point. This means that with beer becoming universal, communications about beer drinking can be universal too. In the beer market Guinness have a major advantage over many competitors because the product is distinctive in its appearance, packaging and taste. The goodness message still provides the basis for the consistency of message which is ideal for communicating across the Asian markets.

Guinness are aware, however, of the need to modify the support for this central brand proposition in the different markets. In Malaysia, Singapore and Hong Kong the TV and press campaign is identical though the execution is slightly different. It is in promotional activity where Guinness is able to tailor the product offering to the local markets although sometimes it is the local laws which make changes necessary. So for the highly developed pub culture in Australia a branded leather jacket is offered in exchange for drinking a given number of pints in recognition of the Australians' session drinking. For the Singaporeans who love games of chance and cars, which, due to strict government policies on pollution and congestion, are expensive to buy and run the promotion was a game of chance in which two BMW cars were given away.

References

Simms, J. (1998) 'A stout defence', *Marketing Business*, March.
The Economist (1997) 'The China Syndrome', 21 June.
Willman, J. (1997) 'Brewers target new areas', *Financial Times*, 8 December.

Part III Cases

Sunlands holidays

The long wait to make a telephone call reminded Thomas Bochardt of the 1950s. The ancient Siemens manual telephone switchboard at Etosha Game Park in Namibia was in stark contrast to the modernity of some parts of the Namibian economy.

Bochardt was in Namibia to finalise a franchising deal based on Sunlands' travel marketing expertise and financial muscle. Twenty-two farms had been selected on the basis of the quality of their location and the quality of the guest service provided at the farm. Sunlands have various motel, hotel and leisure complexes and franchise operations around the world run from company headquarters in Munich, Germany. This was their first venture into Africa.

Namibia is one of Africa's newest countries. It has an estimated population of 1.3 million with one of the lowest population densities in Africa at 1.5 persons per square kilometre. The country has had a chequered history. The earliest inhabitants of Namibia and adjoining Botswana were the San (Bushmen) People. The Portuguese were the first Europeans to show an interest in the country which is very dry and desert-like. In the nineteenth century, Britain and Germany became interested because of the mineral wealth (including diamonds), fishing and opportunities for cattle-ranching. Germany took control of the country from the late 1890s until World War I. South Africa, under a League of Nations Mandate, administered the country until independence was achieved in 1990.

One of the legacies of history is the variety of languages spoken. English and Afrikaans (based on the Dutch language) are the official languages but, in addition, German and the Bantu and the Khosian groups of languages are spoken.

Namibia has an official government tourism policy based on low environmental impact. It wants to avoid some of the worst tourist development excesses found around the world and in other parts of Africa. The policy is to attract low numbers of high-spending international tourists. Tourism is a vital part of the economic development of the country, only mining and agriculture generate more wealth than tourism. The manufacturing base is comparatively weak and depends on South Africa. The country has over 30 per cent unemployment. Rural tourism is thus very attractive to the economic planners.

Namibia has a significant number of attractions for tourists. For example:

1 **Etosha National Park**: one of the best game parks in Africa. It has very good viewing possibilities for seeing lion, elephant and many other species of game.
2 **Fish River Canyon**: second only to the Grand Canyon in the US.
3 **Sossusvlei**: reputed to have the highest sand dunes in the world.
4 **Rock paintings and engravings**: reputed to be the oldest in the world.
5 **Skeleton**: a unique region shaped by the cold Benguela sea current meeting the hot desert coast. It is the graveyard of many ships blown onto its bleak shores.

Namibia is a favourite for film-makers and photographers because of its 300+ days a year of sunshine, clear skies and low costs of living. Fashion photographers and feature film makers (for example, Walt Disney) find that Namibia is an excellent location for filming.

According to the marketing research information available to Bochardt, most tourists in Namibia come from South Africa. Unfortunately, most of these spend little money, they come for camping or fishing trips with their vehicles packed with food bought in South Africa. The 'interesting' tourists come from the US, Asia and Europe. The main existing flow is from the US, Japan and Germany.

The various farms selling guest accommodation promote themselves both independently and collectively through the Namibian Tourist Board. There are variations in the products and services offered by the farms. What they specialise in is a peaceful rural location, close either to spectacular scenery or to game parks with wild animals. Farms typically have five to ten self-contained rooms. Part of the attraction of the farms is the personal interest of the farmer and the family in the venture. Disadvantages of the farms are their limited ability to invest in facilities such as swimming pools and a rather fragmented promotional effort. The Sunlands Holiday franchise would make the difference. It would move the farms into the mainstream of tourism for the twenty-first century.

What concerned Bochardt was the costs of providing facilities. How many customers would want to pay for the extra facilities? Would they stay longer than the typical one to two nights? Did different nationalities want different facilities and different service levels?

The franchise deal was for Sunlands Holidays to create a unified image which would be promoted in suitable countries and to finance the upgrading of accommodation and the provision of some recreational facilities. Each farm would set its own prices within prescribed limits and each farm would pay a negotiated franchise fee based on the services provided by Sunlands. However, the important feature of the personalised service provided by the farm to its guests would remain.

Questions

1 Identify and justify a marketing research plan to enable Thomas Bochardt to make objective marketing decisions with regard to the franchise deal and the twenty-two farms.

2 Explain how promotional approaches and product service packages might be developed and how they might interrelate for Sunlands' venture into franchising with the twenty-two farms in Namibia.

Case comments

Sunlands is a well-established German company. It runs a range of different leisure operations around the world. The company is planning its first venture into Africa. It is proposing a franchise deal in the south west African country of Namibia.

Sunlands has various ways in which it can market its Namibian holidays. Different market segments could be attracted for photography and film-making, for game viewing, for scenic tours, for cultural experiences, etc. The limitation of twenty-two farms and five to ten bedrooms is a factor in the development of the promotional plan. This obviously means that mass media advertising will not be part of the promotional approach. The international marketing mix needs to cover the countries from which tourists will be attracted. It needs to cover the relationship between the type of customer segments, the type of holiday, the product service package and the promotional approaches to reach these customer segments.

Kings Supermarket Inc.

Marks and Spencer (M&S), a giant UK retailer has pioneered the selling of chilled food under the brand name St Michael (pronounced Saint Michael). Now M & S plan to sell similar chilled food products in the US through its recently acquired supermarket chain, Kings Supermarket Inc.

History

From simple beginnings 100 years or so ago, M & S has expanded to become the leading UK retailer with 260 plus stores. Its core product(s) forming the basis of its success has been clothing – ready to wear garments for all the family. Its strategy and positioning has been to offer exceptional value for money. M & S has never sold on a price promotion platform. Discounting is unheard of as was, until recently, advertising and other marketing communication activity. M & S and its brand name St Michael have become synonymous with quality and value, shoppers of all social classes frequent the company's stores. Mrs Thatcher when Prime Minister shopped there regularly.

Having created a reputation in the clothing market M & S began to look for new challenges. Noticing the rise of food supermarkets, M & S decided to diversify away from their core business (clothing) and enter the food market. Their strategy was not to compete 'head to head' with the supermarket giants but instead to develop niche markets – again repeating their formula of exceptional value for money and ignoring price competition. They have been successful, standing today as number three or four in the food supermarket pecking order.

Operating within their existing clothing stores, it was quite impossible for the company to offer customers a comprehensive range of food products – in any case they had no desire to do so. The method of entering the food market was through offering a limited range of products that were different, exciting and which genuinely met consumer needs. Spearheading this challenge were 'complete meal' dishes, single servings. The meals were *not* frozen (such products existed in other supermarket chains) but *chilled*. Chilled food is freshly prepared and needs to be heated or lightly cooked before serving i.e. there is no defrosting process. The range of dishes chosen were semi-exotic as opposed to everyday ones. For example, Sezhuan Chicken, Prawn with Spring Onion and Ginger, Aromatic Crispy Duck are amongst the selection priced variously between £2.50 and £6.99 – and this for a single serving. So they are not cheap, nor are they designed especially for family eating. Rather the stereotyped customer is a professional person with a busy lifestyle who, after a hard day at work, can enjoy a 'special' meal without the bother of preparation. Very few consumers shop exclusively at M & S for food but rather use the store to augment the purchase of everyday items. (However, as the formula has been successful M & S have extended their range of products to include some more mundane products such as bread.) Using the chilled meal concept as a bridgehead strategy has proven very successful for M & S's diversification programme.

Will it work overseas?

M & S are now examining the potential to repeat the formula in the US through its subsidiary Kings Supermarkets. But transporting the UK concept to the US is not simple. Consider the following aspects:

1 **The US consumer**. The American customer may be more unconventional, seeking a wider range of dishes than their British counterparts. Nutritional issues are possibly more important. Low-fat, Hi-fibre stickers are common-place – something that M & S has not had to worry about. The choice of dishes attractive to the UK customer may not have similar appeal. For example Sezhuan Chicken may have no appeal to US customers.

2 **Substitutes**. US supermarkets stock other varieties of take-home and premium easy-to-prepare foods. The traditional US 'deli' (delicatessen), together with salad bars and in-store bakeries offer a wide range of alternatives making chilled food less appealing.

3 **Price**. Chilled food is marketed as semi-exotic or even gourmet (e.g. crispy duck) and is accordingly premium priced. This may limit the US market to certain up-market neighbourhoods e.g. Lower Manhattan in New York. Moreover, traditionally, US food is cheaper than its UK counterpart.

4 **Shopping habits**. Whilst the UK trend to food shopping is towards out of town superstores visited once a week, Marks and Spencers' appeal is to those who top up their weekly shop with daily purchases of chilled and fresh foods. Will the US customer be interested in a daily shopping routine e.g. picking up the chilled meal on the way home from work?

5 **Competition**. Other US food giants are also interested in the chilled food concept. Campbells, General Foods, Kraft and even Nestlé have entered this area. There is no virgin market opportunity here.

6 **Logistics and Suppliers**. These are just two further considerations. Chilled food spoils easily unless a constant temperature is maintained. Shipping from a central base to 264 stores in the UK is feasible but the US is far bigger. Operating and maintaining a distribution network would be more difficult and costly. In moving to the US the company would need to develop new suppliers with the consequent quality control issues – and in a new food category.

7 **The St Michael brand**. In the UK consumer confidence in the company and its brand is second to none. Getting consumers' trust in the new concept of chilled food was not a problem. But in the US awareness levels are zero and in any case the company has chosen to launch under King's brand name.

M & S have retained your services as a marketing consultant to address the overall task of launching into the US market. The issue is strategic not tactical and your initial thoughts include an audit of the marketplace.

Questions

1 What are the particular issues which you recommend M & S pay attention to before entering the US market?

2 On the basis of the information provided in the case, what would be your recommended outline action plan for launching into the US market? (Should you wish to make any assumptions, these must be stated clearly.)

Case comments

Marks and Spencer are a well-established retailer in the UK and have followed a fairly successful international expansion strategy principally in fashion retailing. The marketing of chilled foods overseas is a new venture and obviously raises a number of questions and issues which the reader is asked to address in question one.

The reader needs to consider the marketing mix issues in particular. Special consideration should also be given to the challenges firms face when marketing to countries which are geographically huge, have well-established competition and a sophisticated consumer base.

Putting the fizz into Eastern Europe

A red army is on the march again in Eastern Europe. However, this army is selling Coca-Cola and the American dream, and this huge growth market represents the next stage in fulfilling the firm's mission of 'having one of its drinks within reach of every person on the planet'. Coca-Cola now sells one billion drinks out of the world consumption of 47 billion drinks per day and so has plenty of market growth left to exploit.

Until the fall of communism, Pepsi outsold Coke by four to one, but now Coke outsells Pepsi by two to one. After 1989, Coca-Cola sent Amatil, its Australian and Asian bottling operation into Eastern Europe to build up the market, by using the expertise it had gained in entering emerging markets in Asia. Amatil is now demerging its Eastern European business together with its north Italian bottling operation to form Coca-Cola Beverages (CCB). Coca-Cola, which owns 50.1 per cent, San Miguel of the Philippines and Query of Malaysia are the main shareholders, but will reduce their shareholding when CCB floats in July.

With Pepsi weakened, the local soda drink Kvesa on the wane, CCB sees its main rivals as milk, water, tea and local fizzy drink makers. CCB face the challenge of rolling out the brand across Ukraine, Poland, Romania and the former Yugoslavia, by serving the drinks cold by putting in fridges, using advertising and promotions.

Ukraine appears to CCB to be the most attractive market and it has already built a £100 million bottling plant in Kiev, spent £1 million and, with 2300 workers, is the country's largest employer. So what will stop CCB? The only cloud is the economy. Some 10 million public sector workers are owed three and a half months wages, inflation is predicted to be 18 per cent and the black economy is estimated to be worth more than the official economy. The spectre of violence is everywhere, with 20 businessmen, 15 journalists and 10 bureaucrats assassinated in Ukraine last year. There are some concerns in Russia but step by step policies are emerging which are sensible.

CCB believe that their development in eastern Europe along with those of other firms, such as McDonald's and Proctor and Gamble, will assist the change to a more Western style economy. It is for this reason the CCB believes its activities will be core to Coca-Cola's strategy in five to ten years time.

Questions

1 How will the factors discussed in the case impact on the pricing and distribution strategies of CCB?

2 Make recommendations as to what marketing strategy is appropriate for CCB to follow in Eastern Europe.

Case comments

Eastern Europe is a high-growth market with huge opportunities. However, in view of the information given in the case, conventional marketing mix tools may well not apply. In particular the promotion and distribution activity needs to focus upon expanding the market effectively. The reader needs to consider innovative marketing approaches and assess the risks to CCB involved in the alternatives available.

References

Rushe, D. (1998) 'Coke offshoot aims to fizz in old Soviet bloc', *Sunday Times*, 14 June.

Index